Java 3D Programming

D1319484

Java 3D Programming

Daniel Selman

MANNING

Greenwich
(74° w. long.)

For online information and ordering of this and other Manning books,
go to http://www.manning.com. The publisher offers discounts on this book
when ordered in quantity. For more information, please contact:

Special Sales Department
Manning Publications Co.
209 Bruce Park Avenue   Fax: (203) 661-9018
Greenwich, CT 06830   email: orders@manning.com

11-21-02

Manning Publications Co.   Copyeditor: Maarten Reilingh
209 Bruce Park Avenue   Typesetter: Denis Dalinnik
Greenwich, CT 06830   Cover designer: Leslie Haimes

ISBN 1-930110-35-9
Printed in the United States of America
1 2 3 4 5 6 7 8 9 10 – VHG – 06 05 04 03 02

For Barrie and Mary

brief contents

contents

preface

Over two years ago, I was approached by Manning Publications to write this book. I had just finished an eight-month project using Java 3D for meteorological visualization. For some of that time, Java 3D had still been in beta, so I had been particularly active on the Java 3D Interest mailing list, asking questions, seeking support from the other Java 3D early-adopters, and helping out others where I could.

The Java 3D Interest list became a lifeline on that project, as Java 3D was so new, and the documentation so scarce. We found ourselves frequently on the leading edge of Java 3D development, using (and abusing) it in ways that the architects and designers at Sun had not envisaged. The intelligence and commitment of the people on the Interest list immediately impressed me, and were a welcome relief from other lists I had seen.

Over the past years, I have come to know some of the regular contributors to the list, though we have never met, and the dedicated group of people who strive to support Java 3D, at Sun and outside, bodes well for the continued success of Java 3D. Much of the information in this book has come from discussions with people on the Java 3D Interest list and my own direct experiences using Java 3D—for commercial and private projects. I hope, that by summarizing many of the issues and discussions I have encountered, this book will strengthen the Java 3D community and provide a good reference for programmers picking up Java 3D for the first time.

This book has been very challenging to write. Not only is it my first book, but I quickly discovered what a demanding topic Java 3D could be! I have had to walk a tightrope between veering off on tangents to describe 3D graphics techniques that are better covered in more general texts and reproducing the Sun Java 3D documentation parrot fashion! I have also had to compromise between the immediately useful—workarounds for bugs and installation tips—and the material that is likely to be needed in the longer run as Sun revises Java 3D. Sun has issued several versions of Java 3D and the JDK over the course of writing the book. Each release has brought new bug fixes, workarounds, and changes to the installation procedures. I have updated the examples after each release and revised the text accordingly.

I approached Java 3D as a relatively experienced Java, OpenGL, C, and C++ programmer. The biases in my background may be apparent in my treatment of some of the Java 3D topics, however I have striven for generally useful information wherever possible. I hope you will find this text useful in your programming work.

This book is aimed at intermediate to experienced Java developers. Previous experience of graphics programming (OpenGL and Swing, for example) will be very useful in getting up to speed quickly, but it's not a prerequisite. No book stands alone and you should make good use of the many online resources—including bibliographies—listed in appendix B. If you are building an application with a complex user interface, Jon Barrilleaux's *3D User Interfaces with Java 3D* (from Manning) will prove extremely useful. Readers new to Java 3D should also definitely download Sun's excellent (free) Java 3D tutorial. This book is intended to serve as a companion to the Sun API documentation, and the Java 3D tutorial.

This book covers many of the real-world aspects of building Java 3D applications in more detail than the Sun materials and will help you avoid some of the pitfalls that have befallen your predecessors. While it has not been possible to cover every aspect of the API, this book focuses on areas that generally cause problems for Java 3D programmers, as well as on areas of the API with which I am most experienced. I have only written about topics that I have used in practice and almost every section of the text has an accompanying source code example.

If you find errors, omissions, or just plain disagree—please do not hesitate to contact me through Manning Publication's Author Online forum at http://www.manning.com/selman. I am always interested in hearing about the exciting applications that you are building using Java 3D!

acknowledgments

This book has been a long time in the making, and by now I am deeply indebted to a prodigious list of people: countless individuals on the Java 3D Interest list who routinely engage in insightful conversation on all areas of 3D graphics using Java, the many technical reviewers of the book who guided me and offered constructive criticism and encouragement, as well as the amazingly patient staff at Manning Publications who have taken all my slipped deadlines in stride.

I also thank you, the reader, for risking your hard-earned time and money on my book. I know some of you have been patiently waiting for a very long time. I hope you are as pleased with the results as I am.

While it is hard to single out individuals I would like to especially thank Marjan Bace, my publisher, for believing in the subject matter; Maarten Reilingh, Teresa Barensfeld, and Elizabeth Martin for converting my Javanese into coherent English; Syd Brown and Denis Dalinnik for their graphics and layout expertise; Mary Piergies for shepherding the whole process along; and Ted Kennedy for arranging all the technical reviews. And speaking of technical reviewers, thanks to Bob Gray, Shawn Kendall, Helmuth Trefftz, Jon Barrilleaux, Patrick van Bergen, Hari Srinivasan, Farhat Kaleem, Evan Drumwright, Andreas Kemkes, Claude Duguay, Gordon Watson, B.S. Prabhu, Olivier Fillon, Alex Terrazas, Brandie Lynn, Jim Brackett, John Sutter, Adrian Fletcher, Ken Tallman, and Mark Ollila. Special thanks to Shawn Kendall who reviewed the manuscript and code examples for technical accuracy shortly before the book went to press.

Saving the best for last, thanks to Ann Gile for her love and support—and her ability to give me a good kick in the pants when my motivation was flagging! I truly could not have done it without her by my side.

about this book

Java 3D is a client-side Java application programming interface (API) developed at Sun Microsystems for rendering interactive 3D graphics using Java. Using Java 3D you will be able to develop richly interactive 3D applications, ranging from immersive games to scientific visualization applications.

Who should read it?

Java 3D Programming is aimed at intermediate to experienced Java developers. Previous experience in graphics programming (OpenGL and Swing, for example) will be very useful, but it's not a prerequisite. No book stands alone and you should make good use of the many online resources and books listed in appendix B and the bibliography. Readers new to Java 3D should definitely download Sun's excellent (free) Java 3D tutorial. This book is intended to serve as a companion to the Sun API documentation and the Java 3D tutorial.

How is it organized?

The book has 18 chapters, plus three appendices and a bibliography. Each chapter is fairly self-contained or explicitly references related chapters, allowing you to focus quickly on relevant material for your problem at hand. I have ordered the material so that, if you were starting a project from scratch, progressing in the book would mirror the design questions you would face as you worked through your design study and development efforts. More commonly used material is, in general, closer to the beginning of the book.

Chapter 1 focuses on getting started with Java 3D, system requirements, running the examples in the book, plus a look at the strengths and weaknesses of Java 3D.

Chapter 2 introduces some of the fundamentals of 3D graphics programming, such as projection of points from 3D to 2D coordinates, lighting, and hidden surface removal.

Chapter 3 gets you started with Java 3D programming, from setting up your development environment and resources to running your first application.

Chapter 4 explains the fundamental data structure in Java 3D, the scenegraph. Aspects of good scenegraph design are described using an example application for discussion.

Chapter 5 is a reference to Java 3D's scenegraph nodes, along with usage instructions and examples.

Chapter 6 explains the elements of the Java 3D scenegraph rendering model and guides you in your choice of VirtualUniverse configuration.

Chapter 7 takes a step back and examines data models for 3D applications. Choosing a suitable data model involves understanding your interaction and performance requirements.

Chapter 8 is a reference to creating geometry to be rendered by Java 3D.

Chapter 9 covers the elements of the Java 3D Appearance class, used to control the rendered appearance of the geometric primitives in your scene.

Chapter 10 illuminates the Java 3D lighting model and shows you how to create powerful lighting for your scene.

Chapter 11 introduces the Java 3D behavior model, which allows you to attach code to the objects in your scene. Examples illustrate both keyboard and mouse behaviors for graphical user interfaces.

Chapter 12 expands upon the discussion of behaviors, covering the Interpolator behaviors, used to control geometry attributes using the Alpha class.

Chapter 13 describes how to write your own custom behaviors and register them with Java 3D for invocation. Example behaviors for debugging and complex physical animation as well as others are presented.

Chapter 14 explains how to increase the realism of your scenes by applying bitmaps to your geometry using the process of texture mapping.

Chapter 15 highlights some of the utility classes provided with Java 3D for operations such as triangulation and loading of input data.

Chapter 16 delves into more techniques valuable for interacting with 3D scenes, object interaction using the mouse for selection of 3D objects, and performing collision detection between 3D objects.

Chapter 17 shows, through example, how to build Java 3D applications that use the Swing packages for 2D user interface elements, and can be distributed as Java applets for use from a web browser.

Chapter 18 goes low-level to explain some of the implementation details of the Java 3D API. The aim is to give you a greater appreciation for what is going on behind the scenes and help you optimize your applications.

Appendix A cross-references all the examples by chapter and includes instructions for downloading, installing, and running the example code from the publisher's web site.

Appendix B includes a comprehensive listing of programming and graphics resources online. Print references are provided in the bibliography.

Appendix C explains the Primitive utility class, its geometry cache, and the GeomBuffer class, along with tips and caveats.

Source code

The book contains over 30,000 lines of example code, including some reusable library code that I hope will contribute to the collective understanding of the Java 3D community. Code of particular interest is shown in boldface. Appendix A contains a list of the example Java 3D applications and applets developed for this book, as well as detailed instructions for running the examples. The code itself is identified in the text by an initial reference to its location at http:// www.manning.com/selman, the Manning web site for this book.

Typographical conventions

Italic typeface is used to introduce new terms.

`Courier` typeface is used to denote code samples as well as elements and attributes, method names, classes, interfaces, and other identifiers.

`Courier bold` typeface is used to denote code of special interest.

Code line continuations are indented.

How to use the book

I have tried to organize many of the topics in the book in an order appropriate for developers designing and building a new Java 3D application. I would suggest initially reading or skimming the chapters sequentially to get an overall feel for the design of your application, and then returning to specific chapters and examples for reference material as required.

Please note that the example source code for the book is provided under the GNU General Public License (GPL) (http://www.gnu.org/licenses/licenses.html). I encourage you to modify and distribute the source code in accordance with the spirit of open source and the GPL license.

If you still need help or have questions for the author, please read about the unique Author Online support that is offered from the publisher's web site.

Author Online

Purchase of *Java 3D Programming* includes free access to a private web forum run by Manning Publications where you can make comments about the book, ask technical questions, and receive help from the author and from other users. To access the forum and subscribe to it, point your web browser to http://www.manning.com/selman. This page provides information on how to get on the forum once you are registered, what kind of help is available, and the rules of conduct on the forum.

Manning's commitment to readers is to provide a venue where a meaningful dialog between individual readers and between readers and the author can take place. It is not a commitment to any specific amount of participation on the part of the author, whose contribution to the AO remains voluntary (and unpaid). We suggest you try asking the author some challenging questions, lest his interest stray!

The Author Online forum and the archives of previous discussions will be accessible from the publisher's web site as long as the book is in print.

about the cover illustration

The cover illustration of this book is from the 1805 edition of Sylvain Maréchal's four-volume compendium of regional dress customs. This book was first published in Paris in 1788, one year before the French Revolution. Its title alone required no fewer than 30 words.

> *Costumes Civils actuels de tous les peuples connus dessinés d'après nature gravés et coloriés, accompagnés d'une notice historique sur leurs coutumes, moeurs, religions, etc., etc., redigés par M. Sylvain Maréchal*

The four volumes include an annotation on the illustrations: "gravé à la manière noire par Mixelle d'après Desrais et colorié." Clearly, the engraver and illustrator deserved no more than to be listed by their last names—after all they were mere technicians. The workers who colored each illustration by hand remain nameless.

The colorful variety of this collection reminds us vividly of how culturally apart the world's towns and regions were just 200 years ago. Dress codes have changed everywhere and the diversity by region, so rich at the time, has faded away. It is now hard to tell the inhabitant of one continent from another. Perhaps we have traded cultural diversity for a more varied personal life—certainly a more varied and interesting technological environment.

At a time when it is hard to tell one computer book from another, Manning celebrates the inventiveness and initiative of the computer business with book covers based on the rich diversity of regional life of two centuries ago, brought back to life by Maréchal's pictures. Just think, Maréchal's was a world so different from ours people would take the time to read a book title 30 words long.

What is Java 3D and is it for me?

Java 3D is an application programming interface (API) developed at Sun Microsystems for rendering interactive 3D graphics using the Java programming language. Java 3D is a *client-side* Java API. Other examples of Sun client-side APIs include the Abstract Windows Toolkit (AWT) and Java Foundation Classes (JFC/Swing), which are both Java class libraries for building applications with a Graphical User Interface (GUI). The client-side Java APIs are in contrast to Sun's server-side APIs such as Enterprise Java-Beans (EJB) and the other components of Java 2 Enterprise Edition (J2EE).

Making 3D graphics interactive is a long-standing problem, as evidenced by its long history of algorithms, APIs, and vendors. Sun is not a major player in the 3D graphics domain, although its hardware has long supported interactive 3D rendering. The dominant industry standard for interactive 3D graphics is OpenGL, created by Silicon Graphics (SGI). OpenGL was designed as a cross-platform rendering architecture and is supported by a variety of operating systems, graphics card vendors, and applications. The OpenGL API is written in the C programming language, and hence not directly callable from Java. A number of open source and independent programming efforts have provided simple Java wrappers over the OpenGL API that allow Java programmers to call OpenGL functions, which are then executed in native code that interacts with the rendering hardware. One of the most popular is GL4Java, which you can find at http://www.jausoft.com/gl4java/.

However, there are few advantages to using a Java wrapper over OpenGL, as opposed to coding in C and calling OpenGL directly. Although programmers can use the more friendly Java APIs, they must incur the overhead of repeated calls through the Java Native Interface (JNI) to call the native OpenGL libraries.

Java 3D relies on OpenGL or DirectX to perform native rendering, while the 3D scene description, application logic, and scene interactions reside in Java code. When Sun set out to design Java 3D, although they did not have the resources or industry backing to replace OpenGL, they wanted to leverage more of Java's strengths as an object-oriented programming (OOP) language instead of merely delegating to a procedural language such as C. Whereas OpenGL's level of description for a 3D scene consists of lists of points, lines, and triangles, Java 3D can describe a scene as collections of objects. By raising the level of description and abstraction, Sun not only applied OOP principles to the graphics domain, but also introduced scene optimizations that can compensate for the overhead of calling through JNI.

1.1 STRENGTHS

The foremost strength of Java 3D for Java developers is that it allows them to program in 100 percent Java. In any sizeable 3D application, the rendering code will compose only a fraction of the total application. It is therefore very attractive to have all the application code, persistence, and user interface (UI) code in an easily portable language, such as Java. Although Sun's promise of Write-Once-Run-Anywhere is arguably more of a marketing dream than a reality, especially for client-side programming, Java has made important inroads toward enabling application developers to write applications that can be easily moved between platforms. The platforms of most interest today are Microsoft Windows 98/NT/2000, Sun Solaris, LINUX, and Macintosh OS X.

Java has arguably become *the* language of networked computing and the Internet. High-level support for remote method invocation (RMI), object serialization, platform independent data types, UNICODE string encoding, and the security model all provide persuasive arguments for adopting the Java language for applications that are increasingly gravitating away from a desktop-centric worldview. Many of the state-of-the-art 3D graphics applications being built with Java 3D today are leveraging the strengths of Java as a language for the Internet.

The Java 3D API itself has much to offer the application developer. By allowing the programmer to describe the 3D scene using coarser-grained graphical objects, as well as by defining objects for elements such as appearances, transforms, materials, lights, and so forth, code is more readable, maintainable, reusable, and easier to write. Java 3D uses a higher level scene description model, the *scenegraph*, which allows scenes to be easily described, transformed, and reused.

Java 3D includes a view model designed for use with head-mounted displays (HMDs) and screen projectors. By insulating the programmer from much of the complex trigonometry required for such devices, Java 3D eases the transition from a screen-centric rendering model to a projected model, where rendering in stereo allows for greater realism.

Java 3D also includes built-in support for sampling 3D input devices and rendering 3D spatial sound. By combining all of the above elements into a unified API, Java 3D benefits from a uniformity of design that few other APIs can match.

Java 3D's higher level of abstraction from the mechanics of rendering the scene have also opened the field of interactive 3D graphics to a new class of audience, people who would typically have been considered 3D content creators. Think of 3D graphics creation as a spectrum, with resources and talents distributed across a variety of tasks, as illustrated in figure 1.1.

Many new programmers have moved from Virtual Reality Modeling Language (VRML) into Java 3D. They are 3D content creation specialists; and they require the greater flexibility offered by a programming API, though they are reluctant to learn OpenGL and C. For this audience, Java 3D fills an important niche, allowing them to concentrate on content creation and application logic, without choking on the details of rendering and arcane programming syntax.

1.2   WEAKNESSES

Many of the strengths can be reversed and cited as weaknesses. For some programmers coming *from* OpenGL, there are some OpenGL features that are hard or impossible to achieve within Java 3D. Some of this audience may miss the total control they have over the scene and the rendering process. Many others, however, will quickly learn the mapping from OpenGL functions to Java 3D objects and will appreciate the productivity gains they can achieve using Java 3D.

Although Java 3D includes some clever optimizations, a skilled developer using OpenGL and native C code may be able to achieve higher performance than a Java programmer using Java 3D. If absolute rendering performance is the top-priority for your application then you may be better off using OpenGL or another native rendering API.

One particular problem, inherent in Java, which can be noticeable in performance-critical applications, is the impact of the Java garbage collector (GC). The Java runtime, the Java 3D runtime, and the application code all create objects. All these objects will eventually be garbage, and be collected by the Java Virtual Machine (JVM) GC. While the GC is running there may be an appreciable system slowdown, resulting in several rendered frames being dropped. If garbage collection occurs in the middle of a critical animation sequence, the realism of the rendered scene may be lowered for the user. However, with continued improvements in GC technology, faster hardware, and well-designed and implemented applications, such considerations are no longer prevalent.

The Java client-side APIs, and especially Java 3D, can be difficult to distribute to end users. While the biggest pool of end users run Windows, Sun has had limited success

Content Creation

VRML

```
Material {
    ambientColor   0.200 0.200 0.200
    diffuseColor   0.800 0.400 0.500
    shininess  0.000
}
Cube {
    width   2.000
    height  2.000
    depth   2.000
}
```

Java 3D Programming

```
universe = createVirtualUniverse();
Locale locale = createLocale( universe );
BranchGroup sceneBranchGroup = createSceneBranchGroup();
Background background = createBackground();
```

OpenGL Programming

```
glClearColor(1.0, 1.0, 1.0, 1.0);
glClear(GL_COLOR_BUFFER_BIT);
glColor3f(0.0, 0.0, 0.0);
glMatrixMode(GL_PROJECTION);
glLoadIdentity();
```

Vendor Specific Programming

Figure 1.1   Java 3D fills an important gap between VRML, which is centered around describing 3D content, and OpenGL, which is a C API for rendering points, lines, and triangles

getting Java 2 (JRE 1.2) deployed on the Windows platform. Java 2 is required for Java 3D, although Microsoft's JVM does not support Java 2. This means that end users are required to download Sun's Java 2 implementation, install it, and then download Java 3D and install it, all prior to running your application. If you are deploying your application as an applet, the installation process is potentially more complex as some end users will have to manually copy or edit configuration files before they can view your applet. In addition a suitable version of OpenGL or DirectX must be installed and configured for the end user's hardware and drivers. This lengthy download and installation process can lead to frustration; I think we are some way from seeing mainstream software and games companies offering consumer-grade software products built using Java 3D, or even Java 2. Many modern end users expect the convenience of point-and-click installation and do not have the computer skills to set CLASSPATH variables or debug installation problems.

There is light at the end of the tunnel, however, as the Java WebStart project attempts to make installing and running SDK 1.2 Java applications as easy as running native applications—which may be just as well. At present it does not appear that Microsoft will be shipping *any* JVM with Windows XP.

At present, the biggest groups of Java 3D users appear to be computer scientists, businesspeople, hobbyists, game developers, and programmers. These early adopters are spearheading the deployment of Java 3D for mainstream applications.

1.3 SYSTEM REQUIREMENTS (DEVELOPER AND END USER)

Java is a resource-intensive development and deployment environment and creating interactive 3D graphics is still one of the most challenging tasks for modern PCs. Interactive 3D rendering requires hardware dedicated to 3D rendering, usually provided by third-party display hardware specially adapted for processing 3D scenes. Fortunately, 3D-display hardware has reduced in price radically over the past few years, and today's typical game PCs are able to exceed the capabilities of the expensive dedicated graphics workstations of just a few years ago.

For a realistic immersive 3D experience (first-person 3D games, for example), a consistently high frame rate is required, typically 30 frames per second (FPS) or higher. More powerful rendering hardware will be able to achieve higher frame rates, at higher screen resolutions and with higher resolution texturing, all of which contribute to the overall experience. Modern PCs could typically achieve reasonable frame rates without dedicated rendering hardware, however the processor must execute both application logic and rendering code—to the detriment of both.

Nonimmersive 3D applications (such as visualization or modeling) do not typically require as high a frame rate as immersive applications. However the application logic may become the limiting factor on frame rate, as complex calculations may be necessary prior to rendering every frame.

The frame rate that the end users see is determined by a number of factors:

- *Vertex or transform bound*—Ability of the display hardware to transform and display each vertex in the scene
- *Fill bound*—Ability of the display hardware to shade and texture the scene and push the resulting pixels to the screen
- *Application logic bound*—Ability of the application to prepare the scene for rendering

Different types of application will place different demands on those factors, and the type of application you are writing will often dictate the hardware requirements for development and end users.

The minimum requirements for most interactive 3D applications are:

- 500+ MHz main processor
- Dedicated 3D-display hardware, with at least 16 MB of texture memory. New 3D graphics cards are released regularly so you should research the latest cards within your budget. Ensure that the card has good OpenGL compatibility for use with Java 3D. The Java 3D mailing list is a good source of information on people's experiences with various graphics cards.
- 128+ MB of system RAM

An important part of designing your application should be to set your performance targets. Gather requirements from your user base on typical available hardware and ensure that your application can perform adequately on your target machine configuration. You may need to test using several popular graphics cards to ensure compatibility and performance. You may need to try several driver versions to find the best drivers for your supported cards. Unfortunately, Write-Once-Run-Anywhere does not work out too well in the world of 3D graphics!

Analyze the performance of your application using a tool such as OptimizeIt from VMGEAR (http://www.vmgear.com) to determine whether your frame rate is limited by your application logic or display hardware. Regular use of OptimizeIt will also help you to get the maximum performance from the JVM and increase garbage collection intervals.

1.4 EXPECTED PERFORMANCE

An important part of your application design is to estimate your expected performance and validate your design against your target machine configurations. Aim to build some simple prototypes that will allow you to extrapolate your finished application's performance. It is far easier to revise your designs at this stage than two weeks before completion.

For example, on my home machine—with an AMD 850 MHz processor, nVidia GeForce II Ultra (64 MB RAM) graphics card, and 256 MB RAM—I get about 35 FPS running the Java 3D Fly-Through example application (http://www.javasoft.com/

products/java-media/3D/flythrough.html). The Fly-Through city scene (figure 1.2) is composed of 195,000 triangles, 4,115 `Shape3D` instances, and 1,238 `Appearances` (uncompiled scenegraph).

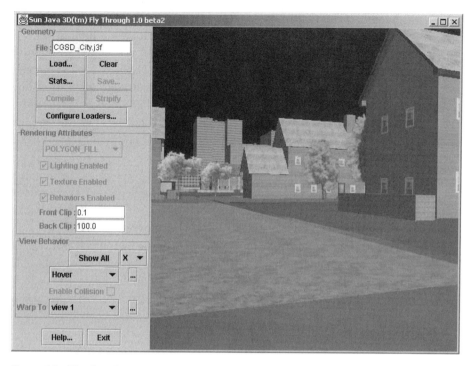

Figure 1.2   The Sun Java 3D example Fly-Through

1.4.1   Memory footprint

Java programs generally tend to require more memory than native programs. This is especially true of programs with a GUI using Swing/JFC. Java 3D can also have high memory requirements, especially if your application loads lots of large bitmaps for texture mapping objects, or defines complex geometry composed of many thousands of vertices.

To give you some idea of Java 3D's memory requirements, table 1.1 shows the total memory required for the Java 3D Fly-Through application. As you can see, bringing up the Swing application requires 25 MB, while opening the city scene pushes memory usage up to over 100 MB.

Table 1.1   Java 3D Fly-Through statistics

Working set	25 MB (no scene loaded)
Working set	108 MB (city scene loaded)

Memory usage will be an important component of your application performance. Performance will be extremely poor if your target users have less physical RAM available than the working set for your application. In this case, the operating system will have to page virtual memory to and from disk.

Another performance criterion that can be important for some applications is startup time. You should set targets for the startup time for your application. The JVM can take a considerable time to start, especially on slower machines with limited RAM. In addition, if you are loading large texture files or 3D object models, your startup time can become very significant. The RAM footprint of your application (including the JVM) and the available system RAM of the end user's computer are the most significant elements affecting startup time. You should take regular startup time measurements while you are in development to ensure that your end users are not frustrated every time they launch your application.

If you are deploying an applet, you should also be aware of the time required for it to download, as well as the graphics resources the applet requires for rendering. Texture images and 3D models can quickly become very large, so some download time targets based on typical end user bandwidth will also prove very useful.

As a reference, I measured the startup time of the Java 3D Fly-Through application. As you can see in table 1.2, launching the application took a very respectable 3 seconds, while loading the 3D content took 14 seconds. Fourteen seconds is a long time, and necessitates some form of progress indicator to reassure users that progress is occurring!

Table 1.2   Java 3D Fly-Through statistics

Start-up time	3 seconds
Loading city scene	14 seconds

1.5   RUNNING THE EXAMPLES

By now, you are probably itching to see Java 3D in action. Please refer to appendix A for a list of the example Java 3D applications and applets developed for this book, as well as detailed instructions for running the examples.

1.6   SUMMARY

Straddling the worlds of content creation and scripting on the one hand and low-level pipeline-based rendering programs on the other, the Java 3D API fills an important gap in 3D graphics APIs. With careful design and implementation, performance of Java 3D applications can rival native OpenGL applications and will exceed JNI-based Java wrappers over OpenGL.

As a Java API, Java 3D is relatively mature, first appearing at the end of 1998. But compared to OpenGL, which first appeared in the early 1990s, Java 3D is still an upstart. For example, OpenGL contains an extension facility that allows vendors to write proprietary extensions to the API—a feature that is not yet implemented in Java 3D, though it is rumored to be appearing in Java 3D 1.4. The Architecture Review Board (ARB) controls additions to OpenGL—while Java 3D may be placed under the Java Community Process (JCP), allowing experts and vendors to influence the direction of the API.

Java 3D is the right choice if you want to program 3D applications using Java. Just as Java introduced many useful abstractions over C++ and includes a rich library of standard APIs, Java 3D introduces abstractions over OpenGL/Direct3D and includes many features that will bring your applications to market faster. Java 3D can be frustrating at times—abstraction is not always a good thing—but it will save you time as you leverage years of API development by Sun's engineers. While absolute performance is sometimes a requirement, 3D graphics hardware, processor, and memory availability are advancing so rapidly that any disparity between Java/Java3D and C/OpenGL is shrinking for all but the most memory-intensive applications.

C H A P T E R   2

3D graphics programming

3D graphics programming is a fairly complex topic, worthy of a book unto itself (and there are many), but this introduction should serve as a good roadmap for further reading and give an appreciation for what Java 3D and your OpenGL or DirectX drivers are doing behind the scenes. In this chapter, I describe some of the fundamental underlying graphics techniques that allow a computer to transform a 3D scene description into a rendered image.

I'll explain much of the needed terminology; however, if you need more information, I recommend the online 3D graphics glossaries from Mondo Media (http://www.mondomed.com/mlabs/glossary.html), 3Dgaming.com (http://www.3dgaming.com/fps/techshop/glossary/), and Chalmers Medialab (http://oss.medialab.chalmers.se/dictionary/).

2.1 *LEARNING 3D GRAPHICS PROGRAMMING*

Given the enormous variety of teaching and learning styles, there probably is no *best* way of teaching 3D graphics programming. I learned 3D graphics programming by experimenting. I wrote my first 3D graphics program about 10 years ago. It was written in C and ran on my venerable Intel 80386 with a whole 256 KB of RAM! Needless to say, it didn't use Java 3D or OpenGL. The program was a modified port of a simple

BASIC program that I "borrowed" from a simple little BASIC programming book. I later ported the program to run on Solaris using the GKS rendering API. The program was a very simple wire frame 3D model viewer and editor. You could load 3D shapes described using ASCII text files and then display them on screen. You could also interactively rotate the shapes about one axis. Times have certainly changed.

The interesting thing about my first 3D effort is that I built upon my general programming knowledge and some simple 2D rendering techniques, such as drawing a line to the screen. That's what we'll do here. In this chapter, we will turn the clock back 10 years and build some sections of that program all over again, this time using Java, Java 2D, and some of the Java 3D utilities. This should remove some of the mystery from the operations performed by 3D graphics libraries like Java 3D and OpenGL. At the end of the day, we are simply converting from 3D coordinates to 2D coordinates and drawing a bunch of points and lines. We can use the source code as a basis for introducing the basics of 3D graphics programming and highlight some of the fundamental operations that a graphics library such as Java 3D provides.

By looking at the example, you'll see the additional operations that a real graphics API provides, and that our homegrown, primitive API does not.

To begin, look at the output from a simple Java 3D program and compare it with the test-bed application MyJava3D. Figure 2.1 was rendered by a simple Java 3D program (the LoaderTest example), which loads a Lightwave OBJ file and renders it to the screen. Figure 2.2 was rendered in MyJava3D using AWT 2D graphics routines to draw the lines that compose the shape.

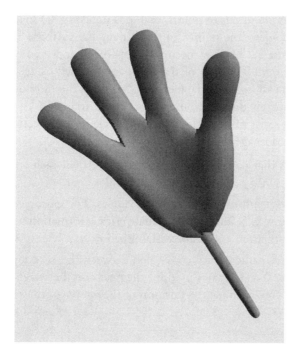

Figure 2.1
Output of a simple Java 3D
application (LoaderTest)

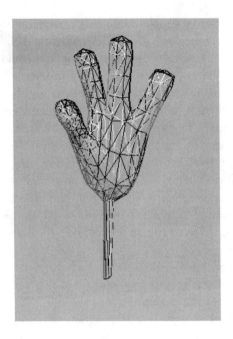

Figure 2.2
Output rendered by MyJava3D—
a wire frame version of the same
hand used for figure 2.1

The Java3D-rendered image is certainly superior. I'll compare the two images in detail later in this chapter. However, the wire frame version (just lines) that was rendered using MyJava3D is also useful.

Note how the triangular surfaces that compose the 3D model are visible in figure 2.2. The model is composed of hundreds of points, each positioned in 3D space. In addition, lines are drawn to connect the points, to form triangular surfaces. The illusion of a solid 3D shape in figure 2.1 has now been revealed—what appeared to be a solid shape is in fact a hollow skin. The skin of the shape is described using hundred of points, which are then drawn as solid triangles. Java 3D filled the interior of the triangles while MyJava3D merely drew the outer lines of each triangle.

Consider the simplest series of operations that must take place to convert the 3D model data into a rendered image:

1 Load the 3D points that compose the vertices (corners) of each triangle. The vertices are indexed so they can be referenced by index later.

2 Load the connectivity information for the triangles. For example, a triangle might connect vertices 2, 5, and 7. The actual vertex information will be referenced using the information and indices established in step 1.

3 Perform some sort of mathematical conversion between the 3D coordinates for each vertex and the 2D coordinates used for the pixels on the screen. This conversion should take into account the position of the viewer of the scene as well as perspective.

4 Draw each triangle in turn using a 2D graphics context, but instead of using the 3D coordinates loaded in step 1, use the 2D coordinates that were calculated in step 3.

5 Display the image.

That's it.

Steps 1, 2, 4, and 5 should be straightforward. Steps 1 and 2 involve some relatively simple file I/O, while steps 4 and 5 use Java's AWT 2D graphics functions to draw a simple line into the screen. Step 3 is where much of the work takes place that qualifies this as a 3D application.

In fact, in the MyJava3D example application, we cheat and use some of the Java 3D data structures. This allows us to use the existing Lightwave OBJ loader provided with Java 3D to avoid doing the tiresome file I/O ourselves. It also provides useful data structures for describing 3D points, objects to be rendered, and so on.

2.2   PROJECTING FROM *3D* WORLD COORDINATES TO *2D* SCREEN COORDINATES

Performing a simple projection from 3D coordinates to 2D coordinates is relatively uncomplicated, though it does involve some matrix algebra that I shan't explain in detail. (There are plenty of graphics textbooks that will step you through them in far greater detail than I could here.)

There are also many introductory 3D graphics courses that cover this material online. A list of good links to frequently asked questions (FAQs) and other information is available from 3D Ark at http://www.3dark.com/resources/faqs.html.

If you would like to pick up a free online book that discusses matrix and vector algebra related to 3D graphics, try Sébastien Loisel's *Zed3D, A compact reference for 3D computer graphics programming*. It is available as a ZIP archive from http://www.math. mcgill.ca/~loisel/.

If you have some money to spend, I would recommend picking up the bible for these sorts of topics: *Computer Graphics Principles and Practice*, by James Foley, Andries van Dam, Steven Feiner, and John Hughes (Addison-Wesley, 1990).

2.2.1   A simple 3D projection routine

Here is my simple 3D-projection routine. The `projectPoint` method takes two `Point3d` instances, the first is the input 3D-coordinate while the second will be used to store the result of the projection from 3D to 2D coordinates (the *z* attribute will be 0). `Point3d` is one of the classes defined by Java 3D. Refer to the Java 3D JavaDoc for details. Essentially, it has three public members, *x*, *y*, and *z* that store the coordinates in the three axes.

From AwtRenderingEngine.java

```java
private int xScreenCenter = 320/2;
private int yScreenCenter = 240/2;
private Vector3d screenPosition = new Vector3d( 0, 0, 20 );
private Vector3d viewAngle = new Vector3d( 0, 90, 180 );
private static final double DEG_TO_RAD = 0.017453292;
private double modelScale = 10;

CT = Math.cos( DEG_TO_RAD * viewAngle.x );
ST = Math.sin( DEG_TO_RAD * viewAngle.x );
CP = Math.cos( DEG_TO_RAD * viewAngle.y );
SP = Math.sin( DEG_TO_RAD * viewAngle.y );

public void projectPoint( Point3d input, Point3d output )
{
 double x = screenPosition.x + input.x * CT - input.y * ST;
 double y = screenPosition.y + input.x * ST * SP + input.y * CT * SP
   + input.z * CP;
 double temp = viewAngle.z / (screenPosition.z + input.x * ST * CP
   + input.y * CT * CP - input.z * SP );

 output.x = xScreenCenter + modelScale * temp * x;
 output.y = yScreenCenter - modelScale * temp * y;
 output.z = 0;
}
```

Let's quickly project some points using this routine to see if it makes sense. The result of running seven 3D points through the projectPoint method is listed in table 2.1.

```
CT: 1
ST: 0
SP: 1
CP: 0
```

Table 2.1 Sample output from the projectPoint method to project points from 3D-world coordinates to 2D-screen coordinates

WX	WY	WZ	SX	SY
1	1	0	250	30
−1	1	0	70	30
1	−1	0	250	210
−1	−1	0	70	210
0	0	0	160	120
1	1	1	255	25
−1	−1	1	65	215

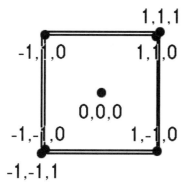

Figure 2.3
The positions of some projected points

Plotting these points by hand using a 2D graphics program (figure 2.3), you can see that they seem to make sense. Projecting the point 0,0,0 places a point at the center of the screen (160,120). While you have symmetry about the corners of the cube, increasing the *Z*-coordinate appears to move the two opposing corners (1,1,1 and –1,–1,1) closer to the viewer.

Taking a look at the `projectPoint` function again, you can see it uses the following parameters:

- Input point *x*, *y*, and z coordinates
- Center of the screen
- Sin and cosine of the viewer's angle of view
- Distance of the screen from the viewer
- Model scaling factor

This very simple projection function is adequate for simple 3D projection. As you become more familiar with Java 3D, you will see that it includes far more powerful projection abilities. These allow you to render to stereo displays (such as head-mounted displays) or perform parallel projections. (In parallel projections, parallel lines remain parallel after projection.)

2.2.2 Comparing output

Look at the outputs from MyJava3D and Java 3D again (figure 2.4). They are very different—so Java 3D must be doing a lot more than projecting points and drawing lines:

- Triangles are drawn filled; you cannot see the edges of the triangles.
- Nice lighting effect can be seen in the curve of the hand.
- Background colors are different.
- Performance is much better—measured by comparing the number of frames rendered per second.

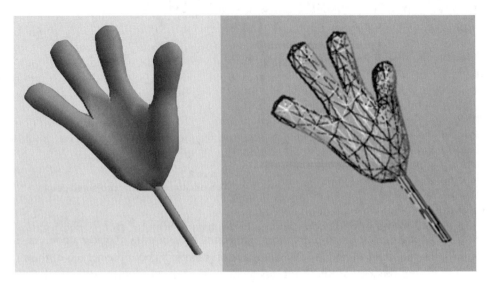

Figure 2.4   Compare the output from Java 3D (left) with the output from MyJava3D (right)

2.2.3   Drawing filled triangles

Java 3D rendered the hand as an apparently solid object. We cannot see the triangles that compose the hand, and triangles closer to the viewer obscure the triangles further away.

You could implement similar functionality within MyJava3D in several ways:

Hidden surface removal

You could calculate which triangles are not visible and exclude them from rendering. This is typically performed by enforcing a winding order on the vertices that compose a triangle. Usually vertices are connected in a clockwise order. This allows the graphics engine to calculate a vector that is normal (perpendicular) to the face of the triangle. The triangle will not be displayed if its normal vector is pointing away from the viewer.

This technique operates in object space—as it involves mathematical operations on the objects, faces, and edges of the 3D objects in the scene. It typically has a computational complexity of order n^2 where n is the number of faces.

This quickly becomes complicated however as some triangles may be *partially* visible. For partially visible triangles, an input triangle has to be broken down into several new wholly visible triangles. There are many good online graphics courses that explain various hidden-surface removal algorithms in detail. Use your favorite search engine and search on "hidden surface removal" and you will find lots of useful references.

Depth sorting (Painter's algorithm)

The so-called Painter's algorithm also operates in object space; however, it takes a slightly different approach. The University of North Carolina at Chapel Hill Computer

Science Department online course Introduction to Computer Graphics (http://www.cs.unc.edu/~davemc/Class/136/) explains the Painter's algorithm (http://www.cs.unc.edu/~davemc/Class/136/Lecture19/Painter.html).

The basic approach for the Painter's algorithm is to sort the triangles in the scene by their distance from the viewer. The triangles are then rendered in order: triangle furthest away rendered first, closest triangle rendered last. This ensures that the closer triangles will overlap and obscure triangles that are further away.

An uncomplicated depth sort is easy to implement; however, once you start using it you will begin to see strange rendering artifacts. The essential problem comes down to how you measure the distance a triangle is from the viewer. Perhaps you would

- Take the average distance of each of the three vertices
- Take the distance of the centroid of the triangle

With either of these simple techniques, you can generate scenes with configurations of triangles that render incorrectly. Typically, problems occur when:

- Triangles intersect
- Centroid or average depth of the triangle is not representative of the depth of the corners
- Complex shapes intersect
- Shapes require splitting to render correctly

For example, figure 2.5 shows some complex configurations of triangles that cannot be depth sorted using a simple algorithm.

The depth of an object in the scene can be calculated if the position of the object is known and the position of the viewer or image plane is known. It would be computationally intensive to have to re-sort all the triangles in the scene every time an object or the viewer's position changed. Fortunately, binary space partition (BSP) trees can be used to store the relative positions of the object in the scene such that they do not need to be re-sorted when the viewpoint changes. BSP trees can also help with some of the complex sorting configurations shown earlier.

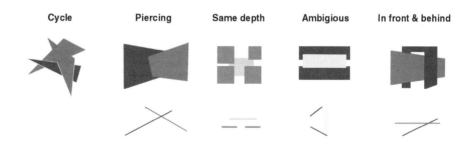

Figure 2.5 Interesting configurations of triangles that are challenging for depth-sorting algorithms

Depth buffer (Z-buffer)

In contrast to the other two algorithms, the Z-buffer technique operates in image space. This is conceptually the simplest technique and is most commonly implemented within the hardware of 3D graphics cards.

If you were rendering at 640 × 480 resolution, you would also allocate a multidimensional array of integers of size 640 × 480. The array (called the depth buffer or Z-buffer) stores the depth of the closest pixel rendered into the image.

As you render each triangle in your scene, you will be drawing pixels into the frame-buffer. Each pixel has a color, and an xy-coordinate in image space. You would also calculate the z-coordinate for the pixel and update the Z-buffer. The values in the Z-buffer are the distance of each pixel in the frame from the viewer.

Before actually rendering a pixel into the frame-buffer for the screen display, inspect the Z-buffer and notice whether a pixel had already been rendered at the location that was closer to the viewer than the current pixel. If the value in the Z-buffer is less than the current pixel's distance from the viewer, the pixel should be obscured by the closer pixel and you can skip drawing it into the frame-buffer.

It should be clear that this algorithm is fairly easy to implement, as long as you are rendering at pixel level; and if you can calculate the distance of a pixel from the viewer, things are pretty straightforward. This algorithm also has other desirable qualities: it can cope with complex intersecting shapes and it doesn't need to split triangles. The depth testing is performed at the pixel level, and is essentially a filter that prevents some pixel rendering operations from taking place, as they have already been obscured.

The computational complexity of the algorithm is also far more manageable and it scales much better with large numbers of objects in the scene. To its detriment, the algorithm is very memory hungry: when rendering at 1024 × 800 and using 32-bit values for each Z-buffer entry, the amount of memory required is 6.25 MB.

The memory requirement is becoming less problematic, however, with newer video cards (such as the nVidia Geforce II/III) shipping with 64 MB of memory.

The Z-buffer is susceptible to problems associated with loss of precision. This is a fairly complex topic, but essentially there is a finite precision to the Z-buffer. Many video cards also use 16-bit Z-buffer entries to conserve memory on the video card, further exacerbating the problem. A 16-bit value can represent 65,536 values—so essentially there are 65,536 depth buckets into which each pixel may be placed. Now imagine a scene where the closest object is 2 meters away and the furthest object is 100,000 meters away. Suddenly only having 65,536 depth values does not seem so attractive. Some pixels that are really at different distances are going to be placed into the same bucket. The precision of the Z-buffer then starts to become a problem and entries that should have been obscured could become randomly rendered. Thirty-two-bit Z-buffer entries will obviously help matters (4,294,967,296 entries), but greater precision merely shifts the problem out a little further. In addition, precision within the

Z-buffer is not uniform as described here; there is greater precision toward the front of the scene and less precision toward the rear.

When rendering using a Z-buffer, the rendering system typically requires that you specify a *near* and a *far clipping plane*. If the near clipping plane is located at $z = 2$ and the far plane is located at $z = 10$, then only objects that are between 2 and 10 meters from the viewer will get rendered. A 16-bit Z-buffer would then be quantized into 65,536 values placed between 2 and 10 meters. This would give you very high precision and would be fine for most applications. If the far plane were moved out to $z = 50,000$ meters then you will start to run into precision problems, particularly at the back of the visible region.

In general, the ratio between the far and near clipping (far/near) planes should be kept to below 1,000 to avoid loss of precision. You can read a detailed description of the precision issues with the OpenGL depth buffer at the OpenGL FAQ and Troubleshooting Guide (http://www.frii.com/~martz/oglfaq/depthbuffer.htm).

2.3 LIGHTING EFFECTS

MyJava3D includes some simple lighting calculations. The lighting equation sets the color of a line to be proportional to the angle between the surface and the light in the scene. The closer a surface is to being perpendicular to the vector representing a light ray, the brighter the surface should appear. Surfaces that are perpendicular to light rays will absorb light and appear brighter. MyJava3D includes a single white light and uses the Phong lighting equation to calculate the intensity for each triangle in the model (figure 2.6).

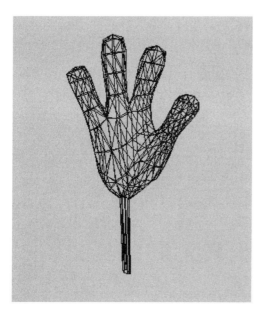

Figure 2.6
MyJava3D rendering without light intensity calculations

The computeIntensity method calculates the color intensity to use when rendering a triangle. It accepts a GeometryArray containing the 3D points for the geometry, an index that is the first point to be rendered, and a count of the number of points (vertices) that compose the item to be rendered.

The method then computes the average normal vector for the points to be rendered by inspecting the normal vectors stored within the GeometryArray. For a triangle (three vertices) this will be the vector normal to the plane of the surface.

The angle between the surface normal and the viewer is then calculated (beta). If the cosine of this angle is less than or equal to zero, the facet cannot be seen by the viewer and an intensity of zero will be returned. Otherwise, the method computes the angle between the light source position vector and the surface normal vector of the surface (theta). If the cosine of this angle is less than or equal to zero, none of the light from the light source illuminates the surface, so its light intensity is set to that of the ambient light. Otherwise, the surface normal vector is multiplied by the cosine of theta, the resulting vector is normalized, and then the light vector subtracted from it and the resulting vector normalized again. The angle between this vector and the viewer vector (alpha) is then determined. The intensity of the surface is the sum of the ambient light, the diffuse lighting from the surface multiplied by the cosine of the theta, and the specular light from the surface multiplied by the cosine of alpha raised to the *glossiness* power. The last term is the Phong shading, which creates the highlights that are seen in illuminated curved objects.

Note that in this simple MyJava3D example only one light is being used to illuminate the scene—in Java3D, OpenGL, or Direct3D many lights can be positioned within the scene and the rendering engine will compute the combined effects of all the lights on every surface.

Please refer to chapter 10 for a further discussion of lighting equations and example illustrations created using Java 3D.

From AwtRenderingEngine.java

```
private int computeIntensity( GeometryArray geometryArray,
  int index, int numPoints )
{
    int intensity = 0;
    if ( computeIntensity != false )
    {
        // if we have a normal vector, compute the intensity
        // under the lighting
        if ( (geometryArray.getVertexFormat( ) & GeometryArray.NORMALS) ==
            GeometryArray.NORMALS )
        {
            double cos_theta;
            double cos_alpha;
            double cos_beta;

            for( int n = 0; n < numPoints; n++ )
                geometryArray.getNormal( index+n, normalsArray[n] );
```

```
            // take the average normal vector
            averageVector( surf_norm, normalsArray, numPoints );
            temp.set( view );
            temp.scale( 1.0f, surf_norm );

            cos_beta = temp.x + temp.y + temp.z;

            if ( cos_beta > 0.0 )
            {
                cos_theta = surf_norm.dot( light );

                if ( cos_theta <= 0.0 )
                {
                    intensity = (int) (lightMax * lightAmbient);
                }
                else
                {
                    temp.set( surf_norm );
                    temp.scale( (float) cos_theta );
                    temp.normalize( );
                    temp.sub( light );
                    temp.normalize( );

                    cos_alpha = view.dot( temp );

                    intensity = (int) (lightMax * ( lightAmbient +
                      lightDiffuse * cos_theta + lightSpecular *
                      Math.pow( cos_alpha, lightGlossiness )));
                }
            }
        }
    }

    return intensity;
}
```

2.4 *PUTTING IT TOGETHER — MYJAVA3D*

The MyJava3D example defines the RenderingEngine interface. This interface
defines a simple rendering contract between a client and a 3D renderer implementation. The RenderingEngine interface defines a simple renderer that can render
3D geometry described using a Java 3D GeometryArray. The GeometryArray
contains the 3D points and normal vectors for the 3D model to be rendered.

In addition to adding GeometryArrays to the RenderingEngine (addGe-
ometry method), the viewpoint of the viewer can be specified (setViewAngle),
the direction of a single light can be specified (setLightAngle), the scaling factor
to be applied to the model can be varied (setScale), and the size of the rendering
screen defined (setScreenSize).

To render all the `GeometryArrays` added to the `RenderingEngine` using the current light, screen, scale, and view parameters, clients can call the render method, supplying a `Graphics` object to render into, along with an optional `GeometryUpdater`. The `GeometryUpdater` allows a client to modify the positions of points or rendering parameters prior to rendering.

From AwtRenderingEngine.java

```java
/**
 * Definition of the RenderingEngine interface. A RenderingEngine
 * can render 3D geometry (described using a Java 3D GeometryArray)
 * into a 2D Graphics context.
 */
public interface RenderingEngine
{
 /**
  * Add a GeometryArray to the RenderingEngine. All GeometryArrays
  * will be rendered.
  */
 public void addGeometry( GeometryArray geometryArray );

 /**
  * Render a single frame into the Graphics.
  */
 public void render( Graphics graphics, GeometryUpdater updater );

 /**
  * Get the current Screen position used by the RenderEngine.
  */
 public Vector3d getScreenPosition();

 /**
  * Get the current View Angle used by the RenderEngine. View
  * angles are expressed in degrees.
  */
 public Vector3d getViewAngle();

 /**
  * Set the current View Angle used by the RenderEngine.
  */
 public void setViewAngle( Vector3d viewAngle );

 /**
  * Get the current View Angle used by the RenderEngine. View
  * angles are expressed in degrees.
  */
 public Vector3d getLightAngle();

 /**
  * Set the current View Angle used by the RenderEngine.
  */
 public void setLightAngle( Vector3d angle );

 /**
```

```
 * Set the Screen size used by the RenderEngine.
 */
public void setScreenSize( int width, int height );

/**
 * Set the scale used by the RenderEngine.
 */
public void setScale( double scale );

/**
 * Get the scale used by the RenderEngine.
 */
public double getScale();
}
```

The RenderingEngine interface is implemented by the AwtRenderingEngine class, which uses simple Graphics rendering calls (drawPolygon, setColor, drawLine, drawPoint) to render the 3D models.

The RenderingEngine instance is driven by a RenderingSurface, an instance of a JPanel that provides a Graphics object for its client area and receives the frames of the rendered scene. The RenderingSurface extends Animating-Surface, which creates a rendering thread, and calls repaint on the JPanel, forcing the scene to be continuously redrawn.

The Surface class, which is the base class for AnimatingSurface (both taken from Sun Java 2D demos), allows you to specify Java 2D rendering hints such as RenderingHints.VALUE_ANTIALIAS_OFF, which switches off antialiasing, and RenderingHints.VALUE_RENDER_SPEED, which tells the Graphics object to optimize for speed rather than rendering quality. It is interesting to see the effect of switching on antialiasing (figure 2.4 is on, figure 2.7 is off), as rendering APIs or 3D graphics hardware does not commonly support this functionality.

The RotatingGeometryUpdater class is used to increase the X-angle of the viewer after each subsequent frame.

From RotatingGeometryUpdater.java

```
/**
 * Implementation of the GeometryUpdater interface
 * that rotates the scene by changing the viewer position
 * and the scale factor for the model.
 */
public class RotatingGeometryUpdater implements GeometryUpdater
{
long lastFrame = -1;

public RotatingGeometryUpdater ( )
{
}

public boolean update( Graphics graphics, RenderingEngine engine,
```

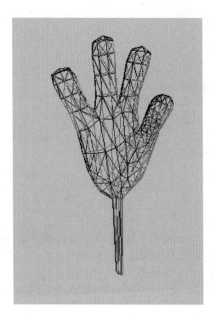

Figure 2.7
MyJava3D rendering with Java2D
antialiasing enabled

```
  GeometryArray geometry, int index, long frameNumber )
  {
   if ( lastFrame != frameNumber )
   {
     lastFrame = frameNumber;
Vector3d viewAngle = engine.getViewAngle( );
 viewAngle.x += 1;
       engine.setViewAngle( viewAngle );
   }

   return false;
  }
}
```

The MyJava3D class pulls all of these elements together. It creates an AwtRendering-Engine instance, loads a GeometryArray from disk using a Java 3D ObjectFile object loader, adds the GeometryArray to the AwtRenderingEngine, constructs a RenderingSurface supplying a RotatingGeometryUpdater, starts the RenderingSurface, and then adds it to the content pane of the JFrame that hosts the application.

From MyJava3D.java

```
/**
 * Render a 3D shape using a 3D rendering engine
 * that was written from scratch using AWT for
 * graphics operations.
 */
```

```java
public class MyJava3D extends JFrame
{
 private static int     m_kWidth = 400;
 private static int     m_kHeight = 400;

 private RenderingEngine    renderingEngine = new AwtRenderingEngine();
 private GeometryUpdater    geometryUpdater = new RotatingGeometryUpdater();
 private RenderingSurface   renderingSurface;

 public MyJava3D( )
 {
    // load the object file
  Scene scene = null;
  Shape3D shape = null;

  // read in the geometry information from the data file
  ObjectFile objFileloader = new ObjectFile( ObjectFile.RESIZE );

  try
  {
   scene = objFileloader.load( "hand1.obj" );
  }
  catch ( Exception e )
  {
   scene = null;
   System.err.println( e );
  }

  if( scene == null )
   System.exit( 1 );

 // retrieve the Shape3D object from the scene
 BranchGroup branchGroup = scene.getSceneGroup( );
 shape = (Shape3D) branchGroup.getChild( 0 );

  // add the geometry to the rendering engine...
  renderingEngine.addGeometry( (GeometryArray) shape.getGeometry() );

  // create a rendering surface and bind the rendering engine
  renderingSurface = new RenderingSurface( renderingEngine,
   geometryUpdater );

  // start the rendering surface and add it to the content panel
  renderingSurface.start();
  getContentPane().add( renderingSurface );

  // disable automatic close support for Swing frame.
 setDefaultCloseOperation( WindowConstants.DO_NOTHING_ON_CLOSE );

 // add the window listener
 addWindowListener(
  new WindowAdapter()
  {
   // handle the system exit window message
   public void windowClosing( WindowEvent e )
   {
```

```
        System.exit( 0 );
                    }
    }
  );
}

public static void main( String[] args )
{
  MyJava3D myJava3D = new MyJava3D();
            myJava3D.setTitle( "MyJava3D" );
            myJava3D.setSize( 300, 300 );
            myJava3D.setVisible( true );
    }
}
```

2.5 SUMMARY

The MyJava3D example application should have demystified some of the magic of 3D rendering and provided the opportunity to experiment with and test your own rendering functionality. A useful exercise would be to add some form of depth sorting or a Z-buffer to the AwtRenderingEngine. With some enhancements, it might be useful in its own right as a lightweight 100 percent Java rendering engine.

The example reinforces how much more convenient it is to leverage a graphics API such as Java 3D. Not only does Java 3D handle (through OpenGL or Direct3D) low-level issues such as Z-buffering, but it also defines classes for specifying geometry and a rendering abstraction called the scenegraph.

The next chapter steps you through creating your first simple Java 3D application, so let's go!

C H A P T E R   3

Getting started, Hello Java 3D!

Now the fun begins. It's time to begin conquering the Java 3D development environment, setting ourselves up for serious Java 3D fun in the chapters to come. I'll introduce a realistic Java 3D application to test your configuration, and allow you to experiment with some of the features described in later chapters. You'll look at a simple Java 3D example, SimpleTest, that illustrates building an AWT-based Java 3D application. The SimpleTest example uses the Sun utility classes MainFrame and Simple-Universe (included with your Java 3D distribution) to hide some of the complexities that we will be delving into in the chapters to come.

3.1 INSTALLATION

Our first step, obviously, is to install everything we need for Java 3D development. Refer to appendix B and the bibliography for useful sources of information or additional help.

3.1.1 Java 2 SDK

Check the Sun web site (http://java.sun.com) and download the latest release. Java 2 SDK 1.3.1 (JDK 1.3.1) is the latest release at the time of print. You can also find it at http://www.javasoft.com/j2se/1.3/. Remove all previous versions of the SDK, JDK, or JRE prior to installing the new SDK. After installation launch the Java plug-in control applet from the Windows Control Panel and set the Java Runtime Environment (JRE) to the newly installed SDK location. This will enable running Java 3D applets using the Java 2 plug-in.

3.1.2   Java 3D 1.2 JDK

Download the latest release of the Java 3D SDK at http://www.javasoft.com/products/ java-media/3D/index.html. The OpenGL version of Java 3D has historically been more stable and ahead of the DirectX release in terms of features. At the time of print the latest release is Java 3D 1.2.1. You should install Java 3D into the same directory as the Java 2 SDK, typically c:\jdk1.3. This will ensure that all your Java 2 demo applications are installed into the same place.

You can then use REGEDIT to edit the Windows registry to remove all references to the JRE installation directory (which is also installed when you install the SDK). Replace all occurrences of c:\program files\javasoft\jre\1.3\... with the SDK installation location, usually c:\jdk1.3\jre\... This will enable running the Java 3D demos from the command line, and ensure that only one Java 2 runtime environment is installed on your machine.

> **IMPORTANT**   Do not run REGEDIT unless you are an experienced Windows user and familiar with editing the registry. It is not strictly necessary to remove all references to the JRE install location.

Test your Java 3D installation by running the HelloUniverse Java 3D demo. First run from the command line by going to the relevant installation directory and then typing:

```
java HelloUniverse
```

You can test the Java 2 plug-in installation by double-clicking the HelloUniverse_plug-in.html file. Your web browser should launch, the Java 2 plug-in window will appear, and the HelloUniverse applet should start.

Once the tests are running you can safely delete the c:\program files\javasoft directory.

3.1.3   Documentation

Java 3D programming involves general Java programming, high-performance programming, 3D graphics algorithms, 2D graphics programming, UI design, and many other issues. A good reference library or collection of electronic bookmarks will save you a lot of time and help you to avoid some of the pitfalls that have befallen your predecessors.

Though far from exhaustive, the list of references which follows should give you some indication of fruitful areas to start researching.

- *Java 2 SDK JavaDoc and reference books*—Java 2 is a complex technology. If you are going to write good Java 3D code you are going to require the latest Java 2 documentation and some good reference books.

- *Swing reference book*—If you are developing an application that uses Swing (JFC) for the UI you will want to get a good Swing reference book. These weighty tomes can save you a lot of time during development. A good place to start is *Swing* by Mathew Robinson and Pavel Vorobiev (http://www.manning.com/Robinson/index.html).

- *Java 3D JavaDoc*—Of course you should ensure that you download the latest API documentation for Java 3D.

- *Sun collateral Java 3D tutorial*—The free Java 3D tutorial from Sun makes a good reference for many introductory topics and for those that like a structured tutorial style book to get started. Find it at http://www.javasoft.com/products/java-media/3D/collateral/.

- *J3D.ORG*—You should check the J3D.ORG web site (http://www.j3d.org/) for FAQs and free example code. Many of the questions and problems that you run into have been faced and answered by other Java 3D users. Many answers are posted on the J3D.ORG web site or in the interest email list archives. J3D.ORG also contains useful utility code, tutorials, and examples that have been contributed by the active Java 3D community.

- *Java 3D interest email list*—You should subscribe to this excellent forum (http://archives.java.sun.com/archives/java3d-interest.html) for asking fellow developers questions. Before posting your questions, take the time to search the archives for similar questions and answers.

- *Java 3D user interface reference*—*Building Java 3D User Interfaces* by Jon Barrilleaux from Manning Publications will be very useful if you are building a complex 3D user interface. Jon answers many of the questions you will run into as you try to use 3D overlays, and presents solutions for the common UI requirements. For more information, surf to http://www.manning.com/Barrilleaux/index.html. There are several other Java 3D books coming into print—check the J3D.ORG web site for the latest information.

- *3D graphics reference books*—If you are new to 3D graphics in general, you may want to pick up a good textbook on the subject. A good reference will cover the general aspects of 3D projections, transformation matrices, clipping, lighting, and rendering. *Computer Graphics: Principles and Practice in C* by James D. Foley, et al. (Addison-Wesley, 1995) is considered by many to be the bible of computer-generated 3D graphics. Many other useful books are reviewed in appendix B.

- *OpenGL reference books*—There is considerable overlap between Java 3D and OpenGL. A good OpenGL reference will give you a greater understanding for what is going on under the covers and allow you to use Java 3D to the fullest. An OpenGL reference can also be useful when you need to extrapolate from the Java 3D documentation and infer the behavior of more advanced operations. The OpenGL "Red Book" is an excellent reference and is also available online at http://ask.ii.uib.no/ebt-bin/nph-dweb/dynaweb/SGI_Developer/OpenGL_PG/. Some general OpenGL related links have been compiled at the OpenGL FAQ and Troubleshooting Guide at http://www.frii.com/~martz/oglfaq/gettingstarted.htm.

3.1.4 Java 2 development environment (optional)

Every developer has their favorite programmer's editor, and an increasing number of Integrated Development Environments (IDEs) are available that support Java 2. They range from free to expensive, and have a wide variety of features. Some of the more popular IDEs for Java 2 development are:

- Kawa, Allaire (http://www.allaire.com/)

All the examples for this book were built using Kawa. Unfortunately, after Allaire was acquired by Macromedia, development of Kawa was discontinued.

- JBuilder, Borland (http://www.inprise.com/jbuilder/)
- Emacs, GNU (http://www.gnu.org/software/emacs/)
- Visual Café, WebGain (http://www.webgain.com/Products/VisualCafe_Overview.html)
- NetBeans (http://www.netbeans.org)
- Eclipse (Open Source, IBM) (http://www.eclipse.org/)
- IntelliJ IDEA (http://www.intellij.com/)

3.1.5 Performance analysis tools (optional)

As you formalize your designs and requirements it is often helpful to drop into a performance measurement tool to see where your code is spending its time. Two popular commercial tools for Java optimization are:

- OptimizeIt, VMGear (http://www.vmgear.com)
- JProbe, Sitraka (http://www.sitraka.com/software/jprobe/)

You can also use the free (but harder to interpret) performance measurement capabilities of the Java 2 JVM. See the documentation for the java -Xprof argument for details.

3.1.6 Java class decompiler (optional)

When things get really sticky and you can't understand what Java 3D is doing it can be useful to decompile the Java 3D class files. You will need to decompress the Java 3D JAR files and extract the class files prior to decompling them. A popular (and free) decompiler is JAD (JAva Decompiler). Find it at http://www.geocities.com/SiliconValley/Bridge/8617/jad.html.

3.2 YOUR FIRST JAVA 3D APPLICATION

The SimpleTest example (figure 3.1) is intended to build upon the HelloUniverse example that comes with the Java 3D distribution. I've attempted to expand upon

Figure 3.1   The SimpleTest example. One hundred lines of Java code give you an animated scene, including a graphical textured background with directional lighting

HelloUniverse by documenting the relationships between the various constructs used in the example and showcasing some of the features of Java 3D that enable you to build fairly complex applications with very little code. This example is 280 lines (less than 100 without comments) and illustrates some fairly complex functionality:

- Background geometry, in this case the scene is placed within a `Sphere`.
- Textured geometry, an image is applied to the inside of the background `Sphere` to give the illusion of a distant skyline.
- Lighting, a single directional light is created to provide depth cues through rendering.
- Geometry, a second smaller `Sphere` is placed within the scene.
- Appearance, the smaller `Sphere` has an `Appearance` and `Material` associated with it that interacts with the directional light to produce a shaded, colored effect.

- Animation, a `PositionInterpolator` behavior is attached to the smaller `Sphere` to move it left and right using a complex time function (`Alpha`).

For instructions on running the examples that accompany the book please refer to appendix A.

   To produce a comparable example using basic OpenGL would require many hundreds of lines of code. You can quickly see the benefits of a Java 3D's higher-level of scene description—the scenegraph.

From SimpleTest.java

```java
import java.applet.Applet;

import javax.media.j3d.*;
import javax.vecmath.*;

import com.sun.j3d.utils.geometry.*;
import com.sun.j3d.utils.universe.*;
import com.sun.j3d.utils.image.TextureLoader;

/*
 * This example builds a simple Java 3D application using the
 * Sun utility classes: MainFrame and SimpleUniverse.
 * The example displays a moving sphere, in front of a
 * background image. It uses a texture image and one light
 * to increase the visual impact of the scene.
 */
public class SimpleTest extends Applet
{
 /*
  * Create a simple Java 3D environment containing:
  * a sphere (geometry), a light,background geometry
  * with an applied texture, and a behavior that will
  * move the sphere along the X-axis.
  */
 public SimpleTest()
 {
 // create the SimpleUniverse class that will
 // encapsulate the scene that we are building.
 // SimpleUniverse is a helper class (utility)
 // from SUN that is included with the core Java 3D
 // distribution.
 SimpleUniverse u = new SimpleUniverse();

 // create a BranchGroup. A BranchGroup is a node in
 // a Tree data structure that can have child nodes
 BranchGroup bgRoot = new BranchGroup();

 // create the Background node and add it to the SimpleUniverse
 u.addBranchGraph( createBackground() );

 // create the behaviors to move the geometry along the X-axis.
 // The behavior is added as a child of the bgRoot node.
 // Anything added as a child of the tg node will be effected by the
```

```
        // behavior (will be moved along the X-axis).
        TransformGroup tg = createBehaviors( bgRoot );

        // add the Sphere geometry as a child of the tg
        // so that it will be moved along the X-axis.
        tg.addChild( createSceneGraph() );

        // because the sphere was added at the 0,0,0 coordinate
        // and by default the viewer is also located at 0,0,0
        // we have to move the viewer back a little so that
        // she can see the scene.
        u.getViewingPlatform().setNominalViewingTransform();

        // add a light to the root BranchGroup to illuminate the scene
        addLights( bgRoot );

        // finally wire everything together by adding the root
        // BranchGroup to the SimpleUniverse
        u.addBranchGraph( bgRoot );
    }

    /*
     * Create the geometry for the scene. In this case
     * we simply create a Sphere
     * (a built-in Java 3D primitive).
     */
    public BranchGroup createSceneGraph()
    {
        // create a parent BranchGroup node for the Sphere
        BranchGroup bg = new BranchGroup();

        // create an Appearance for the Sphere.
        // The Appearance object controls various rendering
        // options for the Sphere geometry.
        Appearance app = new Appearance();

        // assign a Material to the Appearance. For the Sphere
        // to respond to the light in the scene it must have a Material.
        // Assign some colors to the Material and a shininess setting
        // that controls how reflective the surface is to lighting.
        Color3f objColor = new Color3f(0.8f, 0.2f, 1.0f);
        Color3f black = new Color3f(0.0f, 0.0f, 0.0f);
        app.setMaterial(new Material(objColor, black, objColor, black,
          80.0f));

        // create a Sphere with a radius of 0.1
        // and associate the Appearance that we described.
        // the option GENERATE_NORMALS is required to ensure that the
        // Sphere responds correctly to lighting.
        Sphere sphere = new Sphere( 0.1f, Primitive.GENERATE_NORMALS,
          app );

        // add the sphere to the BranchGroup to wire
        // it into the scene.
        bg.addChild( sphere );
        return bg;
```

```
}

/*
 * Add a directional light to the BranchGroup.
 */
public void addLights( BranchGroup bg )
{
 // create the color for the light
 Color3f color = new Color3f( 1.0f,1.0f,0.0f );

 // create a vector that describes the direction that
 // the light is shining.
 Vector3f direction  = new Vector3f( -1.0f,-1.0f,-1.0f );

 // create the directional light with the color and direction
 DirectionalLight light = new DirectionalLight( color, direction );

 // set the volume of influence of the light.
 // Only objects within the Influencing Bounds
 // will be illuminated.
 light.setInfluencingBounds( getBoundingSphere() );

 // add the light to the BranchGroup
 bg.addChild( light );
}

/*
 * Create some Background geometry to use as
 * a backdrop for the application. Here we create
 * a Sphere that will enclose the entire scene and
 * apply a texture image onto the inside of the Sphere
 * to serve as a graphical backdrop for the scene.
 */
public BranchGroup createBackground()
{
 // create a parent BranchGroup for the Background
 BranchGroup backgroundGroup = new BranchGroup();

 // create a new Background node
 Background back = new Background();

 // set the range of influence of the background
 back.setApplicationBounds( getBoundingSphere() );

 // create a BranchGroup that will hold
 // our Sphere geometry
 BranchGroup bgGeometry = new BranchGroup();

 // create an appearance for the Sphere
 Appearance app = new Appearance();

 // load a texture image using the Java 3D texture loader
 Texture tex = new TextureLoader( "back.jpg", this).getTexture();

 // apply the texture to the Appearance
 app.setTexture( tex );
```

```java
    // create the Sphere geometry with radius 1.0.
    // we tell the Sphere to generate texture coordinates
    // to enable the texture image to be rendered
    // and because we are *inside* the Sphere we have to generate
    // Normal coordinates inwards or the Sphere will not be visible.
    Sphere sphere = new Sphere( 1.0f,
                Primitive.GENERATE_TEXTURE_COORDS |
                Primitive.GENERATE_NORMALS_INWARD, app );

    // start wiring everything together,
    // add the Sphere to its parent BranchGroup.
    bgGeometry.addChild( sphere );

    // assign the BranchGroup to the Background as geometry.
    back.setGeometry( bgGeometry );

    // add the Background node to its parent BranchGroup.
    backgroundGroup.addChild( back );

    return backgroundGroup;
}


/*
 * Create a behavior to move child nodes along the X-axis.
 * The behavior is added to the BranchGroup bg, whereas
 * any nodes added to the returned TransformGroup will be
 * effected by the behavior.
 */
public TransformGroup createBehaviors( BranchGroup bg )
{
    // create a TransformGroup.
    //
    // A TransformGroup is a Group node (can have children)
    // and contains a Transform3D member.
    //
    // The Transform3D member contains a 4x4 transformation matrix
    // that is applied during rendering to all the TransformGroup's
    // child nodes. The 4x4 matrix can describe:
    // scaling, translation and rotation in one neat package!

    // enable the TRANSFORM_WRITE capability so that
    // our behavior code can modify it at runtime.
    TransformGroup objTrans = new TransformGroup();
    objTrans.setCapability(TransformGroup.ALLOW_TRANSFORM_WRITE);

    // create a new Transform3D that will describe
    // the direction we want to move.
    Transform3D xAxis = new Transform3D();

    // create an Alpha object.
    // The Alpha object describes a function against time.
    // The Alpha will output a value that ranges between 0 and 1
    // using the time parameters (in milliseconds).
    Alpha xAlpha = new Alpha( -1,
                Alpha.DECREASING_ENABLE |
```

```
                Alpha.INCREASING_ENABLE,
                    1000,
                    1000,
                    5000,
                    1000,
                    1000,
                    10000,
                    2000,
                    4000 );

    // create a PositionInterpolator.
    // The PositionInterpolator will modify the translation components
    // of a TransformGroup's Transform3D (objTrans) based on the output
    // from the Alpha. In this case the movement will range from
    // -0.8 along the X-axis with Alpha=0 to X=0.8 when Alpha=1.
    PositionInterpolator posInt = new PositionInterpolator(  xAlpha,
                objTrans,
                xAxis, -0.8f, 0.8f );

    // set the range of influence of the PositionInterpolator
    posInt.setSchedulingBounds( getBoundingSphere() );

    // wire the PositionInterpolator into its parent
    // TransformGroup. Just like rendering nodes behaviors
    // must be added to the scenegraph.
    objTrans.addChild( posInt );

    // add the TransformGroup to its parent BranchGroup
    bg.addChild( objTrans );

    // we return the TransformGroup with the
    // behavior attached so that we can add nodes to it
    // (which will be effected by the PositionInterpolator).
    return objTrans;
}

/*
 * Return a BoundingSphere that describes the
 * volume of the scene.
 */
BoundingSphere getBoundingSphere()
{
 return new BoundingSphere( new Point3d(0.0,0.0,0.0), 200.0 );
}

/*
 * main entry point for the Application.
 */
public static void main(String[] args)
{
 SimpleTest simpleTest = new SimpleTest();
}
}
```

3.3 EXERCISES FOR THE READER

When you run the example, I would encourage you to make some changes and see their effects. For example:

Colors and lighting

See how the color of the `Material` and the color of the directional light interact to produce the actual rendered color. Sophisticated lighting equations are at work to combine the effects of both at runtime. Try changing the shininess parameter to (80.0f) to increase or decrease the apparent shininess of the smaller `Sphere`.

Try removing the `setMaterial` call and see how rendering is affected.

Animation parameters

The `Alpha` class that is used to control the `PositionInterpolator` can be parameterized using nine variables (figure 3.2) to produce a sophisticated timing function.

I'll discuss the `Alpha` class in depth in chapter 12 (Interpolators), but, for now, try changing some of the `Alpha` parameters and noting the effects.

The axis that the `PositionInterpolator` is moving along can also be easily modified. For example try inserting the line:

```
xAxis.rotY( 1.2 );
```

This will move the `Sphere` along a trajectory more perpendicular to the screen. You can experiment with calls to rotX and rotZ as well. Remember that rotations are described using radians, not degrees.

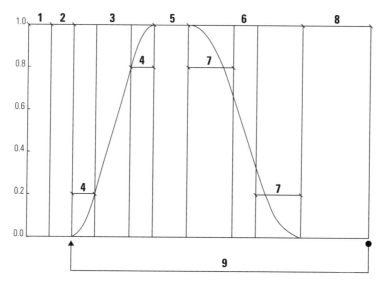

Figure 3.2 The phases of the `Alpha` class: trigger time (1), phase delay (2), increasing alpha (3), increasing alpha ramp (4), at one (5), decreasing alpha (6), decreasing alpha ramp (7), at zero (8), loop count (9)

Background geometry

Try removing the background Sphere, or just remove the texture that was applied to the inside of the Sphere. What happens if you remove the ORed flag `Primitive.GENERATE_NORMALS_INWARD` when the background Sphere is created?

What happens if you remove the `Primitive.GENERATE_TEXTURE_COORDS` flag from the Sphere when it is created?

Load the background image into a graphics editor and experiment by modifying it. Can you see how the rectangular image was applied to the inner surface of the background Sphere?

Scheduling bounds

Experiment by changing the size of the BoundingSphere that describes the application's volume. What effect does it have on the PositionInterpolator and the background?

Capability bits

What happens when you remove the call to:

```
objTrans.setCapability(TransformGroup.ALLOW_TRANSFORM_WRITE);
```

The position of the viewer of the scene

Try removing the call to:

```
u.getViewingPlatform().setNominalViewingTransform();
```

Size of sphere primitives

Try changing the sizes of the Sphere used for background geometry as well as the smaller Sphere in the scene.

3.4 SUMMARY

This example has rather plunged you in at the deep-end of the Java 3D pool. I hope you have enjoyed the guided tour of some of the capabilities of Java 3D. In the chapters to come we will be picking apart many of the features listed and showing you how to get the most out of them for your Java 3D application.

Do not be too concerned if the example code presented in this chapter looks very intimidating, and the descriptions were too vague. You can refer to this example as topics such as scenegraphs, geometry, and appearances are explained in detail in later chapters. This example should have given you a sense of the power of Java 3D and can serve as a good test bed for experimenting with your own applications or trying out the ideas presented in later chapters.

Before you start designing your application, it is important that you understand the data structure that underlies Java 3D rendering—the scenegraph. Once you have a firm grasp of it you will quickly be assembling complex Java 3D functionality that does not suffer from performance problems and is easily reusable.

So now, on to one of the most important concepts in Java 3D—the scenegraph.

CHAPTER 3 GETTING STARTED, HELLO JAVA 3D!

CHAPTER 4

The scenegraph

Is a scenegraph appropriate for your application? If you choose to use a scenegraph for your application you should be able to sketch the required elements out on paper.

In this chapter, I'll introduce the concept of a scenegraph for modeling 3D scenes. I'll present several examples that can be used to guide the scenegraph design process for your application. I'll show you the benefits and drawbacks of using the Java 3D scenegraph along with comparative information for rendering in immediate mode and mixed mode. The possible elements of a Java 3D scenegraph are presented along with usage hints and tips.

4.1 OVERVIEW

Your application's 3D virtual world contains geometric objects with which the user interacts. In Java 3D this virtual world is called the `VirtualUniverse`, the top-level class that contains all the elements that you define within your virtual world. In addition, the `VirtualUniverse` contains nongeometric objects that control or influence the world. `Lights` are a good example of this type of object. In a 3D environment, one cannot see a `Light`, but one can see the effect of the `Light` within its zone of influence.

A concrete example helps to describe some of the details. Imagine a virtual world that models a Formula 1 Grand Prix race (figure 4.1). The model is a simplification of reality. It contains:

- 3 Williams F1 cars
- 2 Ferrari F1 cars
- 3 McLaren F1 cars
- 2 Jordan F1 cars
- 1,000 trees

    300 pine

    300 oak

    400 spruce
- 100 pit crew
- 100 marshals
- 60 advertising billboards

    20 for a sport channel

    20 for a car part manufacturer

    20 for a cigarette manufacturer

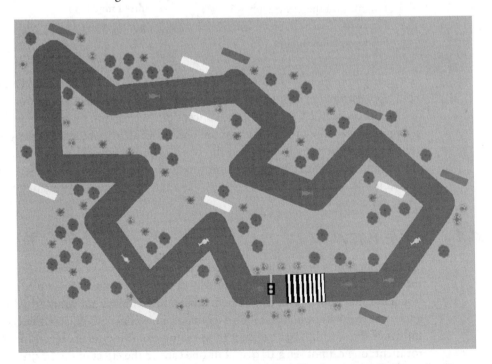

Figure 4.1 An overhead view of our example virtual world—the prototypical race circuit

- 200 straw bales
- 1 racing circuit
- 1 start light
- 1 grass area upon which the race track is situated

Taking a quick sum of the elements we see there are 1,473 objects in this `Virtual-Universe`. However, there are only 16 different types of objects. So, if you had the luxury of a team of 3D graphics artists and modelers, you could send the list away and a few weeks later receive 16 VRML format (for example) 3D graphics files. In fact, one might even define classes and subclasses, breaking the objects into cars, trees, people, billboards, bales, start light, racing circuit, and grass and hence require only eight classes. In this case the 3D graphics artists will produce a single F1 racecar model that can be customized (using color for example) to create the three subclasses McLaren, Williams, and Ferrari.

You should now be wondering how, with 1,473 distinct objects in your scenegraph and only eight classes of objects, you can organize the objects in your world so that you minimize memory overhead and rendering time but maximize programming flexibility.

You should also be aware that some of the objects within the world are dynamic:

- F1 cars
- Pit crew and marshals

Some of the objects are static:

- Straw bales
- Trees
- Billboards
- Race track
- Start light
- Grass

It is important to note in this context that "static" means "does not move relative to the circuit," or "does not move relative to the grass area upon which the circuit sits." It does *not* mean that the items are static relative to the center of the universe or even (potentially) relative to the center of the Earth.

So, static and dynamic in this example have defined movement relationships between the items listed and the *circuit*. You should also therefore think about the spatial relationships between a class of items and all other classes of items. For example, the circuit never moves relative to the grass and maybe the straw bales are always situated 25 meters in front of a billboard; or you model groups of trees in which there was a fixed spatial relationship between the trees within each group.

Some of the objects have appearances that change:

- Dynamically

    Start light (red to green)

- Statically

    F1 cars (Williams, McLaren, or Ferrari insignia)

    People (either pit crew or marshal uniforms)

    Trees (pine, oak, or spruce graphic)

Assume that you are using a low-level graphics API that can only render triangles, points, and lines at a given *x, y, z* coordinate.

Your primitive rendering loop might look like:

1 Run some control logic.

2 Update the *x, y, z* position of dynamic triangles.

3 Update the appearance of triangles whose appearance changes dynamically.

4 Draw the triangles.

5 Go to next frame.

It should be obvious that this approach does not exploit much of the information about the *structure* of the world that you developed initially. The rendering API has no concept of an object and it has no concept of spatial (or otherwise) relationships between objects. This is analogous to sending your initial list of 1,473 objects to the graphics artists and making them do all the work.

What you need is a data structure that you can use both to describe the relationships between objects and exploit to optimize your rendering and memory requirements. Read on.

4.2   WHAT IS A SCENEGRAPH?

A *scenegraph* is a hierarchical data structure that captures the elements of spatial relationships between objects. Technically a scenegraph is a *directed acyclic graph* (DAG). Once you think and model an application hierarchically, the 3D graphics API is provided with a much richer set of information to use to optimize rendering. A scenegraph description also enables application developers to apply object-orientated (OO) principles such as abstraction and reuse to their designs.

In Java 3D, the scenegraph is encapsulated within the `VirtualUniverse` class. The scenegraph is composed of objects derived from the `Node` class. Every instance of the `Node` class has *one* parent `Node`. Additionally, the scenegraph contains objects derived from the `Group` class which encapsulates a collection of `Node` child objects. In this way a hierarchy of `Group`-derived objects can be created with `Node`-derived objects attached to the parent `Group` objects, as shown in figure 4.2.

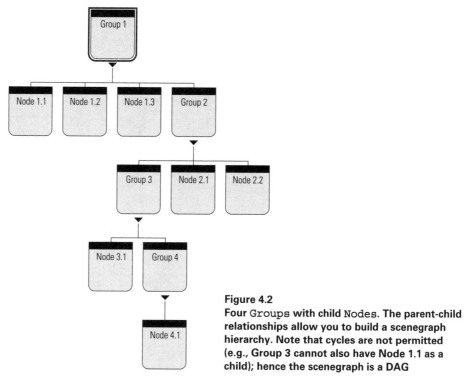

Figure 4.2
Four Groups **with child** Nodes. **The parent-child relationships allow you to build a scenegraph hierarchy. Note that cycles are not permitted (e.g., Group 3 cannot also have Node 1.1 as a child); hence the scenegraph is a DAG**

There are three basic classes of objects within the scenegraph:

- *Management nodes*—Locale, BranchGroup, TransformGroup, View-Platform, Switch, and so forth. These are predominantly derived from Group and manage a collection of child objects.

- *Geometry nodes*—Shape3D, Background, and so forth. These objects are derived from Leaf and define visible geometry within the application's virtual world.

- *Control or influence nodes*—Behaviors, Morph, Light, Sound, Clip, and so forth. These define application behavior and are typically not directly related to the geometry used within the application.

BranchGroup and TransformGroup are both Group nodes (i.e., they can contain child Nodes). A TransformGroup also contains translation, scaling, and rotation information that it applied to its child Nodes. The details of the nodes available in Java 3D are presented in later chapters.

For example, consider how one might compose the scenegraph for the F1 car. The car can be roughly anatomized into seven parts (figure 4.3): four wheels, chassis, rear fin, and front stabilizer.

Each wheel is composed of spokes, a rim, and a tire. In this way the branch of the scenegraph that defines a wheel—that is, the Wheel Group and its three child Nodes, can be reused and duplicated to create the four wheels required for the F1 car.

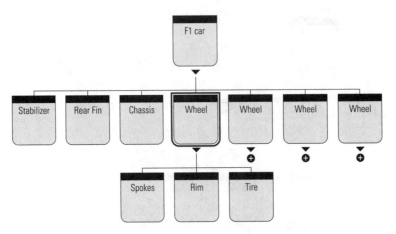

Figure 4.3   Sample scenegraph for the F1 car, plus icons represent unexpanded Groups

The scenegraph also encodes a spatial relationship. When the F1 car is moved, its child Nodes are automatically also moved. For example, the stabilizer might be positioned three meters from the origin of the F1 car in the *x* direction—this spatial relationship will be preserved irrespective of the position of the F1 car's origin. If the wheel is rotated about its axis, the spokes, rim and tire will all be automatically rotated.

The scenegraph allows model complexity to be selectively specified. Just as you have chosen to create the Wheel from three subcomponents, you might choose to further decompose the chassis to introduce more detail into the model. You might have the opportunity to reuse scenegraph branches—perhaps other classes of vehicles at the race circuit require tires that are similar to the F1 tires? Perhaps you need to create piles of tires in the pit?

Various 3D graphics file formats (e.g., VRML) allow models to be created that are composed from subcomponents.

Figure 4.4 shows how the F1 car fits into the overall scenegraph for the F1 racing application.

This scenegraph shown in figure 4.4 embodies the following relationships:

- Moving the grass area upon which the racing circuit sits will also move the circuit and the trees around it.
- Moving the circuit will move the advertising billboards, people at the circuit, cars on the circuit, straw bales, and the start light.
- Moving a F1 car moves its component parts: stabilizer, rear fin, chassis, and wheels.
- Rotating an F1 car's wheels will rotate the wheel's spokes, rim, and tire.

By designing the scenegraph with the spatial relationships in mind, scenegraph elements can be easily reused. Perhaps in the future the racetrack application will be expanded to contain two circuits with an animated transition sequence between them. The transition sequence will use a view from a helicopter flying between the circuits.

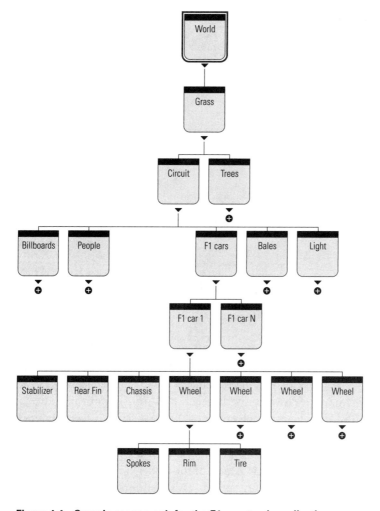

Figure 4.4 Sample scenegraph for the F1 race track application

You'll need to reuse the circuit scenegraph branch and introduce a new element for the helicopter. Figure 4.5 shows how these elements might be introduced into the original scenegraph.

This formulation reuses the whole circuit branch of the scenegraph. The new circuit will have its own surrounding terrain and trees, as well as all the circuit geometry. You'll need to move the helicopter independently of the grass for each circuit, so the helicopter `Group` is added directly into the world `Group`. Moving the world will move the two circuits as well as the helicopter.

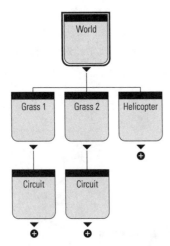

Figure 4.5
Adding a new circuit and
a helicopter to the scenegraph

4.3 JAVA 3D AND THE SCENEGRAPH

This section will cover additional scenegraph elements required by Java 3D to manage and render your scenegraph.

A `VirtualUniverse` contains at least one `Locale` object. A `Locale` defines a geographical region within your scenegraph. `Locales` are covered in depth in chapter 6.

In Java 3D there are two distinct branches within the scenegraph: *scene* and *view*. Up to now we have discussed only the high-level principles behind the scene side of the scenegraph. The scene branch contains the application's scenegraph elements, as discussed in the preceding examples. The view branch contains a `ViewPlatform` node and defines scaling, rotation, and translation information for the view. The view is responsible for rendering the *scene* side of the scenegraph. As shown in figure 4.6, the view attaches to a `ViewPlatform` and reads position and orientation information from the `Nodes` *above* the `ViewPlatform` on the view side of the scenegraph.

The view renders into its attached `Canvas3D` component. `Canvas3D` is a GUI component with an associated native windowing system window.

It is possible to have multiple `ViewPlatforms` in a scenegraph. Multiple `View-Platforms` allow you to define multiple points of view of your scene. By removing the view from a `ViewPlatform` and attaching it to a new `ViewPlatform` you can easily shift between predefined points of view.

It is also possible to have multiple views each rendering into multiple `Canvas3Ds`. For more on these advanced scenegraph features please refer to chapter 6.

An important property of a `Node` in the scenegraph is that it contains boundary (`Bounds` is the Java 3D class) information for the `Node`. The `Bounds` instance is typically a `BoundingSphere` or a `BoundingBox` object. These classes (derived from `Bounds`) define a volume of space within the 3D scene that encloses all the geometry and children of the `Node`. For the F1 car example this would mean that the `Bounds`

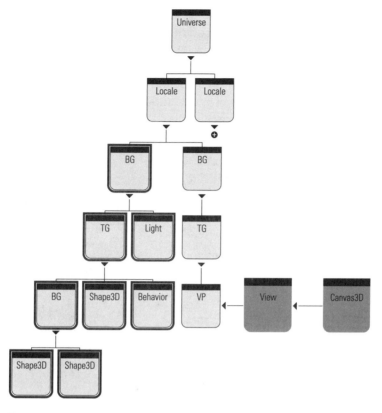

Figure 4.6   Example Java 3D scenegraph. BG: BranchGroup, TG: TransformGroup, VP: ViewPlatform. The *scene* side of the scenegraph has been highlighted (the left branch of the Locale). The right branch of the Locale is the *view* side of the scenegraph

for the F1 car Group node are such that they enclose the geometry for the stabilizer, rear fin, chassis, and four wheel Nodes. In turn, the Bounds for the wheel Group Node are such that they enclose the geometry for the spokes, rim, and tire Nodes.

Java 3D can exploit the hierarchical Bounds information to optimize many scenegraph operations, including rendering. For example, when the Renderer comes to render an F1 car, if it finds that the Bounds of the F1 car Group are outside the current view frustum the Renderer can immediately move on to the next car in the scene. The high-level visibility test on the F1 car Group has saved the Renderer from performing visibility tests on the child Nodes of the F1 car Group.

This implies another important property of a good scenegraph hierarchy: the structure of the scenegraph should provide as much Bounds information as possible to allow the Renderer to optimize rendering. As the scenegraph designer you should be cognizant of the potential Bounds of your scenegraph Nodes. From the full F1 race circuit example you could see that as you move down the scenegraph hierarchy the Bounds of the Groups and Nodes become smaller and smaller.

The Grass Group contains everything within the 3D scene, and as such must always be recursively processed by the Renderer. The Grass Group will be rendered irrespective of the user's point of view of the scene. It would not matter whether the user was riding in-car with a point of view from one of drivers, was orbiting the circuit in a helicopter, or had a view from somewhere around the circuit. If the user can see the virtual world, the Renderer will process the grass Group. Figure 4.7 shows three sample points of view around the circuit.

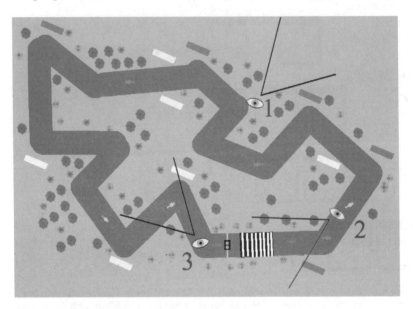

Figure 4.7   The Bounds for the Grass Group enclose everything within the 3D scene. Three FOVs have been defined: #1 is a Marshal's view, #2 is a McLaren driver's view, #3 is a Ferrari driver's view

The trees Group (figure 4.8) contains all the trees within the scene. Since the trees are scattered across the terrain surrounding the race circuit the trees Group will have Bounds that are close to the size of the grass Group. The trees Group will also usually be processed by the scenegraph Renderer (as most points of view around the circuit will intersect trees). Conceivably the viewer of the scene could be positioned at the periphery of the circuit and facing away from the center of the circuit, such that their FOV falls outside of the Bounds of the trees Group. Note that FOV #1 is *not* such a case. Though viewer #1 cannot see any trees, his FOV *does* intersect the trees Group's Bounds object. Each of the trees within the Trees Group will have to be tested against FOV #1—even though none of them actually intersect with FOV #1.

The Circuit Group (figure 4.9) encloses all of the geometry that composes the circuit roadway. This is still a large Group and not significantly smaller than the overall grass Group. It is very unlikely that a viewer of the scene will not be able to view the circuit, which is the central feature of the application.

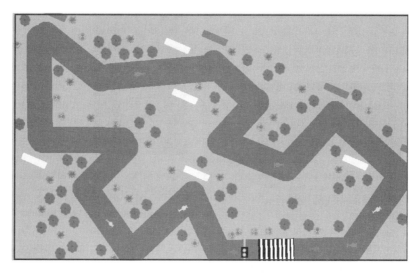

Figure 4.8 The Bounds for the trees enclose all the trees within the 3D scene

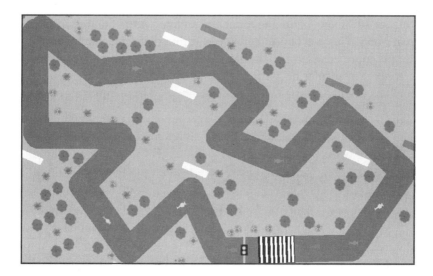

Figure 4.9 The Bounds for the Circuit Group encloses the racing circuit

The F1 car Group (figure 4.10), on the other hand, merely has Bounds that enclose the geometry required for an individual F1 car (a meter by a few meters). It is very likely that a particular F1 car Group will *not* intersect a given FOV. It is highly *unlikely* that a single viewer will be able to see *all* of the F1 cars as they race around the circuit. For example

- FOV #1 intersects with 0 F1 car Groups
- FOV #2 intersects with 1 F1 car Group
- FOV #3 intersects with 1 F1 car Group

Figure 4.10 The Bounds for the F1 car Group encloses the child Nodes that define the geometry for the F1 car

Figure 4.11 The Bounds for the start light Group encloses just the child Nodes that define the geometry for the start light

As there are 10 F1 car Groups in the scenegraph this represents a considerable saving.

The start light Group (figure 4.11) will be even smaller than the F1 car Group (less than a cubic meter). It will rarely intersect with a given FOV, even if we ride in the car with a driver. None of the FOVs defined on figure 4.7 can see the start light.

Figure 4.12 shows bounding rectangles for five classes of objects in the racing circuit virtual world. The level of detail of objects within the world should reflect the theme of the application. For example, the grass around the circuit would probably be modeled as a simple rectangular height field with an applied texture image, while the F1 cars themselves would be complex 3D models composed from hundreds of vertices. On the

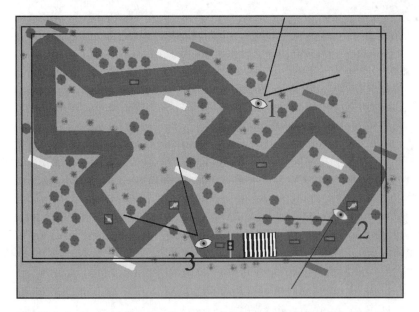

Figure 4.12 Some of the overall Bounds for the scene. Illustrated are Grass, Trees, Circuit, F1 cars, and Start Light. See figure 4.7 for the FOV

other hand, if the application were a landscape design package the grass and trees may be represented using complex geometry. Some of the most challenging applications allow the user to control the application at several levels of detail, dynamically reapportioning the detail within the scene as appropriate. An excellent example of this is the game "Black and White" by Lionhead. The game allows the user to zoom out to control entire countries and to zoom in to view individual character animations and interactions.

4.4   ELEMENTS OF SCENEGRAPH DESIGN

Designing a good scenegraph structure may involve making trade-offs across several factors. The scenegraph should be easy to manipulate at runtime (you may want to dynamically attach and detach entire branches to switch them on or off) as well as easy to customize in the future. You may have to make compromises to get good performance to ensure that Java 3D can process your scenegraph efficiently.

Object-oriented

Object orientation allows easy reuse of scenegraph branches. Ideally, each branch should define a component of the application that can be meaningfully used independently of the other scenegraph branches. You should imagine having to drop the scenegraph branch in question into another application.

Compilable

This property is related to the goal of object orientation. If scenegraph branches can be reused within the scenegraph *without modification* of their appearance or relative position, then Java 3D can further optimize application performance by removing the duplicated branches and replacing them with a reference to a single, unique branch. Learn more about scenegraph compilation in chapter 5. In the F1 example, trees, billboards, and bales might all be good candidates for some form of compilation optimization.

Level of detail independent

A scenegraph branch should be able to have new child `Nodes` added to introduce new complexity into the scene, without disrupting other scenegraph branches.

Polymorphic (customizable)

By replacing child elements of a parent `Group`, you should be able to create new but related scenegraph branches.

Bounds and level of detail aware

Objects with large bounding volumes tend to imply "often visible" which generally implies "performance critical." Do not make objects that are often visible (such as the trees in the Trees `Group`) of such high level of detail that they negatively impact application performance. Using high-detail models for the F1 cars themselves may be less critical as they have smaller `Bounds` and hence fewer of them are visible for most of the time. How you choose to apportion the detail within your scene will always be application/domain-specific or only domain specific, and may be related to the Bounds information of your scenegraph Nodes.

4.5 SCENEGRAPH ADVANTAGES

By now you should be aware of many of the advantages of using a scenegraph. Setting up the scenegraph hierarchy imposes a design rigor upon the application developer. Initially, particularly with scientific visualization applications, the scenegraph may seem unnecessarily restrictive, especially for developers from a low-level OpenGL or DirectX background. However, advanced planning and design will usually prove the utility of the scenegraph model, even for applications that do not initially appear to contain hierarchical graphical objects per se.

Object management

The scenegraph is a data structure. All the Nodes in it can also reference external data through the ScenegraphObject.setUserData method (discussed in chapter 8).

Rendering optimization

Scenegraph node Bounds play an important role in optimizing rendering and behavior scheduling.

Picking support

Mouse object selection operations (picking) are automatically supported by the scenegraph.

Behavior model

Using Java 3D scenegraph behaviors allows scenegraph objects to be automatically rotated, transformed, and scaled using interactive user input, aligned relative to the FOV, animated, morphed, or controlled using a level of detail (LOD) behavior.

Collision detection

The Java 3D scenegraph supports basic collision detection between objects within the scenegraph.

Multiple thread aware

The Java 3D scenegraph traversal, rendering, behavior, and collision detection systems are all thread aware and will make use of multiple threads.

Hierarchical control

Changing the position of a parent Node automatically changes the position of child Nodes accordingly. This is such an important and powerful concept that it is the subject of the next section and example.

4.6 HIERARCHICAL CONTROL

Many 3D applications define a complex scenegraph hierarchy. An important function of the scenegraph is to enforce the geometric and spatial relationships that the scenegraph defines. Just as when the F1 car was moved its constituent parts were also moved. This principle is central to applications that require hierarchical control.

At the scenegraph level, the key to specifying relative positions for `Nodes` within the scenegraph is the `TransformGroup` Node. A `TransformGroup` encapsulates a `Transform3D` instance, which in turn encodes a 4 × 4 scaling, rotation, and translation matrix. The important principle is that a scenegraph `Node`'s rotation, scaling, and translation is always specified *relative* to its parent `Node`'s rotation, scaling, and translation.

To illustrate these principles, in this section I'll show you a Java 3D scenegraph to animate a model of a human arm (figure 4.13). Requirements of the model are:

- Shoulder joint can be rotated
- Elbow joint can be rotated
- Wrist joint can be rotated
- Upper finger joints can be rotated

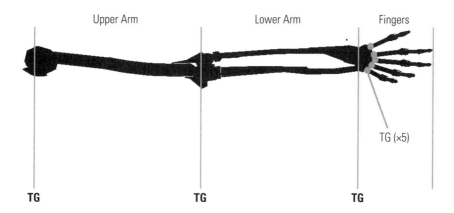

Figure 4.13   The human arm—a hierarchical model

This model is obviously hierarchical. It would be *most* usual if when the elbow joint was rotated the lower arm and the fingers were not also displaced. An important principle of the scenegraph is that the position of a child `Node` *only* depends upon the positions of its parent `Nodes`. In other words, the position of the end of the little finger depends upon

- Length of little finger (defines the offset from the center of rotation)
- Rotation of little finger joint
- Length of wrist
- Rotation of the wrist joint

- Length of lower arm
- Rotation of the elbow joint
- Length of upper arm
- Rotation of the should joint

Converting the rotational requirements into a scenegraph hierarchical model produces a structure such as that in figure 4.14. Note that we have switched to a left-to-right tree representation of the scenegraph hierarchy to save space.

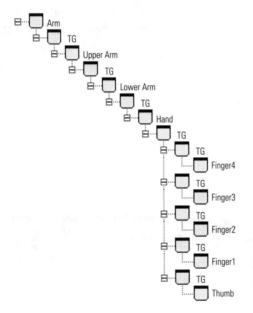

**Figure 4.14
The scenegraph for our
conceptual human arm
model**

As with most things in life, things are not *quite* that simple. There are a few implementation-related issues that must also be resolved through the scenegraph structure. The scenegraph in figure 4.14 would be fine if you required just a *static* model of the human arm, but it would be nice to be able to illustrate the example by rotating the various joints to animate the model (as shown in figure 4.15). To simplify rotating the joints you must introduce another `TransformGroup` into the hierarchy for each limb to store the current joint rotation value. *Two* `TransformGroup`s are thus required, one to store the length of the limb (i.e., the offset of the coordinate system of the *next* limb relative to the current limb's coordinate system) and one to store the joint rotation.

Unfortunately another minor implementation issue arises. The `Cylinder` geometric primitive that you are using to create the limbs in the model is created with 0,0,0 at the center of the cylinder. In other words, if you create a cylinder of length L, it will stretch from $-L/2$ to $L/2$ in the y direction, with a given radius. We would like our cylinders to stretch from 0 to L in the y direction, so an additional `TransformGroup` is required to shift the cylinder upward by $L/2$ in the y direction.

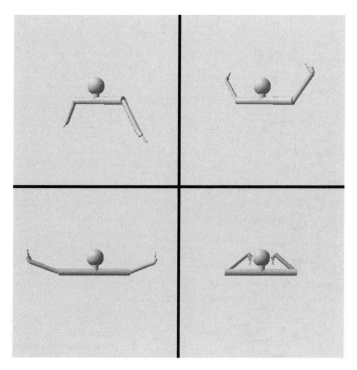

Figure 4.15   Four frames from the ScenegraphTest example to illustrate the simple arm model in action

When these refinements have been made, the scenegraph for the arm looks a little more complicated than our initial design but it still fulfills our rotation requirements for each joint. The completed scenegraph is illustrated in figure 4.16.

To verify the rotational requirements, you can walk up the scenegraph hierarchy from the end of Finger 1. Walking up the hierarchy will tell you what the position of the end of Finger 1 relies upon:

- Finger 1: TG Offset (the length of finger 1)
- Finger 1: TG Joint (the rotation of finger 1)
- Wrist: TG Offset (the length of the wrist)
- Wrist: TG Joint (the rotation of the wrist)
- Lower Arm: TG Offset (the length of the lower arm)
- Lower Arm: TG Joint (the rotation of the lower arm)
- Upper Arm: TG Offset (the length of the upper arm)
- Upper Arm: TG Joint (the rotation of the upper arm)
- Shoulder: TG Shoulder (position/rotation of the shoulder)

The rotational requirements have been satisfied, the scenegraph models the hierarchical structure of the human arm.

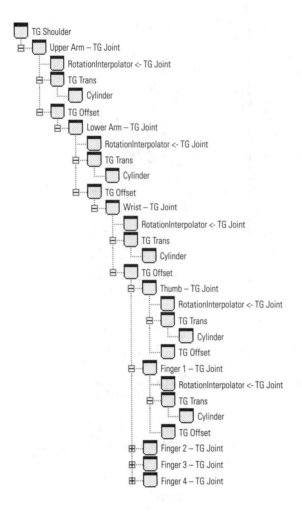

Figure 4.16
The completed scenegraph for the arm model. TG Joint stores the rotation of each joint. TG Trans shifts the geometry for the cylinder upward by L/2. The RotationInterpolator modifies its parent TG Joint to rotate the joints of the model. TG Offset contains the length of the limb, and hence shifts the coordinate system of the next limb (its child)

There are two slightly undesirable implications of the scenegraph as we have designed it. First, the length of the cylinder that we used for the geometry of the arm is unrelated to the length of the limb, inasmuch as the length of the Cylinder effects the next limb in the hierarchy. In this application, TG Offset and the length of the cylinder we created just happen to correspond. Second, the wrist and fingers are poorly modeled, as the fingers should be offset relative to one another. As modeled here the fingers all attach to the same location on the wrist.

4.7 IMMEDIATE MODE VS. RETAINED MODE VS. MIXED MODE

Java 3D does not interact directly with system display hardware to produce the 3D rendering of a scene, but rather relies upon a lower level 3D graphics API: currently either OpenGL or DirectX. The designers of Java 3D have added several locations within the Java 3D rendering loop that application developers can hook into to directly render 3D primitives irrespective of the current scenegraph.

Using Java 3D in *retained mode* does not exploit these capabilities. This is usually the recommended and most common mode for Java 3D. The application developer defines the scenegraph for the application, passes it to Java 3D, and Java 3D is responsible for rendering the scene. Java 3D also coordinates and carries out a lot of the chores related to user interaction.

In complete contrast, using Java 3D in *immediate mode* does not exploit Java 3D's scenegraph abilities at all, and the application developer assumes all responsibility for rendering and user interaction. Java 3D is merely being used as a cross-platform Java wrapper over the native low-level graphics API.

As its name implies, running Java 3D in *mixed mode* exploits some of each of the features of retained mode and some of the features of immediate mode. The application developer *does* define a scenegraph for *some* of the items in the scenegraph but retains responsibility for rendering certain 3D primitives that fall outside of the scenegraph structure.

4.7.1   Immediate mode

Some might say that there is no *pure* immediate mode in Java 3D, as you must always create the View side of the scenegraph to activate the Java 3D rendering loop, within which the immediate mode code will execute. Syntactic quibbles aside, the Immediate-Test.java example renders an array of points in immediate mode and outputs the rendered FPS to standard output.

The minimal Java 3D scenegraph to activate the `View` rendering loop consists of a `VirtualUniverse`, a single `Locale`, and a `BranchGroup` with a single `View-Platform` child `Node`. A `View` is attached to the `ViewPlatform` and a `Canvas3D` is registered with the `View` (figure 4.17).

During the Java 3D rendering loop, the application developer is given several opportunities to prepare and render immediate mode information. The rendering loop calls four methods on the `Canvas3D` registered with the View. By overriding these callback methods, application-specific immediate mode rendering can be performed.

`Canvas3D` callback methods are

- `preRender`: Allow you to prepare any data structures for rendering.
- `renderField`: Can be overridden to perform the rendering.
- `postRender`: Called when rendering is complete.
- `postSwap`: Called once the rendered frame has been made visible to the user.

From ImmediateTest.java

```
//Define a custom Canvas3D that implements Immediate Mode rendering
//and outputs the FPS achieved.
class ImmediateCanvas3D extends Canvas3D
{
```

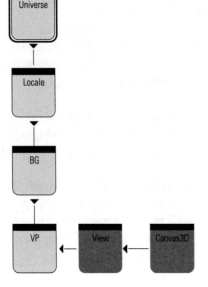

Figure 4.17
The minimal Java 3D scenegraph required for immediate mode rendering. The `Canvas3D` **implements the immediate mode rendering callbacks**

```java
private long              m_nRender = 0;
private long              m_StartTime = 0;

private static final int  nGridSize = 50;
private static final int  m_kReportInterval = 50;

private PointArray        m_PointArray = new PointArray( nGridSize *
 nGridSize, GeometryArray.COORDINATES );

private Transform3D       m_t3d = new Transform3D();
private float             m_rot = 0.0f;

ImmediateCanvas3D(java.awt.GraphicsConfiguration
 graphicsConfiguration)
{
 super( graphicsConfiguration );

 //create the PointArray that we will be rendering
 int nPoint = 0;

 for( int n = 0; n < nGridSize; n++ )
 {
  for( int i = 0; i < nGridSize; i++ )
  {
   Point3f point = new Point3f( n - nGridSize/2,
                                i - nGridSize/2, 0.0f );
   m_PointArray.setCoordinate( nPoint++, point );
  }
 }
}
```

The renderField method renders the actual PointArray that was created in the ImmediateCanvas3D constructor. In addition it tracks how many frames have been rendered and computes a running FPS count. Note that on the first frame the method adds lights and creates material attributes used to render the PointArray. The GraphicsContext3D used for rendering *persists* between rendering so take care not to add lights on every frame, or set material attributes unnecessarily.

At the heart of the renderField method are two calls: the first sets the Model transformation matrix for the GraphicsContext3D, the second calls the draw method on the GraphicsContext3D and passes the PointArray to be rendered:

```
public void renderField( int fieldDesc )
{
 super.renderField( fieldDesc );

 GraphicsContext3D g = getGraphicsContext3D();

 //first time initialization
 if( m_nRender == 0 )
 {
  //set the start time
  m_StartTime = System.currentTimeMillis();

  //add a light to the graphics context
  DirectionalLight light = new DirectionalLight( );
  light.setEnable( true );
  g.addLight( (Light) light );

  //create the material for the points
  Appearance a = new Appearance();
  Material mat = new Material();
  mat.setLightingEnable( true );
  mat.setAmbientColor( 0.5f, 1.0f, 1.0f );
  a.setMaterial( mat );
  a.setColoringAttributes(
   new ColoringAttributes( 1.0f, 0.5f, 0.5f,
                           ColoringAttributes.NICEST ) );

  //enlarge the points
  a.setPointAttributes( new PointAttributes( 4, true ) );

  //make the appearance current in the graphics context
  g.setAppearance( a );
 }

 //set the current transformation for the graphics context
 g.setModelTransform( m_t3d );

 //finally render the PointArray
 g.draw( m_PointArray );

 //calculate and display the frames per second for the
 //immediate mode rendering of the PointArray
 m_nRender++;

 if( (m_nRender % m_kReportInterval ) == 0 )
```

```
  {
    float fps = (float) 1000.0f /
                  ((System.currentTimeMillis() - m_StartTime) /
                  (float) m_kReportInterval);
    System.out.println( "FPS:\t" + fps );

    m_StartTime = System.currentTimeMillis();
  }
}
```

The preRender method is called before every frame is rendered (though a call to renderField). This method sets up the Model transformation matrix that will eventually be used in the renderField call. By increasing the rotation about the y axis of the Model matrix, the PointArray is spun around its vertical axis. Note that the last call in preRender manually calls paint (not something that is usually advisable) to force the next frame to be drawn. In this way, you get a continuous frame-by-frame animation. Figure 4.18 shows a frame rendered by the ImmediateTest example.

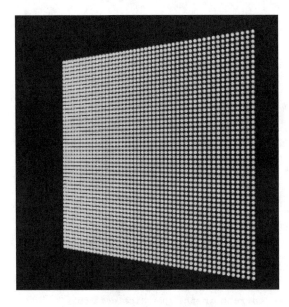

Figure 4.18
Output from the ImmediateTest.java example. The grid of points (a PointArray) has been rendered into the Canvas3D in immediate mode with a Model transformation applied to the GraphicsContext3D

```
public void preRender()
{
  super.preRender();

  //update the model transformation to rotate the PointArray about
  //the Y axis
  m_rot += 0.1;
  m_t3d.rotY( m_rot );

  //move the transform back so we can see the points
  m_t3d.setTranslation( new Vector3d( 0.0, 0.0, -20.0 ) );

  //scale the transformation down so we can see all of the points
```

```
   m_t3d.setScale( 0.3 );

   //force a paint (will call renderField)
   paint( getGraphics() );
  }
}
```

4.7.2   Mixed mode

Rendering in mixed mode consists of nothing more than taking the ImmediateTest example and fleshing out the scenegraph to include geometry information. The MixedTest example adds the following Nodes to the scenegraph:

- Background node: Colors the background of the Canvas3D.
- TransformGroup: Scales the View side of the scenegraph (located above the ViewPlatform).
- RotationInterpolator: Rotates the Transform3D instance inside the Trans-formGroup.
- ColorCube: Adds Cube geometry as a child of the rotating TransformGroup above.

Figure 4.19 shows a sample frame rendered by the MixedTest example.

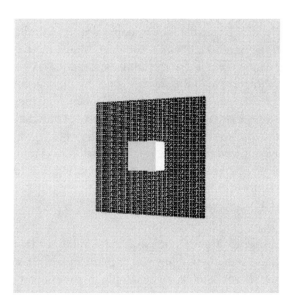

**Figure 4.19
Output from the MixedTest.java example. The grid of points (a PointArray) has been rendered into the Canvas3D in immediate mode while the ColorCube in the center was added to the scenegraph and rendered in retained mode. Also note that a background Node was used to color the background of the Canvas3D, also rendered in retained mode**

From MixedTest.java

```
//Create a TransformGroup and attach a RotationInterpolator to spin
//the ColorCube about its vertical axis
TransformGroup objTrans = new TransformGroup();
```

```
objTrans.setCapability(TransformGroup.ALLOW_TRANSFORM_WRITE);
objTrans.setCapability(TransformGroup.ALLOW_TRANSFORM_READ);

BoundingSphere bounds =
 new BoundingSphere(new Point3d(0.0,0.0,0.0), 100.0);

Transform3D yAxis = new Transform3D();
Alpha rotationAlpha = new Alpha(-1, Alpha.INCREASING_ENABLE,
                        0, 0,
                        4000, 0, 0,
                        0, 0, 0);

RotationInterpolator rotator = new RotationInterpolator(
 rotationAlpha, objTrans, yAxis, 0.0f, (float) Math.PI*2.0f);
rotator.setSchedulingBounds(bounds);

//add the RotationInterpolator to its parent TransformGroup
objTrans.addChild(rotator);

//create the ColorCube and add to its parent TransformGroup
objTrans.addChild( new ColorCube() );
```

Comparing figures 4.18 and 4.19, one might wonder why the grid of points (rendered in immediate mode) has become smaller. The answer is that the MixedTest example introduces a `TransformGroup` on the view side of the scenegraph. This `TransformGroup` shifts the position of the viewer backward relative to the scene so that the ColorCube is visible. The ImmediateTest example also sets a similar backward translation in the `preRender` method, before setting the Model matrix within the `renderField` method. The net effect is that the immediate mode `PointArray` has been translated backward *twice* relative to the viewer—once by the transformation on the View (retained) side of the scenegraph, and once explicitly in the immediate mode code. To render the immediate mode points irrespective of any transformation already applied by virtue of the view side of the scenegraph, one would have to calculate the view transformation, invert it, and multiply it by the desired Model transformation, all before applying it to the `GraphicsContext3D`. By inverting the view transformation, the effect of the transformation will be canceled.

4.7.3   Summary of modes

Java 3D includes simple support to allow you to participate in the rendering cycle for each frame. The four `Canvas3D` methods allow you to perform fairly basic geometry rendering and frame capture. If you choose, these simple methods allow you to dispense with the scene side of the scenegraph and manage, transform, and render the geometry within your scene directly. Before rushing to a decision to use immediate mode, however, I urge you to examine the capabilities of retained mode closely. Java 3D has a strong bias toward retained mode and you could miss out on some important optimizations and features.

Retained mode

- *Pros*

    Rendering of scenegraph elements automatic

    Basic collision detection support

    Scenegraph compilation may optimize rendering

    Picking for geometry selection

    Multiprocessor aware, multithreaded implementation

    Basic user interaction through Behavior model

    Facilitates complex hierarchical animation and control applications

    Supports HMD and stereo display devices

    Built-in support for multiple Views and multiple viewing locations

    OO nature of scenegraph facilitates future extension and reuse

    Built-in support for 3D spatial audio

- *Cons*

    Learning curve of learning a new scenegraph based API

    Some performance penalties incurred related to scenegraph traversal

    Additional state and variable management for highly dynamic scenes

Immediate mode

- *Pros*

    May make porting of existing OpenGL application easier

    Very little new code to learn for OpenGL developers

    No scenegraph traversal overhead

    May be able to implement application-specific rendering optimizations

    Lower memory overhead and direct control of data structures used to control rendering

- *Cons*

    Increased application complexity

    Application will often have to duplicate functionality already built into Java 3D

    Stereo displays must be supported manually

    Third-party 3D object loaders (VRML, etc.) cannot be easily used

Mixed mode

Mix and match from the pros and cons listed above. Decide acceptable application trade-offs between performance and ease of development and extensibility.

4.8 SUMMARY

The scenegraph is the central data structure in Java 3D, and a good understanding of how to design an efficient scenegraph—balancing performance, reusability, and speed of development—will prove invaluable as you move on to design your application and read the chapters to come. You should experiment with the three examples covered in this chapter: ScenegraphTest, ImmediateTest, and MixedTest. By making changes, particularly to the scenegraph structure in the ScenegraphTest example, you will quickly be able to customize the examples to serve as simple prototypes for your own application.

CHAPTER 5

Scenegraph node reference

It is time to look at usage examples and implementation hints and tips for the most commonly used scenegraph elements available in Java 3D. This chapter is intended to supplement the Sun Java 3D API documentation. Whether you are browsing or reading the book chapter by chapter, you may want to skim the detailed implementation advice and move ahead.

5.1 SCENEGRAPH COMPILATION

The Java 3D system supports the concept of a "compiled" scenegraph. Compilation is typically carried out after the scenegraph structure has been built, but before it is displayed. During compilation Java 3D analyzes the elements in the scenegraph, as well as the scenegraph structure, and attempts to perform optimizations to improve rendering time and scenegraph traversal.

Java 3D uses the *capability bits* that have been set on the scenegraph elements to identify which optimizations can be applied to the scenegraph. The capability bits that have been set for an object defines a contract between you (the application developer) and the Java 3D system. If, for example, you have not set the ALLOW_TRANSFORM_WRITE capability on a TransformGroup, the Java 3D system could use the fact that the 4 × 4 transformation matrix within the TransformGroup remains constant to optimize rendering.

The use of capability bits is a powerful mechanism for adding complex optimizations in future versions of Java 3D. At present two main scenegraph optimizations have been implemented: attribute merging/sorting and geometry merging.

To take advantage of the benefits of compilation, you *must* override some of the default settings of the Shape3D-derived objects in your scenegraph. In particular, the pickable property is set by default for Shape3D objects; objects with the pickable property will not be optimized during the compile process.

5.1.1 Appearance merging and sorting

The Appearances assigned to Shape3D objects in the scenegraph are computationally quite expensive for the scenegraph renderer. They take up memory, and when the renderer hits an Appearance, it must make a long and complex series of OpenGL or DirectX calls to the rendering subsystem to add the information within the Appearance to the rendering pipeline. Two optimizations can take place: duplicate Appearance objects can be removed and replaced with a reference to a unique Appearance object, and Shape3D objects can be rendered in an order such that changes in Appearance state are minimized. These optimizations reduce memory consumption and save on calls to the rendering subsystem. Obviously, only Appearance objects that do not have any WRITE capability bits set can be optimized using scenegraph compilation.

5.1.2 Geometry merging

Geometry merging attempts to minimize the number of discrete Shape3D objects in the scenegraph. A scenegraph will benefit from geometry merging if the Shape3D objects fulfill the following criteria:

- Many Shape3Ds with the same attributes and TGs
- Shape3Ds that do not use indexed geometry
- Shape3Ds with no capability bits set on their Appearances
- Shape3Ds without the pickable property

The compilation process will sort and attempt to merge the static subgraphs in the scenegraph. Dynamic subgraphs, that is, Nodes with writable attributes (such as Group.ALLOW_CHILDREN_WRITE), will have their static child Nodes processed while ignoring the dynamic child Nodes.

5.2 NODE

```
java.lang.Object
   |
   +--javax.media.j3d.SceneGraphObject
        |
        +--javax.media.j3d.Node
```

Node is an abstract base class for Group and Leaf Nodes. It defines methods to control bounding volumes (through the Bounds class), automatic computation of Bounds, collision detection and picking (mouse selection). Most important, it allows each Node to have a *single* parent Node. The parent Node allows arbitrarily complex scenegraph structures to be defined.

Group-derived Nodes have the ability to manage a Collection of Node-derived child objects, while Leaf-derived Nodes define the leaves of the scenegraph tree. In other words, Leaf Nodes cannot have child Nodes.

5.3 BOUNDS AND COLLISIONBOUNDS

Java 3D maintains object boundary information for the Nodes in the scenegraph. Every Node in the scenegraph contains a Bounds field that stores the geometric extent of the Node. Java 3D uses the Node Bounds information extensively, for everything from visibility testing to Behavior scheduling.

In addition, Shape3D- and Group-derived objects in the scenegraph (i.e., all geometric objects and geometric container objects) contain the CollisionBounds field. The Java 3D collision detection engine makes use of the CollisionBounds field. A simplistic (and hence poor) collision detection algorithm would iterate through the objects in the scenegraph and test for an intersection between the CollisionBounds for a Shape3D object and the CollisionBounds of every other Shape3D object in the scenegraph.

There are three classes derived from Bounds: BoundingBox, BoundingSphere, and BoundingPolytope. BoundingBox defines a cuboidal volume of space; BoundingSphere, a spherical volume of space; and BoundingPolytope, a set of intersecting planes that define a closed, convex volume.

Node-derived classes also have the option to autocompute their Bounds. This option is enabled by default and allows geometric objects in the scenegraph, as well as their parents, to compute the Bounds field based upon the positions of the geometric primitives (points, lines) from which they are composed.

Consult the following code snippets for the effects of creating an object with various combinations of Bounds and/or CollisionBounds.

From BoundsTest.java

```
//use the defaults
ColorCube cube0 = new ColorCube( 1.0 );
```

RESULTS BoundsAutoCompute: true

Collidable: true

Pickable: true

Bounds: Bounding box: Lower=-1.0 -1.0 -1.0 Upper=1.0 1.0 1.0

CollisionBounds: null

By default, Shape3D objects are created as Collidable and Pickable, and they autocompute their Bounds. No CollisionBounds are assigned, so if collision detection functionality is required, the collision mode USE_GEOMETRY should be used.

```
//explicitly set the Bounds  using a BoundingBox
ColorCube cube1 = new ColorCube( 2.0 );
cube1.setBoundsAutoCompute( false );
Bounds bounds = new BoundingBox( new Point3d( -2, -2, -2),
  new Point3d( 2, 2, 2 ) );
cube1.setBounds( bounds );
cube1.setCollisionBounds( bounds );
```

RESULTS BoundsAutoCompute: false

Collidable: true

Pickable: true

Bounds: Bounding box: Lower = -2.0 -2.0 -2.0 Upper = 2.0 2.0 2.0

CollisionBounds: Bounding box: Lower = -2.0 -2.0 -2.0 Upper = 2.0 2.0 2.0

By calling setBoundsAutoCompute(false), the Bounds and Collision-Bounds for the Shape3D object can be manually specified, as one would expect.

```
//explicitly set the Bounds using a BoundingSphere
ColorCube cube2 = new ColorCube( 4.0 );
cube2.setBoundsAutoCompute( false );
bounds = new BoundingSphere( new Point3d( 0, 0, 0 ), 4 );
cube2.setBounds( bounds );
cube2.setCollisionBounds( bounds );
```

RESULTS BoundsAutoCompute: false

Collidable: true

Pickable: true

Bounds: Bounding box: Lower = -4.0 -4.0 -4.0 Upper = 4.0 4.0 4.0

CollisionBounds: Center = (0.0, 0.0, 0.0) Radius = 4.0

Surprisingly, if a BoundingSphere is used to specify the Bounds and Collision-Bounds for the Shape3D object, the BoundingSphere will be internally converted to a BoundingBox and used for the Bounds. The CollisionBounds uses the original BoundingSphere, however.

```
//auto compute, manual collision
ColorCube cube3 = new ColorCube( 6.0 );
cube3.setBoundsAutoCompute( true );
bounds = new BoundingBox( new Point3d( -10, -10, -10 ),
  new Point3d( 10, 10, 10 ) );
cube3.setCollisionBounds( bounds );
```

RESULTS BoundsAutoCompute: true

Collidable: true

Pickable: true

Bounds: Bounding box: Lower = -6.0 -6.0 -6.0 Upper = 6.0 6.0 6.0

CollisionBounds: Bounding box: Lower = -10.0 -10.0 -10.0 Upper = 10.0 10.0 10.0

```
//auto compute both
ColorCube cube4 = new ColorCube( 6.0 );
cube4.setBoundsAutoCompute( true );
```

RESULTS BoundsAutoCompute: true

Collidable: true

Pickable: true

Bounds: Bounding box: Lower = -6.0 -6.0 -6.0 Upper = 6.0 6.0 6.0

CollisionBounds: null

5.3.1 Bounds and CollisionBounds propagation

There is a final piece to the Bounds story. The scenegraph is a hierarchical data structure, so it makes sense for the Bounds of a parent object to automatically encompass a volume large enough to hold all of its child objects. Java 3D can perform these calculations automatically, as table 5.1 illustrates (from BoundsTest.java).

Table 5.1 Bounds propagation within a branch of the scenegraph

Scenegraph item	Bounds	Autocompute
BranchGroup	null	false
TransformGroup	Bounding Sphere: Center = (0.477, 0.34, 0.23) Radius = 11.00	true
RotationInterpolator	null	true
Group1	Center = (0.0,0.0, 0.0) Radius = 10.39	true
Cube1	Bounding box: Lower = -1.0 -1.0 -1.0 Upper = 1.0 1.0 1.0	true
Cube2	Bounding box: Lower = -2.0 -2.0 -2.0 Upper = 2.0 2.0 2.0	true
Cube3	Bounding box: Lower = -4.0 -4.0 -4.0 Upper = 4.0 4.0 4.0	true
Cube4	Bounding box: Lower = -6.0 -6.0 -6.0 Upper = 6.0 6.0 6.0	true
Cube5	Bounding box: Lower = -6.0 -6.0 -6.0 Upper = 6.0 6.0 6.0	true
Group2	Bounding Sphere: Center = (-0.01,-0.01,0.00) Radius = 8.62	true
PointsArray	Bounding box: Lower = -4.97 -4.98 -5.00 Upper = 4.95 4.96 4.97	true

Group1 contains the five ColorCubes, as created earlier in the section. The largest ColorCube has a BoundingBox of *(–6,–6,–6) –> (6,6,6)*. The radius of the smallest

BoundingSphere to enclose the largest ColorCube is therefore *radius = sqrt(6^2 + 6^2 + 6^2) = 10.392*. This BoundingSphere is automatically created by Java 3D and assigned to the parent Group (Group1) of the ColorCubes. Note that Group1 has the property setBoundsAutoCompute(true).

Group2 contains a Shape3D object composed from 200 random points in a PointArray (positioned between –5 and 5 in the *x*-, *y*-, and *z*-axes). Java 3D automatically creates a BoundingBox to enclose the points composing the Shape3D object—approximately: *(–5,–5,–5) -> (5,5,5)*. The BoundingBox is automatically assigned to the Shape3D object containing the PointArray. The Bounds for the Shape3D object are propagated up the scenegraph hierarchy as a BoundingSphere and assigned to Group2. The center of the BoundingSphere is positioned to minimize the radius (in this case approximately 0,0,0). The radius of the Bounding-Sphere is approximately computed from *radius = sqrt(5^2 + 5^2 + 5^2) = 8.660*.

The parent of Group1, Group2, and RotationInterpolator is Transform-Group. TransformGroup combines the Bounds objects for its children to compute its own Bounds. In this case, as the Bounds of the children are all approximately centered at (0,0,0), which is equal to the Bounds of Group1 (which is the largest).

NOTE   The top-level parent BranchGroup node has the attribute setBounds-AutoCompute(false).

```
//routine to create a Shape3D object made from a point cloud
//of 200 random points
protected Group createPoints()
{
 Group group = new Group();

 final int kNumPoints = 200;
 final double kRadius = 10.0;
 Point3d points[] = new Point3d[kNumPoints];

 for( int n = 0; n < kNumPoints; n++ )
 {
  double randX = (java.lang.Math.random() * kRadius ) - kRadius/2;
  double randY = (java.lang.Math.random() * kRadius ) - kRadius/2;
  double randZ = (java.lang.Math.random() * kRadius ) - kRadius/2;

  points[n] = new Point3d( randX, randY, randZ );
 }

 PointArray pointArray = new PointArray( points.length,
  GeometryArray.COLOR_4 | GeometryArray.COORDINATES );
 pointArray.setCoordinates( 0, points );

 Shape3D shapePoints =
  new Shape3D( pointArray, new Appearance() );

 group.addChild( shapePoints );
 return group;
}
```

Note that the propagation of Bounds up the scenegraph hierarchy (from child to parent) *does not* occur with CollisionBounds. Cube4 has CollisionBounds of *(−10,−10,−10) −> (10,10,10)* but these do not influence the Bounds of the parent Group1. Surprisingly, the CollisionBounds of Cube4 *do not* influence the CollisionBounds of the parent Group1 either. It appears that the application programmer is responsible for manually propagating CollisionBounds from child to parent Nodes.

5.4   *GROUP*

```
java.lang.Object
   |
   +--javax.media.j3d.SceneGraphObject
         |
         +--javax.media.j3d.Node
               |
               +--javax.media.j3d.Group
```

Group defines a scenegraph Node that contains a collection of child Nodes. It defines the following child Node management methods:

```
void addChild(Node child)
java.util.Enumeration getAllChildren()
Node getChild(int index)
void insertChild(Node child, int index)
void moveTo(BranchGroup branchGroup)
int numChildren()
void removeChild(int index)
void setChild(Node child, int index)
```

These methods essentially delegate, in obvious ways, to the internal collection that manages the child Nodes within the Group. Table 5.2 shows the capabilities defined by Group.

Table 5.2   Capabilities defined by Group

Capability bit	Description
ALLOW_CHILDREN_EXTEND	Allows child Nodes to be added to the Group
ALLOW_CHILDREN_READ	Allows reading of child Nodes (e.g., getChild method)
ALLOW_CHILDREN_WRITE	Allows writing of child Nodes (e.g., setChild method)
ALLOW_COLLISION_BOUNDS_READ	Allows reading of collision Bounds
ALLOW_COLLISION_BOUNDS_WRITE	Allows writing of collision Bounds

Group is an important base class for the Java 3D Node management classes, and it can also be instantiated in its own right. For increased flexibility, however, I recommend BranchGroup Nodes because they can be dynamically added or removed from the scenegraph. The classes derived from Group are shown in table 5.3.

Table 5.3 Classes derived from `Group`

Class	Description
BranchGroup	A dynamically insertable and removable Group
OrderedGroup	A Group that renders its children in a defined order, irrespective of location
Primitive	A geometric Group used to manage geometry in the utils package
SharedGroup	A Group that can be reused across the scenegraph and can be attached to multiple parents
Switch	A Group that can conditionally display its child Nodes
TransformGroup	A Group that has an associated geometric transformation containing rotation, translation, and scale information that is applied to its child Nodes before rendering

Note that an instance of any of the `Group`-derived classes, including `SharedGroup`, can only be added to a single location within the scenegraph. Attempting to add a scenegraph node to a scenegraph that already has an assigned parent (i.e., a node that has already been added to the scenegraph) will result in a run-time exception. I discuss reusing scenegraph branches using a `SharedGroup` and a `Link` later in this chapter.

5.4.1 Remove a child Node by reference

It is useful to be able to remove a child `Node` from its parent `Group` without knowing the child `Node`'s index. Unfortunately, because scenegraph `Nodes` are removed from a `Group` using `void removeChild(int index)`, there is no easy way to remove a `Shape3D` object from a `Group` if you do not know the index at which it was originally inserted. In the following example, I remove a `Shape3D` object that corresponds to the internal, application-specific data structure. By storing the application-specific data structure in the `UserData` field of the `Shape3D`, I can retrieve the index of the `Shape3D` and remove it from its parent `Group` object.

`ClassificationObject` is an application-specific data structure that is stored in each child `Node` to identify it. To store the `ClassificationObject` in the `Node`, use

```
node.setUserData( classificationObject );

public void removeChildObject( ClassificationObject targetObj )
{
 //we need to remove the object by index, so we have to iterate
 //through our objects to find it.

 //get an enumeration containing all the child nodes
 Enumeration enum = getAllChildren();

 int nIndex = 0;
 Node obj = null;

 //scan through the child nodes until we find the one that
 //corresponds to our data structure.
 while( enum.hasMoreElements() != false )
```

```
{
 obj = (Node) enum.nextElement();

 if( targetObj != obj.getUserData() )
  nIndex++;
 else
  break;
}

//if we found the object, we can now remove it by index.
if( nIndex < numChildren() )
  removeChild( nIndex );
else
  System.out.println( "Failed to find child object during
    remove operation." );
}
```

Note that in the preceding example, the implicit this is an instance of a class derived from Group that has the capability to remove child Nodes based on an internal data structure.

5.5   SWITCH

```
java.lang.Object
  |
  +--javax.media.j3d.SceneGraphObject
        |
        +--javax.media.j3d.Node
            |
            +--javax.media.j3d.Group
                |
                +--javax.media.j3d.Switch
```

The Switch Node provides the facility to define a Group Node that can conditionally display or hide its child Nodes (see table 5.4).

Table 5.4 Switch Node modes

Effect	Usage example
All child Nodes	new Switch(Switch.CHILD_ALL)
No child Nodes	new Switch(Switch.CHILD_NONE)
A single child Node	switchNode.setWhichChild(nIndex)
Specifiable child Nodes	new Switch(Switch.CHILD_MASK), switchNode.setChildMask(java.util.BitSet childMask)

For example, to create a Switch Node that displays child Nodes at index 3, 6, and 7 use the following:

```
//create the Switch Node
Switch switchGroup = new Switch( Switch.CHILD_MASK );
switchGroup.setCapability( Switch.ALLOW_SWITCH_WRITE );

switchGroup.addChild( createLabel( "Child Node 1", labelScale ) );
switchGroup.addChild( createLabel( "Child Node 2", labelScale ) );
switchGroup.addChild( createLabel( "Child Node 3", labelScale ) );
switchGroup.addChild( createLabel( "Child Node 4", labelScale ) );
switchGroup.addChild( createLabel( "Child Node 5", labelScale ) );
switchGroup.addChild( createLabel( "Child Node 6", labelScale ) );
switchGroup.addChild( createLabel( "Child Node 7", labelScale ) );

//create the logical mask to control Node visibility
java.util.BitSet visibleNodes = new java.util.BitSet(
switchGroup.numChildren() );

//make the third, sixth and seventh nodes visible
visibleNodes.set( 2 );
visibleNodes.set( 5 );
visibleNodes.set( 6 );

//assign the visibility mask to the Switch
switchGroup.setChildMask( visibleNodes );
```

The output of the SwitchTest example is shown in figure 5.1.

The Switch Node can be used to implement *modal* static scenegraphs, that is, scenegraphs that are essentially of a fixed structure but which the user can influence through adding or removing prebuilt sections.

Switch Nodes can also be used to implement simple animation using the SwitchInterpolator Behavior (figure 5.2). The SwitchInterpolator attaches to a Switch Node and cycles the active child of the Switch Node using an Alpha object. For example, a simple 3D "flip-book" style animation could be achieved by adding several versions of a 3D model to a Switch Node and triggering a SwitchInterpolator to cycle from one model to another.

BEWARE If you choose to use the SwitchInterpolator class, do not add the Interpolator as a child of the Switch Node itself, or the moment the Interpolator is activated it will deactivate itself, hence stopping the Interpolator.

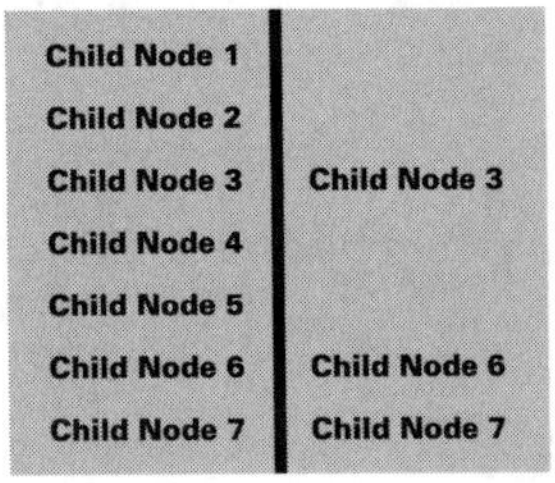

Figure 5.1
The effect of using a BitSet mask and a Switch Node. On the left, the Switch Node has been created with the Switch.CHILD_ALL attribute. On the right, a BitSet has been created to display the third, sixth, and seventh Node through a call to setChildMask. The child elements being controlled by the Switch Node are Text2D objects

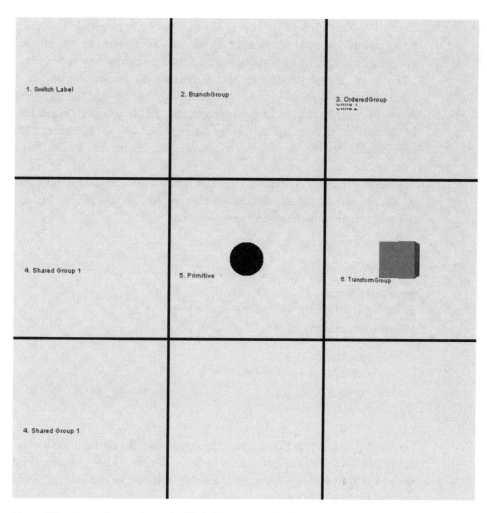

Figure 5.2 Seven frames from the NodesTest example. A `Switch` Node is created with seven child elements, and a SwitchInterpolator is used to cycle between them. Note that the items at index 3 (row 2, column 1) and 6 (row 3, column 1) use a `Link` Node to share a single SharedGroup

5.6 BRANCHGROUP

```
java.lang.Object
  |
  +--javax.media.j3d.SceneGraphObject
      |
      +--javax.media.j3d.Node
          |
          +--javax.media.j3d.Group
              |
              +--javax.media.j3d.BranchGroup
```

BranchGroup defines a Group Node that can be dynamically inserted or removed from a parent Group at runtime. In addition the root parent Group of the scenegraph must be a BranchGroup since only BranchGroups can be inserted into a Locale.

To allow a BranchGroup to be dynamically removed from its parent, the BranchGroup must have the BranchGroup.ALLOW_DETACH capability set. To allow a BranchGroup to be dynamically inserted (or attached) into a parent Group the Group must have the capability Group.ALLOW_CHILDREN_EXTEND. Why these capabilities have been divided between the Group and BranchGroup classes is not quite clear.

BranchGroups are typically used as return values by the methods that build the various components of an application scenegraph. For example, an F1 racing application might define the following abstract class:

```
abstract class F1Object extends Object
{
 BranchGroup   m_BranchGroup = null;

 public F1Object();
 protected BranchGroup createBranchGroup();

 public getBranchGroup()
 {
  if( m_BranchGroup == null )
   m_BranchGroup = createBranchGroup();

  return m_BranchGroup;
 }
}
```

The F1Object abstract class forces the application developer to define the create-BranchGroup virtual method in a derived class. The createBranchGroup method is responsible for creating a BranchGroup containing the child Nodes required to define the Geometry and Behaviors for the F1Object being created. This very simple OO design allows an F1Object Manager class to be defined that maintains a Vector (or List or Map) of generic F1Objects and is responsible for their creation and removal from the applications scenegraph. The objects derived from F1Object are themselves easily reusable because their geometry generation and management routines are all packages with the class itself. The setUserData method (defined in the section on Group Nodes) can be used to track F1Object instances once they have been inserted into the scenegraph.

5.7 ORDEREDGROUP

```
java.lang.Object
   |
   +--javax.media.j3d.SceneGraphObject
        |
        +--javax.media.j3d.Node
             |
             +--javax.media.j3d.Group
                  |
                  +--javax.media.j3d.OrderedGroup
```

The OrderedGroup Node is a less commonly used scenegraph element. It allows an application developer to have basic control over the rendering order of the children of a Group Node.

An OrderedGroup (or DecalGroup which is derived from OrderedGroup) can be useful for defining the rendering order for essentially coplanar surfaces, such as a road lying on terrain, or a cloth covering a table (figure 5.3). Note that both of these examples make implicit assumptions about the range of possible viewing angles for the objects, if the viewer can sit underneath the table, the tablecloth should *not* be rendered before the table! Other uses for an OrderedGroup might be to implement signs or labels for geometric objects—the labels should always be rendered on top of the objects they are labeling, irrespective of the viewer's position.

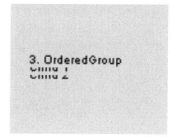

Figure 5.3
The effect of rendering three coplanar child Nodes
using an OrderedGroup. **The item at index 0**
(a Text2D object with the text "3. OrderedGroup"),
overlaps the item at index 1 (Child 1), which overlaps
the item at index 2 (Child 2)

From NodesTest.java

```
OrderedGroup orderedGroup = new OrderedGroup();
orderedGroup.addChild
   ( createLabel( "3. OrderedGroup", labelScale ) );
orderedGroup.addChild( createLabel( "Child 1", labelScale ) );
orderedGroup.addChild( createLabel( "Child 2", labelScale ) );
```

5.8 SHAREDGROUP AND LINK

```
java.lang.Object
   |
   +--javax.media.j3d.SceneGraphObject
         |
         +--javax.media.j3d.Node
               |
               +--javax.media.j3d.Group
                     |
                     +--javax.media.j3d.SharedGroup
```

The SharedGroup Node defines a scenegraph management Node that can be attached to several parent Nodes. The SharedGroup itself can be arbitrarily complex but must occur (as a whole) as a Leaf Node within the scenegraph. A SharedGroup must be wrapped in an instance of a Link object before being added to the scenegraph. The Link must have one unique parent.

SharedGroups *cannot* contain the following Nodes:

- Background
- Behavior-derived
- Clip
- Fog
- Soundscape
- ViewPlatform

```
java.lang.Object
   |
   +--javax.media.j3d.SceneGraphObject
         |
         +--javax.media.j3d.Node
               |
               +--javax.media.j3d.Leaf
                     |
                     +--javax.media.j3d.Link
```

The Link Node is used in association with a SharedGroup. Since the SharedGroup can appear in several locations in the scenegraph, and a Node object can only have a single parent Node, a unique Link Node must be used as a placeholder within the scenegraph for the SharedGroup Node. When the scenegraph is traversed, and the Link Node is encountered, the traversal algorithm will step into the SharedGroup that is internally referenced by the Link Node (figure 5.4).

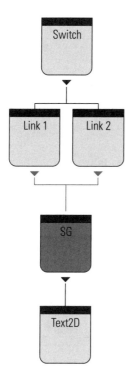

Figure 5.4
A Switch Node with two child Link Nodes. **Both** Link Nodes **reference the same** SharedGroup **(SG). This type of structure is not possible without using** Link Nodes **as a single** Node **can only have one parent** Node

```
//create the SharedGroup
SharedGroup sharedGroup1 = new SharedGroup();

//add geometry to the SharedGroup
sharedGroup1.addChild
  ( createLabel( "4. Shared Group 1", labelScale ) );

//add the first Link for the SharedGroup
switchGroup.addChild( new Link( sharedGroup1 ) );

//add the second Link for the SharedGroup
switchGroup.addChild( new Link( sharedGroup1 ) );

//Note. The InterpolatorTest example also uses SharedGroups
//and Link Nodes in a more substantial manner.
```

SharedGroups can be very useful in minimizing the memory footprint of an application because a single SharedGroup can be referenced hundreds of times within a scenegraph to position repeating geometry within a scene.

5.9 PRIMITIVE

```
java.lang.Object
   |
  +--javax.media.j3d.SceneGraphObject
        |
       +--javax.media.j3d.Node
             |
            +--javax.media.j3d.Group
                  |
                 +--com.sun.j3d.utils.geometry.Primitive
```

Primitive is a Group-derived class that serves as the base class for the geometric primitives (Box, Sphere, Cone, etc.) that are defined in the Java 3D utils package. Objects of the Primitive class should not be instantiated directly, and the Primitive class is very difficult to extend usefully. For a full discussion of the Primitive class, see chapter 8.

5.10 TRANSFORMGROUP

```
java.lang.Object
   |
  +--javax.media.j3d.SceneGraphObject
        |
       +--javax.media.j3d.Node
             |
            +--javax.media.j3d.Group
                  |
                 +--javax.media.j3d.TransformGroup
```

The TransformGroup Node is central to almost all scenegraph designs. A TransformGroup incorporates the rotation, translation, and scaling information that is applied to all of its child Nodes. Without the TransformGroup, scenegraphs would be static, always positioned at 0,0,0, uniformly unit scaled, and without rotation about any of the axes. Not a very interesting interactive scene.

The TranformGroup controls orientation of its child Nodes through the Transform3D object that it encapsulates (figure 5.5). The Transform3D object represents such transformations using a typical 4 × 4 transformation matrix. The 4 × 4 matrix of double precision numbers allows scaling, rotation, and translation information to be stored and applied by a single matrix.

A detailed understanding of the mathematics behind the Transform3D object is very useful, but is beyond the scope of this book. Some useful references for mathematics for 3D graphics are presented in appendix B. Transform3D includes methods that allow application developers to apply transformations while remaining largely ignorant of the underlying implementation.

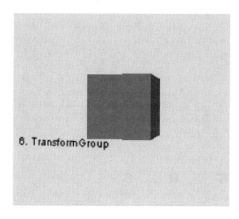

Figure 5.5
A `TransformGroup` is used to rotate a ColorCube and Text2D label to a desired orientation

5.11 SUMMARY

This chapter has introduced many of the `Node` types available in Java 3D. The Java 3D `Nodes` cover the basic requirements of most scenegraphs:

- Propagation of boundary information
- Specification of collision boundary information
- Grouping of `Nodes` into logical units (`Group`)
- Attach and detach Groups (`BranchGroup`)
- Influence the order of rendering within a `Group` (`OrderedGroup`)
- Sharing of `Groups` across the scenegraph hierarchy (`SharedGroup` and `Link`)
- Rotate, translate and scale the children of a Group (`TransformGroup`)

Armed with the information in chapters 4 and 5 you should be able to tackle the high-level scenegraph design for your application. The chapters to come will also be very useful, as we start to discuss how the scenegraph fits into the Java 3D `VirtualUniverse` as well as the rendering model (chapter 6), the data model for your application (chapter 7), and Java 3D's geometry description capabilities (chapter 8).

CHAPTER 6

Defining the universe

One of the fundamental choices you will have to make in your choice of Virtual-Universe configuration is whether to use the SimpleUniverse utility classes or to rely upon the lower level VirtualUniverse classes. By the end of this chapter you should understand the elements of the Java 3D scenegraph rendering model.

Essential elements of the Java 3D scenegraph are covered:

- Defining regions within your universe using Locales
- Attaching the View model to the VirtualUniverse through the View-Platform
- Using multiple Views for rendering
- SimpleUniverse utility classes
- Creating Views, Geometry, and PlatformGeometry for Avatars

6.1 LOCALES AND HIRESCOORD

The VirtualUniverse class contains the virtual world that an application developer populates with Geometry, Behaviors, Lights, and so forth. The Virtual-Universe consists of a collection of Locales. A Locale defines a geographical area within the VirtualUniverse and is anchored at a given 3D coordinate. A Locale uses 256-bit coordinates to specify the anchored *x, y,* and *z* position. The 256-bit coordinates are stored in a HiResCoord object and allow a Locale to be positioned within a virtual space the size of the known (physical) universe yet also maintain a precision of a Planck length (smaller than the size of a proton).

Most applications do not require more than one `Locale`; hence the `Simple-Universe` class creates a `VirtualUniverse` instance with a single `Locale`. `SimpleUniverse` is derived from `VirtualUniverse` and is covered in detail in chapter 3. The default constructor for a `Locale` positions the `Locale` at the origin of the `VirtualUniverse`. Within a `Locale`, doubles or floats are used to specify the positions of objects. If a double is large enough to represent the positions of all the objects within your scene accurately, then a single `Locale` should be sufficient.

However, imagine a scenario: your application is to model parts of the galaxy. The model is to contain the planets orbiting the Sun. On the Earth, the model contains a geometry object a few meters across to represent a house. All the objects in the model are to be created to scale.

How would one go about building such a model for the viewer to be able to switch between three different viewing modes?

- Galaxy: See the Sun with the planets rotating about it.
- Earth: See the planet Earth as it spins about its axis.
- House: View the house on earth.

`Locales` were designed to handle applications such as that just described. The `HiResCoordTest` example implements the application shown in figure 6.1. Creating multiple `Locales` is a fairly lengthy process, so the whole example cannot be included here.

The first problem encountered is how to specify the location of a `Locale`.

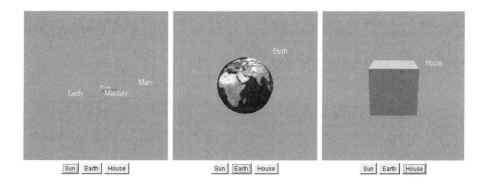

Figure 6.1   Views of the three `Locales` defined in HiResCoordTest.java

```
protected Locale createLocaleEarth( VirtualUniverse u )
{
 int[] xPos = { 0, 0, 0, 0, 0, 0, 0, 0 };
 int[] yPos = { 0, 0, 0, 0, 0, 0, 0, 0 };
 int[] zPos = { 0, 0, 0, 1, 0, 0, 0, 0 };

 HiResCoord hiResCoord = new HiResCoord( xPos, yPos, zPos );
 return new Locale( u, hiResCoord );
}
```

A HiResCoord is created using three 8-element integer arrays. An int is 32 bits, so 8 * 32 = 256 bits.

NOTE   The integer at index 0 contains the most significant bit, while the integer at index 7 contains the least significant bit. The decimal point is defined to lie between indexes 3 and 4, that is,

0x0 0x0 0x0 0x0 . 0x0 0x0 0x0 0x0

The 8-element integer array to specify a coordinate can be considered an 8-digit number in base 2^{32}. The numbers that can be expressed by such an entity are mind-boggling, but table 6.1 (from the API specification) can be used to get you into the right ballpark for the quantity you are trying to express.

Table 6.1   Physical dimensions expressed as a power of 2

2^n Meters	Units
87.29	Universe (20 billion light-years)
69.68	Galaxy (100,000 light-years)
53.07	Light-year
43.43	Solar system diameter
23.60	Earth diameter
10.65	Mile
9.97	Kilometer
0.00	Meter
−19.93	Micron
−33.22	Angstrom
−115.57	Planck length

For example, to specify a distance in light-years (9,460 billion kilometers), find from table 6.1 that $2^{53.07}$ is equal to 9,460 billion kilometers. That is, a 1 at the 53rd bit position will be approximately one light-year. When mapped into the integer array, the 53rd bit is located within the integer at index 3 – 53/32 = 2. It is the 21st bit (53 – 32) within the third integer of the array. The number 2^{21} equals 0x200000, so setting the integer at index 2 of the integer array to 0x200000 will create a HiResCoord instance that stores approximately a light-year.

The integer at index 3 is defined to store meters, so simply setting the integer at index 3 will define a HiResCoord in meters. Conversely, the 20th bit to the right of the decimal point position is approximately a micron.

A useful exercise would be to develop a Java class that returned a HiResCoord for quantities expressed in the various units shown in table 6.1.

```
//creates a Locale that is positioned (2^32 + 5) meters
//away from the origin in the +Z direction.
int[] xPos = { 0, 0, 0, 0, 0, 0, 0, 0 };
int[] yPos = { 0, 0, 0, 0, 0, 0, 0, 0 };
int[] zPos = { 0, 0, 1, 5, 0, 0, 0, 0 };

HiResCoord hiResCoord = new HiResCoord( xPos, yPos, zPos );
```

Once a Locale has been created and positioned, it can be populated with geometry by attaching a BranchGroup containing scenegraph elements:

```
//create the Universe
m_Universe = new VirtualUniverse();

//create the position for the Locale
int[] xPos = { 0, 0, 0, 0, 0, 0, 0, 0 };
int[] yPos = { 0, 0, 0, 0, 0, 0, 0, 0 };
int[] zPos = { 0, 0, 1, 5, 0, 0, 0, 0 };
HiResCoord hiResCoord = new HiResCoord( xPos, yPos, zPos );

//create the Locale and attach to the VirtualUniverse
Locale locale = new Locale( u, hiResCoord );

//create the BranchGroup containing the Geometry for the scene
BranchGroup sceneBranchGroup = createSceneBranchGroup();
sceneBranchGroup.compile();

//add the scene BranchGroup to the Locale
locale.addBranchGraph( sceneBranchGroup );
```

Note that this code will not yet make the geometry visible until a View and a View-Platform are created. This is the subject of the next section.

6.2   VIEW, VIEWPLATFORM, AND LOCALE

Now that a Locale has been created and populated with geometry, Java 3D must be instructed to render the Locale. The key to Java 3D rendering is the View class which attaches to the ViewPlatform instance that is within the scenegraph. The View controls Java 3D rendering and must have an attached Canvas3D component to render into. Multiple Canvas3D instances can be attached to the View, allowing multiple (identical) copies of the View to be rendered simultaneously.

CLIPPING PLANES The clipping planes for the `View` control how much of the scene is rendered. In the example, the front plane is 10 meters from the viewer, while the back clipping plane is 110 meters from the viewer. However, since the viewer has been moved back 20 meters from the origin, the scene will be rendered from −10 to +90 in the Z direction. Note that one cannot set arbitrary clipping planes. The clipping planes have a physical significance in that they define a *view frustum*. The view frustum defines the pyramidal volume of 3D space that is rendered.

The `ViewPlatform` is a simple Java 3D `Leaf Node` and can be added to the `Locale` as shown by the Java3dApplet code:

Based on Java3dApplet.java

```
//create the ViewPlatform BranchGroup
BranchGroup vpBranchGroup = new BranchGroup();

//create a TransformGroup to scale the ViewPlatform
//(and hence View)
TransformGroup tg = new TransformGroup();

//create the ViewPlatform
ViewPlatform vp = new ViewPlatform();
vp.setViewAttachPolicy( View.RELATIVE_TO_FIELD_OF_VIEW );

//attach the ViewPlatform to the TransformGroup
tg.addChild( vp );

//attach the TransformGroup to the BranchGroup
vpBranchGroup.addChild( tg );

//finally, add the ViewPlatform BranchGroup to the Locale
locale.addBranchGraph( vpBranchGroup );
```

Note that the `TransformGroup` created just before the `ViewPlatform` can be used to scale, translate, or rotate the scene rendered by the `View` attached to the `ViewPlatform`. For example:

```
//Move the camera BACK a little. Note that Transformation
//matrices above the ViewPlatform are inverted by the View
//renderer prior to rendering. By moving the camera back 20
//meters, you can see geometry objects that are positioned at 0,0,0.
Transform3D t3d = new Transform3D();
t3d.setTranslation( new Vector3d( 0.0, 0.0, 20.0 ) );
tg.setTransform( t3d );
```

Now we need to create the `View` object itself and attach it to the `ViewPlatform` that was added to the scenegraph.

```
//create the View object
View view = new View();
```

```
//create the PhysicalBody and PhysicalEnvironment for the View
//and attach to the View
PhysicalBody pb = new PhysicalBody();
PhysicalEnvironment pe = new PhysicalEnvironment();
view.setPhysicalEnvironment( pe );
view.setPhysicalBody( pb );

//attach the View to the ViewPlatform
view.attachViewPlatform( vp );

//set the near and far clipping planes for the View
view.setBackClipDistance( 110 );
view.setFrontClipDistance( 10 );
```

Finally, create a `Canvas3D` component (an AWT object) and add it to the `View`'s list of `Canvases` to be rendered into.

```
//create the Canvas3D that the View will render into.
//get the graphics capabilities of the system and create
//the best Canvas3D possible.
GraphicsConfigTemplate3D gc3D = new GraphicsConfigTemplate3D();
gc3D.setSceneAntialiasing( GraphicsConfigTemplate.PREFERRED );
GraphicsDevice gd[] = GraphicsEnvironment.
 getLocalGraphicsEnvironment().getScreenDevices();

Canvas3D c3d = new Canvas3D( gd[0].getBestConfiguration( gc3D ) );

//set the size of the Canvas3D
c3d.setSize( 512, 512 );

//add the Canvas3D to the View so that it is rendered into
view.addCanvas3D( c3d );

//add the Canvas3D component to a parent AWT or Swing Panel
add( c3d );
```

6.3   *SimpleUniverse*

To simplify creating the `View` side of the scenegraph, Sun has provided the `SimpleUniverse` class (figure 6.2). `SimpleUniverse` is defined in the `com.sun.j3d.utils` package and as such should not be considered part of the core Java 3D API. The `SimpleUniverse` class hides some of the complexity of manually defining the `View` side of the scenegraph at the expense of the flexibility of using the core API classes only.

   `SimpleUniverse` is a bit of a misnomer since the class is anything but simple, and this can cause initial confusion because of the plethora of support classes that it relies upon. `SimpleUniverse` introduces five new (non-core-API) classes:

- `Viewer`, a container class that keeps references to the following:

     `ViewerAvatar`, a representation of the viewer of the scene.

     `Canvas3D`, used for rendering the scene.

     AWT `Frame` contains the `Canvas3D` used for rendering.

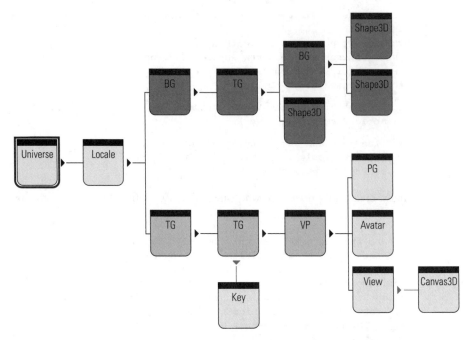

Figure 6.2 The `SimpleUniverse` class encapsulates the details of the view side of the scenegraph (lower branch). The ViewingPlatform has been highlighted and contains a `MultiTransformGroup` composed of two `TransformGroups`. Attached to the `ViewPlatform` are a `PlatformGeometry` Group and a `ViewerAvatar` Group. By attaching a `Key` behavior to one of the `TransformGroups` in the `MultiTransformGroup`, the View, `PlatformGeometry`, and `ViewerAvatar` can all be moved simultaneously and rendered into the `Canvas3D` attached to the view

> `PhysicalBody` references the view's `PhysicalBody`.
>
> `PhysicalEnvironment` references the view's `PhysicalEnvironment`.
>
> View is used for the viewer of the scene.

- `ViewingPlatform` (extends `BranchGroup`) helps set up the `View` side of the scenegraph by creating a hierarchy of `TransformGroups` above the `View-Platform` where the view is attached to the scenegraph. The hierarchy of `TransformGroups` is encapsulated in a `MultiTransformGroup`. In this way a series of transformations can be applied to the view irrespective of transformations that are applied on the geometry side of the scenegraph.

- `ViewerAvatar` (extends `BranchGroup`) contains the geometry used to render the viewer's virtual self in the virtual environment.

- `MultiTransformGroup` is a simple encapsulation of a `Vector` of `Trans-formGroups`.

- `PlatformGeometry` (extends `BranchGroup`) contains the geometry associated with the viewer's `ViewingPlatform`. For example, in a multiplayer gaming scenario, each player might be able to drive one of several vehicles. A `Viewing-Platform` would represent each vehicle in the scenegraph, and the geometry for the vehicle would be attached to the `ViewingPlatform`. The player would be represented by geometry attached to the `ViewerAvatar`, which in turn would govern another player's view of the player, while the `ViewingPlatform` would contain the geometry to describe the internal characteristics of the vehicle the player was riding in. By attaching the view to different `ViewingPlatforms`, the player can move between vehicles.

In the PlatformTest example, two avatars (Dan and Jim) and three views are created: overhead, Dan's, and Jim's (figures 6.3–6.5). Each `Avatar` is assigned `ViewerAvatar` geometry (a simple `Cone` pointing in the direction of view) and `PlatformGeometry` (a text label to identify the avatar).

The example is too lengthy to be included in its entirety but some illustrative excerpts have been extracted:

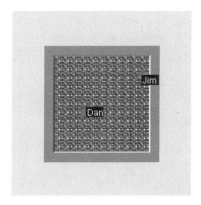

Figure 6.3   Overhead view of the virtual arena with two avatars: Dan and Jim

Figure 6.4   The view for avatar Jim — Jim can see Dan

Figure 6.5   The view for avatar Dan — Dan can see Jim

```java
//This method creates the SimpleUniverse View and ViewPlatform
//scenegraph elements to create an avatar that has an associated
//Canvas3D for rendering, a PlatformGeometry, ViewerAvatar, and a
//KeyNavigator to allow movement of the ViewerAvatar with the
//keyboard.
ViewingPlatform createViewer( Canvas3D c, String szName,
  Color3f objColor, double x, double z )
{
 //create a Viewer and attach to its canvas. A Canvas3D can
 //only be attached to a single Viewer.
 Viewer viewer2 = new Viewer( c );

 //create a ViewingPlatform with 1 TransformGroup above the
 //ViewPlatform
 ViewingPlatform vp2 = new ViewingPlatform( 1 );

 //create and assign the PlatformGeometry to the Viewer
 vp2.setPlatformGeometry( createPlatformGeometry( szName ) );

 //create and assign the ViewerAvatar to the Viewer
 viewer2.setAvatar( createViewerAvatar( szName, objColor ) );

 //set the initial position for the Viewer
 Transform3D t3d = new Transform3D();
 t3d.setTranslation( new Vector3d( x, 0, z ) );
 vp2.getViewPlatformTransform().setTransform( t3d );

 //set capabilities on the TransformGroup so that the
 //KeyNavigatorBehavior can modify the Viewer's position
 vp2.getViewPlatformTransform().setCapability(
  TransformGroup.ALLOW_TRANSFORM_WRITE );
 vp2.getViewPlatformTransform().setCapability(
  TransformGroup.ALLOW_TRANSFORM_READ );

 //attach a navigation behavior to the position of the viewer
 KeyNavigatorBehavior key = new KeyNavigatorBehavior(
  vp2.getViewPlatformTransform() );
 key.setSchedulingBounds( m_Bounds );
 key.setEnable( false );

 //add the KeyNavigatorBehavior to the ViewingPlatform
 vp2.addChild( key );

 //set the ViewingPlatform for the Viewer
 viewer2.setViewingPlatform( vp2 );

 return vp2;
}

//creates and positions a simple Cone to represent the Viewer.
//The Cone is aligned and scaled such that it is similar to a 3D
//"turtle".
ViewerAvatar createViewerAvatar( String szText, Color3f objColor )
{
 ViewerAvatar viewerAvatar = new ViewerAvatar();
```

```
//rotate the Cone so that it is lying down and the sharp end
//is pointed toward the Viewer's field of view.
TransformGroup tg = new TransformGroup();
Transform3D t3d = new Transform3D();
t3d.setEuler( new Vector3d( Math.PI / 2.0, Math.PI, 0 ) );
tg.setTransform( t3d );

//create appearance and material for the Cone
Appearance app = new Appearance();
Color3f black = new Color3f(0.4f, 0.2f, 0.1f);
app.setMaterial(new Material(objColor, black, objColor,
  black, 90.0f));

//create the Primitive and add to the parent BranchGroup
tg.addChild( new Cone( 1, 3, Primitive.GENERATE_NORMALS, app ) );
viewerAvatar.addChild( tg );

return viewerAvatar;
}

//create a simple Raster text label used to help identify
//the viewer.
PlatformGeometry createPlatformGeometry( String szText )
{
 PlatformGeometry pg = new PlatformGeometry();
 pg.addChild( createLabel( szText, 0f, 2f, 0f ) );

 return pg;
}

//creates a simple Raster text label (similar to Text2D)
private Shape3D createLabel( String szText, float x,
  float y, float z )
{
 BufferedImage bufferedImage = new BufferedImage( 25, 14,
  BufferedImage.TYPE_INT_RGB );
 Graphics g = bufferedImage.getGraphics();
 g.setColor( Color.white );
 g.drawString( szText, 2, 12 );

 ImageComponent2D imageComponent2D = new ImageComponent2D(
  ImageComponent2D.FORMAT_RGB, bufferedImage );

 //create the Raster for the image
 javax.media.j3d.Raster renderRaster = new javax.media.j3d.Raster(
            new Point3f( x, y, z ),
            javax.media.j3d.Raster.RASTER_COLOR,
            0, 0,
            bufferedImage.getWidth(),
            bufferedImage.getHeight(),
            imageComponent2D,
            null );

 return new Shape3D( renderRaster );
}
```

6.3.1 Avatars and platform geometry

The `SimpleUniverse` class allows you to attach geometry to the viewer of your 3D scene. There are two methods of attaching viewer geometry using the `Simple-Universe` class: `ViewingPlatform.setPlatformGeometry` or `Viewer.set-Avatar`. The `ViewingPlatform` can be accessed from the `SimpleUniverse` by calling `getViewingPlatform` or calling `getViewer` to access the `Viewer` object. There does not seem to be any difference between these two methods.

There is nothing magical about the geometry that represents the viewer; it may be easier, and more consistent in your application, to represent the viewer using a separate `BranchGroup` attached to the root of your scenegraph. `SimpleUniverse` is defined in the Java 3D utilities package (`com.sun.java.j3d.utils`) along with the `Viewer`, `ViewerAvatar`, and `ViewingPlatform` classes. These classes are merely defined for convenience; it may be safer to use the core Java 3D scenegraph management classes.

That said, here is a short example of using `setPlatformGeometry` to assign geometry for the `Viewer`; the output is shown in figures 6.6–6.7.

Figure 6.6   A frame rendered by `AvatarTest`. The viewer's avatar is the large cube to the right of the frame

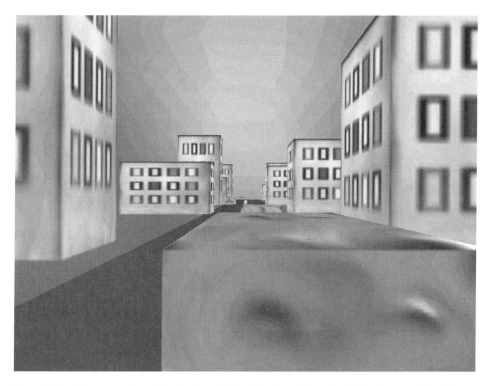

Figure 6.7 A frame rendered by `AvatarTest`. The viewer's avatar is the large cube in the center of the frame

```
//Create a simple scene and attach it to the virtual universe
SimpleUniverse u = new SimpleUniverse();

//Add everything to the scene graph—it will now be displayed.
BranchGroup scene = sg.createSceneGraph();
u.addBranchGraph(scene);

PlatformGeometry pg = sg.createPlatformGeometry();

//set the just created PlatformGeometry.
ViewingPlatform vp = u.getViewingPlatform();
vp.setPlatformGeometry(pg);

//or

Viewer viewer = u.getViewer();

ViewerAvatar viewerAvatar = new ViewerAvatar();
viewerAvatar.addChild( sg.createViewerAvatar() );

viewer.setAvatar( viewerAvatar );
```

6.4　BACKGROUND GEOMETRY

Background geometry is assumed to be positioned at infinite distance, that is, no perspective calculations need to be performed. It is also assumed that it has been tessellated onto a unit sphere. In addition, a background color, an image, and the bounds within which the background is active can be specified. Background geometry is rendered after the background image has been drawn. See figures 6.8–6.10.

Figure 6.8　Sphere background geometry. A texture image was applied to the sphere and normal vectors generated such that the texture is visible when viewed from within the sphere

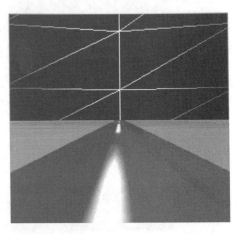

Figure 6.9　Sphere used as background geometry, rendered as a wireframe with an applied texture image

**Figure 6.10
The texture image used to generate the "sunset" effect used in AvatarTest.java. Note that the texture coordinates set by the sphere primitive require that the sunset portion of the image be split in half and inverted**

```
//To set a Background image:
ImageComponent2D image = new TextureLoader(
  "sky.jpg", this).getScaledImage( 1300,1300 );
Background back = new Background( image );
back.setApplicationBounds( getBoundingSphere() );

//To set Background Geometry:
Background back = new Background();
BranchGroup bgGeometry = new BranchGroup();

Appearance ap = new Appearance();
Texture tex = new TextureLoader( "back.jpg", this).getTexture();
ap.setTexture( tex );

Sphere sphere = new Sphere( 1.0f, Primitive.GENERATE_TEXTURE_COORDS |
  Primitive.GENERATE_NORMALS_INWARD, ap );

bgGeometry.addChild( sphere );
back.setGeometry( bgGeometry );
```

The foregoing examples have the effect of setting a background image. However, the second approach, using a texture-mapped sphere with the image applied, has an advantage: the texture image is automatically scaled when it is applied to the sphere. In the first example, the background image must be manually scaled to correspond to the size of the rendering window. If the rendering window is resizable, the image must be rescaled or it will merely be painted into the top left corner of the rendering window. Applying the image as a texture may also render considerably faster depending upon your rendering hardware.

In the second example, note that the normal vectors generated for the Sphere must point *inward* because the viewer is *inside* the generated Sphere and views the texture applied to the inside of the Sphere. Alternately, the sphere's PolygonAttributes can be set to CULL_NONE to render triangles with Normal vectors pointing away from the viewer.

6.5 USING MULTIPLE VIEWS

Multiple views can be a useful technique for rendering different views of the created scene. Multiple views are often used in CAD or 3D-editor applications to display the three orthogonal views of an object (side, top, front) as well as an interactive camera view. For complex 3D manipulation, multiple views are sometimes the only way to give the user the required degree of control for interactive object manipulation.

There are a few issues that you should be aware of if you opt to use multiple views.

6.5.1 Billboards and LOD behaviors

Java 3D implements Billboard (rotate the object to face the viewer) and LOD (vary the geometry of objects depending on distance from viewer) as operations that directly manipulate the scenegraph. This obviously has implications when there is more than one viewer: if the Billboard Behavior rotates an object to face Viewer1, it cannot simultaneously rotate the object to face Viewer2.

If there is more than one active View, the Billboard and LOD Behaviors will use the orientation and distance information from the *first* View attached to the live ViewPlatform. This is defined as the *primary* View for the Behavior and can be returned using the Behavior.getView() method.

The OrientedShape3D class defines a variant of the Shape3D class that is always aligned to face the viewer, irrespective of View.

Sun will be offering more complete support for multiple Views in forthcoming releases, so check the latest details at the Sun Java 3D site.

6.6 SUMMARY

By now you should have some good ideas as to how you will assemble your application from the components supplied by the Java 3D API, as well as many of the capabilities of the API. The VirtualUniverse class provides flexibility in defining your application's view of your virtual world while the SimpleUniverse class abstracts some of the underlying details and provides a good starting point for simple applications or prototypes. Java 3D's view model includes built-in support for some powerful features: multiple Locales for very large worlds, rendering to stereoscopic displays, geometry to represent both the view and the viewer, and a physical environment for the view. We have only been able to touch on many of the capabilities—many more are introduced in later chapters. If you are interested in using the VirtualUniverse class directly please refer to chapter 17 and the SwingTest example, which builds up the scenegraph from scratch using VirtualUniverse.

In the next chapter, we will start to discuss the important question of the data model you should adopt for your application. Your data model design will ideally be efficient for rendering, while flexible and maintainable enough to satisfy your application and development goals.

C H A P T E R   7

Data model design

By thinking about the requirements of your data model in a conscious way early on in your development cycle, you can make Java 3D rendering an implementation of a view into your data model—rather than the data model itself.

Fundamentally you will have to decide upon an internal data model suitable for your application. This will be one of the following types:

- Surface (skin) model
- Voxel (volume) model
- Mathematical parametric model

The decisions you make in this chapter will probably have the greatest impact upon your application performance. From the outset you should be intimately aware of the performance objectives for your application and the features your data model will have to support.

7.1   CHOOSING A DATA MODEL

When designing your 3D application the obvious place to start is to consider your user's view of the application. Everything that is rendered (drawn) by the underlying Java 3D scenegraph renderer can be described as geometry. Discussions of geometry are generally independent of such issues as user interaction, view parameters and rotation, rendering attributes, and object lighting.

The geometry defined in your scene is rendered by the Java 3D renderer using the current view parameters and the geometry's attributes, such as color, material, and lighting. The choice of geometry description will probably be the most influential factor in deciding eventual application performance. Deciding the geometry description will always entail making several compromises between contradictory factors such as rendering speed and quality, size of data models, asset managements and load time.

A simple 3D model viewer might simply load a 3D model file (perhaps in VRML format), use a Java 3D file loader to convert the model into Java 3D objects, then render it. For interactive applications however (such as games requiring complex character animation) or scientific visualization applications dealing with large data sets, such a simple approach will rarely suffice.

3D character animation may require that a data model support animation using inverse kinematics, that it implement skin-and-bones animation systems that can be scripted, or that it have data from motion capture devices played back through the characters. The Cosm team (http://www.cosm-game.com) is busy creating an online world built using Java and Java 3D that includes skin-and-bones character animation. You can also download some sample code for skin-and-bones animation from http://www.j3d.org.

Motion capture is becoming an increasingly important technology for the level of realism required by the latest games. Dedicated motion capture labs, such as EdVEC in Scotland (http://www.edvec.ed.ac.uk), provide sophisticated camera equipment to capture 3D motion and data models.

Scientific visualization applications are generally required to visualize extremely complex data sets, which may not have an obvious representation as 3D objects. Key elements of these applications choose informative 3D data representations, process the raw data, and ensure that the processed data can be rendered efficiently. Visualization data sets may be N-dimensional (meteorology or MRI data for example) or may have to be created from thousands of 2D images as in the Visible Human Project (http://www.nlm.nih.gov/research/visible/visible_human.html).

Algorithms to construct surfaces from 3D data points, adaptive meshes, and dynamic levels of detail may all be required to generate compelling interactive worlds from the raw input data. It is hard to overstate the importance of understanding your feature and performance objectives as you design your data model. Java 3D provides little support for anything other than simple point, line, and triangle rendering, so you may need a convenient internal representation (*model*), which can then be converted into a representation for rendering (*view*). The rendering representation may need to make assumptions as to the current available hardware, or it may be adaptive and modify the representation based on a target frame-rate for the application.

7.1.1   Surface models

Typically, geometry is described as a collection of triangles, or faces, that define an approximation of the outer skin of the object. Importantly, most rendering hardware is optimized to render triangles. Unfortunately, defining objects using a triangular skin description loses many important properties of a 3D model.

A triangulation, by its nature, makes assumptions regarding the rendering hardware available to an application. The application developer may want to create an application that renders an object on a low-end system using 100 triangles, while rendering the object using 10,000 triangles on high-end systems. Such formulations can be accommodated by using a LOD description that allows an application to load several definitions of an object and choose the one most appropriate given the object's position in the scene and system performance. It may also be possible to dynamically retriangulate the points that compose the surface of the model. This technique is commonly applied to terrain using variants of the ROAM algorithm. The Virtual Terrain site (http://www.vterrain.org) contains may good links to terrain rendering.

Any skin (surface triangulation) description cannot, by its nature, contain information for the internal characteristics of an object. Skin descriptions are merely concerned with surface appearance, and generally assume homogenous (or irrelevant) internal characteristics. Solid modeling operations—operations such as generating two new objects by slicing a plane through an object—are also difficult to implement using a triangular skin description.

Figures 7.1 and 7.2 show a 3D-facial model rendered as a simple skin model. A pair of carefully calibrated cameras was used to capture the model (including a photo realistic texture image). Surface construction was then performed on the input data to generate triangles, calculate normal vectors, and texture coordinates. Finally the processed data was saved as a VRML file and interactively rendered.

If your geometry is very dynamic, as in character animation, you should definitely consider using Java 3D *geometry-by-reference* support. Releases of Java 3D earlier than version 1.2 would always copy the arrays of data values you passed to it into internal

Figure 7.1
**Skin description. Each triangular face is
rendered using an applied texture image**

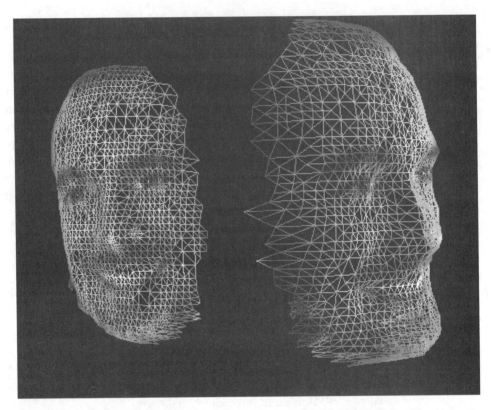

Figure 7.2   Skin description. Each triangular face is rendered using three lines with a texture image applied

data structures. Java 3D version 1.2 introduced a geometry-by-reference feature that eliminates the copying, and greatly improves performance through increased rendering speed and reduced heap allocation and garbage collection. See the `GeometryArray` class and `GeometryUpdater` interface for details of using geometry-by-reference.

7.1.2   Volumetric and mathematical models

Voxel description may be more appropriate if internal object characteristics are not homogenous or if complex object operations must be performed that will significantly alter surface geometry. Voxels are simple building blocks for an object (often cubes), and can possess individual material attributes, allowing nonuniform material descriptions. Thus a pyramid might be described by a sequence of stacked voxels (cubes). Slicing a pyramid with a plane can generate a complex series of geometric shapes; and developing robust algorithms for generating new triangular skin descriptions from an original skin description for a pyramid is a nontrivial problem. Using a voxel-level description, however, the problem is far simpler: if the centroid of a given voxel lies on one side of the slicing plane, assign it to object A, otherwise assign it to object B. Boolean operations, such as calculating the intersection of two arbitrary objects, are also far easier to implement. Applications must typically use a voxel description internally, and generate a skin surface description for rendering. This allows the application to optimize rendering performance (which is required for every frame) while not sacrificing the ability to perform solid modeling operations (which is required occasionally).

Voxel descriptions are often associated with medical visualization applications, particularly for magnetic resonance imaging (MRI) visualization. MRI equipment provides an array of coordinates along with an MRI reading for each coordinate. MRI data can be rendered as an array of cubes with the MRI reading for each cube assigned as a color or transparency for the cube. Finding surfaces across voxels (isosurfaces) may require using the Marching Cubes Algorithm or one of its variants. See W.E. Lorensen, et al., "Marching Cubes: a high resolution 3D surface reconstruction algorithm," *Computer Graphics*, vol. 21, no. 4, pp 163–169 (Proc. of SIGGRAPH), 1987, and Alan Watt, et al., *Advanced Animation and Rendering Techniques*, Addison-Wesley, 1992.

Voxel descriptions also suffer from inherent assumptions regarding the performance of rendering hardware, as the object modeler must decide the voxel resolution required for an object (or part of an object). See figures 7.3, 7.4, and 7.5.

Mathematical object descriptions are useful in that they do not contain assumptions about rendering performance—if an object is described as a sphere, with radius 2.5 meters, the rendering system can render the object in a manner appropriate for the underlying hardware. Non-Uniform Relational B-Splines (NURBS) are commonly

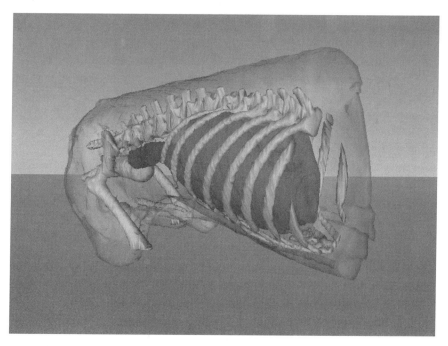

Figure 7.3 Transparent volume rendering of Lucky's (the virtual dog) abdomen. Courtesy Edinburgh Virtual Environment Centre (http://www.edvec.ed.ac.uk)

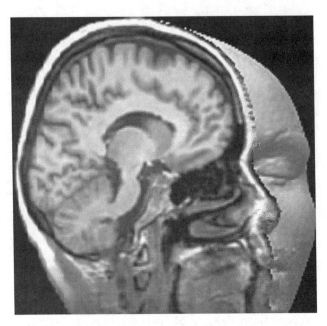

Figure 7.4   Voxel rendering of human skull from MRI data.
Courtesy Ohio State University (http://www.cis.ohio-state.edu/volviz/)

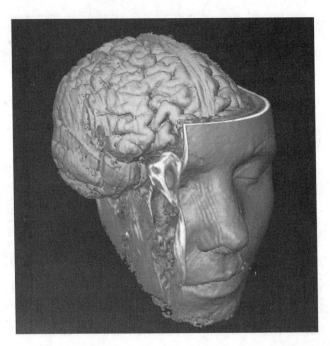

Figure 7.5   Volume rendering of human skull with two sections removed to show internal detail.
Courtesy State University of New York at Stony Brook (http://www.cs.sunysb.edu/~vislab/)

CHAPTER 7   DATA MODEL DESIGN

used in technical modeling applications as they describe an object's surface mathematically and in a manner that can be rendered (with varying accuracy) compatibly with the hardware available.

It is important to reiterate, however, that current 3D video cards used to accelerate rendering deal exclusively in simple strips of triangles. Thus, no matter what level of description you choose for your application, your objects will need to be decomposed into strips of triangles. The low-level graphics language itself may handle this transformation; OpenGL can render NURBS, for example (figure 7.6). Java 3D does not have the ability to render NURBS directly, the application developer must write code to convert the NURBS into triangles prior to rendering.

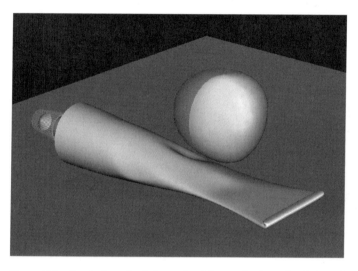

Figure 7.6   Rendering of a tube and a deformed sphere, both described using NURBS. Image produced using Amapi 3D (http://www.eovia.com)

VOXELS OR SKIN DESCRIPTION? You can use some of the items in this list to guide you in your choice of an internal data model:

- Object geometry is static or only varies simply (such as scaling along an access): Skin
- Objects need to be decomposed using Boolean operations: Voxels
- Objects need to have internal material attributes: Voxels
- Internal attributes are uniform or irrelevant: Skin

7.1.3   Implementing in Java 3D

The Java 3D and OpenGL APIs are both focused around rendering skin-based models. The geometric primitives available for rendering points, lines, and triangles are all most suited to rendering surface geometry. Some OpenGL demos, however, implement volume rendering—converting, at runtime, an internal volume-based representation to a surface-based representation for rendering. Doug Gehringer, an engineer at Sun, has written a Java 3D volume rendering demo that is available at http://www.j3d.org.

Volume rendering (on Solaris, only) can also be approximated in Java 3D using the Solaris Texture3D support. Texture3D rendering allows a three-dimensional raster to be mapped onto three-dimensional geometry for rendering.

I have also successfully approximated volume rendering using Java 3D for meteorological visualization by rendering points and providing interactive controls to dynamically apply a rendering threshold to the points. The JavaMet example, included with this book, uses a cloud of points to simulate simple volume rendering. Each point in the cloud has an associated frequency, and the end user can interactively control which points are rendered by adjusting the upper and lower frequency limits (figure 7.7).

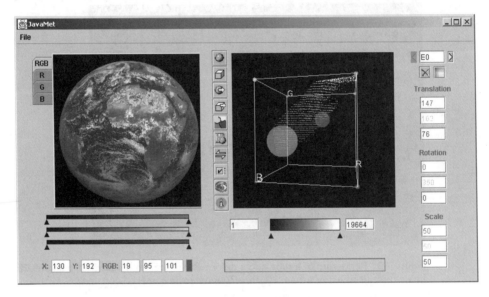

Figure 7.7 The JavaMet application renders the red, green, and blue channels of the image on the left as a series of 3D voxels in the 3D view on the right. Each voxel has a frequency associated with it, and the voxel threshold can be interactively modified using the slider below the 3D view

7.2   PERFORMANCE OBJECTIVES

One of the biggest issues you will face when developing 3D applications is performance, which usually translates to *rendering time*. Rendering time defines how long the Java 3D renderer will take to render a single frame that is a view of your 3D scene. This, in turn, defines the FPS that will be achievable for your application. For games applications and smooth animation, a rate of 20 or more FPS is desirable. Obviously, the FPS that your application will achieve is inherently linked to the hardware that it is running on. When designing your application it is therefore vital to specify your performance objectives on specific platforms. For example, you might want the application to achieve 30 FPS on a 500 MHz PC running Windows 98 with an nVidia GeForce MX video card. This typical system configuration (or target machine) must be the yardstick by which you judge your application and all the decisions you make while designing your application should be evaluated in the context of their impact on the performance of the application running on your target machine (or machines). During the initial design phase, you should run simulated tests on your target machine to evaluate your design decisions and assess whether the performance objectives are achievable.

A trap that developers sometimes fall into is to introduce features that look great on their development machines (which are typically high-end) but cause an overall degradation in performance on users' machines (which are typically closer to the performance of the target machine).

Almost all 3D applications are interactive, that is, the user is able to influence the current point of view or camera and hence the rendered view. The required frame rate is often related to the mode of user interaction: for 3D CAD visualization input is largely mouse or tablet driven and motion is usually confined to a small number of objects and is not continuous. Lower rates of five or more FPS may be acceptable. For interactive 3D games a frame rate is required that allows users to suspend belief and accept that they are moving within the scene. Lower frame rates provide a choppier motion and quickly destroy the impression of smooth movement, 20 or more FPS is typically required.

7.2.1   Rendering quality

Rendering quality depends on such factors as geometry description, low-level graphics language, rendering hardware, and display hardware. Typically the only factor under the developer's direct control is geometry description. The following will influence the visual appearance of rendered geometry:

- Complexity of model description. Such complexity is usually defined in terms of the number of vertices or surfaces.

- Application of different lighting and shading models. Lighting and shading models can be used to influence perceived surface characteristics, such as smoothness of the model (Gauraud shading), or to add specular highlights to the model (Phong shading),

- Complexity of texture images applied to the model. High-resolution texture images are less likely to suffer from becoming pixelated when magnified.

- Java 3D rendering settings. Java 3D and the lower-level graphics language compromise internally between speed and accuracy of rendering. There are settings to tell Java 3D to err on the side of speed or accuracy for everything from perspective calculation through to lighting and fog calculations.

Rendering quality is a difficult balancing act, and a compromise must typically be struck between the complexity of model description plus texture images on the one hand and rendering time on the other. It may be necessary to dynamically change the model description based on the distance of the object from the viewer using a level of detail approach.

Unfortunately, not all software and hardware renderers are created equal, and noticeable differences will be perceived between DirectX and OpenGL rendering as well as between different makes (and versions) of 3D accelerator cards and drivers. To compound matters, certain makes of 3D cards will incorrectly render certain configurations of geometric primitives. The only advice that can be given is to ensure applications are tested on as wide a variety of hardware and software platforms as possible.

7.2.2 Load time

Load time is not typically of paramount importance, but loading large complex geometric models and texture images can become very time consuming, particularly if the models are loaded across the Internet. Like other objectives, load-time objectives should be set and adhered to throughout the development phase.

Before your application's data can be loaded, the JVM must be loaded from disk and started. The time taken to load the JVM is heavily dependent upon available physical memory, and it can take *minutes* to load the JVM on machines with less than 64 MB. You must seriously consider using delayed loading techniques for application data to ensure that the user is not left waiting for several minutes for your application to complete startup.

7.2.3 Memory footprint

The total memory footprint (all allocated memory) of a Java 3D application is unfortunately quite large. Most of the memory allocated will probably be used by the JVM and the Java 3D subsystem. If models and textures are very large, however, they can come to play a significant part in determining runtime memory requirements. Determine the minimum amount of physical memory required on your target machine and endeavor to keep your application's memory footprint within physical memory. Any paging of memory to or from disk (virtual memory) will probably cause your application to be so slow as to be unusable. For Java 3D applications, and certainly applications that also use Swing, the minimum memory requirements for reasonable performance is 64 MB. Running the simplest Java 3D example, HelloUniverse, requires upward of 20 MB.

7.2.4 Development time and asset management

Complex geometry for visualization will either be loaded into your application in a standard 3D graphics file format (such as VRML), a proprietary 3D graphics format, or as raw data that must be processed to produce geometry for rendering. For data in a standard 3D graphics format, one of many available Sun or third-party ObjectLoaders can be used. For data in a proprietary format a custom ObjectLoader can be written that adheres to the interfaces required for ObjectLoaders. Raw numerical data must be processed using application-specific methods. These could include triangulation, surface fitting, geometry assignment and generation, color assignment, and so on.

Many different data loaders (`ObjectLoaders`) have been developed and these are constantly being refined and supplemented. Some of the most popular are the VRML, DXF, and Lightwave data file loaders. These allow 3D graphics designers to work in parallel to define geometry, while Java 3D programmers can concentrate their efforts on UI, application logic, and behavior programming.

7.3   SUMMARY

As you have probably gathered, designing the data model for your application is a complex undertaking. This chapter points out a few landmarks as you work through your design. The requirements of your data model are intimately linked to your application's feature set—the data model for a 3D-combat game will be significantly different from the data model for a MRI visualization application. You should research algorithms that can provide some measure of hardware performance independence and separate your internal data model from that used by Java 3D for rendering. Although Java 3D provides adequate data structures for describing geometry, if you rely on these data structures for your own internal data model, you may be making invalid assumptions about available hardware and precluding the incorporation of your own application-specific optimizations in the future.

C H A P T E R   8

Geometry reference

Just as life offers many choices, Java 3D provides many geometry generation options. By reading the relevant section for the geometry option you are interested in using, you can quickly come up to speed on typical usage and learn useful programming tips.

The sections in this chapter describe the mechanics and implementation issues for the geometry generation options available in Java 3D. These are:

- The Shape3D classes (part of the core javax.media.j3d package)
- Primitive derived classes (from com.sun.java.j3d.utils), including Box, Cone, Sphere, and so on
- Text (2D and 3D) generation

8.1   SHAPE3D

```
java.lang.Object
   |
   +--javax.media.j3d.SceneGraphObject
        |
        +--javax.media.j3d.Node
             |
             +--javax.media.j3d.Leaf
                  |
                  +--javax.media.j3d.Shape3D
```

The Shape3D class is essential to defining viewable geometry in Java 3D. The Shape3D class packages the geometry information for a visual object along with the appearance information that governs how the geometry is rendered. The Appearance class is covered in chapter 9 and includes a variety of rendering attributes (material, line, surface attributes, etc.).

In addition, each Shape3D maintains a Bounds object for use in collision detection and intersection testing between PickRays (lines) and other Shape3D objects in the scene.

As is customary, Shape3D ensures access to internal variables and attributes is subject to the capability bits that have been set for the Shape3D object.

An example class derived from Shape3D is the ColorCube class. The source code for the ColorCube class is available in the com.sun.java.j3d.utils.geometry package where ColorCube is defined. The basic principle is to define geometry using one of the Geometry-derived classes such as QuadArray and then assign the geometry to the Shape3D using setGeometry(...). GeometryArray-derived classes can also store the normal vectors, colors, and texture coordinates for each vertex defined.

8.1.1 The user data field

A useful feature, defined in Shape3D's SceneGraphObject base class, is that each Shape3D has a user data object associated with it. This allows an arbitrary Object-derived class to be attached to the Shape3D object using:

```
public void setUserData(java.lang.Object userData);
public java.lang.Object getUserData();
```

The user data object can then be queried in response to scenegraph operations, for example selecting with the mouse. A selection utility will typically return the Shape3D object that was selected and an application-specific data structure will need to be retrieved to apply the results of the selection operation—this can be stored in the user data field of the Shape3D object.

The user data field can also be used to remove a scenegraph object once it has been added—a useful function. This technique is described in chapter 5.

8.2 PRIMITIVE

```
java.lang.Object
  |
  +--javax.media.j3d.SceneGraphObject
      |
      +--javax.media.j3d.Node
          |
          +--javax.media.j3d.Group
              |
              +--com.sun.j3d.utils.geometry.Primitive
```

Primitive is not part of the Java 3D package (javax.media.j3d) but has been defined in the Java 3D utilities package (com.sun.java.j3d.utils). The Primitive class serves as the base class for several simple geometric shapes that can

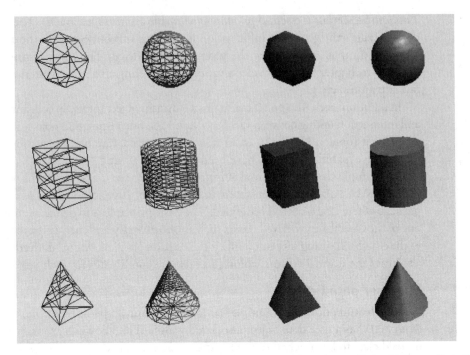

Figure 8.1 Geometric objects derived from `Primitive`: sphere, box, cylinder, and cone. Note the different resolution options and how the `Primitives` are triangulated when drawn as wire frames

act as building blocks for Java 3D developers. The Java 3D `Primitive`-derived classes have been illustrated in figure 8.1.

`Primitive` is derived from `Group`—that is, it is *not* a `Shape3D` object. This is important—a `Primitive` is *not* a shape or geometric object, but is rather a collection of `Shape3D` objects. `Primitive` provides methods to access the subcomponents of the `Group`. There is therefore an important distinction between modifying the characteristics of the `Primitive` (`Group` settings) and modifying the properties of the child `Shape3D` objects (`Shape3D` settings such as `Material`, `Appearance`, etc.)

Because of serious class design issues regarding the `Primitive` base class, I cannot recommend that any of the `Primitive`-derived classes be used in a Java 3D application of any complexity. The fundamental issue is that the `Primitive` class defines a "has-a" relationship for its geometry. That is, a single `Primitive` is defined such that it is a container for its geometric parts. For example, `Box` has six geometric parts: FRONT, BACK, LEFT, RIGHT, TOP, and BOTTOM. To facilitate this relationship the `Primitive` class is derived from `Group`.

The Java 3D scenegraph, however, can only have `Leaf`-derived geometric objects as leaf nodes, and many operations, such as picking for mouse-based selection, are performed on `Shape3D`-derived objects. This lack of compatibility between `Shape3D` objects and `Primitive` objects is something that Sun will address with future releases of Java 3D.

     CHAPTER 8   GEOMETRY REFERENCE

Additionally, it is not generally possible to derive a class from `Primitive` because the class is not designed to be extensible. For example Primitive.java contains the following code:

```
static final int SPHERE = 0x01;
static final int CYLINDER = 0x02;
static final int CONE = 0x04;
static final int BOX = 0x08;
```

This extremely non-object-oriented approach to differentiating between instances of objects derived from `Primitive` essentially makes it impossible for application developers to safely create new `Primitive`-derived classes. In general, classes at the top of a class hierarchy should not have knowledge of derived classes.

Example code for all of the `Primitive`-derived classes is defined in the Sun Conic-World Java 3D demo directory. The ConicWorld demo creates a variety of `Primitive` objects with various lighting, material, and texture attributes.

The following subsections describe the simple geometric `Primitives` defined in `com.sun.j3d.utils.geometry`.

8.2.1 Box

```
java.lang.Object
   |
   +--javax.media.j3d.SceneGraphObject
       |
       +--javax.media.j3d.Node
           |
           +--javax.media.j3d.Group
               |
               +--com.sun.j3d.utils.geometry.Primitive
                   |
                   +--com.sun.j3d.utils.geometry.Box
```

Box defines a simple six-sided cube, illustrated in figure 8.2. Unfortunately for Swing developers this name conflicts with the Swing class `javax.swing.Box` so if your application uses Swing you should reference the Java 3D class explicitly, as in the following:

```
com.sun.j3d.utils.geometry.Box box =
 new com.sun.j3d.utils.geometry.Box( 0.5f, 0.5f, 0.5f, null);
```

Figure 8.2
The Box Primitive

Box contains the following Shape3D objects:

- FRONT = 0;
- BACK = 1;
- RIGHT = 2;
- LEFT = 3;
- TOP = 4;
- BOTTOM = 5;

The identifiers are used as indices into the Primitive Group Node. In other words, to retrieve the FRONT face of the cube, you must call:

```
Shape3D frontFace = box.getShape( Box.FRONT );
```

This is defined in Box.java as:

```
public Shape3D getShape(int partId)
{
 if (partId < FRONT || partId > BOTTOM)
        return null;
    return (Shape3D)((Group)getChild(0)).getChild(partId);
}
```

The faces of the Box are Shape3D objects and are children of the first Node added to the Group. The first Node of the Group is a TransformGroup object that allows the Box to be moved as a whole. Thus, modifying the scale, rotation, and translation of the TransformGroup's Transform3D applies the scale, rotation, and translation to all of its child Nodes also.

The Sun example ConicWorld/BoxExample.java provides an example of creating Boxes and loading and applying texture images to Boxes.

```
//Set Appearance attributes
//first, create an appearance
Appearance ap = new Appearance();

//create a colored material
Color3f aColor  = new Color3f(0.1f, 0.1f, 0.1f);
Color3f eColor  = new Color3f(0.0f, 0.0f, 0.0f);
Color3f dColor  = new Color3f(0.8f, 0.8f, 0.8f);
Color3f sColor  = new Color3f(1.0f, 1.0f, 1.0f);
Material m = new Material(aColor, eColor, dColor, sColor, 80.0f);

//enable lighting and assign material
m.setLightingEnable(true);
ap.setMaterial(m);

//render the Box as a wire frame
PolygonAttributes polyAttrbutes = new PolygonAttributes();
polyAttrbutes.setPolygonMode( PolygonAttributes.POLYGON_LINE );
polyAttrbutes.setCullFace( PolygonAttributes.CULL_NONE ) ;
ap.setPolygonAttributes( polyAttrbutes );
```

```
//create the box and assign the appearance
Box BoxObj = new Box(1.5f, 1.5f, 0.8f, Box.GENERATE_NORMALS |
Box.GENERATE_TEXTURE_COORDS, ap);

//load and assign a texture image and set texture parameters
TextureLoader tex = new TextureLoader( "texture.jpg", "RGB", this);
if (tex != null)
 ap.setTexture(tex.getTexture());
TextureAttributes texAttr = new TextureAttributes();
texAttr.setTextureMode(TextureAttributes.MODULATE);
ap.setTextureAttributes(texAttr);
```

8.2.2 Cone

```
java.lang.Object
  |
  +--javax.media.j3d.SceneGraphObject
       |
       +--javax.media.j3d.Node
            |
            +--javax.media.j3d.Group
                 |
                 +--com.sun.j3d.utils.geometry.Primitive
                      |
                      +--com.sun.j3d.utils.geometry.Cone
```

Cone defines a simple Cone Primitive with a radius and a height, illustrated in figures 8.3 and 8.4. It is a capped cone centered at the origin with its central axis aligned along the Y-axis. The center of the Cone is defined to be the center of its bounding box (rather than its centroid). If the GENERATE_TEXTURE_COORDS flag is set, the texture coordinates are generated so that the texture gets mapped onto the Cone similarly to a Cylinder, except without a top cap.

Cone consists of the following Shape3D objects:

- int BODY = 0;
- int CAP = 1;

Figure 8.3
The Cone Primitive
(low resolution)

Figure 8.4
The Cone Primitive
(high resolution)

By default, 15 surfaces are generated for the sides of the Cone. This can be increased or decreased by using the most customizable constructor:

```
public Cone(float radius, float height, int primflags,
    int xdivision, int ydivision, Appearance ap)
```

The geometry for the Cone consists of a Cylinder tapering from the supplied radius at one end to zero radius at the other end. A disk is created using the same number of divisions as the Cylinder and aligned to close the open end of the Cylinder.

8.2.3   Cylinder

```
java.lang.Object
   |
   +--javax.media.j3d.SceneGraphObject
         |
         +--javax.media.j3d.Node
               |
               +--javax.media.j3d.Group
                     |
                     +--com.sun.j3d.utils.geometry.Primitive
                           |
                           +--com.sun.j3d.utils.geometry.Cylinder
```

The Cylinder Primitive defines a capped cylinder, illustrated in figure 8.5. Cylinder is composed from three Shape3D components: Body, Top disk, and Bottom disk.

Figure 8.5
The Cylinder Primitive

- int BODY = 0;
- int TOP = 1;
- int BOTTOM = 2;

The default number of surfaces created for the body is 15 along the *X*-axis and 1 along the *Y*-axis, the disks are created as 15-sided polygons. Again, use the most complex form of the constructor to vary the number of surfaces generated for the cylinder:

```
public Cylinder(float radius, float height, int primflags,
    int xdivision, int ydivision, Appearance ap) {
```

8.2.4   Sphere

```
java.lang.Object
  |
  +--javax.media.j3d.SceneGraphObject
       |
       +--javax.media.j3d.Node
            |
            +--javax.media.j3d.Group
                 |
                 +--com.sun.j3d.utils.geometry.Primitive
                      |
                      +--com.sun.j3d.utils.geometry.Sphere
```

The `Sphere` `Primitive` defines a sphere with 15 divisions in both the *X*- and *Y*-axes, illustrated in figures 8.6 through 8.8. Use the most customizable form of the constructor to vary the number of surfaces created for the `Sphere`:

```
public Sphere(float radius, int primflags, int divisions,
  Appearance ap)
```

| **Figure 8.6**
 The `Sphere` Primitive
 (low resolution) | **Figure 8.7**
 The `Sphere` Primitive
 (high resolution) | **Figure 8.8**
 `Sphere` Primitive with
 an applied texture image
 of the Earth |

8.2.5   Primitive flags

All of the `Primitives` have a primitive flags (`primflags`) argument in one of their constructors. Primitive flags influence the attributes applied to the `Shape3D` geometry when it is generated internally for the `Primitive`. The available primitive flags are shown in table 8.1.

Table 8.1   Primitive flags for `Primitive` derived classes

Primitive flag	Effect
ENABLE_APPEARANCE_MODIFY	Set ALLOW_APPEARANCE_READ and ALLOW_APPEARANCE_WRITE capabilities on the generated geometry's Shape3D nodes.
ENABLE_GEOMETRY_PICKING	Set ALLOW_INTERSECT capability on the generated geometry.
GENERATE_NORMALS	Generate normal vectors along with geometry.

continued on next page

Table 8.1 Primitive flags for `Primitive` derived classes *(continued)*

Primitive flag	Effect
GENERATE_NORMALS_INWARD	Normal vectors flipped along the surface.
GENERATE_TEXTURE_COORDS	Generate texture coordinates along with geometry.
GEOMETRY_NOT_SHARED	Generate geometry that will not be shared by another scene graph node.

After a `Primitive` has been generated, the capabilities for the `Shape3D` subparts can also be accessed by calling

```
getShape( partid ).setCapability( ALLOW_INTERSECT );
```

Note that the `setPrimitiveFlags` method should not be used, as it does not have any effect once the `Primitive` has been created.

Unless primitive flags are explicitly supplied, the default GENERATE_NORMALS primitive flag is used. In other words, both vertex coordinates and normal vectors are generated (to allow surfaces to be lighted).

8.2.6 Primitives and the geometry cache

The `Primitive`-derived classes use a very simplistic cache to minimize the CPU time used to create the geometry for each class. An analysis of this capability is included in appendix C.

8.3 *GEOMBUFFER*

The `Primitive`-derived classes internally make use of the `GeomBuffer` helper class. This class allows geometry to be defined using an API similar to OpenGL's stateful display list geometry definition API. This capability is discussed in more detail in appendix C and may be useful for porting OpenGL programs.

8.4 *RASTERS*

```
java.lang.Object
   |
   +--javax.media.j3d.SceneGraphObject
       |
       +--javax.media.j3d.NodeComponent
           |
           +--javax.media.j3d.Geometry
               |
               +--javax.media.j3d.Raster
```

The `Raster` class serves double duty in Java 3D. It can be used to either render an image into the 3D scene at a given location or to read the depth components of the 3D scene. The first application is much more common and easier to describe because it truly represents geometry definition.

8.4.1 Rendering an image using a Raster

A `Raster` object can be used to simply paste a 2D image into the 3D view. The `Raster` has a 3D location associated with it, and this serves as the upper-left corner of the rendered image. Note however that the image for the `Raster` is rendered *as-is* and will not have any scaling, translation, or rotation applied to it—regardless of the `Raster`'s position within the scenegraph. A `Raster` might be appropriate for graphical coordinate axis labels, for example. Since `Raster` is derived from `Geometry` it must be encapsulated by a `Shape3D` `Node` before it can be added to the scenegraph.

There are six basic steps to using a Raster:

1 Create the `BufferedImage`.
2 Read in or generate the image data.
3 Create the `ImageComponent2D` to wrap the `BufferedImage`.
4 Create the `Raster` to wrap the `ImageComponent2D`.
5 Create the `Shape3D` to contain the `Raster`.
6 Add the `Shape3D` to the scenegraph.

For example:

```
//create the image to be rendered using a Raster
BufferedImage bufferedImage =
 new BufferedImage( 128, 128, BufferedImage.TYPE_INT_RGB);

//load or do something to the image here…

//wrap the BufferedImage in an ImageComponent2D
ImageComponent2D imageComponent2D =
 new ImageComponent2D( ImageComponent2D.FORMAT_RGB,
                        bufferedImage);
imageComponent2D.setCapability( ImageComponent.ALLOW_IMAGE_READ );
imageComponent2D.setCapability( ImageComponent.ALLOW_SIZE_READ );

//create the Raster for the image
m_RenderRaster = new Raster(  new Point3f( 0.0f, 0.0f, 0.0f ),
                              Raster.RASTER_COLOR,
                              0, 0,
                              bufferedImage.getWidth(),
                              bufferedImage.getHeight(),
                              imageComponent2D,
                              null );

m_RenderRaster.setCapability( Raster.ALLOW_IMAGE_WRITE );
m_RenderRaster.setCapability( Raster.ALLOW_SIZE_READ );

//wrap the Raster in a Shape3D
Shape3D shape = new Shape3D( m_RenderRaster );
```

8.4.2 Retrieving scene depth components using a Raster

The other, more unusual, application for a `Raster` is to use it to retrieve the depth components of the 3D scene. These are stored in the Z-buffer, a multibyte array that stores the depth into the scene for each rendered pixel. The depth to the first occurrence of geometry is stored in the Z-buffer, and floating point values are scaled such that the closest value to the user is zero while the farthest value is one.

Querying the Z-buffer directly is quite uncommon, but may be useful for such application-specific functionality as hit testing or rendering.

The following example illustrates overriding the `Canvas3D postSwap` method to retrieve the contents of the Z-buffer for the scene using a `Raster` object. The Z-buffer `Raster` is then used to dynamically update an image `Raster` so that the depth components can be rendered graphically. The output from the RasterTest illustrating this technique is shown in figure 8.9.

Figure 8.9   Two frames from RasterTest. Each frame contains a rotating cube and a `Raster` displaying the depth components of the entire frame. The `Raster` is visible because it also has a depth component

From RasterTest.java

```
//size of the window, and hence size of the depth component array
private static int    m_kWidth = 300;
private static int    m_kHeight = 300;

//the Raster used to store depth components
private Raster     m_DepthRaster = null;

//the Raster used to render an image into the 3D view
private Raster     m_RenderRaster = null;

//an array of integer values for the depth components
private int[]     m_DepthData = null;

//create the image to be rendered using a Raster
BufferedImage bufferedImage = new BufferedImage( 128, 128, Buffered-
Image.TYPE_INT_RGB );
ImageComponent2D imageComponent2D = new ImageComponent2D(
ImageComponent2D.FORMAT_RGB, bufferedImage );
imageComponent2D.setCapability( ImageComponent.ALLOW_IMAGE_READ );
```

```java
imageComponent2D.setCapability( ImageComponent.ALLOW_SIZE_READ );

//create the depth component to store the 3D depth values
DepthComponentInt depthComponent = new DepthComponentInt( m_kWidth,
 m_kHeight );
depthComponent.setCapability( DepthComponent.ALLOW_DATA_READ );

//create the Raster for the image
m_RenderRaster = new Raster( new Point3f( 0.0f, 0.0f, 0.0f ),
                            Raster.RASTER_COLOR,
                            0, 0,
                            bufferedImage.getWidth(),
                            bufferedImage.getHeight(),
                            imageComponent2D,
                            null );

m_RenderRaster.setCapability( Raster.ALLOW_IMAGE_WRITE );
m_RenderRaster.setCapability( Raster.ALLOW_SIZE_READ );

//create the Raster for the depth components
m_DepthRaster = new Raster( new Point3f( 0.0f, 0.0f, 0.0f ),
                            Raster.RASTER_DEPTH,
                            0, 0,
                            m_kWidth,
                            m_kHeight,
                            null,
                            depthComponent );

//create a custom Canvas3D with postSwap overridden
GraphicsConfigTemplate3D gc3D = new GraphicsConfigTemplate3D();
gc3D.setSceneAntialiasing( GraphicsConfigTemplate.PREFERRED );
GraphicsDevice gd[] = GraphicsEnvironment.getLocalGraphicsEnviron-
ment().getScreenDevices();

RasterCanvas3D c3d =
 new RasterCanvas3D( this, gd[0].getBestConfiguration( gc3D) );
c3d.setSize( getCanvas3dWidth( c3d ), getCanvas3dHeight( c3d ) );

//create a Shape3D object for the Raster containing the Image
Shape3D shape = new Shape3D( m_RenderRaster );

//add the Raster's Shape3D to the Scenegraph
objRoot.addChild( shape );

//take the Depth Raster and update the Render Raster containing
//the image based on the depth values stored in the Depth Raster.
//create a temporary BufferedImage for the depth components
BufferedImage tempBufferedImage =
 new BufferedImage( m_DepthRaster.getDepthComponent().getWidth(),
                    m_DepthRaster.getDepthComponent().getHeight(),
                    BufferedImage.TYPE_INT_RGB );

//allocate an array of integers to store the depth components
//from the Depth Raster
m_DepthData =
 new int[ m_DepthRaster.getDepthComponent().getWidth() *
        m_DepthRaster.getDepthComponent().getHeight () ];
```

```java
//copy the depth values from the Raster into the integer array
((DepthComponentInt) m_DepthRaster.getDepthComponent()).
 getDepthData( m_DepthData );

//assign the depth values to the temporary image. the integer
//depths will be interpreted as integer rgb values.
tempBufferedImage.setRGB(
  0, 0,
  m_DepthRaster.getDepthComponent().getWidth (),
  m_DepthRaster.getDepthComponent().getHeight(),
  m_DepthData, 0,
  m_DepthRaster.getDepthComponent().getWidth() );

//get a graphics device for the image
Graphics g = tempBufferedImage.getGraphics();
Dimension size = new Dimension();
m_RenderRaster.getSize( size );

//The Depth Raster is a different size than the Render Raster.
//i.e., if the Depth Raster is canvas width by canvas height and
//the Render Raster is of arbitrary size, we rescale the image here.
g.drawImage( tempBufferedImage,
             0, 0,
             (int) size.getWidth(),
             (int) size.getHeight(), null);

//finally, assign the scaled image to the RenderRaster
m_RenderRaster.setImage(
 new ImageComponent2D( BufferedImage.TYPE_INT_RGB,
                       tempBufferedImage) );

//Canvas3D overridden method to read the depth components
// of the 3D view into a Raster object and notify the Applet
class RasterCanvas3D extends Canvas3D
{
 RasterTest       m_RasterTest = null;

 public RasterCanvas3D( RasterTest rasterTest,
                        GraphicsConfiguration gc)
 {
  super( gc );
  m_RasterTest = rasterTest;
 }

 public void postSwap()
 {
  super.postSwap();
  getGraphicsContext3D().readRaster(
   m_RasterTest.getDepthRaster() );

  //notify the applet to update the render object used
  //to display the depth values
  m_RasterTest.updateRenderRaster();
    }
}
```

8.5 TEXT2D

```
java.lang.Object
  |
  +--javax.media.j3d.SceneGraphObject
      |
      +--javax.media.j3d.Node
          |
          +--javax.media.j3d.Leaf
              |
              +--javax.media.j3d.Shape3D
                  |
                  +--com.sun.j3d.utils.geometry.Text2D
```

Text2D creates a texture-mapped rectangle that displays a text string. The size of the rectangle and its texture map are customizable through the constructor. The resulting Shape3D object is a transparent (except for the text) rectangle located at 0, 0, 0 and extending up the positive *Y*-axis and out the positive *X*-axis.

Text2D essentially creates an image when it is constructed and draws the text string into the image. This texture image is then applied (once) at construction to the rectangular geometry.

NOTE The setRectangleScaleFactor/getRectangleScaleFactor methods may appear to have no effect, but note the following Sun bug report: the setRectangleScaleFactor method will not change text size unless the setString method is called. It must therefore be called before any calls to setString are made.

As a Text2D object is merely a rectangle with a texture applied to its front, it is interesting to consider the trade-off between creating the Text2D object with larger font sizes and scaling the Text2D object as a whole. On the one hand, creating a Text2D object with a larger font size will create a larger rectangle, and larger texture image will be applied to the rectangle. Applications require more memory to handle larger texture images, and increased memory requirements could become significant if large numbers of Text2D objects are created with large font sizes. On the other hand, creating a Text2D object with a small font and then scaling the object using a TransformGroup will result in smaller

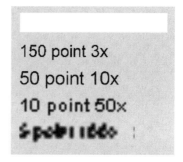

Figure 8.10 Five instances of Text2D: 400 point 1x scale, 150 point 3x scale, 10 point 50x scale and 5 point 100x scale. Note that the system was unable to render text at a size of 400 points

texture images and lower memory requirements, but image resolution will be compromised as the texture image is scaled. These trade-offs are illustrated in figure 8.10.

A more interesting Text2D implementation would have the ability to regenerate its texture image based on the Text2D object's distance from the viewer. In this way the Text2D could automatically incorporate LOD-type behavior, creating high-resolution text string images when viewed up close, and saving memory by dynamically creating low-resolution text string images when viewed from afar.

Also, be aware that because a Text2D object applies the string as a texture image, the texture image is only viewable from the "right side" of the Text2D object. To use the Text2D object as a label a Billboard type behavior will have to be used to ensure the back face of the Text2D object is never visible to the viewer.

8.6   TEXT3D

```
java.lang.Object
  |
  +--javax.media.j3d.SceneGraphObject
       |
       +--javax.media.j3d.NodeComponent
            |
            +--javax.media.j3d.Geometry
                 |
                 +--javax.media.j3d.Text3D
```

The Text3D class generates 3D geometry for a given font, with a given extrusion, as shown in figure 8.11. In contrast to the Text2D class, which merely generates an image of the text string in a given font, Text3D creates a true complex 3D object that forms the text string supplied. The font and pitch describe the generated geometry in the X and Y dimensions, whereas a FontExtrusion object describes the font in the Z direction.

Figure 8.11
A Text3D instance rendered as a wireframe

Although Text3D is relatively straightforward to use, it is often more of a problem, in applications that use Text3D objects as labels, to ensure that the Text3D object is always aligned relative to the viewer so as to be easily visible.

The following example creates a simple 10-point SansSerif 3D-text label and encapsulates it in a Shape3D object.

```
Font3D f3d = new Font3D( new Font( "SansSerif", Font.PLAIN, 10),
                         new FontExtrusion () );
Text3D label3D = new Text3D( f3d, "Hello World", locationPoint );

Shape3D sh = new Shape3D( label3D );
```

The names of the available font families (e.g., SansSerif) can be retrieved using

`java.awt.GraphicsEnvironment.getAvailableFontFamilyNames`

A `FontExtrusion` object can be used to control the depth of text as follows:

```
//describe the FontExtrusion contour using X,Y coordinates
//that in mathematical parlance are "monotonic  in X"
double X1 = 0;
double Y1 = 0;
double X2 = 3;
double Y2 = 0;
Shape extrusionShape = new java.awt.geom.Line2D.Double(X1, Y1, X2, Y2);
FontExtrusion fontEx = new FontExtrusion( extrusionShape) ;
Font3D f3d = new Font3D( new Font( "TimesRoman",
                                   Font.PLAIN, nSize),
                         fontEx);
```

This example will create a `Text3D` object that is 3 units deep instead of the default 0.2 units.

Unfortunately, there are serious usability issues that may influence your decision to use a `Text3D` object. These are described in the following subsections.

8.6.1   Complex geometry

`Text3D` objects can contain many hundreds of vertices. Creating lots of `Text3D` objects may quickly consume memory and impact performance. The number of vertices created is proportional to the pitch of the font used, as well to the font itself. Using small sans serif fonts will generate fewer vertices than large serif fonts. This is particularly relevant if your application uses the Java 3D collision detection methods; internally `Text3D` creates a `GeometryArray` object for each letter. If you create many `Text3D` objects with many letters, each containing many vertices, collision detection will quickly consume all available processor time.

`Text3D` objects generate vertex coordinates and Normal vectors for their geometry. This implies that they can be displayed and lighted, but *cannot* have a texture image applied to them.

8.6.2 SetString problems

There is essentially no way to modify the contents of a Text3D object at runtime, for example, to create dynamic or context sensitive labels. The misleading setString method does not destroy the previously generated geometry within the Text3D object, but appends new geometry to the object (figure 8.12). In addition, it does not honor the font, pitch, and other dimensions that were specified when the Text3D object was created. setString(null) can be used to *not* display the Text3D object, though this is probably not useful as there would be no way to restore the object without generating more geometry. Note that setString("") causes a NullPointerException. I expect Sun to address these bugs in the immediate future so check your implementation version.

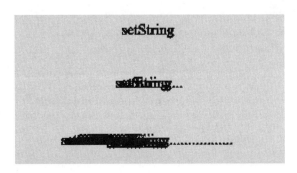

Figure 8.12
Three frames generated by the Text3DTest example. Each subsequent call to setString (called after each frame) *adds* geometry to the Text3D. The result is that geometry gets ever more complex

8.7 MORPH

```
java.lang.Object
  |
  +--javax.media.j3d.SceneGraphObject
        |
        +--javax.media.j3d.Node
              |
              +--javax.media.j3d.Leaf
                    |
                    +--javax.media.j3d.Morph
```

The Morph Node is similar to a normal Shape3D Node except that is can have multiple GeometryArray objects associated with it. You can therefore put four versions of the same geometry into a Morph object and progressively morph between them by adjusting the weights associated with each GeometryArray.

Table 8.2 shows the coordinates for the first point from four GeometryArrays, along with the weight for each. First, each coordinate is multiplied by the weight of its GeometryArray, and then the sum of all weighted coordinates is taken as the resulting coordinate.

Table 8.2 Example of morphing using four weighted points

GeometryArray	Weight	X	Y	Z	W x X	W x Y	W x Z
1	0.5	10	10	0	5	5	0
2	0.25	20	5	0	5	1.25	0
3	0.125	−5	−10	0	−0.625	−1.25	0
4	0.125	−10	−2	0	−1.25	−0.25	0
Resulting Point					8.125	4.75	0

Note that the sum of the GeometryArray weights should equal 1.

As you would expect, there has to be a one-to-one correspondence between the points in each GeometryArray. There is no *feature* information, so Java 3D merely uses the indices of each coordinate in the array to compute the resulting coordinates. In addition, all the GeometryArrays must have the same vertex format, the GeometryArrays must be of the same type, and must have comparable texture coordinate specifications.

Please refer to the Sun Java 3D Morphing example to see the Morph Node in action.

8.8 SUMMARY

This chapter has introduced a lot of the nitty-gritty details of using the various scene-graph Nodes to define Geometry. At the heart of all these options is the Shape3D Node and the GeometryArray class for containing arrays of vertex coordinates, colors, and texture coordinates. This chapter is intended to augment the official documentation so please refer to your JavaDoc for information on the various APIs.

Now that you know how to create your geometry you are probably wondering how you can control its appearance—both at creation time, and dynamically at runtime. The next chapter introduces the Appearance class that you associate with a Shape3D instance to do just that.

C H A P T E R   9

Setting geometry appearances

The Java 3D `Appearance` class enables you to set rendering attributes for the geometric primitives in your scene—at startup, during scenegraph creation, or dynamically at runtime. After reading this chapter, you should be able to dynamically modify the appearance of the geometry within your scenegraph.

9.1   INTRODUCTION

Java 3D contains a host of classes to specify the rendering attributes for geometric primitives, such as color, texture, back-face removal, and so on. Java 3D defines "has-a" relationships between the classes that control overall rendering appearance. For example, an `Appearance` *has* a `Material` class, a `PolygonAttributes` class, a `Rendering-Attributes` class, and so on. This is one of the best-designed areas of Java 3D; with a little experience you can quickly learn to navigate the various classes that, when combined, specify object appearance. Compared with learning the plethora of separate OpenGL methods to specify appearance, the OO nature of the Java 3D design pays dividends.

An instance of an `Appearance` object is associated with each `Shape3D` geometric object in the scenegraph. The `Appearance` object defines rendering state information that must be applied to the rendering pipeline before the raw geometry within the `Shape3D` is rendered.

It is useful to think of the Java 3D renderer traversing through the defined scenegraph; when it encounters `TransformGroups`, it applies matrix transformations; when it encounters a `Shape3D Node`, it applies the `Shape3D`'s `Appearance` state—all before executing the `Shape3D` object to generate native graphics API calls.

What follows is an overview of the `NodeComponent`-derived classes that define a Java 3D rendering state for a `Shape3D` object. Emphasis is placed on areas of potential confusion or typical problems. Consult the detailed Sun API reference for a method-by-method summary of the classes. I have prefaced each section with a table listing the capability bits that control access to the specific feature being discussed. The tables include references to OpenGL functions where appropriate and useful.

One of the lengthier examples of the book accompanies this chapter: AppearanceTest (illustrated in figure 9.1) allows you to dynamically modify most of the `Appearance` attributes on a simple scene. I encourage you to examine the code for the example and run it as you work through this chapter—most of the sections will be significantly clarified by this interactive example.

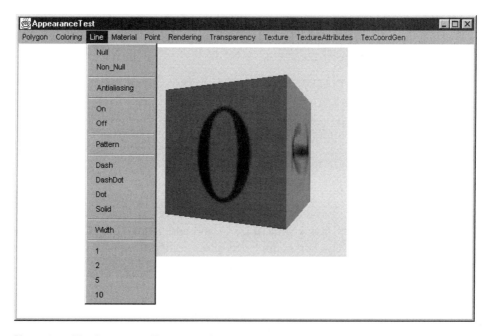

Figure 9.1   The AppearanceTest example application allows `Appearance` **settings to be modified at runtime**

9.2   APPEARANCE

```
java.lang.Object
   |
  +--javax.media.j3d.SceneGraphObject
        |
       +--javax.media.j3d.NodeComponent
            |
           +--javax.media.j3d.Appearance
```

The Appearance class contains member variables that together define an appearance state for a Shape3D object. A Shape3D object basically contains Geometry and Appearance. The Appearance class itself does not define any of the properties that control Shape3D appearance, but instead packages Appearance subcomponents, such as PolygonAttributes, RenderingAttributes, and so on.

The Appearance class controls access to its member variables through the familiar, but rigorous, process of setting capability bits. That is, the application developer must specify which Appearance member variables will be modified after the Appearance is attached to a *live* scenegraph. A live scenegraph is one that has either been compiled or has been rendered.

The capability bits that control access to the member variables of the Appearance class are:

- COLORING_ATTRIBUTES
- LINE_ATTRIBUTES
- MATERIAL
- POINT_ATTRIBUTES
- POLYGON_ATTRIBUTES
- RENDERING_ATTRIBUTES
- TEXGEN
- TEXTURE_ATTRIBUTES
- TEXTURE
- TRANSPARENCY

Preface the listed items with ALLOW_ and add _READ or _WRITE for read or write access respectively. For example, to allow read/write access to the Material and PolygonAttributes member variables, you would put the following in your code:

```
Appearance app = new Appearance();
app.setCapability( ALLOW_MATERIAL_READ );
app.setCapability( ALLOW_MATERIAL_WRITE );
app.setCapability( ALLOW_POLYGON_ATTRIBUTES_READ );
app.setCapability( ALLOW_ POLYGON_ATTRIBUTES_WRITE );
```

Four separate calls must be made to the `setCapability` method—it is not possible to OR together the various capabilities. ORing together capability bits will lead to very unpredictable behavior.

Public accessor methods to access the member variable are defined as:

```
app.setMaterial( new Material() );
app.setPolygonAttributes( new PolygonAttributes() );

PolygonAttributes polyAttribs = app.getPolygonAttributes();
Material material = app.getMaterial();
```

9.3   COLORINGATTRIBUTES

```
java.lang.Object
   |
   +--javax.media.j3d.SceneGraphObject
         |
         +--javax.media.j3d.NodeComponent
               |
               +--javax.media.j3d.ColoringAttributes
```

Table 9.1   Capability bits for the `ColoringAttributes` class

COLOR
SHADE_MODE
OpenGL Reference: glColor

The `ColoringAttributes` within a `Shape3D`'s `Appearance` are used to control the color of a `Shape3D` *if* a `Material` has not also been assigned to the `Appearance`. If a `Material` has been assigned, the `ColoringAttributes` are ignored and the more complex color and lighting information within the `Material` class are used instead. See table 9.1.

The colors of any vertices within the `Shape3D` that have per-vertex colors applied are unchanged by the `ColoringAttributes`.

The next example, from AppearanceTest.java, creates a standard `Box` and then replaces the LEFT face with a new face created with new geometry and per-vertex colors. When a `ColoringAttributes` object is assigned to the `Appearance` for the `Box` it will set the color for the five original faces but will not effect the LEFT face which has per-vertex colors assigned, as illustrated in figure 9.2.

```
int nScale = 50;

Box box = new Box( nScale,nScale,nScale,
                   Primitive.GENERATE_NORMALS |
                   Primitive.GENERATE_TEXTURE_COORDS,
                   m_Appearance);

Shape3D frontFace = box.getShape( Box.LEFT );
```

Figure 9.2
A Box primitive with an applied
ColoringAttribute. The LEFT
face has been removed and replaced
with a QuadArray that includes
per-vertex colors that are unaffected
by the ColoringAttributes

```
//create a new LEFT face so we can assign per-vertex colors
GeometryArray geometry =
 new QuadArray( 4, GeometryArray.COORDINATES |
                   GeometryArray.NORMALS |
                   GeometryArray.COLOR_4 |
                   GeometryArray.TEXTURE_COORDINATE_2 );

nScale = 40;

final float[] verts =
{
 // new LEFT face
 -1.0f * nScale, -1.0f * nScale,  1.0f * nScale,
 -1.0f * nScale,  1.0f * nScale,  1.0f * nScale,
 -1.0f * nScale,  1.0f * nScale, -1.0f * nScale,
 -1.0f * nScale, -1.0f * nScale, -1.0f * nScale
};

final float[] colors =
{
 // left face
 1,0,0,0,
 0,1,0,0.2f,
 0,0,1,0.8f,
 0,0,0,1,
};

float[] tcoords =
{
 // texture coordinates for LEFT face
 1, 0,
 1, 1,
 0, 1,
 0, 0
};
```

```
Vector3f normalVector = new Vector3f(-1.0f,  0.0f,  0.0f);
```

geometry.setColors(0, colors, 0, 4);

```
for( int n = 0; n < 4; n++ )
 geometry.setNormal( n, normalVector );
```

```
geometry.setTextureCoordinates( 0, tcoords, 0, 4 );
geometry.setCoordinates( 0, verts );
```

9.4   *LINEATTRIBUTES*

```
java.lang.Object
  |
  +--javax.media.j3d.SceneGraphObject
       |
       +--javax.media.j3d.NodeComponent
            |
            +--javax.media.j3d.LineAttributes
```

Table 9.2   Capability bits for the `LineAttributes` class

ANTIALIASING
PATTERN
WIDTH
OpenGL Reference: glLineStipple, glLineWidth

The `LineAttributes` class controls the style of lines used to draw the edges of surfaces. See table 9.2. The available styles are:

- Antialiasing: on or off
- Pattern: dash, dash dot, dot, or solid
- Line width: In pixels

To see the effect of the `LineAttributes` class, the `Appearance` must be set to render in `LINE` (wire frame) mode:

```
Appearance app = new Appearance();
PolygonAttributes polyAttribs = new PolygonAttributes( PolygonAt-
tributes.POLYGON_LINE, PolygonAttributes.CULL_NONE, 0 );
app.setPolygonAttributes(polyAttribs );
```

See section 9.7.1 for more detail on `PolygonAttributes`. Figures 9.3–9.6 show examples rendered using various `LineAttribute` styles.

The lines rendered in `LINE` mode are effected by color, lighting, and texture applied to surfaces.

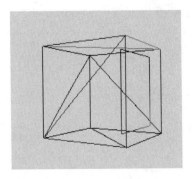

Figure 9.3   Rendering in LINE mode with a null LineAttributes

Figure 9.4   Rendering with a LineAttributes of width 10 without antialiasing

Figure 9.5   Rendering with a LineAttributes of width 10 with antialiasing

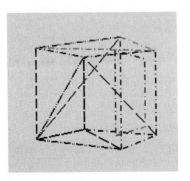

Figure 9.6   Rendering with a LineAttributes of width 2 with a Dash Dot pattern

9.5   MATERIAL

```
java.lang.Object
   |
   +--javax.media.j3d.SceneGraphObject
        |
        +--javax.media.j3d.NodeComponent
             |
             +--javax.media.j3d.Material
```

Table 9.3   Capability bits for the Material class

COMPONENT
OpenGL Reference: glColorMaterial, glMaterial

The Material class specifies surface rendering characteristics (table 9.3) using the following parameters:

- Surface colors

  Ambient

  Diffuse

  Emissive

  Specular

- Lighting enable: Controls whether lighting is enabled for the Shape3D.

- Shininess: Gloss parameter that controls the effect of specular lighting.

The effects of the various colors specified within the Material are described in detail in the context of lighting in chapter 10. Figure 9.7 shows a cube rendered with an applied Material, and per-vertex colors on four vertices of the cube.

Figure 9.7
**Appearance with an applied Material
with Ambient, Diffuse, Emissive, and Specular
colors. Lighting calculations determine the
shade of each surface**

9.6 POINTATTRIBUTES

```
java.lang.Object
   |
   +--javax.media.j3d.SceneGraphObject
        |
        +--javax.media.j3d.NodeComponent
             |
             +--javax.media.j3d.PointAttributes
```

Table 9.4   Capability bits for PointAttributes class

ANTIALIASING
SIZE
OpenGL Reference: glPointSize, GL_POINT_SMOOTH

The PointAttributes class specifies rendering information for rendered points (table 9.4). PointAttributes encapsulates two appearance properties:

- ANTIALIASING: Boolean to specify whether points are antialiased
- SIZE: The size of each point in pixels

If antialiasing is enabled, points are rendered as circular; if antialiasing is disabled, points are rendered as square (size pixels by size pixels) as shown in figures 9.8 and 9.9.

NOTE The time taken to render a point (at least without hardware acceleration) is proportional to the size of the point in pixels.

Note that a single point, when antialiased, approximates a sphere, in that it is never possible to view the point "edge-on" as a disc. When points are rendered without antialiasing, the point approximates a cube with each front face always perpendicular to the viewer. Figures 9.10 and 9.11 illustrate.

The figures are taken from the PointTest.java example. The example defines the points to be rendered, as well as `Appearances`, as follows:

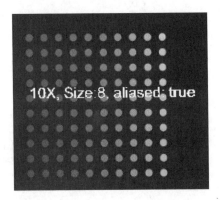

Figure 9.8   An array of colored points of size 8 pixels with antialiasing

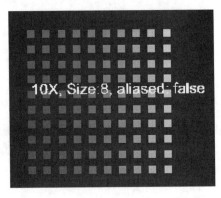

Figure 9.9   The same as in figure 9.8 but without antialiasing set in the `PointAttributes`

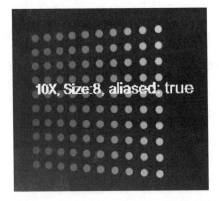

Figure 9.10   When rotated, antialiased points appear as spheres

Figure 9.11   When rotated, nonantialiased points appear as squares aligned with the viewer

```
//create a BranchGroup containing an nNumPoints x nNumPoints
//array of points
//the size of the points is set to nPointSize and antialiasing
//is set to bAliased
private BranchGroup createPoints( final int nPointSize, final int
  nNumPoints, boolean bAliased )
{
 BranchGroup bg = new BranchGroup();

 //create a Text3D label describing the points
 String szText = new String();
 szText += ( nNumPoints + "X, Size:" + nPointSize + ", aliased: "
  + bAliased );

 Font3D f3d = new Font3D( new Font( "SansSerif", Font.PLAIN, 1), new
  FontExtrusion() );
 Text3D label3D = new Text3D( f3d, szText, new Point3f(-5,0,0) );
 Shape3D sh = new Shape3D( label3D );
 bg.addChild( sh );

 //create the PointArray used to hold the geometry for the points
 PointArray pointArray = new PointArray( nNumPoints * nNumPoints,
  GeometryArray.COORDINATES | GeometryArray.COLOR_3 );

 //populate the PointArray that we will be rendering
 int nPoint = 0;
 final double factor = 1.0 / nNumPoints;

 for( int n = 0; n < nNumPoints; n++ )
 {
  for( int i = 0; i < nNumPoints; i++ )
  {
   Point3f point = new Point3f( n - nNumPoints/2,
                                i - nNumPoints/2, 0.0f );
   pointArray.setCoordinate( nPoint, point );
   pointArray.setColor( nPoint++,
                        new Color3f( 0.5f, (float) (n * factor),
                        (float) (i * factor) ) );
  }
 }

 //create the Appearance for the points
 Appearance pointApp = new Appearance();

 //enlarge the points and set antialiasing
 pointApp.setPointAttributes( new PointAttributes
  ( nPointSize, bAliased ) );

 //create a Shape3D for the PointArray and assign the appearance
 Shape3D pointShape = new Shape3D( pointArray, pointApp );

 //add the Shape3D to the BranchGroup and return
 bg.addChild( pointShape );
 return bg;
}
```

9.7 POLYGONATTRIBUTES

```
java.lang.Object
   |
  +--javax.media.j3d.SceneGraphObject
        |
       +--javax.media.j3d.NodeComponent
             |
            +--javax.media.j3d.PolygonAttributes
```

Table 9.5 Capability bits for the `PolygonAttributes` class

CULL_FACE
MODE
NORMAL_FLIP
OFFSET
OpenGL Reference: glCullFace, glFrontFace, glPolygonMode

The `PolygonAttributes` class encapsulates properties for how polygons are rendered (table 9.5). Polygon rendering is controlled by the following properties:

- Cull face: Determines which surfaces of the polygon are rendered. Either all surfaces or the backward-facing surfaces or the front-facing surfaces are rendered. Backward-facing surfaces are backward facing by virtue of the direction of their normal vector (calculated from the winding order of the vertices). That is, the vector normal to the surface is currently pointing away from the viewer.

- Rendering mode: Renders either the polygon as a filled triangular surface or just the edges of the surface as lines or just the vertices of the surface as points.

- Normal vector compensation: Flips the orientation of surface normal vectors. This mode is useful for geometry that is defined using clockwise winding when counter-clockwise winding should be used for surface normal vector calculation.

- Z-value offset: Shifts the geometry attached to the parent `Appearance` *away* from the eye (viewer) by the specified amount. By specifying an offset on one `Shape3D` it can be moved in front of or behind the other `Shape3D`. Because of differences in OpenGL/DirectX hardware implementation, however, it is very difficult to achieve consistent results using this method.

For example, to allow write access to the `CULL_FACE` property, use the following:

```
PolygonAttributes polyAttribs = new PolygonAttributes();
polyAttribs.setCapability(PolygonAttributes.ALLOW_CULL_FACE_WRITE );
```

Table 9.6 Cull face parameters

CULL_BACK
CULL_FRONT
CULL_NONE

Cull face parameters (table 9.6) can be implemented as follows:

```
polyAttribs.setCullFace( PolygonAttributes.CULL_BACK );
```

Table 9.7   Mode parameters

POLYGON_FILL

POLYGON_LINE

POLYGON_POINT

Polygon fill-mode parameters are shown in table 9.7. For example, to set line-only (wire frame) mode, use the following:

```
polyAttribs.setPolygonMode( PolygonAttributes.POLYGON_LINE );
```

Figures 9.12 through 9.15 illustrate how normal vector flipping can influence both the lighting calculations, (compare the shading of the horizontal faces in figure 9.12 with figure 9.13), and surface culling (figure 9.14, 9.15).

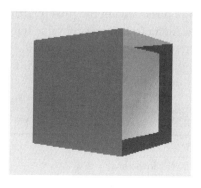

Figure 9.12   CULL_NONE, NORMAL_FLIP = false

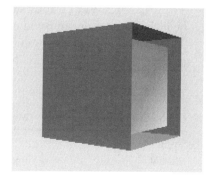

Figure 9.13   CULL_NONE, NORMAL_FLIP = true

Figure 9.14   CULL_FRONT, NORMAL_FLIP = false

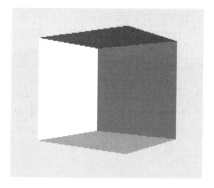

Figure 9.15   CULL_FRONT, NORMAL_FLIP = true

9.8 RENDERINGATTRIBUTES

```
java.lang.Object
   |
   +--javax.media.j3d.SceneGraphObject
        |
        +--javax.media.j3d.NodeComponent
             |
             +--javax.media.j3d.RenderingAttributes
```

Table 9.8 Capability bits for the `RenderingAttributes` class

ALPHA_TEST_FUNCTION

ALLOW_ALPHA_TEST_VALUE

ALLOW_DEPTH_ENABLE

OpenGL Reference: glAlphaFunc

The `RenderingAttributes` class allows pixels within the final rendered scene to be included or excluded based on the pixel Alpha (transparency) value (table 9.8).

Assuming an Alpha test value of `A`, the test conditions listed in table 9.9 and shown in figure 9.16 are available.

Table 9.9 Alpha test modes

Alpha test function	Meaning
ALWAYS	Always render pixel regardless of A
EQUAL	Render pixel if pixel transparency = A
GREATER	Render pixel if pixel transparency > A
GREATER_OR_EQUAL	Render pixel if pixel transparency >= A
LESS	Render pixel if pixel transparency < A
LESS_OR_EQUAL	Render pixel if pixel transparency <= A
NEVER	Never render pixel regardless of A
NOT_EQUAL	Render pixel if pixel transparency != A

The interpolation of transparency values across primitives (quads or triangles) can sometimes be surprising. Figure 9.17 illustrates what happens to a `QuadArray` when it is rotated. In this case vertexes 0 and 1 have a transparency of 0.0, and vertexes 1 and 2 have a transparency of 1.0.

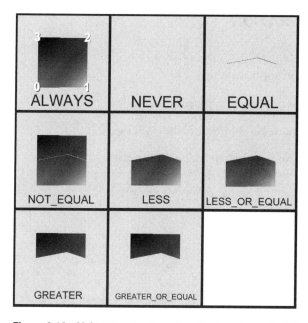

Figure 9.16 Using `RenderingAttributes` to control the portions of a `QuadArray` that are rendered. Vertex 0 has transparency 0.0, vertex 1 has transparency 0.2, vertex 2 has transparency 0.8, and vertex 3 has transparency 1.0. In all cases the `Alpha` test value was set to 0.5

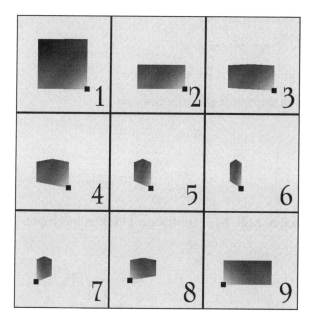

Figure 9.17 The lower two vertices have transparency 0.0, while the upper two vertices have transparency 1.0. The `Alpha` test value is 0.5 and `Alpha` test function is `LESS`. Note that, as the `QuadArray` rotates, the transparency interpolation changes as a function of the rotation and an apparent spike appears in the middle of the quad

9.9   TexCoordGeneration

```
java.lang.Object
   |
   +--javax.media.j3d.SceneGraphObject
          |
          +--javax.media.j3d.NodeComponent
                 |
                 +--javax.media.j3d.TexCoordGeneration
```

Table 9.10   Capability bits for the TexCoordGeneration class

ENABLE

FORMAT

MODE

PLANE

OpenGL Reference: glTexGen

Java 3D's texture capabilities (table 9.10) are discussed in detail in chapter 14.

9.10   TextureAttributes

```
java.lang.Object
   |
   +--javax.media.j3d.SceneGraphObject
          |
          +--javax.media.j3d.NodeComponent
                 |
                 +--javax.media.j3d.TextureAttributes
```

Table 9.11   Capability bits for the TextureAttributes class

BLEND_COLOR

MODE

TRANSFORM

OpenGL Reference: glTexParameter

Java 3D's texture capabilities (table 9.11) are discussed in detail in chapter 14.

9.11   Texture

```
java.lang.Object
   |
   +--javax.media.j3d.SceneGraphObject
          |
          +--javax.media.j3d.NodeComponent
                 |
                 +--javax.media.j3d.Texture
```

Table 9.12 Capability bits for the `Texture` class

BOUNDARY_COLOR
ENABLE
FILTER
IMAGE
MIPMAP_MODE
OpenGL Reference: glTexImage2D.

Java 3D's texture capabilities (table 9.12) are discussed in detail in chapter 14.

9.12   *TRANSPARENCYATTRIBUTES*

```
java.lang.Object
   |
   +--javax.media.j3d.SceneGraphObject
        |
        +--javax.media.j3d.NodeComponent
             |
             +--javax.media.j3d.TransparencyAttributes
```

Table 9.13 Capability bits for the `TransparencyAttributes` class

MODE
VALUE
OpenGL Reference: glBlendFunc

The `TransparencyAttributes` class allows the transparency of objects to be specified. Transparency is set using an Alpha value (table 9.13). Alpha values range from 0.0, representing complete opacity, to 1.0, representing complete transparency. Like color, transparency can either be set on a per-vertex basis or, by using the `TransparencyAttributes` class, for an entire `Shape3D`. Per-vertex transparency (set using COLOR_4 per-vertex colors) takes precedence over the transparency value specified in the `Shape3D`'s `TransparencyAttributes`. The examples to follow will help to illustrate this.

Transparency should be used with care, because, as the OpenGL reference indicates, it is a blending operation between pixels that have their source geometry located at different positions within the scene.

Using transparency slows rendering considerably because the renderer must track the transparency of every pixel in the frame. Without transparency the color of a pixel in the frame is dictated by the color of the geometry closest to the viewer. All other geometry that would be mapped into the frame pixel location can be discarded since it is occluded by the geometry closest to the viewer. If some of the elements in the scenegraph are transparent, however, the renderer must perform a sequence of complex blending operations between the colors generated for a single pixel in the frame.

Figure 9.18
Five Sphere **primitives with varying transparency, from left to right 100%, 70%, 50%, 30%, and 10%. All of the** Spheres **have the same color (black)**

Here is what the Microsoft/Silicon Graphics OpenGL reference says about using transparency: "Transparency is best implemented using glBlendFunc (GL_SRC_ALPHA, GL_ONE_MINUS_SRC_ALPHA) with primitives sorted from farthest to nearest. Note that this transparency calculation does not require the presence of alpha bitplanes in the frame buffer. You can also use glBlendFunc (GL_SRC_ALPHA, GL_ONE_MINUS_SRC_ALPHA) for rendering antialiased points and lines in arbitrary order." The key phrase in the description is, "with primitives sorted from farthest to nearest." This is where the problems with using transparency in Java 3D occur. Because transparency is a Shape3D object attribute, Java 3D users naturally assume that they merely have to set the object or vertex transparency and Java 3D will take care of everything else. Sadly, this is not the case, as Java 3D provides very little support for sorting the primitives "from farthest to nearest." This should be changing however, as Java 3D 1.3 will implement depth-sorted transparency—as demonstrated as a Sun presentation at the JavaOne 2001 conference.

Traditional 3D rendering techniques rely on the Z-buffer to ensure objects nearer to the viewer are rendered on top of objects further away.

The Z-buffer is essentially an array of depth values, one element in the array for each pixel in the frame. As the scene is rendered, the Z-buffer is updated with the distance of the source location for each pixel from the viewer. The Color buffer tracks the color of the closest source location for each pixel in the frame, as shown in the following sequences:

- Rendering for Surface 1

    Prerender pixel at location 5,10.

    Get depth to geometry for pixel (10 meters).

    Update Z-buffer with depth to geometry and update Color buffer with color of pixel.

- Rendering for Surface 2

    Prerender pixel at location 5,10.

    Get depth to geometry for pixel (15 meters).

    Do *not* update Z-buffer as 15 > 10 and do *not* update Color buffer as pixel is not closer to viewer.

In this way, when all the geometry in the scene has been prerendered, the Z-buffer contains the depth values for each pixel to the nearest geometry and the Color buffer contains the color for each pixel. When transparency is used, however, the color of a pixel cannot be solely determined from the color of the closest geometry; instead, a complex blend of the colors of all geometry gets mapped to the pixel location. In general, the blending will only be calculated correctly if the geometry is rendered from back to front, which is of course view-dependent.

The problem therefore becomes one of sorting geometry from front to back before rendering takes place. For general scenes this is extremely difficult, especially for scenes that are composed of overlapping or interpenetrating objects. Such objects will have to be decomposed into nonpenetrating subsections before rendering.

Without sorting, you will only get reasonable results if most of your objects are opaque and you have only a few, nonoverlapping, transparent surfaces. The Java 3D rendering order is as follows:

1. Opaque objects
2. Ordered objects (OrderedGroups)
3. Transparent objects

Within the opaque and transparent groups no sorting is performed. Therefore, transparent objects will overlap opaque or ordered objects in front of them, whereas, because transparent objects are not depth-sorted, there are no guarantees that transparent objects will be rendered correctly.

Figures 9.19 through 9.29 illustrate some of the potential rendering problems. The scene for the following figures was composed of a single Box primitive with one face (LEFT) removed. The LEFT face was replaced with a new, slightly smaller face that included per-vertex colors (COLOR_4). The code used to replace the LEFT face follows:

```
//create a Box with Normal vectors and texture coordinates
Box box = new Box(nScale,nScale,nScale,
          Primitive.GENERATE_NORMALS |
          Primitive.GENERATE_TEXTURE_COORDS, m_Appearance );

Shape3D frontFace = box.getShape( Box.LEFT );

//create a new left face so we can assign per-vertex colors
GeometryArray geometry = new QuadArray( 4,  GeometryArray.COORDINATES |
          GeometryArray.NORMALS |
          GeometryArray.COLOR_4 |
          GeometryArray.TEXTURE_COORDINATE_2 );

nScale = 40;

//define the geometry for the left face
final float[] verts =
{
  -1.0f * nScale, -1.0f * nScale,  1.0f * nScale,
  -1.0f * nScale,  1.0f * nScale,  1.0f * nScale,
```

```
       -1.0f * nScale,  1.0f * nScale, -1.0f * nScale,
       -1.0f * nScale, -1.0f * nScale, -1.0f * nScale
};

//define the colors for the left face. Note we are using RGBA
//colors and include per-vertex transparency
final float[] colors =
 {
 1,0,0,0,
 0,1,0,0.2f,
  0,0,1,0.8f,
  0,0,0,1,
};

//define the texture coordinates for the left face
float[] tcoords =
{
 1, 0,
 1, 1,
 0, 1,
 0, 0
};

//define the normal vector for the new left face
Vector3f normalVector = new Vector3f(-1.0f,  0.0f,  0.0f);

//assign the colors to the QuadArray
geometry.setColors( 0, colors, 0, 4 );

//assign the normal vector for each vertex in the QuadArray
for( int n = 0; n < 4; n++ )
 geometry.setNormal( n, normalVector );

//assign the texture coordinates for each vertex in the QuadArray
geometry.setTextureCoordinates( 0, tcoords, 0, 4 );

//finally, assign the vertices themselves into the QuadArray
geometry.setCoordinates( 0, verts );
```

NOTE   All rendering was performed with `PolygonAttributes.CULL_NONE`; so *all* the faces of the `Box` were rendered.

9.12.1   A warning about transparency

Consider carefully what you are trying to achieve if you choose to use transparency as an Appearance attribute in your scene. It is very difficult to know exactly what will be rendered by Java 3D in either NICEST or SCREEN_DOOR mode, and without some form of application-specific sorting algorithm, which must be carried out potentially on every frame, problems will probably occur.

The issues with transparency really do not reside at the Java3D level, but Java 3D has not done a good job of insulating the Java 3D developer from the underlying issues in the OpenGL/DirectX implementation. I am hopeful that Sun can address many of these issues in Java 3D 1.3.

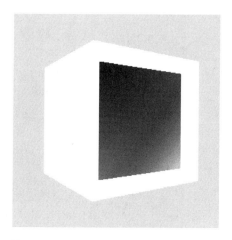

Figure 9.19   Coloring = null, Material = null, Transparency = null

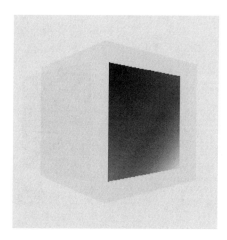

Figure 9.20   Coloring = green, Material = null, Transparency = null. Note that the QuadArray with per-vertex colors is unaffected

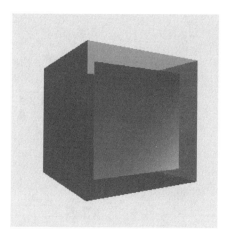

Figure 9.21   Coloring = null, Ambient: white Diffuse: white Emissive: blue, Transparency = null. Lighting is now active and affects the QuadArray with per-vertex colors

Figure 9.22   Coloring = null, Material = null. Transparency = 0—NICEST. Here we have set up transparency for both the Box (100% opaque) and the QuadArray (per-vertex transparency). Even though the QuadArray should be visible at the front of the Box, it is being rendered *behind* the Box. This would be a case that could be solved using a simple sorting algorithm because the centroid of the Box is behind the centroid of the QuadArray and hence it should be rendered before the QuadArray

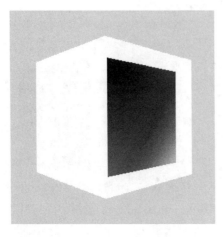

Figure 9.23   Coloring = null, Material = null. Transparency = 0—SCREEN_DOOR. Here, when we switch to SCREEN_DOOR transparency, the rendering order problem disappears

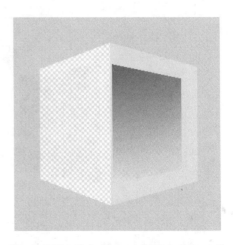

Figure 9.24   Coloring = null, Material = null. Transparency = 0.5—NICEST. When the Box is semitransparent, the problem with rendering order is not apparent because you can see the QuadArray through the Box

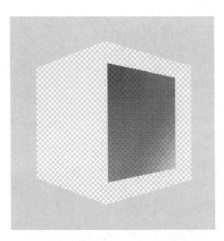

Figure 9.25   Coloring = null, Material = null. Transparency = 0.5—SCREEN_DOOR. Using stippling to simulate transparency is not as realistic as using true color blending

Figure 9.26   Coloring = null, Material = null. Transparency = 0.8—NICEST. We have increased the transparency of the Box and rotated it so that the QuadArray is now at the rear of the Box. No problems apparent here

Figure 9.27 Coloring = null, Material = null. Transparency = 0.8—SCREEN_DOOR. We have increased the transparency of the Box and rotated it so that the QuadArray is now at the rear of the Box. Using SCREEN_DOOR transparency, the QuadArray has now disappeared

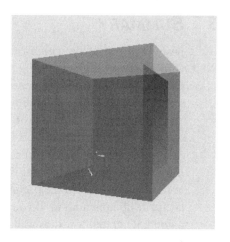

Figure 9.28 Coloring = null, Ambient: white, Diffuse: white, Emissive: blue, Transparency = 0.5—NICEST. The scene renders correctly— but continuously renders, cycling over the back faces and then redrawing the front faces

Figure 9.29 Coloring = null, Ambient: white, Diffuse: white, Emissive: blue, Transparency = 0.5—SCREEN_DOOR. No problems apparent here

9.13 SUMMARY

Java 3D provides you with a rich set of capabilities for controlling the appearance of your geometry. By combining aspects of the `Appearance` class, such as materials, transparency, textures, or rendering attributes, you can achieve visually effective scenes with very little programming.

The high-level object-oriented API allows you to easily navigate through the dozens of appearance capabilities and is a real productivity improvement over a lower-level API such as OpenGL. In some areas (for example, transparency), however, it can be important to understand what is going on under the covers, as Java 3D does a poor job at insulating you from the peculiarities of the underlying implementation or providing adequate documentation. If you require additional information I strongly recommend a good 3D graphics text as well as an OpenGL/DirectX reference.

C H A P T E R   1 0

Lights

Lighting is an important topic in 3D graphics. The lights that you choose for your scene can have a profound impact, making it appear, for examples, highly atmospheric or almost photographically realistic or flat and artificial. There are two basic problems with setting up lighting for your scene. The first is to understand how lighting is calculated, as well as understanding the mechanics of setting up lighting parameters and doing the necessary programming. The second problem is aesthetic and involves making artistic decisions regarding how you want your scene to appear. Because lights can also be computationally expensive, you need to use them carefully and ensure you are striking the right balance between frame rate and responsiveness on the one hand and a richly shaded scene on the other.

Figures 10.2 through 10.15 show a scene viewed under different lighting conditions. The illustrations give an indication of the lighting effects that are possible using Java 3D and provide a starting point for designing your own scene lighting. You'll want to run the example application to see the color illustrations for the full effect. You can also refer to the ebook edition of this book, available from the publisher's web site at http://www.manning.com/selman, which contains color illustrations.

The LightTest example application allows you to interactively modify lighting parameters and view the results.

10.1 LIGHTS

Careful use of lights can make the difference between a flat, unconvincing 3D scene and an atmospheric, immersive virtual reality. The shading that results from applying lighting to a 3D scene provides many of the important visual cues that convey the depth information for the scene.

There are four basic types of light defined in Java 3D and most 3D rendering APIs:

- *Ambient lights*—Applied to the whole scene.
- *Directional lights*—Positioned at infinity and shine in a given direction.
- *Point lights*—Radiating outward from a given point in 3D space within the scene.
- *Spotlights*—Radiating outward from a given point and with a given spread angle, to allow the width of the light's beam to be specified.

Lights positioned within the scene influence the colors that are applied to surfaces. Lights are *not* visible entities in themselves, but they affect the colors of the surfaces of objects within the scene. For example, there is no built-in support for displaying shafts of light that illuminate fog or dust before falling onto the surfaces of objects in the scene. Other lighting side effects, like lens-flare, are also not supported. Such visual effects, now commonly seen is 3D games such as Quake, are not implemented in either OpenGL or DirectX and hence not supported in Java 3D.

Once the lights are positioned within the scene, complex lighting equations govern the resulting color and shading of a surface. The result, a rendered shaded surface, relies on many factors, such as:

- *Surface Properties*
    angle of surface relative to light sources
    material properties: ambient, diffuse, emissive and specular colors, shininess (or gloss)
    surface simulation: e.g., bumpy or wrinkled
    vertex colors
    transparency
    applied texture image
    shading model (Lambert, Gouraud, Phong)

- *Light Properties*
    position
    color
    direction
    attenuation: how the intensity of the light decreases with distance
    concentration
    spread angle
    extent (Bounds)

10.1.1   Lighting equations

A mathematical equation (from the Java 3D Specification) determines the color of a pixel given the positions and colors of lights, `Material` properties of the pixel's surface, normal vector for the surface, and position of the viewer. The lighting equation used in Java 3D is a simplification of the OpenGL lighting equation.

$$Me + Ma \cdot \sum_{i}^{Numamb} (Lc_i) + \sum_{i}^{Numlt} (atten_i \cdot spot_i \cdot (diff_i + spec_i))$$

Note that
- Multiplication
- Dot product

$$diff_i = (L_i \bullet N) \cdot Lc_i \cdot Md$$

$$spec_i = (S_i \bullet N)^{shin} \cdot Lc_i \cdot Ms$$

Note that if $(L_i \bullet N) \le 0$, then $diff_i$ and $spec_i$ are set to 0.

$$atten_i = 1/(Kc_i + Kl_i \cdot d_i + Kq_i \cdot d_i^2)$$

Note that for directional lights, $atten_i$ is set to 1.

$$spot_i = \max((-L_i \cdot D_i), 0)^{exp_i}$$

Note that if the vertex is outside the spotlight cone, as defined by the cutoff angle, $spot_i$ is set to 0. For directional and point lights, $spot_i$ is set to 1.

    The lighting equation is a subset of OpenGL in that the Java 3D ambient and directional lights are not attenuated and only ambient lights contribute to ambient lighting.

    The parameters used in the lighting equation are:

    E = Eye vector

    Ma = Material ambient color

    Md = Material diffuse color

    Me = Material emissive color

    Ms = Material specular color

    N = Vertex normal

    $shin$ = Material shininess

The per-light values are:

    d_i = Distance from vertex to light

D_i = Spotlight direction

exp_i = Spotlight exponent

Kc_i = Constant attenuation

Kl_i = Linear attenuation

Kq_i = Quadratic attenuation

L_i = Direction from vertex to light

Lc_i = Light color

S_i = Specular half-vector = $\| (L_i + E) \|$

The basic principle of the lighting equations is fairly simple—if a surface is close to 90 degrees to a light ray, then the surface will be brightly lit. That is, large quantities of the light reaching the surface are absorbed by the surface and hence visible. The color used to brightly light the surface will be related to the color of the light as well as the color of the surface.

10.1.2 Normal vectors and lighting

The lighting equation requires that you define a normal vector for each vertex that you want to be lit. The lighting equation will interpolate the surface color between the vertices in the surface based on the vertex position and normal vector. There are a number of algorithms used to interpolate surface color between vertices, described in the sections that follow.

Lambert shading

The simplest lighting model merely colors a surface in proportion to its angle relative to the viewer. This is commonly referred to as *Lambert* or *cosine shading*. To establish the intensity of the surface, the model uses the cosine of the angle between the ray of light hitting the surface and the surface normal. As the light source comes to be closer to perpendicular to the surface, so the angle between the light ray and the surface normal decreases and the surface lightens. When the light is at right angles to the surface, the angle is zero and the intensity is at a maximum.

Lambert shading is extremely fast to calculate and produces a marked improvement in depth perception for the scene. It produces faceted models, as if each surface had been cut from glass, and tends to emphasize the edges between surfaces.

Often it is preferable that the individual surfaces that comprise the model be calculated to approximate a smooth edge, but, by emphasizing the surface decomposition as much as the model itself, Lambert shading can make the model appear artificial. In 1971, Henri Gouraud published an improved shading model that generates smooth shading across surfaces—preserving the depth cues inherent in Lambert shading while not emphasizing the edges between surfaces.

Gouraud shading

In Gouraud shading, instead of assigning a single intensity to a surface, the average intensities at each vertex are calculated. Once the average intensity of each vertex is calculated the intensities are then interpolated along each scan line between these averages to give a smooth appearance. A given vertex might be shared between several surfaces, and hence its normal vector can influence the intensity of each of the surfaces to which it contributes.

Phong shading

Two years after Gouraud, Bui Tuong Phong developed an algorithm to incorporate specular highlights into the intensity interpolation algorithm developed by Gouraud. So-called Phong shading computes an approximate normal vector for each point along the scan lines. These intermediate normal vectors can then be used to calculate an intensity based partly on the interpolated Gouraud shading component and partly from a point's normal vector.

Consider a triangular surface where the averaged normal vector for two of the vertices was a little less than 90 degrees while the averaged normal vector for the third vertex was a little more than 90 degrees. If the surface were Gouraud shaded, the interpolated intensities would be fairly uniform across the surface (as the cosine of the angle for each normal vector would be approximately equal). However, the planar surface is *probably* intended to model a smooth surface fitted between the vertices of the surface. If this is the case, then at some point *across* the surface, the normal vector must reach 90 degrees. This point, within the surface, should therefore be assigned a higher intensity than any of the vertices at the edges of the surface. Phong shading, by interpolating the normal vectors across the surface, as well as Gouraud intensity, can introduce local highlights that would otherwise be merely averaged into the intensity of the surface as a whole. Phong introduced a new coefficient for each surface, called *shiniess,* that controls how radically the surface responds to light and influences the size of a surface's specular highlight.

An interesting compromise must be made between Lambert and Gouraud shading, as the averaging behavior of Gouraud shading must be balanced with the facet display behavior of Lambert shading. Using Gouraud shading, it is easy to display a coarsely triangulated sphere that is beautifully and smoothly shaded and has Phong specular highlights applied, but whose edges are straight—and belie the faceted nature of the model.

- Lambert shading varies the intensity of a surface based on its angle relative to a light source.
- Gouraud shading smoothes Lambert shading across a surface and between surfaces.
- Phong shading can add specular highlights to Gouraud shading.

Notice that these three components are visible in the Java 3D lighting equations given in section 10.1.1. As should be clear from these equations, lights are expensive computationally and you should design your scene's lighting requirements in the context of general application performance and usability. With artful design, however, apparently complex lighting can be created with a fairly modest number of lights. The surface smoothing characteristics of the lighting equations can also be gainfully employed to give coarsely meshed models a smoother appearance. If the models in the scene contain fewer vertices, the scene may render quicker, even with the added overhead of a more complex shading model.

NO NORMALS...
NO SHADING It is critical to note that, however you decide to light your models, all of the shading algorithms rely on the normal vectors that have been assigned to the vertices of the models. As an application developer it is your responsibility to tell the renderer about the normal vector for each of your vertices, just as it is your responsibility to tell the render about the position of each vertex! The Java 3D `NormalGenerator` class can be used to generate the normal vectors for a model. Failure to assign normal vectors will typically result in a uniformly shaded model that offers no depth cues through shading surfaces.

10.1.3   Lighting and material properties

Examining the lighting equation one can see how the various material properties for the surface interplay.

The emissive (*Me*) and ambient (*Ma*) color of the surface are combined irrespective of vertex-normal vectors, and the position or color of lights in the scene.

The diffuse color (*Md*) of the surface is combined with the color of each light (*Lci*) and applied relative to the angle between each light and each vertex normal. If the light and the normal vector are perpendicular there is no diffuse color component applied.

The material specular color (*Ms*) is combined with the light color (*Lci*) in proportion to the calculated specular component.

In other words,

- The color of a light is combined with the diffuse and specular material color for a surface.

- The emissive and ambient colors of a surface are irrespective of light color or position.

10.1.4   What about shadows?

Note that the discussion has been devoid of any mention of shadows cast by objects onto other objects in the scene. This is because there is *no* built-in support for automatic shadow calculation in Java 3D or the lower level rendering APIs such as OpenGL or Direct3D.

Although this often comes as a surprise and a disappointment to many people new to rendering APIs, if you consider how you might go about calculating shadows for arbitrary 3D scenes, it quickly becomes apparent that a general purpose algorithm is unsuitable for interactive 3D graphics. The sheer amount of calculations that need to be performed means that application-specific cheats have to be developed that are able to mimic some of the effects of shadow casting. Lightweight shadow calculation algorithms are available in the OpenGL literature.

Realistic effects such as reflection, refraction, and shadows are best left to noninteractive applications that can make use of ray-tracing techniques. These techniques follow individual light rays as they bounce around the scene, having their color modified along the way, until they finally intersect with a pixel for display.

10.2   *LIGHT NODE*

```
java.lang.Object
   |
   +--javax.media.j3d.SceneGraphObject
          |
          +--javax.media.j3d.Node
                 |
                 +--javax.media.j3d.Leaf
                        |
                        +--javax.media.j3d.Light
```

Light is an abstract base class for the four types of Light Leaf Node available in Java 3D: AmbientLight, DirectionalLight, PointLight, and SpotLight.

This section is illustrated using the LightTest.java example program. LightTest is one of the longer examples in the book. It allows the four types of light to be positioned within the scene, and for the light properties to be modified at runtime. You can thus view the results interactively. The program will certainly not win any awards for UI design, but all the parameters for all the Java 3D Light classes can be modified at runtime. In addition, geometry is also created to represent the lights themselves: a Cone, whose base is set to the color of the light, denotes the SpotLight, while a large Cone through the center of the scene denotes the direction and color of the Directional-Light. A small Sphere is created for the PointLight.

The LightTest example, shown in figure 10.1, creates the four lights and a simple 3D scene consisting of several Spheres with a checkered floor composed from a QuadArray.

10.2.1   Light properties

Light defines all the properties necessary for a simple ambient light. An ambient light shines equally everywhere within its zone of influence and does not possess position or direction. Such a light is of course a practical impossibility, much like frictionless surfaces or the perfect collisions beloved of physicists.

Color

A Light has a color. If no color is specified a 100 percent white light is created.

Influencing bounds

A Bounds object is associated with each Light. The Bounds object defines the zone of influence for the Light. Note that for Lights that possess positional information (SpotLight and PointLight) the Bounds is completely independent of the position of the Light. It is the application developer's responsibility to ensure that the Bounds of the Light and the position of the Light correspond in some sensible application-specific manner.

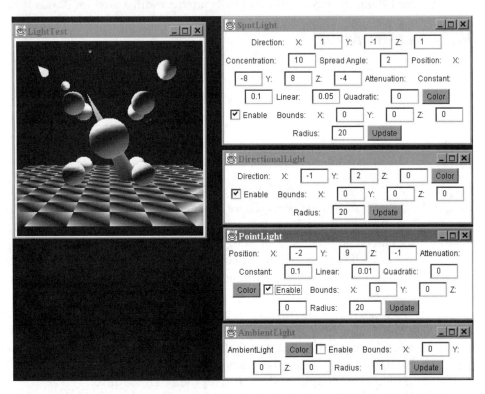

Figure 10.1 The LightTest example program allows you to interactively modify lighting parameters for the four types of light object in Java 3D: SpotLight, DirectionaLight, PointLight, and AmbientLight. The Cone at the top left of the figure depicts the SpotLight, the small Sphere at the top middle of the figure depicts a PointLight, while the large cone at the center of the scene depicts the DirectionalLight's direction vector

Scope

Defining scopes for lights is an additional mechanism to restrict the zone of influence of a Light. An object in the scene will be lit only if it falls within the Bounds of a light *and* the Group containing the object is included in the scope of the Light. In other words, the scope information for a light takes precedence over the Bounds information for the Light. By default, Lights do not contain any scopes, and the Bounds set for the Light will solely define its zone of influence.

State

The state for lights is very simple—ON or OFF.

10.3 AMBIENTLIGHT

AmbientLight simply inherits the properties defined in the base-class Light object. AmbientLight instances illuminate a scene evenly, without direction or attenuation characteristics. AmbientLights are useful in illuminating the dark areas left by the other types of Light. Because an AmbientLight does not possess a direction, it lights a scene with an even, flat light. Because this kind of light does very little to increase 3D perception, it is typically used in combination with one of the other lights.

AmbientLights are very simply handled by the rendering engine (illumination is independent of surface orientation). Thus, they are, computationally, the cheapest of the types of Light.

> **NOTE** AmbientLight is a cheap approximation of many diffuse light sources, such as in a well-lit office building with many windows and overhead lighting.

10.4 DIRECTIONALLIGHT

A DirectionalLight is a light that is assumed to shine from an infinite distance—for example, to model sunlight. It allows a Vector3f object to be assigned to the light to specify the direction. DirectionalLight can be very useful in providing simple 3D cues to the user of an application.

Illumination of surfaces depends upon the orientation of the surface relative to the DirectionalLight vector, so a DirectionalLight is computationally more expensive that an AmbientLight.

> **NOTE** DirectionalLight is an approximation of a shaft of light entering a scene, such as a shaft of sunlight entering a room through one glass wall.

10.5 POINTLIGHT

A PointLight is a light that shines from a given point within the 3D scene. Although the light source itself is invisible, the effects of the light vary with distance and orientation of the surface upon which it falls. A PointLight is computationally more expensive than a DirectionalLight because each object in the scene must have both orientation and distance relative to the light evaluated.

A PointLight contains attenuation properties that define how the brightness falls off with distance. The attenuation contains three components:

- *Constant*—Subtracted from the intensity of the light irrespective of distance. That is, dimming the light at its source.
- *Linear*—Subtracted for every unit moved away from the light source. The light at 2 meters is twice as bright as the light at 4 meters.
- *Quadratic*—Subtracted as a function of a square of the distance from the light. The light at 2 meters is four times as bright as the light at 4 meters.

> **NOTE** A `PointLight` is an approximation of a point light source, such as a light bulb hanging from the ceiling of a large room. As one moves further toward the corners of the room the illumination from the light lessens (attenuates).

10.6 SPOTLIGHT

A `SpotLight` is a light that shines from a given location and in a given direction.

The `SpotLight` is the most computationally expensive of the light types, as distance from the light source, surface orientation, and distance from the center of the conical beam must all be evaluated for all objects within a `SpotLight`'s zone of influence.

A `SpotLight` contains two properties:

- *Spread angle*—Width of the beam in radians
- *Concentration*—Strength of the beam within the conical region

> **NOTE** A `SpotLight` is an approximation of a typical directional light source, such as a flashlight, car headlight, or desk lamp. The width of the conical beam for the `Spotlight` can be varied, along with the position and attenuation of the light.

Figures 10.2 through 10.9 illustrate the effects of applying the different types of light to a simple scene.

The relevant parameters for the lights are shown in tables 10.1 through 10.3.

Table 10.1 Spotlight

SpotLight parameter	Value
Direction	1, −1, 1
Concentration	10
Spread angle	2
Position −8, −8, −4	
Attenuation	Constant 0.1 Linear 0.05 Quadratic 0.0

Table 10.2 DirectionalLight

DirectionalLight parameter	Value
Direction	−1, 2, 0

Table 10.3 PointLight

PointLight parameter	Value
Position	–2, 9, –1
Attenuation:	Constant 0.1 Linear 0.01 Quadratic 0.0

Figure 10.2 `SpotLight`

Figure 10.3 `SpotLight` **and**
`DirectionalLight`

Figure 10.4 `SpotLight,`
`DirectionalLight,` **and** `PointLight`

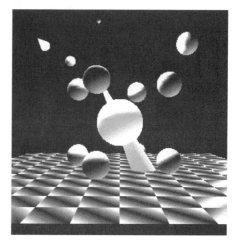

Figure 10.5 `SpotLight, Directional-`
`Light, PointLight,` **and** `AmbientLight.`
Note that the `Bounds` **of the** `AmbientLight`
have been set such that only the central
large sphere (and the cone depicting the
`DirectionalLight` **are influenced**

Figure 10.6 `DirectionalLight` **and**
`PointLight`

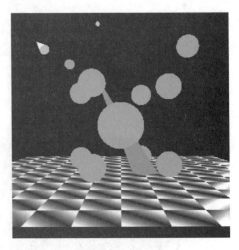

Figure 10.7 `AmbientLight`

Figure 10.8 `PointLight` **and**
`AmbientLight`

Figure 10.9 `DirectionalLight`,
`PointLight`, **and** `AmbientLight`

Figures 10.10 through 10.12 illustrate the effect of varying the `SpreadAngle` for a single `SpotLight`.

Figures 10.13 through 10.15 illustrate varying the attenuation parameters of a `SpotLight`. As the linear and quadratic components of the attenuation are increased, the boundary between lit and unlit surfaces becomes increasingly blurred because the light attenuates more rapidly with distance.

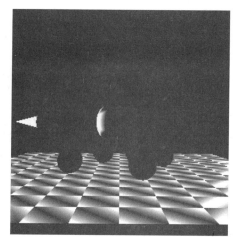

Figure 10.10 SpotLight.SpreadAngle is 0.2 radians

Figure 10.11 SpotLight.SpreadAngle is 0.5 radians

Figure 10.12 SpotLight.SpreadAngle is 2 radians

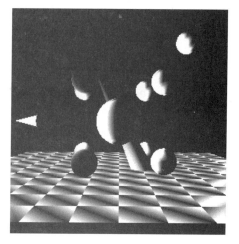

Figure 10.13 SpotLight.**Attenuation:** Constant **is 0.05,** Linear **is 0.0,** Quadratic **is 0.0**

10.7 *LIGHTING, MATERIAL ATTRIBUTES, AND PER-VERTEX COLORS*

The Lights in a scene, an object's material attributes (specifying ambient, emissive, diffuse, and specular color for an object), and the colors that have been assigned to the vertices of an object all interact to produce the final rendered surface.

If lighting or color information is not displayed correctly, note the following points:

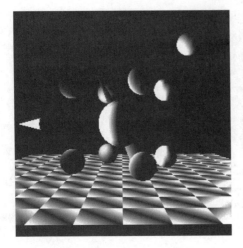

Figure 10.14 SpotLight. **Attenuation: Constant is 0.05, Linear is 0.01, Quadratic is 0.0**

Figure 10.15 SpotLight. **Attenuation: Constant is 0.05, Linear is 0.01, Quadratic is 0.01**

- If the colors of a GeometryArray are modified at runtime (using setColors) the geometry may also be reset using setGeometry (Java 3D 1.1).
- If per-vertex colors have been assigned (using setColors), and a Material has been assigned to a Shape3D, the per-vertex colors will override the *diffuse* component of the Material object.
- If per-vertex colors have been assigned and a Material has *not* been assigned, the Shape3D will be unlit and colored *solely* by the per-vertex colors.

Java 3D 1.2 includes the setIgnoreVertexColors method in the Rendering-Attributes class that allows this default behavior to be overridden.

10.8 SUMMARY

I hope this chapter has inspired you to create some great lighting effects for your 3D world. As you can see, the possible ways to combine the lights and their different parameters are almost endless. I encourage you to run the LightTest example to learn how the different lighting parameters can be combined to create the effect you want. After you have a sense for the number of lights you will require, you should test your application with representative geometry loaded to ensure that your choice of lights performs well on your target hardware platform.

C H A P T E R   1 1

Behaviors—navigation, alignment, and LOD

Java 3D includes a rich set of built-in behaviors that can be used for everything from automatically modifying the transparency of objects to keyboard navigation and collision detection.

Some behaviors automatically execute complex code to modify objects within the scenegraph, so take care to ensure that behavior processing does not bog down application performance. With prudent design and knowledge of some of the limitations, behaviors can be a powerful asset in quickly developing or prototyping application logic.

By the time you finish this chapter, you should have a broad knowledge of the behaviors built into Java 3D and a good sense of how to develop your own behaviors. By mixing and matching your own behaviors and built-in behaviors, you should be able to design your application logic within Java 3D's behavior model.

11.1 INTRODUCTION

We should start by taking a look at the general Java 3D behavior architecture. What *is* a behavior anyway?

Just as you can add geometry (Shape3D), transformations (TransformGroup), or lights (Light) to the scenegraph, Java 3D also allows you to add blocks of executable *code* to the scenegraph. This code is packaged within a class derived from Behavior and is automatically executed by Java 3D in response to a set of criteria. In Java 3D, the criteria for a Behavior being executed are called *wake up criteria* and are defined using classes derived from WakeUpCondition.

The behavior architecture is based on the following series of events and notifications:

1 Create a Behavior and register its WakeUpCondition.
2 Java 3D enters its Behavior processing loop.
3 Java 3D checks whether the WakeUpCondition for the current Behavior is satisfied.
4 Java 3D calls Behavior.processStimulus if the WakeUpCondition is met.
5 Behavior code executes within processStimulus call.
6 Behavior sets its next WakeUpCondition.
7 The next Behavior is processed by the Behavior processing loop.

The behavior architecture facilitates good application design and code reuse because a scenegraph branch can contain not only the complex geometry for a hierarchical scenegraph element but also the code to *control* the scenegraph element. For example, an application might define a car that drives around a race-circuit (figure 11.1). The application allows the user to replay a prerecorded racing sequence. Just as the car itself has been decomposed into a hierarchical model, behaviors can also be modeled hierarchically. A Behavior attached to each wheel of the car will rotate the wheel and its child nodes (spokes, etc.), while a Behavior attached to the top-level node of the car allows the entire car to be moved through a prerecorded trajectory using a Behavior to interpolate between positions.

Good, reusable, class design results. Every wheel has the ability to be rotated, while every car on the track can be replayed through a trajectory. The higher level elements in the scenegraph need have no knowledge of these properties of the car object—indeed they can be added and refined as the application is developed.

At least, that's the goal. As with everything in computers, things are never that simple and some careful design must go into ensuring that your application's Behaviors can be executed efficiently. Imagine your application with 50 cars, each with four wheels; that comes out to 200 Behaviors to be scheduled, their WakeUp criteria checked, and their processStimulus methods to be called—potentially on every frame. Not a very efficient way to rotate the wheels on the cars! Perhaps a better way would be to create a *single* Behavior that could rotate *every* car's wheels on the circuit—not as architecturally clean a design but a lot more efficient and scaleable.

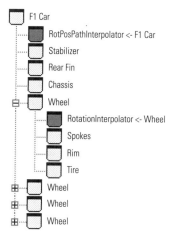

Figure 11.1
A scenegraph branch for the Formula 1 racing car. The branch contains five Behaviors, **the first (**RotPosPathInterpolator**) to replay the car through a recorded trajectory, and four** RotationInterpolator Behaviors**—one to rotate each wheel**

Section 11.2 on the Behavior class will describe the capabilities of all general Behaviors and show you with the basics of writing your own Behaviors.

11.2 BEHAVIOR CLASS

```
java.lang.Object
   |
   +--javax.media.j3d.SceneGraphObject
         |
         +--javax.media.j3d.Node
               |
               +--javax.media.j3d.Leaf
                     |
                     +--javax.media.j3d.Behavior
```

The Behavior class defines the following basic components of the behavior architecture:

Scheduling bounds

The behavior processor executes a Behavior only if the scheduling Bounds for the Behavior intersect the ViewPlatform's activation region. That is, you define the 3D volume within which the Behavior is to be activated. For the racing car example, you might define that a car's wheels are to be rotated only if the car is within 20 meters of the viewer.

The scheduling Bounds for a Behavior are specified using the setScheduling-Bounds or setSchedulingBoundingLeaf methods. If a BoundingLeaf is specified, it takes precedence over Bounds set using setSchedulingBounds.

The Bounds for the ViewPlatform are set using the ViewPlatform.set-ActivationRadius method. When the Bounds for a Behavior and the View-Platform's activation radius intersect, the Behavior is scheduled for processing.

Enable State

Behaviors can be manually switched on or off by modifying their enable states using the setEnable method.

WakeUp Condition

The Java 3D behavior processor calls the processStimulus method when the WakeUp condition for the behavior has been met. The WakeUp condition for a Behavior is set using the wakeupOn method. There are two opportunities to register or update a Behavior's WakeUp condition: at the end of the initialize method and at the end of the processStimulus method. The different types of WakeUpCondition classes are described in the coming sections.

processStimulus method

A Behavior does all of its application- or behavior-specific work within the processStimulus method. Because a Behavior could have been activated by a variety of WakeUp criteria, an Enumeration is passed to the processStimulus method to allow the Behavior to evaluate exactly why it was activated and take appropriate action.

After executing its behavior-specific code, the Behavior *must* call the wakeupOn method to register continued interest in its WakeUp condition. If the Behavior does not call wakeupOn, it will not be activated again.

initialize method

The Java 3D behavior processor calls the initialize method to allow each Behavior in the scenegraph to set its initial WakeUpCondition.

11.2.1 When do Behaviors run?

A Behavior's processStimulus methods will be called if all the following conditions are met:

- The Behavior has been added to the scenegraph.
- The Behavior's scheduling Bounds intersect the ViewPlatform's activation region.
- The Behavior is enabled.
- The Behavior's WakeUpCondition is true. The WakeUpCondition is set in the initialize method and must be reset after each call to processStimulus.
- View.isBehaviorSchedulerRunning() returns true.

11.3 ANATOMY OF A TYPICAL BEHAVIOR

A typical Behavior implements the following three methods: constructor, initialize, and processStimulus.

Constructor

The Behavior constructor typically receives references to the scenegraph elements that will be affected by the Behavior. For example, a Behavior to move an object would receive a reference to the object's parent TransformGroup. These external references will be stored in member variables so that they can be accessed within the processStimulus method when the Behavior is activated.

initialize method

The initialize method must be overridden to register the initial WakeUp conditions for the Behavior. The WakeupCondition object for the Behavior will typically be stored in a member variable so that the WakeupCondition can be reapplied at the end of the processStimulus method.

The last line of the initialize method will call the wakeupOn method to register the WakeupCondition object for the Behavior.

processStimulus method

A simple Behavior can ignore the Enumeration passed to the processStimulus method—the Behavior knows why it was activated and can proceed to the application-specific code. A more complex or composite Behavior will have to query the Enumeration and first determine what mode it was activated in before it can execute the appropriate Behavior code.

Within the Behavior's processStimulus code, the Behavior will call methods on the member variables it stored in the constructor. For example, the Behavior might call Transform3D methods and then call TransformGroup.setTransform to update the position or orientation of an object.

At the end of the processStimulus method, the Behavior will almost certainly call the wakeupOn method, with a previously stored WakeupCondition, to ensure that it receives continued notifications and is rescheduled for processing.

11.4   OVERVIEW OF THE BUILT-IN BEHAVIORS

There are 26 classes derived from Behavior in Java 3D. To describe each in detail is beyond the scope of this chapter. Please refer to the Sun API documentation for a description of each Behavior's methods. Interpolator, mouse, and keyboard Behaviors are described in more detail in subsequent sections.

See table 11.1 for help in selecting an appropriate built-in Behavior for your application.

Table 11.1   Built-in behaviors

Behavior name			Description
Billboard			Aligns a TransformGroup relative to the Viewer
Interpolator			Abstract base class for all Interpolators
	ColorInterpolator		Interpolates diffuse color of a Material
	PathInterpolator		Abstract base class for all PathInterpolators (linear Interpolation)
		PositionPath-Interpolator,	Interpolates the translation of a TransformGroup along a path
		RotationPath-Interpolator	Interpolates the rotation of a TransformGroup along a path
		RotPosPath-Interpolator,	Interpolates the translation and rotation of a TransformGroup along a path
		RotPosScale-PathInterpolator	Interpolates the translation, rotation and scale of a TransformGroup along a path
	Position-Interpolator		Interpolates the translation of a TransformGroup between two points
	Rotation-Interpolator		Interpolates the rotation of a TransformGroup between two values
	ScaleInterpolator		Interpolates the scale of a Transform-Group between two values
	SwitchValue-Interpolator		Interpolates between two Switch values, switching on the children of the Switch Node
	TCBSplinePath-Interpolator		Abstract base class for the Spline path Interpolators
		RotPosScale-TCBSplinePath-Interpolator	Performs cubic spline interpolation between key frames for the translation, rotation and scale of a TransformGroup
Transparency-Interpolator			Interpolates the transparency of a TransparencyAttribute between two values
KeyNavigator-Behavior			Simple keyboard navigation by modifying a TransformGroup in response to key presses
LOD			Abstract base class for LOD behaviors that modify a Switch Node

continued on next page

Table 11.1   Built-in behaviors *(continued)*

Behavior name		Description
	DistanceLOD	Selects child of the Switch Node based on distance from viewer
MouseBehavior		Abstract base class for the Mouse behaviors
	MouseRotate	Modifies the rotational components of a TransformGroup based on mouse input
	MouseTranslate	Modifies the translation components of a TransformGroup based on mouse input
	MouseZoom	Modifies the scale components of a TransformGroup based on mouse input
PickMouse-Behavior		Abstract base class for the mouse picking behaviors
	PickRotate-Behavior	Modifies the rotational components of a picked TransformGroup based on mouse input
	PickTranslate-Behavior	Modifies the translation components of a picked TransformGroup based on mouse input
	PickZoomBehavior	Modifies the scale components of a picked TransformGroup based on mouse input

11.5   OVERVIEW OF WAKEUP CRITERIA

Java 3D includes 14 Wakeup criteria (or triggers) for Behaviors. These simple criteria are specified and derived from the WakeupCriterion class. In addition, Boolean combinations of simple criteria can be specified using the classes derived from WakeupCondition.

For example, you can either define a Behavior that is activated every time an object is moved (i.e., WakeupOnTransformChange, which is a WakeupCriterion):

```
wakeupOn( new WakeupOnTransformChange( tg ) );
```

Or define a Behavior that is activated every time an object is moved *and* a specified number of frames have elapsed (i.e., WakeupAnd, which is a WakeupCondition):

```
WakeupCriterion criterionArray[] = new WakeupCriterion[2];
criterionArray[0] = new WakeupOnTransformChange( tg );
criterionArray[1] = new WakeupOnElapsedFrames( 20 );

WakeupCondition wakeUpCondition = new WakeupAnd( criterionArray );
wakeupOn( wakeUpCondition );
```

11.5.1 WakeupCriterion

```
java.lang.Object
  |
  +--javax.media.j3d.WakeupCondition
       |
       +--javax.media.j3d.WakeupCriterion
```

The WakeupCriterion derived classes (table 11.2) define the atomic events that can be used on their own or combined using the WakeupCondition (table 11.3).

Table 11.2   WakeupCriterion for triggering behaviors

Name	Behavior is called
WakeupOnActivation	The first time the Viewplatform's activation region intersects this object's scheduling region.
WakeupOnAWTEvent	Specific AWT event occurs.
WakeupOnBehaviorPost	Specific behavior object posts a specific event.
WakeupOnCollisionEntry	Specified object collides with any other object in the scene graph.
WakeupOnCollisionExit	Specified object no longer collides with any other object in the scene graph.
WakeupOnCollisionMovement	Specified object moves while in collision with any other object in the scene graph.
WakeupOnDeactivation	First detection of a Viewplatform's activation region no longer intersecting with this object's scheduling region.
WakeupOnElapsedFrames	Specific number of frames have elapsed.
WakeupOnElapsedTime	Specific number of milliseconds have elapsed.
WakeupOnSensorEntry	First time Viewplatform intersects the specified boundary.
WakeupOnSensorExit	First detection of a Viewplatform no longer intersecting the specified boundary.
WakeupOnTransformChange	Transform within a specified TransformGroup changes
WakeupOnViewPlatformEntry	First time Viewplatform intersects the specified boundary.
WakeupOnViewPlatformExit	First detection of a Viewplatform no longer intersecting the specified boundary.

11.5.2 WakeupCondition

```
java.lang.Object
  |
  +--javax.media.j3d.WakeupCondition
```

The WakeupCondition-derived classes are used to specify Boolean combinations of WakeupCriterion classes (table 11.3). In this way composite Wakeup conditions can be specified.

Table 11.3 `WakeupConditions` **for combining** `WakeupCriterion` **instances**

Name	Description
WakeupAnd	Any number of wakeup conditions ANDed together.
WakeupAndOfOrs	Any number of OR wakeup conditions ANDed together.
WakeupOr	Any number of wakeup conditions ORed together.
WakeupOrOfAnds	Any number of AND wakeup conditions ORed together.
WakeupCriterion	See table 11.2 for simple criteria.

A composite `Wakeup` condition can be created by the following code:

From StretchBehavior.java

```
protected WakeupCondition  m_WakeupCondition = null;

//create the WakeupCriterion for the behavior
WakeupCriterion criterionArray[] = new WakeupCriterion[2];
criterionArray[0] = new WakeupOnAWTEvent( KeyEvent.KEY_PRESSED );
criterionArray[1] = new WakeupOnElapsedFrames( 1 );

//save the WakeupCriterion for the behavior
m_WakeupCondition = new WakeupOr( criterionArray );
```

11.5.3   Summary

The behavior model provides a powerful mechanism to enable application code to be called in a demand-driven manner. Events that occur within the scenegraph can trigger code to be executed, analogous to event processing for GUI elements.

`Behaviors` can be very useful, but they hinge upon Java 3D's behavior processor to call them when their `WakeUp` criteria has been met. Your `Behaviors` can only be as functionally rich as combinations of `WakeUp` criteria will allow—there is no point writing a `Behavior` that should be invoked when the user scratches his head, because Java 3D will never invoke it.

Java 3D provides a relatively complete set of `WakeupCondition`-derived classes; however, not *all* eventualities have been covered, and there may be occasions where there is not a suitable `WakeupCondition`-derived class. For example, there is currently no equivalent to VRML's `VisibilitySensor Node`. Chapter 13 builds upon these concepts and illustrates how to write your own custom `Behaviors`.

The next sections will describe some of the most useful built-in behaviors: keyboard and mouse navigation, aligning objects relative to the viewer, and choosing different object models based on the distance from the viewer.

11.6 USING KEYBOARD BEHAVIORS

The Java 3D keyboard behavior responds to AWT key-press events (KeyEvent.KEY_PRESSED and KeyEvent.KEY_RELEASED) and modifies the 4x4 transformation matrix within a TransformGroup. The changes to the TransformGroup can affect the size, position, and rotation of the TranformGroup's child Nodes.

Keyboard navigation is typically used to simulate moving the viewer of a 3D scene, as opposed to manipulating individual objects within a scene. Mouse behaviors, described in section 11.7, are usually used for object manipulation, although there is considerable overlap between the two areas.

In terms of visual effect, there is no difference between moving the viewer (by attaching the keyboard behavior to a TransformGroup on the view side of the scenegraph) and moving the scene itself (by attaching the keyboard behavior to a root TransformGroup on the scene side of the scenegraph). Figure 11.2 shows a diagram of the typical scenegraph structure that illustrates these two approaches.

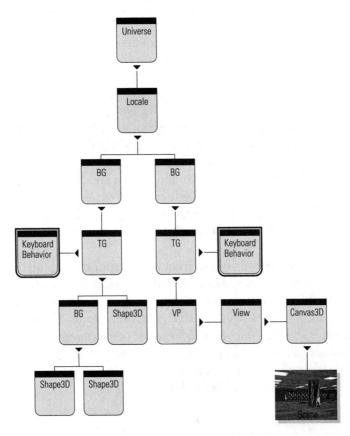

Figure 11.2 A Java 3D scenegraph. A keyboard behavior can be added either to the scene side of the scenegraph (left) or to the view side of the scenegraph (right)

There are advantages and disadvantages to both approaches. If the keyboard behavior is added on the scene side of the scenegraph, you really *are* moving the scene. For a single view and with a single `ViewPlatform`, this will not be noticeable; however, once there are multiple views of the scene or predefined views have been set up using numerous `ViewPlatforms`, the effects of moving the scene will be noticeable.

The advantage of attaching the behavior to the scene side of the scenegraph is that most keyboard behaviors expect this to be the case (including the built-in behavior). Remember that the *inverse* of the multiplication of the `Transform3Ds` above the `ViewPlatform` is used to set the view projection matrix. If the keyboard behavior is added on the view side of the scenegraph, the motion and rotation keys are reversed.

If you need to support multiple views, add the keyboard behavior to the view side of the scenegraph and modify the behavior to account for the reversal in movement direction. Otherwise, it will probably be easier to add the behavior to a root `Trans-formGroup` on the scene side of the scenegraph.

11.6.1 KeyNavigatorBehavior

```
java.lang.Object
  |
  +--javax.media.j3d.SceneGraphObject
       |
       +--javax.media.j3d.Node
            |
            +--javax.media.j3d.Leaf
                 |
                 +--javax.media.j3d.Behavior
                      |
                      +--com.sun.j3d.utils.behaviors.keyboard.
                         KeyNavigatorBehavior
```

The `KeyNavigatorBehavior` is the built-in Java 3D keyboard navigation behavior—part of the utilities package. The `KeyNavigatorBehavior` is very easy to use and it typically consists of: creating a `KeyNavigatorBehavior` object and passing it the `TransformGroup` that the `Behavior` should modify, setting the scheduling `Bounds` for the `Behavior`, ensuring the `ALLOW_TRANSFORM_WRITE` capability bit is set on the `TransformGroup`, and adding the `KeyNavigatorBehavior` to the scenegraph.

From AppearanceTest.java

```java
//create the TransformGroup that the Key behavior will affect
TransformGroup zoomTg = new TransformGroup();
zoomTg.setCapability( TransformGroup.ALLOW_TRANSFORM_WRITE );
zoomTg.setCapability( TransformGroup.ALLOW_TRANSFORM_READ );

//create the Key behavior and add to the scenegraph
KeyNavigatorBehavior key = new KeyNavigatorBehavior( zoomTg );
```

```
key.setSchedulingBounds( createApplicationBounds() );
key.setEnable( true );
objRoot.addChild( key );
```

The keyboard controls for the `KeyNavigatorBehavior` are implemented in the `KeyNavigator` class, which performs the matrix modifications based on key presses. The `KeyNavigator` class has a fairly sophisticated implementation that includes a large number of movement key combinations and acceleration of movement. The key events that the `KeyNavigator` class handles are shown in table 11.4.

Table 11.4 `KeyNavigatorBehavior` keyboard controls

Key press	Effect
DOWN_ARROW	move backward
UP_ARROW	move forward
RIGHT_ARROW	rotate right
LEFT_ARROW	rotate left
PAGE_UP	rotate upward
PAGE_DOWN	rotate downward
ALT + RIGHT_ARROW	move right
ALT + LEFT_ARROW	move left
ALT + PAGE_UP	move upward
ALT+ PAGE_DOWN	move downward
EQUALS (HOME_NOMINAL)	stop movement
SHIFT	fast movement, rotation and scale
SHIFT + META	slow movement, rotation, and scale
PLUS_SIGN	increase Scale
MINUS_SIGN	decrease Scale

11.6.2   Writing a simple keyboard behavior

Simple keyboard processing is easy to accomplish; for example, the following class simply modifies a `TransformGroup` in response to presses of the left and right arrow keys.

```java
public class CarSteering extends Behavior
{
 private WakeupOnAWTEvent    wakeupOne = null;
 private WakeupCriterion[]   wakeupArray = new WakeupCriterion[1];
 private WakeupCondition     wakeupCondition = null;

 private final float         TRANSLATE_LEFT = -0.05f;
 private final float         TRANSLATE_RIGHT = 0.05f;

 TransformGroup              m_TransformGroup = null;

 public CarSteering( TransformGroup tg )
 {
  m_TransformGroup = tg;

  wakeupOne = new WakeupOnAWTEvent(KeyEvent.KEY_PRESSED);
  wakeupArray[0] = wakeupOne;
  wakeupCondition = new WakeupOr(wakeupArray);
 }


 //Override Behavior's initialize method to set up wakeup criteria
 public void initialize()
 {
  //Establish initial wakeup criteria
  wakeupOn(wakeupCondition);
 }

 //Override Behavior's stimulus method to handle the event.
 public void processStimulus(Enumeration criteria)
 {
  WakeupOnAWTEvent ev;
  WakeupCriterion genericEvt;
  AWTEvent[] events;

  while (criteria.hasMoreElements())
  {
   genericEvt = (WakeupCriterion) criteria.nextElement();

   if (genericEvt instanceof WakeupOnAWTEvent)
   {
    ev = (WakeupOnAWTEvent) genericEvt;
    events = ev.getAWTEvent();
    processAWTEvent(events);
   }
  }

  //Set wakeup criteria for next time
  wakeupOn(wakeupCondition);
 }

 //Process a keyboard event
 private void processAWTEvent(AWTEvent[] events)
 {
  for( int n = 0; n < events.length; n++)
```

```
{
 if( events[n] instanceof KeyEvent)
 {
 KeyEvent eventKey = (KeyEvent) events[n];

 if( eventKey.getID() == KeyEvent.KEY_PRESSED )
 {
  int keyCode = eventKey.getKeyCode();
  int keyChar = eventKey.getKeyChar();

  Vector3f translate = new Vector3f();

  Transform3D t3d = new Transform3D();
  m_TransformGroup.getTransform( t3d );
  t3d.get( translate );

  switch (keyCode)
  {
   case KeyEvent.VK_LEFT:
    translate.x += TRANSLATE_LEFT;
   break;

   case KeyEvent.VK_RIGHT:
    translate.x += TRANSLATE_RIGHT;
   break;
  }
  t3d.setTranslation( translate );
  m_TransformGroup.setTransform( t3d );
  }
 }
 }
}
}
```

Writing custom behaviors is covered in greater detail in chapter 13.

11.6.3 Implementing DOOM and DOOM-style keyboard navigation

In my experience, many of the people interested in implementing keyboard navigation would like to use it in an immersive, first-person perspective 3D scene (figure 11.3). When I set out to write the examples to illustrate keyboard behaviors, this must have been at the front of my mind, because the KeyNavigateTest example ended up looking a lot like DOOM or Id's early favorite, Wolfenstein 3D (http://idsoftware.com/).

Writing the example was a lot of fun, and it includes a number of features that should be of interest to people writing immersive, first-person perspective applications:

- Simple keyboard navigation is used: forward, backward, rotate left, rotate right.
- A 3D world can be created from a simple 2D map—defined using a standard image file.
- Five types of objects can be dynamically created within the world: walls, bookcases, pools of water, flaming torch (animated), and Guards (animated).

CHAPTER 11 BEHAVIORS—NAVIGATION, ALIGNMENT, AND LOD

Figure 11.3 The `KeyNavigateTest` example in action. DOOM all over again

- Collision detection is used to ensure walls and bookcases are impenetrable.

- Simple behaviors attached to the guards allow them to move around within the world.

- Simple texture image techniques animate the texture images for torches to give an impression of flames.

The example is obviously fairly lengthy and cannot be discussed in depth here, so only highlights will be described. I was impressed by how functional the example became with a relatively small amount of code. This is due in part to Java 3D's high-level features and in part to the extensive use I made of the reusable classes within the `org.selman.java3d.book` package.

Loading and creating the world from a 2D map

One nice feature of the example is that the definition of the 3D world is a 2D map (figure 11.4). The map is loaded from a standard GIF image, and the colors of the pixels within the image are queried one by one.

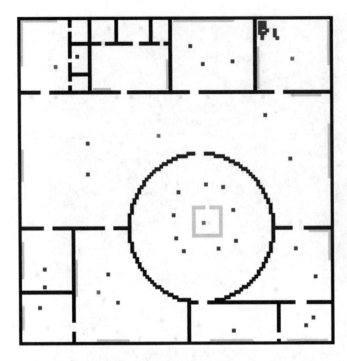

Figure 11.4
A map for the
KeyNavigateTest
example application.
Colored pixels within
the image denote
the different classes of
objects: bookcases, walls,
guards, water, and lights

The RGB (red, green, blue) color of each pixel in the image is compared against the color values that are used to denote each class of object within the world. These colors are defined as follows:

From KeyNavigateTest.java

```
//walls are black pixels
private final int m_ColorWall = new Color( 0,0,0 ).getRGB();

//guards are red pixels
private final int m_ColorGuard = new Color( 255,0,0 ).getRGB();

//lights are yellow pixels
private final int m_ColorLight = new Color( 255,255,0 ).getRGB();

//bookcases are green pixels
private final int m_ColorBookcase = new Color( 0,255,0 ).getRGB();

//water is blue pixels
private final int m_ColorWater = new Color( 0,0,255 ).getRGB();
```

The createMap routine loops over the pixels in the image and delegates responsibility for creating the individual elements of the 3D world to the createMapItem method.

```java
//create elements of the Map and add to the Group g
public Group createMap( Group g )
{
 System.out.println( "Creating map items" );

 Group mapGroup = new Group();
 g.addChild( mapGroup );

 //load the map image using the texture loader
 Texture tex = new TextureLoader( m_szMapName, this).getTexture();
 m_MapImage = ((ImageComponent2D) tex.getImage( 0 )).getImage();

 //query the size of the map image
 float imageWidth = m_MapImage.getWidth();
 float imageHeight = m_MapImage.getHeight();

 //the size of our world is related to the size of the image
 FLOOR_WIDTH = imageWidth * 8;
 FLOOR_LENGTH = imageHeight * 8;

 //loop over each pixel in the image and call createMapItem
 for( int nPixelX = 1; nPixelX < imageWidth-1; nPixelX++ )
 {
  for( int nPixelY = 1; nPixelY < imageWidth-1; nPixelY++ )
   createMapItem( mapGroup, nPixelX, nPixelY );

  float percentDone = 100 * (float) nPixelX / (float) (imageWidth-2);
  System.out.println( "    " + (int) (percentDone) + "%" );
 }

 //finally, create the external perimeter wall all around the world
 createExternalWall( mapGroup );

 return mapGroup;
}
```

The `createMapItem` method compares the color of the incoming pixels with the
colors of the predefined classes of objects and delegates object creation as necessary.

```java
//create an object from a pixel location based on the color of
//the pixel
void createMapItem( Group mapGroup, int nPixelX, int nPixelY )
{
 //get the color of the pixel
 int color = m_MapImage.getRGB( (int) nPixelX, (int) nPixelY );

 //compare with our defined colors and delegate the object creation
 if( color == m_ColorWall )
  createWall( mapGroup, nPixelX, nPixelY );

 else if( color == m_ColorGuard )
  createGuard( mapGroup, nPixelX, nPixelY );

 else if( color == m_ColorLight )
  createLight( mapGroup, nPixelX, nPixelY );
```

```
else if( color == m_ColorBookcase )
 createBookcase( mapGroup, nPixelX, nPixelY );

else if( color.hashCode() == m_ColorWater.hashCode() )
 createWater( mapGroup, nPixelX, nPixelY );
}
```

For example, the `createWall` method is used to create a cuboidal section of wall every time a black pixel is encountered.

```
//create a section of wall at a given pixel location
void createWall( Group mapGroup, int nPixelX, int nPixelY )
{
 //get the world coordinates for the center of the pixel location
 Point3d point = convertToWorldCoordinatesPixelCenter(
  nPixelX, nPixelY );

 //use a shared Appearance for all Wall objects to minimize
 //texture memory
 if( m_WallAppearance == null )
  m_WallAppearance = new Appearance();

 //get the size in world coordinates of a pixel in the image
 Vector3d squareSize = getMapSquareSize();

 //create a Cuboid object that models a section of Wall and
 //assign an Appearance. Cuboid is defined in the
 //org.selman.java3d.book package
 Cuboid wall = new Cuboid( this, mapGroup, ComplexObject.GEOMETRY |
                                           ComplexObject.TEXTURE );
 wall.createObject(  m_WallAppearance,
          new Vector3d( point.x, m_kFloorLevel, point.z ),
          new Vector3d( squareSize.x/2, m_kCeilingHeight/2,
          squareSize.z/2), "wall.gif", null, null );
}
```

Storing the world description in an image is very convenient and allows several worlds to be quickly generated using a standard bitmap editor. Three maps are included with the example: small_map.gif (32 × 32 pixels), large_map (64 × 64 pixels), and huge_map (128 × 128 pixels).

Implementing collision detection

To implement simple collision detection to prevent the viewer from walking through walls or bookcases, a modified keyboard behavior was used. The KeyCollision-Behavior class is derived from KeyBehavior, written by Gary Moss and Andrew Cain, included with permission in the org.selman.java3d.book package.

The KeyCollisionBehavior takes a reference to a CollisionDetector interface in its constructor. If the CollisionDetector.isCollision method returns true, the modified Transform3D is *not* applied to the TransformGroup and no movement will occur.

```
//The KeyCollisionBehavior class adds simple collision detection
//to a keyboard behavior
public class KeyCollisionBehavior extends KeyBehavior
{
 private CollisionChecker  m_CollisionChecker = null;

 public KeyCollisionBehavior( TransformGroup tg,
    CollisionDetector collisionDetector )
 {
  super( tg );

  m_CollisionChecker = new CollisionChecker( tg,
    collisionDetector, true );
 }

 //before the TransformGroup is updated, we need to ensure
 //that we are not going to walk into anything solid.
 protected void updateTransform()
 {
  if( m_CollisionChecker.isCollision( transform3D ) == false )
   transformGroup.setTransform(transform3D);
 }

 //disallow rotation up or down
 protected void altMove(int keycode)
 {
 }

 //disallow moving up or down
 protected void controlMove(int keycode)
 {
 }
}
```

The main `Applet` class implements the `CollisionDetector` interface with its single method, `isCollision`, as follows. The first method does a quick check to ensure that we are still within the boundaries of our world; if this passes, then the second method is used to check which pixel in the map image corresponds to our 3D world coordinate position (only the x and z coordinates are used).

```
//return true if the Transform3D would put us into collision
//with a "solid" object in the world.
public boolean isCollision( Transform3D t3d, boolean bViewSide )
{
 //get the translation from the Transform3D
 t3d.get( m_Translation );

 //we need to scale up by the scale that was applied to the root TG
```

```
//on the view side of the scenegraph
if( bViewSide != false )
 m_Translation.scale( 1.0 / getScale() );

Vector3d mapSquareSize = getMapSquareSize();

//first check that we are still inside the "world"
//because we can't walk outside it
if(  m_Translation.x < -FLOOR_WIDTH + mapSquareSize.x ||
    m_Translation.x > FLOOR_WIDTH - mapSquareSize.x ||
    m_Translation.y < -FLOOR_LENGTH + mapSquareSize.y ||
    m_Translation.y > FLOOR_LENGTH - mapSquareSize.y )
     return true;

//then do a pixel based look up using the map
if( bViewSide != false )
 return isCollision( m_Translation );

return false;
}
```

If the very fast check that we are still inside the world passes, then we need to look up the pixel in the map image that our *new* position will fall within. Once we have queried the color of that pixel, we will know if we can enter that location.

```
//return true if the given x,z location in the world
//corresponds to a wall section
protected boolean isCollision( Vector3d worldCoord )
{
 Point2d point = convertToMapCoordinate( worldCoord );
 int nImageWidth = m_MapImage.getWidth();
 int nImageHeight = m_MapImage.getHeight();

 //outside of image
 if( point.x < 0 || point.x >= nImageWidth ||
   point.y < 0 || point.y >= nImageHeight )
   return true;

 int color = m_MapImage.getRGB( (int) point.x, (int) point.y );

 //we can't walk through walls or bookcases
 return( color == m_ColorWall || color == m_ColorBookcase );
}
```

This very simple grid-based collision detection algorithm works fairly well for this application since it exploits knowledge of the scene, as well as constraint on the user's movement. Incidentally, the guard objects that move around the scene also hook into the same `CollisionDetection` interface implemented by the application object. For these objects, however, bViewSize = true, and they are allowed to penetrate through walls and bookcases to catch the unwary by surprise.

Another neat feature of the example is the use of transparent bitmaps for both water and flaming torches. The flaming torches also use a computationally inexpensive and simple form of texture animation, which is discussed in the next section.

Simple texture image animation for flaming torches

To provide an animated effect for the flaming torch objects, a simple behavior was used to modify the `Transform3D` within the objects `TextureAttributes`. Even slight movement of the texture image was found to give quite pleasing results (figure 11.5).

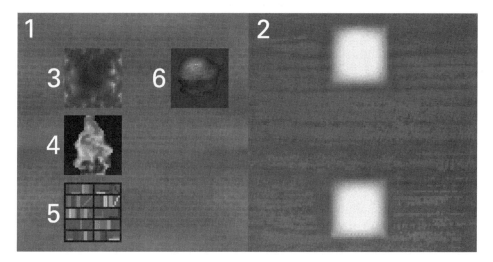

Figure 11.5 The texture images used by the `KeyNaviagateTest` example application. Floor 128 x 128 (1), ceiling 128 x 128 (2), walls 32 x 32 transparent background (3), lights 32 x 32 transparent background (4), bookcases 32 x 32 (5), and water 32 x 32 (6)

The sample's `Light` class defines the geometry and simple texture animation behavior for the light. `Light` is derived from the reusable `ComplexObject` class (defined in the `org.selman.java3d.book` package).

From Light.java

```
public class Light extends ComplexObject
{
 private TextureAttributes m_TextureAttributes = null;

 public Light( Component comp, Group g, int nFlags )
 {
  super( comp, g, nFlags );
 }
 protected Group createGeometryGroup( Appearance app,
  Vector3d position, Vector3d scale, String szTextureFile,
  String szSoundFile )
 {
  Group g = new Group();

  //draw all the faces of the object
  app.setPolygonAttributes(
```

```
    new PolygonAttributes( PolygonAttributes.POLYGON_FILL,
                           PolygonAttributes.CULL_NONE, 0, false )
  );

  //The texture image for the light includes transparent areas for
  //the background. By making the object fully transparent, we can just
  //draw an irregularly shaped texture image.
  app.setTransparencyAttributes(
   new TransparencyAttributes(
    TransparencyAttributes.BLENDED, 1.0f )
   );

  //assign a TextureAttributes object to the Appearance and keep
  //a reference to it so we can modify it
  m_TextureAttributes = new TextureAttributes(
    TextureAttributes.REPLACE,
    new Transform3D(), new Color4f(0,0,0,1),
    TextureAttributes.FASTEST );
   app.setTextureAttributes( m_TextureAttributes );

  //apply the texture image
  if( (m_nFlags & ComplexObject.TEXTURE) == ComplexObject.TEXTURE )
   setTexture( app, szTextureFile );

  //create the geometry for the Light—a simple Cone
  Cone cone = new Cone( 1, 1, Primitive.GENERATE_TEXTURE_COORDS,
    app );

  //add the geometry to its parent group
  g.addChild( cone );

  //add a behavior to animate the TextureAttributes
  attachBehavior( new TextureAnimationBehavior(
    m_TextureAttributes ) );

  return g;
 }
}
```

The TextureAnimationBehavior performs the work of modifying the Trans-
form3D within Light's TextureAttributes object. Every 300 milliseconds, the
Transform3D is randomly modified to move the texture image around the *Y*-axis of
the Cone.

```
class TextureAnimationBehavior extends Behavior
{
 //the wake up condition for the behavior
 protected WakeupCondition  m_WakeupCondition = null;
 protected Transform3D    m_Transform3D = null;
 protected TextureAttributes m_TextureAttributes = null;

 public TextureAnimationBehavior( TextureAttributes texAttribs )
 {
  m_TextureAttributes = texAttribs;
```

```java
  m_Transform3D = new Transform3D();
  m_TextureAttributes.setCapability(
    TextureAttributes.ALLOW_TRANSFORM_WRITE );

  //create the WakeupCriterion for the behavior
  WakeupCriterion criterionArray[] = new WakeupCriterion[1];
    criterionArray[0] = new WakeupOnElapsedTime( 300 );

  //save the WakeupCriterion for the behavior
  m_WakeupCondition = new WakeupOr( criterionArray );
  }

public void initialize()
{
  //apply the initial WakeupCriterion
  wakeupOn( m_WakeupCondition );
}

public void processStimulus( java.util.Enumeration criteria )
{
    while( criteria.hasMoreElements() )
  {
    WakeupCriterion wakeUp = (WakeupCriterion)
      criteria.nextElement();

    if( wakeUp instanceof WakeupOnElapsedTime )
    {
      //make a small random change to the Transform3D and apply it
      //to the TextureAttributes
      m_Transform3D.rotY( Utils.getRandomNumber( 0.4, 0.4 ) );
      m_TextureAttributes.setTextureTransform( m_Transform3D );
    }
  }

  //assign the next WakeUpCondition, so we are notified again
  wakeupOn( m_WakeupCondition );
  }
}
```

Note that the Light objects do *not* use a shared Appearance object, or else all the random changes to the Light texture images would be synchronized. When the example application is run, sometimes the Water objects and the Light objects are not rendered in the correct order. This is because both objects are transparent, and Java 3D does not have (full) built-in support for determining the rendering order of transparent objects. An application-specific fix for the example application would be to force the Water objects (which are always on the floor) to render before the Light objects (which are always off the floor) using an OrderedGroup, as shown in figure 11.6.

Sun will be improving the support for transparent objects in the 1.3 release of Java 3D. (Sun demonstrated an application that rendered multiple transparent objects from multiple viewpoints at JavaOne 2001.)

Figure 11.6 A frame rendered by `KeyNavigateTest` with the small_map.gif world loaded. Note that the middle torch is rendered behind the water on the ground

11.6.4   Conclusions

I have discussed a lot more than keyboard navigation and have arguably strayed off topic. However, I hope you found the real-world discussion of how to integrate first-person keyboard navigation into an immersive world interesting. Section 11.7 describes mouse behaviors and focuses on manipulating individual objects within the world using the mouse.

11.7   *USING MOUSE BEHAVIORS*

A mouse behavior is typically used to allow the user to interactively manipulate a graphical object within a 3D scene. Using a standard 2D mouse as a 3D input device can be problematic and has been extensively studied by human computer interaction (HCI) experts. Although I don't think that anyone could claim that any of the techniques are intuitive, a number of usable standards have emerged for translating mouse movements into changes in translation, rotation, and scale in three dimensions.

If you decide to use the standard 2D mouse as a 3D input device, I suggest you review the literature and study the 3D applications that your target audience is likely to be familiar with. Emulate the paradigms that your users are experienced with wherever possible—it is unlikely that your application is *so* unique that no one has previously encountered your UI problems.

The simplest way to implement direct manipulation using the mouse is to use Java 3D's built-in mouse behaviors. Be aware, however, that this is only *one* solution to a problem that is an ongoing research topic.

As an aside, you can also purchase a 3D mouse, which is a virtual reality input device that can track its position within three dimensions. The 3D mice fall outside the scope (and budget) of this text; however, it should be possible to integrate them with Java 3D using the Java 3D Sensor architecture.

11.7.1 Java 3D and the mouse

So, all this begs the question, how does Java 3D support the standard mouse as an input device? The answer is that the behavior model again comes into play. Mouse behaviors respond to AWT events such as mouse-click, mouse-drag, and mouse-release and convert the mouse events' *x* and *y* pixel coordinates into changes that are applied to a `Transform3D`, which is in turn applied to a `TransformGroup`. Any child `Nodes` beneath the `TransformGroup` will be moved, scaled, or rotated based on the changes in their parents' `TransformGroup`.

Java 3D's mouse behaviors are included in the Java 3D utility package (`com.sun.j3d.utils.behaviors.mouse`), which underscores their status as works in progress. The three basic mouse behaviors are

- `MouseRotate`: Rotates an object when the left mouse button is pressed.
- `MouseTranslate`: Translates an object when the right mouse button is pressed.
- `MouseScale`: Scales an object when the left mouse button is pressed and the ALT key is held down.

The Java 3D mouse behaviors are all derived from a common base class, `Mouse-Behavior`.

```
java.lang.Object
  |
  +--javax.media.j3d.SceneGraphObject
        |
        +--javax.media.j3d.Node
              |
              +--javax.media.j3d.Leaf
                    |
                    +--javax.media.j3d.Behavior
                          |
                          +--com.sun.j3d.utils.behaviors.mouse.MouseBehavior
```

Since the basic mouse behaviors are fairly easy to use, you merely create the behavior object passing in the `TransformGroup` that the behavior is to affect, optionally set the behavior's scheduling bounds, add the behavior to the scenegraph, and voila! The objects underneath the `TransformGroup` should now move, rotate, or scale based on your mouse movements, as shown in the following code example.

```
//create a TransformGroup that we will be rotating
TransformGroup subTg = new TransformGroup();

//The WRITE capability must be set so that the behavior can
//change the Transform3D in the TransformGroup
subTg.setCapability(TransformGroup.ALLOW_TRANSFORM_WRITE);

//add a ColorCube as a child of the TransformGroup
subTg.addChild( new ColorCube(10.0) );

//attach a MouseRotate behavior so we can rotate the color cube
//with the left mouse button
MouseRotate mouseRot = new MouseRotate( subTg );
subTg.addChild( mouseRot );
```

The three built-in mouse behaviors are fine for simple applications or quick prototyping; however, they have a number of drawbacks in serious applications. Section 11.7.3 will define three new mouse behaviors that fix some of these problems and provide a more robust framework to use in applications.

The Java 3D VRML viewer (see http://www.j3d.org for details) also includes a number of mouse and keyboard behaviors and full source code. In particular, it defines behaviors appropriate for VRML world navigation:

- FlightBehavior.java allows the user to fly through a 3D world, controlling roll, pitch, yaw, and velocity.
- KeyBehavior.java is another keyboard navigation class.

So, don't reinvent the wheel; consult, modify, or derive from the available navigation behaviors whenever you can.

11.7.2 Building improved mouse behaviors

The built-in mouse behaviors are pretty basic in their functionality and often don't offer enough flexibility for use in a real-world application. Application developers typically rewrite these behaviors from scratch, using the source code for the built-in mouse behaviors as a guide in order to integrate mouse processing into UI display logic or implement application-specific features.

I have included three mouse behaviors that fix a number of problems and extend the built-in behaviors. These behaviors classes are:

- TornadoMouseRotate
- TornadoMouseTranslate
- TornadoMouseScale

The behaviors, defined in the org.selman.java3d.book package, have a number of advantages over the built-in behaviors (figure 11.7). Each of the Tornado mouse behaviors can have a registered TornadoChangeListener to receive notifications of mouse behavior processing. The TornadoChangeListener interface allows the following notifications to be handled:

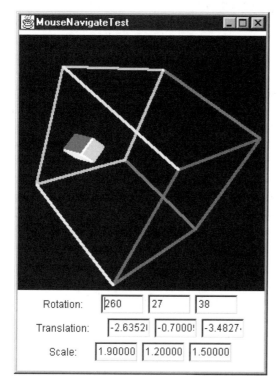

Figure 11.7
The MouseNavigateTest example enables the user to interactively rotate, translate, and scale a ColorCube object within the boundaries of the larger cube. The current position, rotation, and scale of the object are displayed in the UI elements below the Canvas3D

- onStartDrag—called when a mouse drag is started
- onEndDrag—called when a mouse drag is completed
- onApplyTransform—called when manipulation is complete and an object is being updated
- onAdjustTransform—called when a new Transform3D is being calculated

In addition, the three behaviors also accept behavior-specific interfaces:

- RotationChangeListener—Allows TornadoMouseRotate to pass the new angles about the *x, y,* and *z* axes to the caller.
- ScaleChangeListener—Allows TornadoMouseScale to pass the new scales along the *x, y,* and *z* axes to the caller.
- TranslationChangeListener—Allows TornadoMouseTranslate to pass the new translation along the *x, y,* and *z* axes to the caller.

These interfaces allow the `MouseNavigateTest` example to display the rotation, translation, and scale of an object in UI elements *while* the user is manipulating the object.

One significant problem with the built-in `MouseTranslate` behavior is that it *always* moves objects in the *x-y* plane. This does not cause any problems when the `MouseTranslate` behavior is added at the top of the scenegraph hierarchy. However, if a `TransformGroup` is used to rotate the scene such that the *x-y* plane is no longer parallel to the screen, and a child `TransformGroup` is added with an attached `MouseTranslate` behavior, the objects beneath the child `TransformGroup` will *still* move in the *x-y* plane and not parallel to the screen.

The `Tornado` mouse behaviors have built-in support for fixing this problem, and the abstract method `TornadoMouseBehavior.isRelativeToObjectCoordinates` controls whether object movement should compensate for `Transform-Groups` *above* the `TransformGroup` being manipulated using the mouse. This is pretty hard to describe in words, so I suggest you run the `MouseNavigateTest` example and you will see that the small cube is translated along a plane parallel to the screen, even though it is a child of a `TransformGroup` that has itself had a rotation applied.

The Tornado mouse behaviors also put a clamp on the range of changes permitted using translation or scaling. It is very easy using the built-in behaviors to lose objects because they are either translated outside the visible world or scaled wrong (too large or too small). The `TornadoMouseTranslate` and `TornadoMouseScale` behaviors accept minimum and maximum values for translation and scaling in the *x*, *y*, and *z* axes and will ensure that the objects are kept within these limits. In the `MouseNavigate-Test` example, it is not possible to translate the small cube outside of the larger cube, and scaling is permitted only between 50 and 200 percent along each axis. More explicit control over the speed of scaling, rotation, and translation is also offered, since each of the constructors accepts various scaling parameters.

Moreover, the Tornado mouse behaviors are not coded to specifically affect a `TransformGroup` but to accept a generic object via the `setObject` method. A runtime check is made on the class type of the `Object`, and if the object is a `Trans-formGroup` (which is typical), the `TransformGroup` is modified using an updated `Transform3D`. If the `Object` is *not* a `TransformGroup`, it is up to the developer to modify the `Object` in some way based on interface notifications or in a derived class. The classes were designed with derivation in mind and are highly customizable, so they form a good basis for application-specific derived classes.

Example usage of the new behaviors, from *MouseNavigateTest.java*

```
//Note that we are creating a TG above the TG that is being
//controlled by the mouse behaviors. The Sun mouse translate behavior
//would fail in this instance because all movement would be in the
//x-y plane irrespective of any TG above the object. The
//TornadoMouseTranslate behavior always moves an object parallel
//to the image plane
TransformGroup objTrans1 = new TransformGroup();
```

```java
Transform3D t3d = new Transform3D();
objTrans1.getTransform( t3d );
t3d.setEuler( new Vector3d(0.9,0.8,0.3) );
objTrans1.setTransform( t3d );

TransformGroup objTrans = new TransformGroup();
objTrans.setCapability(TransformGroup.ALLOW_TRANSFORM_WRITE);
objTrans.setCapability(TransformGroup.ALLOW_TRANSFORM_READ);

//create the mouse scale behavior and set limits
TornadoMouseScale mouseScale = new TornadoMouseScale( 5, 0.1f );
mouseScale.setMinScale( new Point3d( 0.5,0.5,0.5 ) );
mouseScale.setMaxScale( new Point3d( 2,2,2 ) );
mouseScale.setObject( objTrans );
mouseScale.setChangeListener( this );
mouseScale.setSchedulingBounds( getApplicationBounds() );
objTrans.addChild( mouseScale );

//create the mouse rotate behavior
TornadoMouseRotate mouseRotate =
  new TornadoMouseRotate( 0.001, 0.001 );
mouseRotate.setObject( objTrans );
mouseRotate.setChangeListener( this );
mouseRotate.setSchedulingBounds( getApplicationBounds() );
objTrans.addChild( mouseRotate );

//create the mouse translate behavior and set limits
TornadoMouseTranslate mouseTrans =
  new TornadoMouseTranslate( 0.005f );
mouseTrans.setObject( objTrans );
mouseTrans.setChangeListener( this );
mouseTrans.setMinTranslate( new Point3d( -4,-4,-4 ) );
mouseTrans.setMaxTranslate( new Point3d( 4,4,4 ) );
mouseTrans.setSchedulingBounds( getApplicationBounds() );
objTrans.addChild( mouseTrans );

//add the small cube
objTrans.addChild( new ColorCube(0.5) );

//create some axes for the world to show it has been rotated,
//and just use a larger wireframe ColorCube
ColorCube axis = new ColorCube(5.0);
Appearance app = new Appearance();
app.setPolygonAttributes( new PolygonAttributes(
  PolygonAttributes.POLYGON_LINE,
  PolygonAttributes.CULL_NONE, 0 ) );
axis.setAppearance( app );
objTrans1.addChild( axis );

//add the TransformGroup we are controlling with the mouse to
//the parent TransformGroup
objTrans1.addChild( objTrans );
```

11.8 BILLBOARD BEHAVIOR

```
java.lang.Object
   |
   +--javax.media.j3d.SceneGraphObject
         |
         +--javax.media.j3d.Node
               |
               +--javax.media.j3d.Leaf
                     |
                     +--javax.media.j3d.Behavior
                           |
                           +--javax.media.j3d.Billboard
```

The following is from Sun's Java 3D documentation: "The `Billboard` behavior node operates on the `TransformGroup` node to cause the local +z axis of the `TransformGroup` to point at the viewer's eye position. This is done regardless of the transforms above the specified `TransformGroup` node in the scene graph. `Billboard` nodes provide the most benefit for complex, roughly symmetric objects. A typical use might consist of a quadrilateral that contains a texture of a tree."

This means that you can define some geometry and then attach a `Billboard` behavior to the `TransformGroup` controlling the position of the geometry. The `Billboard` behavior will ensure that the geometry is oriented consistently to the viewer. Unlike real billboards, Java 3D `Billboards` are equipped with stepper motors so that they are always perpendicular to you, regardless of your position relative to them. For example, your application might define a 3D virtual environment to model a town. To allow people using the environment to easily navigate the town, you might wish to have a sign with the name of each building attached to the roof of the building. How do you ensure that people will always see the front of all the signs, regardless of their position in the town? By attaching a `Billboard` behavior to each sign, Java 3D will automatically rotate the sign such that the face of the sign is perpendicular to each viewer's line of sight.

> **NOTE** This approach would work fine if there were only a few signs in the town but would quickly become unrealistic as the number of signs increased. If the number of signs is large, instead of creating large numbers of `Billboard` behaviors, which will compromise performance, the orientations of the signs can be manually updated when the view direction is modified. Alternatively aligned geometry could be used (such as `Raster` or `OrientedShape3D`). `Behaviors` can be computationally intensive and so must be used with care.

The most general method to create a `Billboard` is:

```
public Billboard(TransformGroup tg, int mode, Point3f point)
```

This allows the `Billboard` to be attached to a graphical object's `Transform-Group`, which contains the rotation components that control the orientation of the graphical object.

In addition, two modes of rotation are supported:

- ROTATE_ABOUT_AXIS—Specifies that rotation should be about the specified axis.
- ROTATE_ABOUT_POINT—Specifies that rotation should be about the specified point and the children's Y-axis should match the view object's *y* axis.

Use ROTATE_ABOUT_AXIS with an axis of (0,1,0) to align billboards in a virtual environments where the user is in a world where +*y* is up (i.e., where the user is walking through a scene). Use ROTATE_ABOUT_POINT with the point set to the center of desired rotation. This is a useful mode for generalized 3D movement. It rotates around the center of rotation such that +*z* aligns with the eye and +*y* aligns with the +*y* axis of the view. This mode is useful because the text labels are always right side up.

The following code extract creates two 3D text labels and attaches a `Billboard` behavior to each. The first `Billboard` is created to ROTATE_ABOUT_AXIS, while the second is created to ROTATE_ABOUT_POINT. The whole scene is then set to rotate about the *y* axis, using a `RotationInterpolator` to simulate the scene spinning about the 0,0,0 coordinate—or the camera panning around the scene aimed at the 0,0,0 coordinate. While the `RotationInterpolator` strives to rotate the scene, the `Billboard` behaviors attempt to preserve the spatial relationship between the 3D text labels and the viewer. The `Billboard` behaviors ensure that the text labels are always facing the viewer. For contrast, a simple cube is created without a `Billboard` behavior—the cube rotates as expected (figure 11.8).

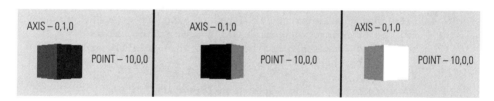

Figure 11.8   Three frames rendered by `BillboardTest`. Note that although the entire scene is rotating, the `Billboard` behaviors attached to the two `Text3D` instances ensure that the `Text3D` labels are always visible. Some jitter is visible as the labels are rotated before the `Billboard` behavior can compensate

From BillboardTest.java

```java
protected BranchGroup createSceneBranchGroup()
 {
  BranchGroup objRoot = super.createSceneBranchGroup();

  TransformGroup objTrans = new TransformGroup();
  objTrans.setCapability(TransformGroup.ALLOW_TRANSFORM_WRITE);
  objTrans.setCapability(TransformGroup.ALLOW_TRANSFORM_READ);

  BoundingSphere bounds = new BoundingSphere(
    new Point3d(0.0,0.0,0.0), 100.0);

  Transform3D yAxis = new Transform3D();
```

```
Alpha rotationAlpha = new Alpha(-1, Alpha.INCREASING_ENABLE,
 0, 0,
 4000, 0, 0,
 0, 0, 0);

RotationInterpolator rotator = new RotationInterpolator(
  rotationAlpha, objTrans, yAxis, 0.0f, (float) Math.PI*2.0f);
rotator.setSchedulingBounds(bounds);
objTrans.addChild(rotator);

objTrans.addChild( createBillboard( "AXIS - 0,1,0",
          new Point3f( -40.0f, 40.0f, 0.0f ),
          Billboard.ROTATE_ABOUT_AXIS,
          new Point3f( 0.0f, 1.0f, 0.0f ),
          bounds ) );

objTrans.addChild( createBillboard( "POINT - 10,0,0",
          new Point3f( 40.0f, 00.0f, 0.0f ),
          Billboard.ROTATE_ABOUT_POINT,
          new Point3f( 10.0f, 0.0f, 0.0f ),
          bounds ) );

objTrans.addChild( new ColorCube(20.0) );

objRoot.addChild( objTrans );

return objRoot;
}

//create a Text3D label at a given location and attach a
//Billboard behavior to the label to align it with the Viewer
private TransformGroup createBillboard( String szText,
   Point3f locationPoint, int nMode, Point3f billboardPoint,
   BoundingSphere bounds )
{
 TransformGroup subTg = new TransformGroup();
 subTg.setCapability(TransformGroup.ALLOW_TRANSFORM_WRITE);

 Font3D f3d = new Font3D( new Font( "SansSerif", Font.PLAIN, 10),
    new FontExtrusion() );
 Text3D label3D = new Text3D( f3d, szText, locationPoint );

 Shape3D sh = new Shape3D( label3D );

 subTg.addChild( sh );

 //attach a Billboard behavior to the TransformGroup containing
 //the Text3D label
 Billboard billboard = new Billboard(
   subTg, nMode, billboardPoint );
 billboard.setSchedulingBounds( bounds );
 subTg.addChild( billboard );

 return subTg;
}
```

`Billboard` behaviors are great for orienting simple signs or shapes when the viewer is navigating in a walk-through type simulation. Unfortunately, bugs prevent these behaviors from being particularly useful for orienting geometry when faced with generalized pitch, roll, and yaw navigation (you should check this with the latest Java 3D version). Also, `Billboards` only control the orientation of the geometry they are attached to—they cannot guarantee that the geometry is always visible or consistently scaled. For simple labels, a `Raster` object positioned in 3D space may be more appropriate depending upon the application and requirements.

11.9   USING LOD BEHAVIORS

LOD is a mechanism to dynamically modify the rendered geometry in a scene based on the position of the viewer. A LOD behavior performs a function similar to MIPMAPS for texture images (chapter 14) in that it allows you to specify a high-resolution model when the viewer is close up and a number of lower resolution models for when the viewer is farther away.

LOD behaviors are essentially optimizations that you can apply to your scenegraph to ensure that the time spent rendering a frame is spent rendering detail that the user is actually going to *see*, and should be the focus of their attention. For example, a model of an office building might be dynamically selected based on the viewer approaching the object: first a simple cube, then a texture mapped cube, then a series of stacked texture mapped cubes and finally a full-blown architectural model loaded from a VRML file. It would be very wasteful of CPU and rendering resources to always render the high-detail model of the building— yet the appearance of the lower resolution models is not sufficiently interesting when the viewer is up close, so a LOD behavior allows for a good trade-off of the two considerations.

Current computer games (such as the very visually impressive Black and White by Lionhead) use dynamic LOD algorithms extensively. The ROAM algorithm and Quad-trees are both commonly applied to large-scale interactive 3D terrain rendering. Two good references for adaptive meshes and the ROAM algorithm are http://www.llnl.gov/graphics/ROAM and http://uo.soex.com/engine/ROAM.html.

11.9.1   DistanceLOD Class

```
java.lang.Object
   |
  +--javax.media.j3d.SceneGraphObject
       |
       +--javax.media.j3d.Node
           |
           +--javax.media.j3d.Leaf
               |
               +--javax.media.j3d.Behavior
                   |
                   +--javax.media.j3d.LOD
                       |
                       +--javax.media.j3d.DistanceLOD
```

LOD itself is an abstract class. The only class derived from it is `DistanceLOD` which implements a LOD behavior based on the distance of the viewer from a point. Conceivably you could derive your own custom LOD behaviors from the abstract base class to implement application specific LOD functionality, or to switch the state of objects based on UI input.

The `SplineInterpolatorTest` example application uses a simple `Distance-LOD` behavior. Two versions of the 3D world are created, a high resolution version to be used when the viewer is less than 180 meters away and a low resolution version to be used when the viewer is more than 180 meters away.

The two versions of the world are created within separate `Groups` and added to a single `Switch Node`—the high resolution world is added first.

A `DistanceLOD` object is then created and initialized with an array of distances—as we only have two versions of the world we just have to pass in a single distance value to select between them. If we had n distance values in the distances array, and hence $n + 1$ models in the `Switch Node`, the formula for selecting between them is shown in table 11.5.

Table 11.5

Index selected	Distance (d)
0	if $d <=$ distances[0]
i	if distances[$i - 1$] < d <= distances[i]
n	if $d >$ distances[$n - 1$]

The `DistanceLOD` is then passed a reference to the `Switch Node` that it is going to control using the `LOD.addSwitch` method.

From SplineInterpolatorTest.java

```
//create a Switch group that contains two versions of the world:
//the first is a high resolution version, the second is a lower
//resolution version.
public Group createLodLand( Group g )
{
 Switch switchNode = new Switch();
 switchNode.setCapability( Switch.ALLOW_SWITCH_WRITE );

 Group hiResGroup = createLand( switchNode );
 createEnvirons( switchNode );

 //create a DistanceLOD that will select the child of the Switch
 //node based on distance. Here we are selecting child 0 (high res)if
 //we are closer than 180 units to 0,0,0 and child 1 (low res)
 //otherwise.
 float[] distanceArray = {180};

 DistanceLOD distanceLod = new DistanceLOD( distanceArray );
 distanceLod.setSchedulingBounds( getApplicationBounds() );
```

```
   distanceLod.addSwitch( switchNode );

   g.addChild( distanceLod );
   g.addChild( switchNode );

   return hiResGroup;
}

//create a high resolution representation of the world:
//a single texture mapped square and a larger (water colored)
//square to act as a horizon.
public Group createLand( Group g )
{
 Land land = new Land( this, g,
    ComplexObject.GEOMETRY | ComplexObject.TEXTURE );
 Group hiResGroup = land.createObject( new Appearance(),
   new Vector3d(), new Vector3d( LAND_WIDTH,1,LAND_LENGTH ) ,
   "boston.gif", null, null );

 Appearance app = new Appearance();
 app.setColoringAttributes( new ColoringAttributes(
    WATER_COLOR_RED/255f, WATER_COLOR_GREEN/255f,
    WATER_COLOR_BLUE/255f, ColoringAttributes.FASTEST ) );

 Land base = new Land( this, hiResGroup, ComplexObject.GEOMETRY );
 base.createObject( app, new Vector3d(0,-5,0), new Vector3d(
   2 * LAND_WIDTH,1,2 * LAND_LENGTH ), null, null, null );

 return hiResGroup;
}

//create a low resolution version of the world and
//applies the low resolution satellite image
public Group createEnvirons( Group g )
{
 Land environs = new Land( this, g,
    ComplexObject.GEOMETRY | ComplexObject.TEXTURE );
 return environs.createObject( new Appearance(), new Vector3d(),
    new Vector3d( 2 * LAND_WIDTH,1, 2 * LAND_LENGTH) ,
    "environs.gif", null, null );
}
```

11.10 SUMMARY

This chapter has introduced the Java 3D behavior model and described the most common built-in behaviors for UI interaction as well as the LOD and Billboard behaviors. The next chapter will introduce another important class of behaviors—Interpolator—used to vary objects within your scene as a function of time.

C H A P T E R   1 2

Using Interpolator behaviors

The `Interpolator` class defines the functionality for an important and powerful set of behaviors that deserve extra mention. The behaviors derived from `Interpolator` allow an object's current state to be interpolated between a set of defined states as a function of time.

This chapter introduces the `Interpolator` classes and the `Alpha` class, which is used to control the speed of interpolation.

12.1   THE INTERPOLATOR CLASS

```
java.lang.Object
  |
  +--javax.media.j3d.SceneGraphObject
       |
       +--javax.media.j3d.Node
            |
            +--javax.media.j3d.Leaf
                 |
                 +--javax.media.j3d.Behavior
                      |
                      +--javax.media.j3d.Interpolator
```

Java 3D includes a rich set of behaviors for interpolating an object between states. These behaviors are important for many animation and visualization applications and are covered in detail in this section. `Interpolator` behaviors can be used to interpolate an object's:

- *Color*—Linearly between diffuse material colors
- *Path*—Position along a specified path
- *Position*—Linearly between positions
- *Rotation*—Linearly between rotations
- *Scale*—Linearly between scale values
- `Switch value`—Toggle `Switch` Node's visible child based on time
- *Spline path*—Position along a specified spline path
- *Transparency*—Linearly between transparency values

All the `Interpolation` classes require an `Alpha` object. The `Alpha` class is used to convert the current time to a value between 0 and 1—this value is then used by the `Interpolator` to perform its specific action. The `Alpha` class is described in section 12.2.

12.2 THE ALPHA CLASS

```
java.lang.Object
  |
  +--javax.media.j3d.Alpha
```

A good understanding of the `Alpha` class is key to using all the `Interpolator` behaviors. The `Alpha` class defines a function that converts the current time (in milliseconds) to a value between 0 and 1 (*alpha value*). The alpha value can then be used by the `Interpolator` to produce the desired interpolation between specified end states.

For example, a `PositionInterpolator` might be used to move an object between position (0,0,0) and (0,0,5) in 10 seconds. To achieve the desired result, an `Alpha` object must be created that returns 0 at 0 seconds and 1 at 10 seconds. The `PositionInterpolator` can then use the `Alpha` object to create the desired *z* coordinate (table 12.1).

Table 12.1   Coordinate calculation using Alpha

Time (seconds)	Alpha	Z Coordinate
0	0	0 * 5 = 0
5	0.5	0.5 * 5 = 2.5
10	1	1 * 5 = 5

The `Alpha` class uses a parameterized function to convert time values to alpha values between 0 and 1.

Figure 12.1 illustrates the basic shape of the functions that can be created using the `Alpha` class. Nine parameters can be used to create a customized `Alpha` function are listed there.

The *increasing alpha phase* (3) is composed of three potential sections, as is the *decreasing alpha phase* (6). The values of *increasing alpha ramp* (4) and *decreasing alpha ramp* (7) define symmetrical acceleration and deceleration of the Alpha value at the beginning and end of the phase. These quadratic sections help to smooth the transition from 0 to 1 (*increasing alpha*) or 1 to 0 (*decreasing alpha*). Note that the Alpha value varies linearly between the quadratic sections. The `loopCount` parameter (9) allows `Alpha` functions to be repeated (a fixed number of times or infinitely) by joining `Alpha` functions end to end.

Run the AlphaTest example and interactively modify the nine parameters to get a good feel for how to parameterize an `Alpha` object for your application (figure 12.2).

NOTE While testing the AlphaTest example, I ran into an interesting bug in the Alpha class. If *either* the increasing alpha ramp or decreasing alpha ramp parameter is set to zero, the other will also be set to zero. You can work around this bug by setting the parameter to 1 millisecond instead of 0 milliseconds.

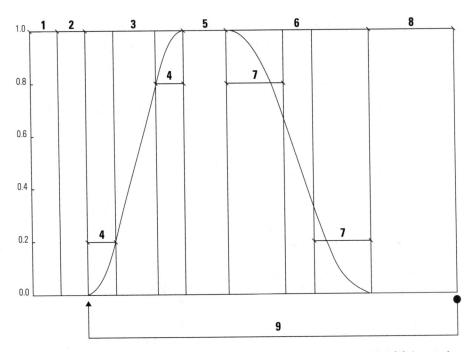

Figure 12.1 The phases of the Alpha class: `triggerTime` (1), phase delay (2), increasing alpha (3), increasing alpha ramp (4), at one (5), decreasing alpha (6), decreasing alpha ramp (7), at zero (8), and `loopCount` (9)

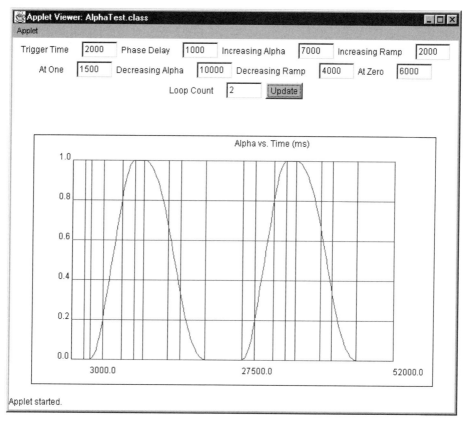

Figure 12.2 The AlphaTest example allows an `Alpha` object to be parameterized interactively and plots the resulting Alpha function

12.2.1 Using a custom Alpha class

You can, of course, derive your own class from `Alpha` to implement your own `Alpha` function. The `FileAlpha` class from the CustomAlphaTest examples loads times and alpha values from a text file and linearly interpolates between them.

From the file Values.xls from the CustomAlphaTest example

```
0      0
1000   0.1
3000   0.4
4000   0.2
6000   0.8
10000  0.5
12000  0.1
14000  1.0
16000  0.1
```

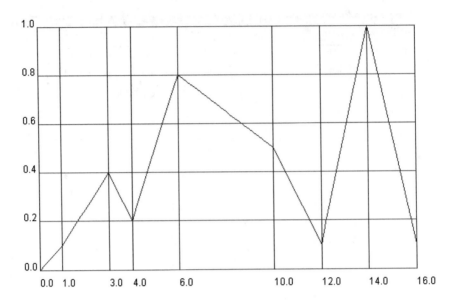

Figure 12.3 The `FileAlpha` class loads times and Alpha values from a file and linearly interpolates between them to provide a highly flexible Alpha function

The text file defines an ordered series of time and alpha value pairs (figure 12.3). Times are specified in milliseconds.

The `FileAlpha` class overrides the following `Alpha` methods.

```
public void setStartTime(long l)
public long getStartTime()
public void setLoopCount( int i )
public int getLoopCount()
public boolean finished()
public float value( long time )
```

Please refer to the `FileAlpha` class for details.

The `CustomAlphaTest` is also interesting in that it interpolates the position of a `ColorCube` using the `FileAlpha` and plots the value and time of the `FileAlpha` on the graph shown in figure 12.3.

12.2.2 Summary

An `Alpha` class is very simple—it converts a time value in milliseconds to a value between 0 and 1. The built-in `Alpha` class defines all the parameters for an `Alpha` function to implement a common class of onset, peak, offset activation functions.

A custom `Alpha` function, such as `FileAlpha`, is a very powerful mechanism to feed application-specific data into one of the `Interpolator`-derived classes. An application might define an `Alpha` class that samples data straight from a communications port, or reads precomputed data from a file. The output from the custom `Alpha` class can then be used to parameterize a wide variety of `Interpolators`.

Alpha classes are used in conjunction with Interpolators, but they do not do anything visible themselves. Their prime purpose in Java 3D is to provide input to the Interpolator classes. Interpolators are the subjects of section 12.3, so read on.

12.3 EXAMPLE OF INTERPOLATOR USAGE

```
java.lang.Object
  |
  +--javax.media.j3d.SceneGraphObject
       |
       +--javax.media.j3d.Node
            |
            +--javax.media.j3d.Leaf
                 |
                 +--javax.media.j3d.Behavior
                      |
                      +--javax.media.j3d.Interpolator
```

The Java 3D Interpolators were explored using the InterpolatorTest and the SplineInterpolatorTest examples. The InterpolatorTest example demonstrates using the following Interpolators:

SwitchValueInterpolator

The SwitchValueInterpolator is used to cycle through the children of a Switch Node based on the output from an Alpha object. The SwitchValueInterpolator maps the output from the Alpha into a current visible child Node using the following algorithm:

```
float f = alpha.value();
int i = firstSwitchIndex +
  (int)(f * (float)(childCount - 1) + 0.5F);
target.setWhichChild(i);
```

Note that the Switch Node passed to the SwitchInterpolator must have the Switch.ALLOW_SWITCH_WRITE capability.

```
//create the Switch Node
Switch switchNode = new Switch();

//set the WRITE capability
switchNode.setCapability( Switch.ALLOW_SWITCH_WRITE );

//add children to switchNode here…

//create the Alpha for the Interpolator
Alpha alpha = new Alpha(  -1,
        Alpha.INCREASING_ENABLE | Alpha.DECREASING_ENABLE,
        500,
        100,
        5000,
        2000,
        1000,
        5000,
```

```
        2000,
        500 );

//create the SwitchInterpolator and pass the Alpha
//and a Switch Node
Interpolator switchInterpolator =
 new SwitchValueInterpolator( alpha, switchNode );

//add the Interpolator to a parent BranchGroup
//and set Scheduling Bounds
BranchGroup bg = new BranchGroup();
bg.addChild( interpolator );
interpolator.setSchedulingBounds( getApplicationBounds() );
```

ColorInterpolator

The `ColorInterpolator` can be used to linearly interpolate the `Material` diffuse color of an `Appearance` between two extremes. Note that the `Material` must have the `ALLOW_COMPONENT_WRITE` capability bit set.

```
//create an Appearance
Appearance app = new Appearance();

//create a Material and assign an initial color
Color3f objColor = new Color3f(1.0f, 0.7f, 0.8f);
Color3f black = new Color3f(0.0f, 0.0f, 0.0f);
Material mat =
 new Material(objColor, black, objColor, black, 80.0f);

//ensure the Interpolator has WRITE access to the Material
mat.setCapability( Material.ALLOW_COMPONENT_WRITE );

//assign the Material to the Appearance
app.setMaterial( mat );

//create the Interpolator-by default interpolate
//between black and white
Interpolator interpolator =
 new ColorInterpolator( alpha, app.getMaterial() );
```

PositionInterpolator

The `PositionInterpolator` can be used to linearly interpolate between two *x, y, z* positions. The `PositionInterpolator` modifies a `TransformGroup`, which will in turn affect the position of all its child `Nodes`. The `TransformGroup` must have the `ALLOW_TRANSFORM_WRITE` capability set.

```
//create the TransformGroup
TransformGroup tg = new TransformGroup();
tg.setCapability(TransformGroup.ALLOW_TRANSFORM_WRITE);
tg.setCapability(TransformGroup.ALLOW_TRANSFORM_READ);

//create the Interpolator—by default interpolate
//between x = 0 and x = 1
Interpolator interpolator = new PositionInterpolator ( alpha, tg );
```

RotationInterpolator

The `RotationInterpolator` can be used to linearly interpolate between two sets of axis angle rotations. The `RotationInterpolator` modifies a `Transform-Group`, which will in turn affect the position of all its child `Nodes`. The `Transform-Group` must have the `ALLOW_TRANSFORM_WRITE` capability set.

```
//create the Interpolator—by default interpolate
//between Y angle = 0 and Y angle = 2π
Interpolator interpolator = new RotationInterpolator ( alpha, tg );
```

ScaleInterpolator

The `ScaleInterpolator` can be used to linearly interpolate between two scale values for an axis. The `ScaleInterpolator` modifies a `TransformGroup`, which will in turn affect the position of all its child `Nodes`. The `TransformGroup` must have the `ALLOW_TRANSFORM_WRITE` capability set.

```
//create the Interpolator—by default interpolate
//between a uniform scale of 0 and 1
Interpolator interpolator = new ScaleInterpolator ( alpha, tg );
```

TransparencyInterpolator

The `TransparencyInterpolator` can be used to linearly interpolate between two transparency values. The `TransparencyInterpolator` modifies an `Appearance`'s `TransparencyAttributes`. The `TransparencyAttributes` must have the `ALLOW_VALUE_WRITE` capability set.

```
//create the TransparencyAttributes
TransparencyAttributes transparency = new TransparencyAttributes();

//set the required capability bit
transparency.setCapability(
  TransparencyAttributes.ALLOW_VALUE_WRITE );

//set the transparency mode
transparency.setTransparencyMode( TransparencyAttributes.NICEST );

//assign the transparency to an Appearance
app.setTransparencyAttributes( transparency );

//create the interpolator and interpolate
//between 0 (opaque) and 0.8.
Interpolator interpolator = new TransparencyInterpolator( alpha,
app.getTransparencyAttributes(), 0, 0.8f );
```

RotPosScalePathInterpolator

The `RotPosScalePathInterpolator` is the most flexible of all the `PathInterpolators`. As its name suggests, it allows the rotation, position, and scale of a `TransformGroup` to be modified.

Rotations, positions, and scales are specified at a series of Alpha values (or *knots*). The rotation, position, and scale defines a *pose* that, along with the time information, allows the `Interpolator` to linearly interpolate between poses based on the Alpha value and the defined knots.

As the name knots implies, a useful way to visualize the interpolator is as a string stretched taut between a number of points. Each point is called a knot, and as well as having an Alpha value (time) when the interpolator is to *reach* the knot it also possesses position, scale, and rotation information (a pose). The distance between knots defines the speed at which the interpolation between values must occur.

Knots are specified using float values between 0 and 1, where 0 is the knot used at Alpha value 0 and 1 is the knot used at Alpha time 1. The array of knot values defines a mapping from Alpha value to pose information. The knot values must *increase* from 0 to 1 in the knot array.

```
//define the knots array that map from Alpha to pose index
float[] knots = {0.0f, 0.1f, 0.2f, 0.3f, 0.4f,
                 0.6f, 0.8f, 0.9f, 1.0f};

//create array with 9 poses: containing rotation, position
//and scale values
Quat4f[] quats = new Quat4f[9];
Point3f[] positions = new Point3f[9];
float[] scales = {0.2f, 0.5f, 0.8f, 2.3f, 5.4f,
                  0.6f, 0.4f, 0.2f, 0.1f};

//define the rotation values for each of the 9 poses
quats[0] = new Quat4f(0.3f, 1.0f, 1.0f, 0.0f);
quats[1] = new Quat4f(1.0f, 0.0f, 0.0f, 0.3f);
quats[2] = new Quat4f(0.2f, 1.0f, 0.0f, 0.0f);
quats[3] = new Quat4f(0.0f, 0.2f, 1.0f, 0.0f);
quats[4] = new Quat4f(1.0f, 0.0f, 0.4f, 0.0f);
quats[5] = new Quat4f(0.0f, 1.0f, 1.0f, 0.2f);
quats[6] = new Quat4f(0.3f, 0.3f, 0.0f, 0.0f);
quats[7] = new Quat4f(1.0f, 0.0f, 1.0f, 1.0f);
quats[8] = quats[0];

//define the positions for each of the 9 poses
positions[0]= new Point3f(0.0f,  0.0f, -1.0f);
positions[1]= new Point3f(1.0f, -2.0f, -2.0f);
positions[2]= new Point3f(-2.0f,  2.0f, -3.0f);
positions[3]= new Point3f(1.0f,  1.0f, -4.0f);
positions[4]= new Point3f(-4.0f, -2.0f, -5.0f);
positions[5]= new Point3f(2.0f,  0.3f, -6.0f);
positions[6]= new Point3f(-4.0f,  0.5f, -7.0f);
positions[7]= new Point3f(0.0f, -1.5f, -4.0f);
positions[8]= positions[0];

//create the interpolator and pass Alpha, TransformGroup,
//knots, and pose information
RotPosScalePathInterpolator rotPosScalePathInterplator = new RotPosScale-
PathInterpolator(
  alpha,
  tg,
```

```
new Transform3D(),
knots,
quats,
positions,
scales );
```

As you can see, the rotation angles are specified using the Quat4f class. The Quat4f class specifies a rotation as a quaternion. The following is a description of quaternions, taken from the excellent "Matrix and Quaternion FAQ." The FAQ can be found online and it currently maintained by Andreas Junghanns at http://www.cs.ualberta.ca/~andreas/math/matrfaq_latest.html.

"Quaternions extend the concept of rotation in three dimensions to rotation in four dimensions. This avoids the problem of "gimbal-lock" and allows for the implementation of smooth and continuous rotation. In effect, they may be considered to add an additional rotation angle to spherical coordinates: longitude, latitude, and rotation angles. A Quaternion is defined using four floating point values |x y z w|. These are calculated from the combination of the three coordinates of the rotation axis and the rotation angle."

Unfortunately most people do not *think* readily in quaternions, so the following two conversion functions are useful to help create quaternions from axis or Euler angles. The algorithms for the functions were taken from the "Matrix and Quaternion FAQ." I encourage you to check the FAQ for updates, optimizations and corrections to this code.

From InterpolatorTest.java

```
//Quat4f createQuaternionFromAxisAndAngle
//( Vector3d axis, double angle )
{
 double sin_a = Math.sin( angle / 2 );
 double cos_a = Math.cos( angle / 2 );

 //use a vector so we can call normalize
 Vector4f q = new Vector4f();

 q.x = (float) (axis.x * sin_a);
 q.y = (float) (axis.y * sin_a);
 q.z = (float) (axis.z * sin_a);
 q.w = (float) cos_a;

 //It is best to normalize the quaternion
 //so that only rotation information is used
 q.normalize();

 //convert to a Quat4f and return
 return new Quat4f( q );
}

//Quat4f createQuaternionFromEuler( double angleX,
//double angleY, double angleZ )
{
```

```
//simply call createQuaternionFromAxisAndAngle for each axis
//and multiply the results
Quat4f qx = createQuaternionFromAxisAndAngle(
    new Vector3d(1,0,0), angleX );
Quat4f qy = createQuaternionFromAxisAndAngle(
    new Vector3d(0,1,0), angleY );
Quat4f qz = createQuaternionFromAxisAndAngle(
    new Vector3d(0,0,1), angleZ );

//qx = qx * qy
qx.mul( qy );

//qx = qx * qz
qx.mul( qz );

return qx;
}
```

■

12.3.1 Design of the InterpolatorTest example

The InterpolatorTest example creates a Switch Node and attaches a Switch-Interpolator. A custom Alpha class (RandomAlpha) is used to generate Alpha values for the SwitchInterpolator. The RandomAlpha generates a random Alpha value (between 0 and 1) every 10 seconds. This causes the SwitchInterpolator to randomly switch between child Nodes every 10 seconds.

The Switch Node has six child Nodes:

1 Group containing a ColorInterpolator: Operates on an Appearance.

2 Group containing a PositionInterpolator: Operates on a Trans-formGroup.

3 Group containing a RotationInterpolator: Operates on a Trans-formGroup.

4 Group containing a ScaleInterpolator: Operates on a TransformGroup.

5 Group containing a TransparencyInterpolator: Operates on an Appearance.

6 Group containing a RotPosScaleInterpolator: Operates on a Trans-formGroup.

Each Group also contains a Link Node to a common SharedGroup. The SharedGroup contains a TransformGroup with a child Shape3D. The parent TransformGroup is passed to each Interpolator that requires a Transform-Group, while the Shape3D's Appearance is passed to each Interpolator that requires an Appearance. A Text2D is also created with the name of the Interpolator as text so that the current active Interpolator can be seen. See figure 12.4.

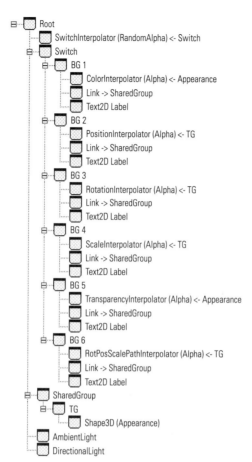

Root
   SwitchInterpolator (RandomAlpha) <- Switch
  Switch
    BG 1
      ColorInterpolator (Alpha) <- Appearance
      Link -> SharedGroup
      Text2D Label
    BG 2
      PositionInterpolator (Alpha) <- TG
      Link -> SharedGroup
      Text2D Label
    BG 3
      RotationInterpolator (Alpha) <- TG
      Link -> SharedGroup
      Text2D Label
    BG 4
      ScaleInterpolator (Alpha) <- TG
      Link -> SharedGroup
      Text2D Label
    BG 5
      TransparencyInterpolator (Alpha) <- Appearance
      Link -> SharedGroup
      Text2D Label
    BG 6
      RotPosScalePathInterpolator (Alpha) <- TG
      Link -> SharedGroup
      Text2D Label
  SharedGroup
    TG
      Shape3D (Appearance)
  AmbientLight
  DirectionalLight

Figure 12.4
The basic scenegraph design for
the InterpolatorTest example

The InterpolatorTest example exploits a useful feature of Behaviors: when the Switch changes its active child Node, the Behaviors of the inactive child Nodes are no longer scheduled. In this way, the SwitchInterpolator that randomly selects child Nodes (using the RandomAlpha class) also activates a single Behavior—inactive Behaviors are no longer processed even though they are still enabled.

The RandomAlpha class is very simple:

```
//This class defines an Alpha class that returns
//a random value every N milliseconds.
public class RandomAlpha extends Alpha
{
 protected long       m_LastQueryTime = 0;
 protected float      m_Alpha = 0;
 protected final int    m_kUpdateInterval = 10000;

 public RandomAlpha()
 {
 }
```

```
//core method override returns the Alpha value for a given time
public float value( long time )
{
 if( System.currentTimeMillis()
       - m_LastQueryTime > m_kUpdateInterval )
 {
  m_LastQueryTime = System.currentTimeMillis();
  m_Alpha = (float) Math.random();
 }

 return m_Alpha;
}
}
```

12.4 USING A CUBIC-SPLINE INTERPOLATOR

Java 3D includes a class to perform cubic-spline interpolation of position, rotation, and scale between key frames. The class uses the Kochanek-Bartels (K-B) algorithm to allow smooth interpolation between key frames (*knots*), which specify pose and interpolation information. Unlike linear interpolation, which suffers from potential discontinuities at control points (knots), K-B interpolation, while guaranteeing that the path passes through all the control points, varies the path smoothly. Instead of a piece of taut string strung between control points, the analogy is closer to a springy rod that passes through each point.

The K-B algorithm is fairly complex, and a discussion of the mathematics behind the algorithm is beyond the scope of this practical book. There are a number of very good online resources that describe the algorithm in detail. In addition, because the Interpolator class that implements the algorithm is in the Java 3D utils package, all the source code is available for inspection.

The good news is that the algorithm is extremely flexible and allows very fine control over the interpolated path. Each key frame, along with all the pose information (position, rotation, scale), also defines the following three parameters:

- Tension (–1 to +1)
- Continuity (–1 to +1)
- Bias (–1 to +1)

As with most terms in this book, a picture is worth a thousand words, so see figures 12.5, 12.6, and 12.7, which illustrate the K-B parameters.

Tension parameter

The tension parameter controls the length of the curve segments either side of a key frame. The higher the tension, the shorter the segments.

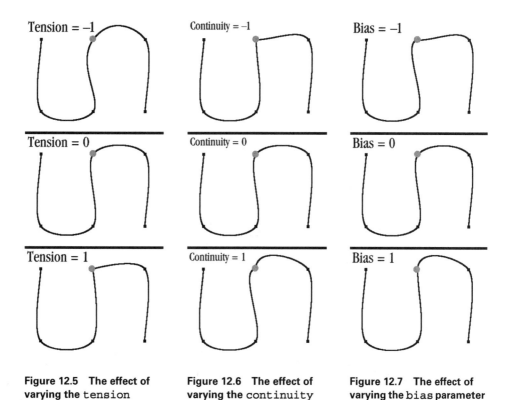

Figure 12.5 The effect of varying the `tension` parameter at a key frame on a 2D K-B spline curve

Figure 12.6 The effect of varying the `continuity` parameter at a key frame on a 2D K-B spline curve

Figure 12.7 The effect of varying the `bias` parameter at a key frame on a 2D K-B spline curve

Continuity

The `continuity` parameter enables you to purposefully introduce discontinuities into the path. The path can either mimic a sharp corner at the key frame (−1) or overshoot the key frame and slingshot back (1).

Bias

The `bias` parameter enables you to apportion `tension` at a key frame to each curve segment either side of the key frame. In this way the path is skewed about the key frame, with the segment on one side of the key frame slacker than the segment on the other side.

12.4.1 The SplineInterpolatorTest example

`SplineInterpolatorTest` is one of the most ambitious examples of the book. When I thought of animating an object using a spline curve, I thought of tracking a camera along a spline curve and rendering the results. My initial idea was to model an architectural or city fly-over, and the example grew from there.

`SplineInterpolatorTest` creates a virtual model of the city of Boston. The example loads a predefined spline curve from a file and takes the viewer on a virtual flight around the city (figures 12.8, 12.9, and 12.10).

The virtual city is composed of the following elements:

- A square with a high-resolution satellite image of the city texture mapped onto it.
- A larger square with a lower resolution satellite image applied.
- A large blue square to act as a base for the model and supply a consistent horizon.
- A cloudy sky backdrop texture mapped onto a `Background Sphere`.
- Some randomly created texture mapped buildings (`Boxes`).

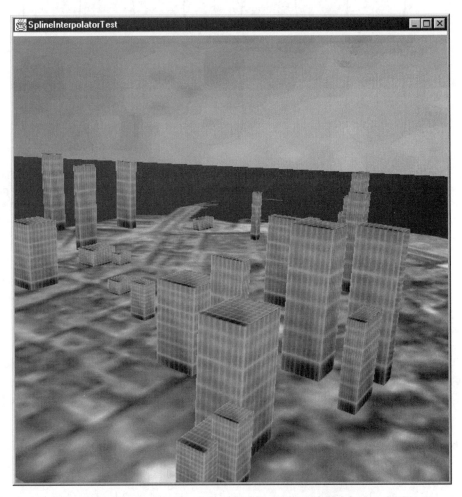

Figure 12.8 A frame from the `SplineInterpolatorTest` example. Take a virtual fly-over of Boston city center

Figure 12.9 When viewed from afar, the `SplineInterpolatorTest` dynamically switches to a low-resolution image of the whole of the city. One of the orbiting helicopters is visible in the frame

Figure 12.10
Looking up at one of the
helicopters orbiting the city

- Three helicopters each flying a spline curve loaded from a file. The geometry for the helicopters is also loaded from a file.
- Sound support. Each helicopter has an attached `PointSound` source. The 3D sound engine generates 3D spatial sound from the three sound sources.

The rendered results are very pleasing, and the smoothness of the spline based animation gives a nice impression of movement and acceleration through the generated world. The satellite images were downloaded from the Microsoft Terraserver satellite image database. Terraserver is very useful in that different resolution images (i.e., from 32 meters per pixel down to 1 meter per pixel) can be easily downloaded. It allows a LOD behavior to be used, so that a high-resolution image appears when the viewer is close to the city and a lower resolution image appears when the viewer is far above the city. Both texture images are 256 × 256 pixels in size, and hence should be supported by hardware renderers.

To support the functionality required for the example, a base class was created for defining the behaviors, geometry, and appearance for the objects in the world. For an application of this complexity, the approach taken in most example code, which is to throw everything in the `Applet` class, was clearly not going to work. What was required was an OO design that empowered the objects within the world with the abilities they required. These abilities include:

- Create geometry.
- Load geometry from a disk file.
- Assign a texture image.
- Assign a sound.
- Assign a spline path and `Alpha` object to animate the object.
- Load a spline path from a disk file.

These chores are handled by the `ComplexObject` class, which allows the main code of the application to deal with the objects themselves, and not with `Transform-Groups`, sounds, appearances, and the like. This keeps the reusable functionality low in the class hierarchy and puts the application-specific details in super classes and the main `Applet` class itself.

The code for the example is obviously too long to be shown in full, so some interesting highlights will be discussed. The source code for `ComplexObject` is in the `org.selman.java3d.book` package.

12.4.2 Creating the LOD behavior

```
//create a Switch group that contains two versions of the world:
//The first is a high resolution version, and the second is a
//lower resolution version.
public Group createLodLand( Group g )
{
 Switch switchNode = new Switch();
```

```
switchNode.setCapability( Switch.ALLOW_SWITCH_WRITE );

Group hiResGroup = createLand( switchNode );
createEnvirons( switchNode );

//Create a DistanceLOD that will select the child
//of the Switch node based on distance. Here we are
//selecting child 0 (high res) if we are closer
//than 180 units to 0,0,0, and child 1 (low res) otherwise.
float[] distanceArray = {180};

DistanceLOD distanceLod = new DistanceLOD( distanceArray );
distanceLod.setSchedulingBounds( getApplicationBounds() );
distanceLod.addSwitch( switchNode );

g.addChild( distanceLod );
g.addChild( switchNode );

return hiResGroup;
}
```

12.4.3   Reading spline key frames from disk

The following code is used to read in a series of key frames from a disk file. Defining key frames by hand takes a lot of trial and error, so it is very desirable to be able to quickly modify the key frame file and rerun the application rather than having to recompile.

A utility method was written to read the data for a series of key frames from a disk file. The format of the file is as follows:

1 Alpha time

2 Position x,y,z

3 Rotation x,y,z

4 Scale x,y,z

5 Tension (–1 to 1)

6 Continuity (–1 to 1)

7 Bias (–1 to 1)

8 Linear Interpolation (0 or 1)

For example, the spline curve that the viewer is interpolated along is defined as follows, from rotate_viewer_spline.xls:

```
0.0
5 6 5
-0.4 0 0
1 1 1
0 1 0
0

0.3
2 4 10
1.0  0.2 0
1 1 1
```

```
0 0 0
0

0.5
-2 4 8
-0.3 0.6 0.2
1 1 1
-1 1 -1
0

0.7
-2 5 10
-0.4 -0.6 0.5
1 1 1
-1 1 -1
0

0.8
-1 4 5
-0.6 -0.9 -0.2
1 1 1
1 1 1
0

0.9
0 10 15
-1.2 0 0
1 1 1
1 0 1
0

1.0
0 52 0
-1.5 0 0
1 1 1
0 1 1
0
```

The utility method to read and create the key frame array is simply the following:

From Utils.java in the org.selman.java3d.book package

```java
static public TCBKeyFrame[] readKeyFrames( URL urlKeyframes )
{
 StringBuffer szBufferData = readFile( urlKeyframes );

 if( szBufferData == null )
  return null;

 Vector keyFramesVector = new Vector();

 //create a tokenizer to tokenize the input file at whitespace
 java.util.StringTokenizer tokenizer =
   new java.util.StringTokenizer( szBufferData.toString() );

 /*
  * Each keyframe is defined as follows:
```

```java
 * - knot (0 >= k <= 1)
 * - position (x,y,z)
 * - rotation (rx,ry,rz)
 * - scale (x,y,z)
 * - tension (-1 >= t <= 1)
 * - continuity (-1 >= c <= 1)
 * - bias (-1 >= b <= 1)
 * - linear (int - 0 or 1)
 */
while( true )
{
 try
 {
  float knot = Float.parseFloat( tokenizer.nextToken() );

  float posX = Float.parseFloat( tokenizer.nextToken() );
  float posY = Float.parseFloat( tokenizer.nextToken() );
  float posZ = Float.parseFloat( tokenizer.nextToken() );

  float rotX = Float.parseFloat( tokenizer.nextToken() );
  float rotY = Float.parseFloat( tokenizer.nextToken() );
  float rotZ = Float.parseFloat( tokenizer.nextToken() );

  float scaleX = Float.parseFloat( tokenizer.nextToken() );
  float scaleY = Float.parseFloat( tokenizer.nextToken() );
  float scaleZ = Float.parseFloat( tokenizer.nextToken() );

  float tension = Float.parseFloat( tokenizer.nextToken() );
  float continuity = Float.parseFloat( tokenizer.nextToken() );
  float bias = Float.parseFloat( tokenizer.nextToken() );

  int linear = Integer.parseInt( tokenizer.nextToken() );

  //create the actual keyframe from the data just read
  TCBKeyFrame keyframe = new TCBKeyFrame(
   knot,
   linear,
   new Point3f( posX, posY, posZ ),
   createQuaternionFromEuler( rotX, rotY, rotZ ),
   new Point3f( scaleX, scaleY, scaleZ ),
   tension,
   continuity,
   bias );

  keyFramesVector.add( keyframe );
 }
 catch( Exception e )
 {
  break;
 }
}

//create the return structure and populate
TCBKeyFrame[] keysReturn =
  new TCBKeyFrame[ keyFramesVector.size() ];
```

```
for( int n = 0; n < keysReturn.length; n++ )
 keysReturn[n] = (TCBKeyFrame) keyFramesVector.get( n );

//return the array
return keysReturn;
}
```

12.4.4 Creating the texture-mapped sky backdrop

To create the background for the example we create a Sphere, assign a texture image to the Sphere and then assign the Sphere to a Background node. Note that because the viewer of the scene is within the Sphere the normal vectors assigned to the vertices of the Sphere must be created with the Primitive.GENERATE_NOR-MALS_INWARD option.

From SplineInterpolatorTest.java

```
//we want a texture-mapped background of a sky
protected Background createBackground()
{
 //add the sky backdrop
 Background back = new Background();
 back.setApplicationBounds( getApplicationBounds() );

 BranchGroup bgGeometry = new BranchGroup();

 //create an appearance and assign the texture image
 Appearance app = new Appearance();
 Texture tex = new TextureLoader( "sky.gif", this).getTexture();
 app.setTexture( tex );

 Sphere sphere =
  new Sphere( 1.0f, Primitive.GENERATE_TEXTURE_COORDS |
                    Primitive.GENERATE_NORMALS_INWARD,
             app );

 bgGeometry.addChild( sphere );
 back.setGeometry( bgGeometry );

 return back;
}
```

12.4.5 Controlling the extent of the audio for the helicopters

The distance over which the PointSounds created for the three helicopters can be heard is controlled by three factors: (1) the ViewPlatform's activation radius, (2) the scheduling bounds of the Sound, and (3) distance/gain parameters of the PointSound itself.

A PointSound is potentially audible when the ViewPlatform's activation radius intersects the scheduling bounds for the Sound. The actual volume of the mixed sound is controlled by the distance/gain parameters for the PointSound.

```
//Return the scheduling bounds for the Helicopter's sound
protected Bounds getSoundSchedulingBounds( boolean bCollide )
{
 return new BoundingSphere( new Point3d(0,0,0), 20 );
}
```

The `getSoundDistanceGain` method returns an array of `Point2f` objects that define how the volume of the sound attenuates with distance. In the following example the sound is at 20 percent of its maximum intensity at 2 units distance and at 5 percent of maximum intensity at 20 units distance.

```
protected Point2f[] getSoundDistanceGain( boolean bCollide )
{
 Point2f[] gainArray = new Point2f[2];

 gainArray[0] = new Point2f( 2, 0.2f );
 gainArray[1] = new Point2f( 20, 0.05f );

 return gainArray;
}
```

12.5 SUMMARY

This discussion of `Interpolators` and the `SplineInterpolatorTest` example should have alerted you to some of the power of the interpolator behaviors built into Java 3D. The support for such high-level features as interpolators in Java 3D is a real time saver. Just think about having to implement this functionality by hand.

C H A P T E R   1 3

Writing custom behaviors

Some behaviors automatically execute complex code to modify objects within the scenegraph, so care must be taken to ensure that behavior processing does not bog down application performance. With careful design and knowledge of some of the limitations, behaviors can be a powerful asset in quickly developing or prototyping application logic.

By the end of this chapter you should have a good sense of how to develop your own behaviors. By mixing and matching your own and the built-in behaviors, you should be able to design your application logic within Java 3D's behavior model.

13.1   THE BEHAVIORTEST EXAMPLE

There are occasions when the built-in behaviors do not provide enough functionality to capture the logic of your application. By creating your own classes derived from `Behavior`, you can easily integrate your application logic into Java 3D's behavior processing framework.

The `BehaviorTest` example application uses four behaviors: the built-in `RotationInterpolator` and three custom behaviors of varying complexity: `ObjectSizeBehavior`, `ExplodeBehavior`, and `StretchBehavior`. See figure 13.1.

`ObjectSizeBehavior` is the simplest, and it calculates the smallest `BoundingBox` that encloses a `Shape3D`'s geometry. The `BoundingBox` is recalculated every 20 frames, and the size of the `BoundingBox` is written to standard output. Note that the basic anatomy of a behavior described in section 11.3 is adhered to here.

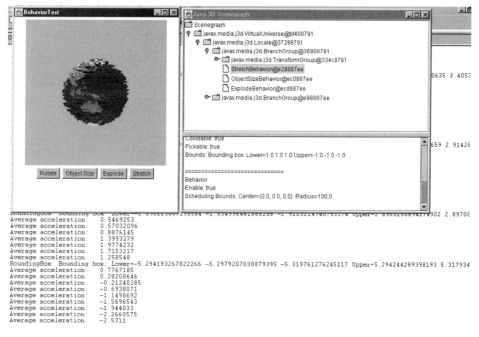

```
BoundingBox: Bounding box  Lower=-2.070221001290584 -2.0343904010000200 -2.910321470733174 Upper=2.090320004274902 2.89708
Average acceleration:    0.5469253
Average acceleration:    0.57032096
Average acceleration:    0.8876145
Average acceleration:    1.3993279
Average acceleration:    1.9774232
Average acceleration:    1.7153217
Average acceleration:    1.258548
BoundingBox: Bounding box  Lower=-5.294193267822266 -5.2979207038879395 -5.3197761276245117 Upper=5.294244289398193 5.317934
Average acceleration:    0.7767185
Average acceleration:    0.28208646
Average acceleration:    -0.21240285
Average acceleration:    -0.6938071
Average acceleration:    -1.1498692
Average acceleration:    -1.5696543
Average acceleration:    -1.944033
Average acceleration:    -2.2660575
Average acceleration:    -2.5311
```

Figure 13.1   The BehaviorTest example application. StretchBehavior is used to modify the geometry of the Sphere after every frame, while ObjectSizeBehavior reports the Bounds for the object after every 20 frames

ExplodeBehavior is more complex. Given a Shape3D object, it explodes the object after a specified number of milliseconds by rendering the Shape3D as points and modifying the coordinates within the Shape3D's GeometryArray. The transparency of the object is gradually increased so that the object fades into the background.

StretchBehavior is the most complex of the custom behaviors. It operates upon a specified GeometryArray and animates the vertices within the array as if they were weights attached by springs to the origin. StretchBehavior listens for key presses and increases the acceleration of each vertex when a key is pressed. The increased acceleration causes the vertices to move away from the origin, which causes an increase in the restraining force from the spring. The vertices oscillate back and forth, finally coming to rest at their original position.

13.2   *OBJECTSIZEBEHAVIOR*

The ObjectSizeBehavior class implements a simple behavior that calculates and prints the size of an object based on the vertices in its GeometryArray.

```java
class ObjectSizeBehavior extends Behavior
{
//the wake up condition for the behavior
protected WakeupCondition   m_WakeupCondition = null;

//the GeometryArray for the Shape3D that we are querying
protected GeometryArray   m_GeometryArray = null;

//cache some information on the model to save reallocation
protected float[]        m_CoordinateArray = null;

protected BoundingBox    m_BoundingBox = null;
protected Point3d        m_Point = null;;

public ObjectSizeBehavior( GeometryArray geomArray )
{
 //save the GeometryArray that we are modifying
 m_GeometryArray = geomArray;

 //set the capability bits that the behavior requires
 m_GeometryArray.setCapability(
  GeometryArray.ALLOW_COORDINATE_READ );
 m_GeometryArray.setCapability(
  GeometryArray.ALLOW_COUNT_READ );

 //allocate an array for the coordinates
 m_CoordinateArray =
  new float[ 3 * m_GeometryArray.getVertexCount() ];

 //create the BoundingBox used to calculate the size of the object
 m_BoundingBox = new BoundingBox();

 //create a temporary point
 m_Point = new Point3d();

 //create the WakeupCriterion for the behavior
 WakeupCriterion criterionArray[] = new WakeupCriterion[1];
  criterionArray[0] = new WakeupOnElapsedFrames( 20 );

 //save the WakeupCriterion for the behavior
 m_WakeupCondition = new WakeupOr( criterionArray );
}

public void initialize()
{
 //apply the initial WakeupCriterion
 wakeupOn( m_WakeupCondition );
}

public void processStimulus( java.util.Enumeration criteria )
{
 while( criteria.hasMoreElements() )
 {
  WakeupCriterion wakeUp =
```

```
      (WakeupCriterion) criteria.nextElement();

    //every N frames, recalculate the bounds for the points
    //in the GeometryArray
    if( wakeUp instanceof WakeupOnElapsedFrames )
    {
     //get all the coordinates
     m_GeometryArray.getCoordinates( 0, m_CoordinateArray );

     //clear the old BoundingBox
     m_BoundingBox.setLower( 0,0,0 );
     m_BoundingBox.setUpper( 0,0,0 );

     //loop over every vertex and combine with the BoundingBox
     for( int n = 0; n < m_CoordinateArray.length; n+=3 )
     {
      m_Point.x = m_CoordinateArray[n];
      m_Point.y = m_CoordinateArray[n+1];
      m_Point.z = m_CoordinateArray[n+2];

      m_BoundingBox.combine( m_Point );
     }

     System.out.println( "BoundingBox: " + m_BoundingBox );
    }
   }

   //assign the next WakeUpCondition, so we are notified again
   wakeupOn( m_WakeupCondition );
  }
 }
```

To use the behavior one could write:

```
Sphere sphere = new Sphere( 3, Primitive.GENERATE_NORMALS | Primi-
tive.GENERATE_TEXTURE_COORDS, 32, app );

m_SizeBehavior = new ObjectSizeBehavior( (GeometryArray) sphere.get-
Shape().getGeometry() );
m_SizeBehavior.setSchedulingBounds( getApplicationBounds() );
objRoot.addChild( m_SizeBehavior );
```

This code snippet creates the behavior and passes the geometry for a Sphere to the constructor, sets the scheduling bounds for the behavior and adds it to the scenegraph. Do not forget to *add* the behavior to the scenegraph, or it will not get scheduled.

Output from the behavior is simply:

```
Bounding box: Lower=-5.048 -5.044 -5.069 Upper=5.040 5.060 5.069
Bounding box: Lower=-5.048 -5.044 -5.069 Upper=5.040 5.060 5.069
Bounding box: Lower=-5.048 -5.044 -5.069 Upper=5.040 5.060 5.069
```

The behavior verifies the size of the geometry for the Shape3D every 20 frames. Note that the behavior follows the general anatomy of a behavior as was described in section 11.3.

When writing a behavior you should be very aware of the computational cost of the processing within the `processStimulus` method and how often the behavior is likely to be invoked. The `ObjectSizeBehavior`'s `processStimulus` method is called once every 20 frames, so any processing that is performed is going to have a fairly big impact on application performance. Whenever possible, avoid creating `Objects` (using the new operator) within the `processStimulus` method if it is going to be invoked frequently. Any `Objects` created by the behavior using the new operator and not assigned to a member variable will have to be garbage-collected. Not only is creating objects a relatively costly operation, but garbage collection can cause your application to noticeably pause during rendering.

For example, instead of creating a new `BoundingBox`, which would have had size 0, a single `BoundingBox` object was resized using:

```
m_BoundingBox.setLower( 0,0,0 );
m_BoundingBox.setUpper( 0,0,0 );
```

With Java 3D in general, you should avoid burning (allocate, followed by garbage-collect) `Objects` as much as possible, and minimize the work that the garbage collector has to perform.

13.3 EXPLODEBEHAVIOR

The constructor for the `ExplodeBehavior` is as follows:

```
public ExplodeBehavior( Shape3D shape3D,
                        int nElapsedTime, int nNumFrames,
                        ExplosionListener listener )
```

The behavior attaches to the `Shape3D` specified and explodes the object after nElapsedTime milliseconds (figure 13.2). The explosion animation takes nNumFrames to complete, and, once complete, a notification is passed to the caller via an `ExplosionListener` interface method.

To model the simple explosion, the behavior switches the `Shape3D`'s appearance to rendering in points (by modifying the `PolygonAttributes`) and sets the point size (using `PointAttributes`). The transparency of the `Shape3D` is then set using `TransparencyAttributes`. The vertices of the `Shape3D`'s geometry are then moved away from the origin with a slight random bias in the $x+$, $y+$, and $z+$ direction.

The `ExplodeBehavior` moves through the following life cycle:

1 The behavior is created.

2 Initialize is called by Java 3D.

3 `WakeUp` condition is set to be `WakeupOnElapsedTime( n milliseconds )`.

4 `processStimulus` is called after n milliseconds.

5 The `Appearance` attributes are modified for the `Shape3D`.

6 The `WakeUp` condition is set to `WakeupOnElapsedFrames( 1 )`.

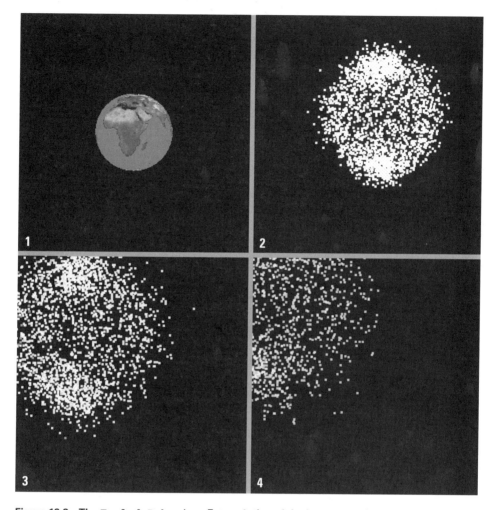

Figure 13.2 The `ExplodeBehavior`: Frame 1, the original `Shape3D`; frames 2–4, some frames of the explosion animation

7 `processStimulus` is called after every frame.

8 The `GeometryArray`'s vertex coordinates is modified.

9 Coordinates are reassigned.

10 If frame number < number of frames for animation

- Set the `WakeUp` condition to `WakeupOnElapsedFrames( 1 )`

11 Else

- Restore the original `Shape3D` `Appearance` and coordinates.
- Notify the `ExplosionListener` that the behavior is done.
- Call `setEnable( false )` to disabled the behavior.

The `processStimulus` method for the `ExplodeBehavior` is as follows.

```java
public void processStimulus( java.util.Enumeration criteria )
{
 while( criteria.hasMoreElements() )
 {
  WakeupCriterion wakeUp =
    (WakeupCriterion) criteria.nextElement();

  if( wakeUp instanceof WakeupOnElapsedTime )
  {
   //we are starting the explosion,
   //apply the appearance changes we require
   PolygonAttributes polyAttribs =
    new PolygonAttributes( PolygonAttributes.POLYGON_POINT,
                           PolygonAttributes.CULL_NONE, 0 );
   m_Shape3D.getAppearance().setPolygonAttributes( polyAttribs );

   PointAttributes pointAttribs = new PointAttributes( 3, false );
   m_Shape3D.getAppearance().setPointAttributes( pointAttribs );

   m_Shape3D.getAppearance().setTexture( null );

   m_TransparencyAttributes =
    new TransparencyAttributes( TransparencyAttributes.NICEST, 0 );
   m_TransparencyAttributes.setCapability(
     TransparencyAttributes.ALLOW_VALUE_WRITE );
   m_Shape3D.getAppearance().setTransparencyAttributes(
     m_TransparencyAttributes );
  }
  else
  {
   //we are mid explosion, modify the GeometryArray
   m_nFrameNumber++;

   m_GeometryArray.getCoordinates( 0, m_CoordinateArray );

   m_TransparencyAttributes.
    setTransparency( ((float) m_nFrameNumber) /
    ((float) m_nNumFrames) );
   m_Shape3D.getAppearance().
    setTransparencyAttributes( m_TransparencyAttributes );

   for( int n = 0; n < m_CoordinateArray.length; n+=3 )
   {
    m_Vector.x = m_CoordinateArray[n];
    m_Vector.y = m_CoordinateArray[n+1];
    m_Vector.z = m_CoordinateArray[n+2];

    m_Vector.normalize();

    m_CoordinateArray[n] += m_Vector.x * Math.random() +
     Math.random();
```

```
      m_CoordinateArray[n+1] += m_Vector.y * Math.random() +
      Math.random();
      m_CoordinateArray[n+2] += m_Vector.z * Math.random() +
      Math.random();
    }

    //assign the new coordinates
    m_GeometryArray.setCoordinates( 0, m_CoordinateArray );
  }
}

if( m_nFrameNumber < m_nNumFrames )
{
  //assign the next WakeUpCondition, so we are notified again
  wakeupOn( m_FrameWakeupCondition );
}
else
{
  //we are at the end of the explosion
  //reapply the original appearance and GeometryArray coordinates
  setEnable( false );
  m_Shape3D.setAppearance( m_Appearance );

  m_GeometryArray.setCoordinates( 0, m_OriginalCoordinateArray );

  m_OriginalCoordinateArray = null;
  m_GeometryArray = null;
  m_CoordinateArray = null;
  m_TransparencyAttributes = null;

  //if we have a listener notify them that we are done
  if( m_Listener != null )
    wakeupOn( m_Listener.onExplosionFinished( this, m_Shape3D ) );
}
```

13.4 *STRETCHBEHAVIOR*

StretchBehavior implements a more complex behavior. The behavior modifies the coordinates within a GeometryArray based on simulated forces applied to the geometric model. Forces are modeled as springs from the origin to every vertex. Every vertex has a mass and an applied force, and hence an acceleration. Pressing a key will increase the acceleration at each vertex, upsetting the force equilibrium at vertices. The model will then start to oscillate in size under the influence of the springs. Because there are variations in mass between vertices, the model will distort slightly as it oscillates— the heavier vertices displacing less than the lighter ones. A damping effect is modeled by losing a portion of the vertex acceleration after each iteration. See figure 13.3.

NOTE   This is a computationally expensive behavior.

StretchBehavior responds to two WakeUp conditions: after every frame and after a key press. The WakeUp conditions for the behavior are specified as follows:

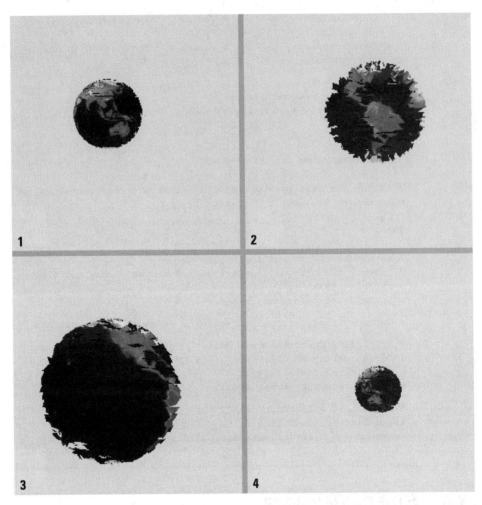

Figure 13.3 The StretchBehavior: Frame 1, the original Shape3D; frames 2–4, the vertices within the Shape3D's geometry are oscillating as the vertices are affected by the springs from each vertex to the origin. The model is a Sphere primitive with an applied texture image. The Sphere was created with a resolution value of 32

```
//create the WakeupCriterion for the behavior
WakeupCriterion criterionArray[] = new WakeupCriterion[2];
criterionArray[0] = new WakeupOnAWTEvent( KeyEvent.KEY_PRESSED );
criterionArray[1] = new WakeupOnElapsedFrames( 1 );

//save the WakeupCriterion for the behavior
m_WakeupCondition = new WakeupOr( criterionArray );
```

As usual, the WakeupCriterion is passed to the behavior inside the initialize method:

```java
public void initialize()
{
 //apply the initial WakeupCriterion
 wakeupOn( m_WakeupCondition );
}
```

The `processStimulus` method of the behavior, which is called on every frame and in response to a key press, performs all the basic physics calculations and updates the positions of the coordinates within the `GeometryArray`.

From StretchBehavior.java

```java
public void processStimulus( java.util.Enumeration criteria )
{
 //update the positions of the vertices—regardless of criteria
 float elongation = 0;
 float force_spring = 0;
 float force_mass = 0;
 float force_sum = 0;
 float timeFactor = 0.1f;
 float accel_sum = 0;

 //loop over every vertex and calculate its new position
 //based on the sum of forces due to acceleration and the spring
 for( int n = 0; n < m_CoordinateArray.length; n+=3 )
 {
  m_Vector.x = m_CoordinateArray[n];
  m_Vector.y = m_CoordinateArray[n+1];
  m_Vector.z = m_CoordinateArray[n+2];

  //use squared lengths, as sqrt is costly
  elongation = m_LengthArray[n/3] - m_Vector.lengthSquared();

  //Fspring = k*Le
  force_spring = m_kSpringConstant * elongation;
  force_mass = m_AccelerationArray[n/3] * m_MassArray[n/3];

  //calculate resultant force
  force_sum = force_mass + force_spring;

  //a = F/m
  m_AccelerationArray[n/3] = (force_sum / m_MassArray[n/3]) *
   m_kAccelerationLossFactor;
  accel_sum += m_AccelerationArray[n/3];

  m_Vector.normalize();

  //apply a portion of the acceleration as change
  //in coordinate based on the normalized vector
  //from the origin to the vertex
  m_CoordinateArray[n] +=
    m_Vector.x * timeFactor * m_AccelerationArray[n/3];
  m_CoordinateArray[n+1] +=
    m_Vector.y * timeFactor * m_AccelerationArray[n/3];
```

```
    m_CoordinateArray[n+2] +=
      m_Vector.z * timeFactor * m_AccelerationArray[n/3];
  }

  //assign the new coordinates
  m_GeometryArray.setCoordinates( 0, m_CoordinateArray );

  while( criteria.hasMoreElements() )
  {
   WakeupCriterion wakeUp =
    (WakeupCriterion) criteria.nextElement();

   //if a key was pressed increase the acceleration at the vertices
   //a little to upset the equilibrium
   if( wakeUp instanceof WakeupOnAWTEvent )
   {
    for( int n = 0; n < m_AccelerationArray.length; n++ )
     m_AccelerationArray[n] += 0.3f;
   }
   else
   {
    //otherwise, print the average acceleration
    System.out.print( "Average acceleration:\t"
    + accel_sum/m_AccelerationArray.length + "\n" );
   }
  }

  //assign the next WakeUpCondition, so we are notified again
  wakeupOn( m_WakeupCondition );
}
```

After pressing a key has disturbed the equilibrium of the model, it can take a considerable length of time to return to equilibrium. In figure 13.4 the model took over 500 frames to stabilize.

13.5   USING BEHAVIORS FOR DEBUGGING

A library of custom Behavior classes can be a very useful debugging aid, as they can be quickly added and removed from the scenegraph as needed. It is a simple step to conditionally add the debugging behaviors for development builds and remove them for production builds. For example, I have used the following two behaviors extensively:

1 BoundsBehavior is attached to a scenegraph Node and creates a wire frame ColorCube or Sphere to graphically represent the Bounds (BoundingBox or BoundingSphere) for the object at runtime.

2 FpsBehavior can be added anywhere in the scenegraph and writes the rendered FPS to the standard output window.

Both behaviors can be found in the org.selman.java3d.book package and are illustrated in the BehaviorTest example application.

CHAPTER 13   WRITING CUSTOM BEHAVIORS

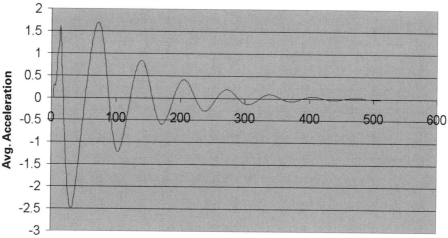

Figure 13.4 The `StretchBehavior` causes the `Sphere` to oscillate in size. By plotting the average vertex acceleration, you can see that the model took in excess of 500 frames to stabilize. The parameters used were Spring Constant 0.8, Acceleration Loss Factor 0.98, and Vertex Mass 50 + 2.5 (average)

13.5.1 Calculating the rendered FPS using a behavior

A useful method of displaying the rendered FPS in a Java 3D application is to add the following `Behavior` class anywhere within the scenegraph. A behavior-based calculation is easier to add and remove to a program than overriding the `Canvas3D` `postSwap` method.

NOTE   If accuracy is paramount, `postSwap` may provide more accurate results because `Behavior` processing typically runs on an independent thread to rendering.

From FpsBehavior

```
//this class implements a simple behavior
//that output the rendered Frames Per Second.
public class FpsBehavior extends Behavior
{
 //the wake up condition for the behavior
 protected WakeupCondition  m_WakeupCondition = null;
 protected long         m_StartTime = 0;

 private final int       m_knReportInterval = 100;

 public FpsBehavior()
 {
  //save the WakeupCriterion for the behavior
  m_WakeupCondition =
```

```
      new WakeupOnElapsedFrames( m_knReportInterval );
}

public void initialize()
{
 //apply the initial WakeupCriterion
 wakeupOn( m_WakeupCondition );
}

public void processStimulus( java.util.Enumeration criteria )
{
 while( criteria.hasMoreElements() )
 {
  WakeupCriterion wakeUp =
    (WakeupCriterion) criteria.nextElement();

  //every N frames, report the FPS
  if( wakeUp instanceof WakeupOnElapsedFrames )
  {
   if( m_StartTime > 0 )
   {
    final long interval = System.currentTimeMillis() - m_StartTime;
    System.out.println( "FPS: " + (double) m_knReportInterval / (
     interval / 1000.0));
   }

   m_StartTime = System.currentTimeMillis();
  }
 }

 //assign the next WakeUpCondition, so we are notified again
 wakeupOn( m_WakeupCondition );
 }
}
```

13.6 SUMMARY

The BehaviorTest example allows many behaviors to affect a single texture-mapped Sphere. RotationInterpolator rotates the entire scene, Object-SizeBehavior prints the size of the Sphere every 20 frames, ExplodeBehavior explodes the Sphere every 10 seconds, StretchBehavior models the vertices of the Sphere as weights attached to springs anchored at the origin, and BoundsBehavior tracks the Bounds of the Sphere.

Tying all these behaviors together into a single application allows complex application logic to be built up from relatively simple building blocks. The interactions between the behaviors can be explored by running the example and switching the behaviors on and off using the AWT buttons at the bottom of the Frame.

I hope the examples presented in this section have demystified Java 3D's behaviors. You should now start breaking down your application logic into good, reusable, OO chunks and distributing them across your scenegraph. You should aim to empower your scenegraph objects with the abilities to detect, process, and respond to user interactions.

Keep a careful eye on application performance at all times, because excessive behavior processing can slow your frame rate or make your application appear unresponsive. Do not be afraid of writing more complex behaviors that can affect whole classes of objects within your scenegraph. In this way you may be able to limit the number of behaviors in the scenegraph and use a manager design philosophy, where each behavior manages a given class of objects within the scenegraph, instead of attaching single instances of a behavior to a single object.

CHAPTER 14

Using texture images

The process of applying a bitmap to geometry is called *texture mapping* and is often a highly effective way of achieving apparent scene complexity while still using a relatively modest number of vertices. By the end of this chapter, you should be able to generate texture coordinates and apply a texture image to your geometry (e.g., figure 14.1).

If you are familiar with the process of texture mapping and texture coordinates, you may want to skim the first few sections and jump straight to the specifics of the Java 3D implementation.

As colors can only be associated with *vertices* in the model, if texture mapping was not used, a vertex would have to be located at every significant surface color transition. For highly textured surfaces such as wood or stone, this would quickly dominate the positions of the vertices rather than the geometric shape of the object itself. By applying an image to the geometric model, the *apparent* complexity of the model is increased while preserving the function of vertices for specifying relative geometry within the model.

Modern 3D computer games have used texture mapping extensively for a number of years, and first-person-perspective games such as Quake by Id software immerses the user in a richly texture-mapped world.

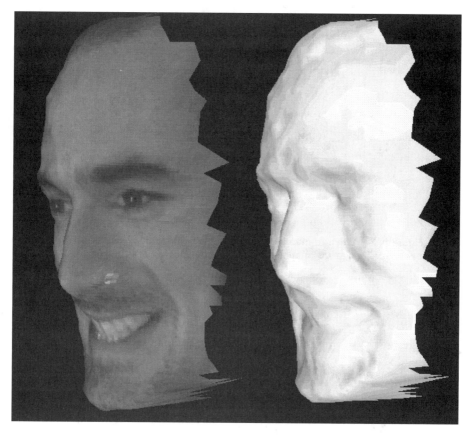

Figure 14.1 By applying a bitmap to the geometric model (left), very realistic results can be achieved even with a fairly coarse geometric mesh

14.1   INTRODUCTION

Texture mapping is exactly what it says. As an application developer, you are defining a mapping from 3D coordinates into texture coordinates. Usually this equates to defining a coordinate mapping to go from a vertex's 3D coordinates to a 2D pixel location within an image.

Defining coordinate mappings sounds pretty complicated, but in practice it can be as simple as saying the vertex located at position (1,1,1) should use the pixel located at (20,30) in the image named texture.jpg.

Looking at figure 14.2 it should be obvious that the renderer does some pretty clever stuff when it maps a texture onto a geometric model. The texture used was 64 × 64 pixels in size, but when it was rendered, the faces of each cube were about 200 × 200 pixels. So, the renderer had to resize the texture image on the fly to fit the face of each cube. Even tougher, you can see that what started out as a square texture image turned into a parallelogram as perspective and rotation were applied to the cube.

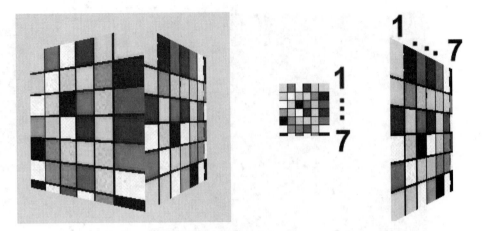

Figure 14.2 A texture-mapped cube (left); the texture image, actual size (middle); and the how the texture image was mapped onto one of the faces of the cube (right)

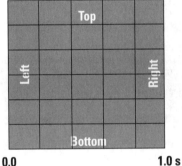

Figure 14.3
Texture coordinates range from 0.0 to 1.0 with the origin at the bottom left of the texture image. The horizontal dimension is commonly called *s* and the vertical dimension is called *t*

You should also be able to see that as the texture has been enlarged it has become pixilated. This is because several eventual screen pixels are all mapped to the same pixel within the texture image. This is a common problem with texture mapping and is visible in texture-mapped games such as Quake, as well.

To discuss the details of mapping between 3D vertex coordinates and texture pixels, some terminology must be introduced. Figure 14.3 illustrates texture coordinates. Instead of mapping to pixel locations directly (which would be relative to the size of the texture image), we use texture coordinates. Texture coordinates range from 0.0 to 1.0 in each dimension, regardless of the size of the image. We know therefore that the coordinates $s = 0.5$, $t = 0.25$ are always located halfway across the image and three-quarters of the way down from the *top* of the image. Note that the origin of the texture coordinate system is at the bottom left of the image, in contrast to many windowing systems that define the origin at the top left.

A pixel within an image that is used for texture mapping is often referred to as a *texel*.

There are essentially two types of texture mapping, static and dynamic. Defining a static mapping is the most commonly used and easiest form of texture mapping and is the subject of section 14.1.1.

14.1.1 Static mapping using per-vertex texture coordinates

Static mapping defines a static relationship between vertex coordinates and texture coordinates. This is usually implemented by simply assigning a texture coordinate to each vertex in the model (table 14.1).

Table 14.1   Static mapping

Vertex 143:
coordinate: 3,–6,7
color: red = 184, green = 242, blue = 32
normal vector 0.5, 0.2, -0.3
texture coordinate: 0.3, 0.6

Vertex 143 has been assigned a number of attributes: coordinate (position), color, normal vector, and a texture coordinate.

The `TextureTest` example that follows can be used to experiment with the relationship among images, texture coordinates, and 3D vertex coordinates (figure 14.4).

`TextureTest` loads the following information from a simple ASCII text file:

- Name of texture image
- Size of geometry in the x direction
- Geometry y scaling factor
- Number of vertices
- Texture coordinates for Vertex 1
- Texture coordinates for Vertex 2
- Texture coordinates for Vertex N

For example, the data for the image in figure 14.4 is shown in table 14.2.

Table 14.2   Data for the image in figure 14.4

Width 400 Height 400						
Vertex	**x**	**y**	**x'**	**y'**	**tx**	**ty**
0	159	99	159	301	0.40	0.75
1	125	126	125	274	0.31	0.69
2	110	163	110	237	0.28	0.59

continued on next page

Table 14.2 Data for the image in figure 14.4 (continued)

Vertex	x	y	x'	y'	tx	ty
3	102	243	102	157	0.26	0.39
4	118	304	118	96	0.30	0.24
5	179	363	179	37	0.45	0.09
6	220	364	220	36	0.55	0.09
7	264	335	264	65	0.66	0.16
8	287	289	287	111	0.72	0.28
9	295	204	295	196	0.74	0.49
10	279	132	279	268	0.70	0.67
11	253	104	253	296	0.63	0.74
12	207	95	207	305	0.52	0.76

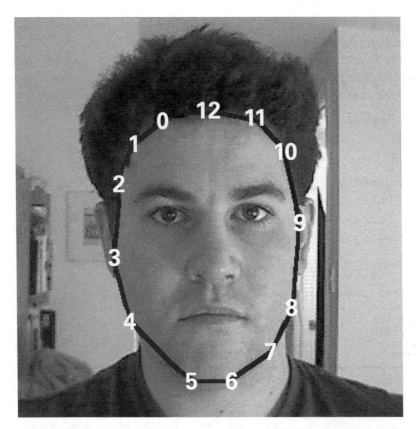

Figure 14.4 The `TextureTest` example loads an image and a list of texture coordinates and displays a portion of the image in a 3D scene by texture mapping it onto a `TriangleArray`

- The *x, y* columns are the pixel locations in the image that are returned by a bitmap editor. The origin for these 2D coordinates is at the top-left of the image. The *x'* and *y'* coordinates compensate for this by flipping the *y* coordinate ($y' =$ height $- y$). The texture coordinates *tx* and *ty* are suitable for Java 3D ($tx = x'/$ width and $ty = y'/$height). It is very easy to perform the coordinate conversions using a spreadsheet.

- The ASCII file is therefore:

```
daniel.gif    (name of the image file)
5             (size in the x direction)
1.0           (y scale factor)
13            (number of texture coordinates)
0.40    0.75  (texture coordinate 1, x y)
0.31    0.69
0.28    0.59
0.26    0.39
0.30    0.24
0.45    0.09
0.55    0.09
0.66    0.16
0.72    0.28
0.74    0.49
0.70    0.67
0.63    0.74
0.52    0.76  (texture coordinate 13, x y)
```

The Microsoft Excel spread sheet file daniel coords.xls with the `TextureTest` example contains the formulae necessary for the coordinate transformation (figure 14.5).

IMPORTANT   The texture coordinates are specified in counterclockwise order. This is a requirement imposed by the `com.sun.j3d.utils.geometry.Triangulator` utility, which converts the polygon created from the texture coordinates into a `TriangleArray`.

The `createTextureGeometry` method performs most of the work related to assigning texture coordinates to vertices. There are eight basic steps:

1 Read Texture coordinates from file.

2 Generate vertex coordinates based on scaling and translating texture coordinates.

3 Load the texture image using the `com.sun.j3d.utils.image.Texture-Loader` class and assign to an `Appearance`.

```
//load the texture image and assign to the appearance
TextureLoader texLoader = new TextureLoader( texInfo.m_szImage,
Texture.RGB, this );
Texture tex = texLoader.getTexture();
app.setTexture( tex );
```

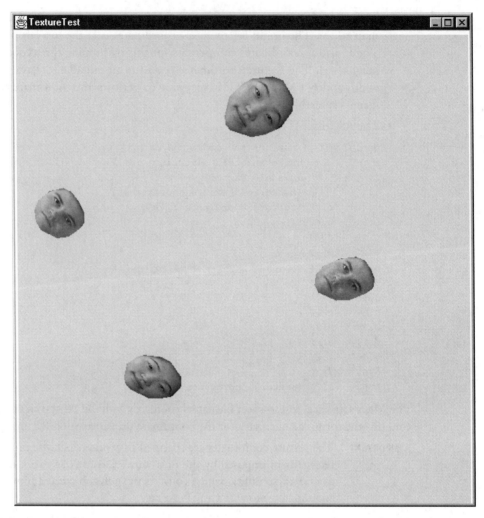

Figure 14.5 The `TextureTest` example in action. Four texture-mapped `TriangleArrays` have been created from two sets of texture coordinate data and images. The `TriangleArrays` are rotated using an `Interpolator`

4 Create a `GeometryInfo` object to store the texture and vertex coordinates (`POYGON_ARRAY`).

```
//create a GeometryInfo for the QuadArray that was populated.
GeometryInfo gi = new GeometryInfo( GeometryInfo.POLYGON_ARRAY );
```

5 Assign the texture and vertex coordinates to the `GeometryInfo` object.

```
//assign coordinates
gi.setCoordinates( texInfo.m_CoordArray );
gi.setTextureCoordinates( texInfo.m_TexCoordArray );
```

6 Triangulate the `GeometryInfo` object.

```
//use the triangulator utility to triangulate the polygon
int[] stripCountArray = {texInfo.m_CoordArray.length};
int[] countourCountArray = {stripCountArray.length};

gi.setContourCounts( countourCountArray );
gi.setStripCounts( stripCountArray );

Triangulator triangulator = new Triangulator();
triangulator.triangulate( gi );
```

7 Generate Normal vectors for the `GeometryInfo` object.

```
//generate normal vectors for the triangles,
//not strictly necessary as we are not lighting the scene
//but generally useful
NormalGenerator normalGenerator = new NormalGenerator();
normalGenerator.generateNormals( gi );
```

8 Create a `Shape3D` object based on the `GeometryInfo` object.

```
//wrap the GeometryArray in a Shape3D and assign appearance
new Shape3D( gi.getGeometryArray(), app );
```

Please refer to TextureTest.java for the full example. The important methods are listed in full next.

```
//create a TransformGroup, position it, and add the texture
//geometry as a child node
protected TransformGroup createTextureGroup( String szFile,
 double x, double y, double z, boolean bWireframe )
{
 TransformGroup tg = new TransformGroup();
 Transform3D t3d = new Transform3D();
 t3d.setTranslation( new Vector3d( x,y,z ) );
 tg.setTransform( t3d );

 Shape3D texShape = createTextureGeometry( szFile, bWireframe );

 if( texShape != null )
  tg.addChild( texShape );

 return tg;
}


//return a Shape3D that is a triangulated texture-mapped polygon
//based on the texture coordinates and name of texture image in the
//input file
protected Shape3D createTextureGeometry( String szFile,
 boolean bWireframe )
{
 //load all the texture data from the file and
 //create the geometry coordinates
 TextureGeometryInfo texInfo = createTextureCoordinates( szFile );
```

```java
if( texInfo == null )
{
 System.err.println( "Could not load texture info for file:" +
                     szFile );
 return null;
}

//print some stats on the loaded file
System.out.println( "Loaded File: " + szFile );
System.out.println( "   Texture image: " + texInfo.m_szImage );
System.out.println( "   Texture coordinates: " +
                    texInfo.m_TexCoordArray.length );

//create an Appearance and assign a Material
Appearance app = new Appearance();

PolygonAttributes polyAttribs = null;

//create the PolygonAttributes and attach to the Appearance,
//note that we use CULL_NONE so that the "rear" side
//of the geometry is visible with the applied texture image
if( bWireframe == false )
{
 polyAttribs = new PolygonAttributes(
   PolygonAttributes.POLYGON_FILL,
   PolygonAttributes.CULL_NONE, 0 );
}
else
{
 polyAttribs = new PolygonAttributes(
   PolygonAttributes.POLYGON_LINE,
   PolygonAttributes.CULL_NONE, 0 );
}

app.setPolygonAttributes( polyAttribs );

//load the texture image and assign to the appearance
TextureLoader texLoader = new TextureLoader( texInfo.m_szImage,
 Texture.RGB, this );
Texture tex = texLoader.getTexture();
app.setTexture( tex );

//create a GeometryInfo for the QuadArray that was populated.
GeometryInfo gi = new GeometryInfo( GeometryInfo.POLYGON_ARRAY );
gi.setCoordinates( texInfo.m_CoordArray );
gi.setTextureCoordinates( texInfo.m_TexCoordArray );

//use the triangulator utility to triangulate the polygon
int[] stripCountArray = {texInfo.m_CoordArray.length};
int[] countourCountArray = {stripCountArray.length};

gi.setContourCounts( countourCountArray );
gi.setStripCounts( stripCountArray );

Triangulator triangulator = new Triangulator();
triangulator.triangulate( gi );
```

```java
//Generate normal vectors for the triangles, not strictly necessary
//as we are not lighting the scene, but generally useful.
NormalGenerator normalGenerator = new NormalGenerator();
 normalGenerator.generateNormals( gi );

//wrap the GeometryArray in a Shape3D and assign appearance
return new Shape3D( gi.getGeometryArray(), app );
}

/*
 * Handle the nitty-gritty details of loading the input file
 * and reading (in order):
 * - texture file image name
 * - size of the geometry in the X direction
 * - Y direction scale factor
 * - number of texture coordinates
 * - each texture coordinate (X Y)
 * This could all be easily accomplished using a scenegraph loader,
 * but this simple code is included for reference.
 */
protected TextureGeometryInfo createTextureCoordinates(
 String szFile )

{
 //create a simple wrapper class to package our return values
 TextureGeometryInfo texInfo = new TextureGeometryInfo();

 //allocate a temporary buffer to store the input file
 StringBuffer szBufferData = new StringBuffer();

 float sizeGeometryX = 0;
 float factorY = 1;
 int nNumPoints = 0;
 Point2f boundsPoint = new Point2f();

 try
 {
  //attach a reader to the input file
  FileReader fileIn = new FileReader( szFile );

  int nChar = 0;

  //read the entire file into the StringBuffer
  while( true )
  {
   nChar = fileIn.read();

   //if we have not hit the end of file
   //add the character to the StringBuffer
   if( nChar != -1 )
    szBufferData.append( (char) nChar );
   else
    //hit EOF
    break;
  }
```

```
//create a tokenizer to tokenize the input file at whitespace
java.util.StringTokenizer tokenizer =
 new java.util.StringTokenizer( szBufferData.toString() );

//read the name of the texture image
texInfo.m_szImage = tokenizer.nextToken();

//read the size of the generated geometry in the X dimension
sizeGeometryX = Float.parseFloat( tokenizer.nextToken() );

//read the Y scale factor
factorY = Float.parseFloat( tokenizer.nextToken() );

//read the number of texture coordinates
nNumPoints = Integer.parseInt( tokenizer.nextToken() );

//read each texture coordinate
texInfo.m_TexCoordArray = new Point2f[nNumPoints];
Point2f texPoint2f = null;

for( int n = 0; n < nNumPoints; n++ )
{
  texPoint2f = new Point2f(  Float.parseFloat(
          tokenizer.nextToken() ),
          Float.parseFloat( tokenizer.nextToken() ) );

  texInfo.m_TexCoordArray[n] = texPoint2f;

  //keep an eye on the extents of the texture coordinates
  // so we can automatically center the geometry
  if( n == 0 || texPoint2f.x > boundsPoint.x )
   boundsPoint.x = texPoint2f.x;

  if( n == 0 || texPoint2f.y > boundsPoint.y )
   boundsPoint.y = texPoint2f.y;
 }
}
catch( Exception e )
{
 System.err.println( e.toString() );
 return null;
}

//build the array of coordinates
texInfo.m_CoordArray = new Point3f[nNumPoints];

for( int n = 0; n < nNumPoints; n++ )
{
  //scale and center the geometry based on the texture coordinates
texInfo.m_CoordArray[n] = new Point3f( sizeGeometryX  *
 texInfo.m_TexCoordArray[n].x - boundsPoint.x/2),
 factorY * sizeGeometryX *
 (texInfo.m_TexCoordArray[n].y - boundsPoint.y/2), 0 );
 }

 return texInfo;
}
```

As the `TextureTest` example illustrates, using a static mapping from vertex coordinates is relatively straightforward. Texture coordinates are assigned to each vertex, much like vertex coordinates or per-vertex colors. The renderer will take care of all the messy details of interpolating the texture image between projected vertex coordinates using projection and sampling algorithms.

Texture coordinates themselves are usually manually calculated or are the product of an automated texture-mapping process (such as 3D model capture or model editor).

Note that although we have called this section static mapping, there is nothing to prevent you from modifying the texture coordinates within a `GeometryArray` at runtime. Very interesting dynamic effects can be achieved through reassigning texture coordinates.

Care must be taken to ensure that texture images do not become too pixilated as they become enlarged and stretched by the sampling algorithm. The MIPMAP technique covered in detail in Section 14.3.4 is useful in this regard in that different sizes of different texture images can be specified.

Needless to say, texture images consume memory, and using large 24-bit texture images is an easy way to place a heavy strain on the renderer and push up total memory footprint. Of course, the larger the texture image, the less susceptible it is to becoming pixilated so a comfortable balance must be found between rendering quality, rendering speed, and memory footprint. You should also be very aware that different 3D rendering hardware performs texture mapping in hardware only if the texture image falls within certain criteria. Modern 3D rendering cards typically have 16 MB or more of texture memory, and 64 MB is now not uncommon. Most rendering hardware will render texture images of up to 512 × 512 pixels. You should consult the documentation for the 3D rendering cards that your application considers important.

14.1.2   Dynamic mapping using TexCoordGeneration

In contrast to a hard-coded static mapping between vertex coordinates and texture coordinates, dynamic texture mapping enables the application developer to define a mapping that is resolved by the renderer at runtime. Dynamic mapping is fairly unusual but is very useful for certain scientific visualization applications—where the position of a vertex in 3D space should correlate with its texture coordinate.

Rather than having to manually update the texture coordinate whenever a vertex moves, the application developer defines a series of planes that the renderer uses to calculate a texture coordinate.

The `TexCoordTest` example application explores the three texture coordinate generation options in Java 3D. These are `TexCoordGeneration.EYE_LINEAR`, `TexCoordGeneration.OBJECT_LINEAR`, and `TexCoordGeneration.SPHERE_MAP` (figures 14.6–14.11). Each will be described in turn in the sections that follow.

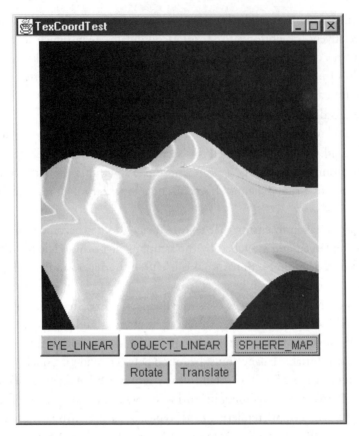

Figure 14.6 The `TexCoordTest` example application in action. The vertices in the undulating landscape do not have assigned texture coordinates, but rather a `TexCoordGeneration` object is used to calculate texture coordinates dynamically

OBJECT_LINEAR mode

The OBJECT_LINEAR texture coordinate generation mode calculates texture coordinates based on the relative positions of vertices. The `TexCoordTest` example creates a simulated landscape that has contours automatically mapped onto the landscape Everything above the $y = 0$ plane is texture-mapped green, while everything below is texture-mapped blue.

Figure 14.7 illustrates the texture image used in the `TexCoordTest` example for dynamic texture mapping. The texture image is 64 × 64 pixels and merely contains a single row of pixels that is of interest—the rest of the image is ignored. The bottom row of the image ($t = 0$) defines the colors to be dynamically applied to the landscape. The midpoint of the row ($s = 0.5$) defines the elevation = 0 (sea level) contour, while everything to the left of the midpoint is used for elevations below sea level, and everything to the right is used for elevations above sea level. Different colored pixels for contours are evenly spaced from the midpoint.

Figure 14.7 **The texture image used to perform dynamic mapping of texture coordinates in the** `TexCoordTest` **example application**

To map contours onto the landscape we merely need to define a mapping from the y coordinate of the landscape to the s coordinate of the texture image. That is, we are defining a 1D-to-1D mapping from vertex coordinates to texture coordinates.

A vertex's position is defined using three dimensions (x, y, z), while a texture coordinate can potentially be expressed in three dimensions (although typically only s and t are used).

We define a plane for each of the texture coordinates (s, t, and sometimes r). The s texture coordinate is given by a vertex's position relative to the s plane, the t coordinate is given by a vertex's position relative to the t plane, and so on. Planes are defined by specifying the direction of the vector perpendicular (normal) to the plane.

For example, to create our mapping from y vertex coordinate to s texture coordinate:

```
TexCoordGeneration texGen =
  new TexCoordGeneration( TexCoordGeneration.OBJECT_LINEAR,
                          TexCoordGeneration.TEXTURE_COORDINATE_2,
                          new Vector4f( 0,
                                        (float)
                                        (1.0/(2 * yMaxHeight)),
                                        0,
                                        0.5f ),
                          new Vector4f( 0,0,0,0 ),
                          new Vector4f( 0,0,0,0 ) );
```

The parameters to the `TexCoordGeneration` constructor do the following:

1. Specify the texture coordinate generation mode that we are using, in this case, `OBJECT_LINEAR`.
2. Specify that we are generating 2D texture coordinates (s and t).
3. Define the mapping from vertex coordinate to s coordinate.
4. Define the mapping from vertex coordinate to t coordinate.
5. Define the mapping from vertex coordinate to r coordinate (which is unused when 2D texture coordinates are used).

The mapping from vertex coordinates to s coordinates we defined was:

(0, (float) (1.0/ (2 * yMaxHeight)), 0, 0.5f)

This equates to:

s texture coordinate = (0.0 * vertex x) + (1.0/ 2 * yMaxHeight * vertex y) + (0.0 * vertex z) + 0.5;

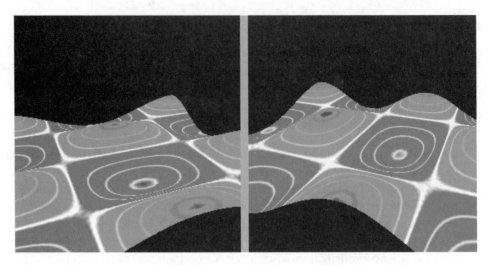

Figure 14.8 Using `OBJECT_LINEAR` **texture coordinate generation**

That is, the *t* texture coordinate is equal to a scaled version of the *y* vertex coordinate plus an offset of 0.5. We use an offset of 0.5 because we defined the midpoint of the texture image as the elevation = 0 contour.

From the equation you can see that:

Vertex $y = y$MaxHeight, s = 1.0

Vertex $y = 0.0$, $s = 0.5$

Vertex $y = - y$MaxHeight, $s = 0.0$

That is, we have successfully defined a mapping from vertex *y* coordinate in the range ± *y*MaxHeight to *s* texture coordinates in the range 0.0 to 1.0. The texture coordinate is independent of a vertex's *x* and *z* coordinates.

Using the `OBJECT_LINEAR` mode, the landscape has texture coordinates automatically calculated, coloring areas above sea level green (light gray) and areas below sea level blue (dark gray). As the landscape as a whole is rotated and translated, the texture coordinates are unaffected. The vertex coordinates in the local coordinate system of the landscape are unchanged, despite the *origin* of the landscape's coordinate being shifted.

EYE_LINEAR mode

The `EYE_LINEAR` texture coordinate generation mode is very similar to the `OBJECT_LINEAR` mode with one important difference. The positions of vertices in their *local* coordinate system are no longer used; rather the positions of vertices in the *world* coordinate system are used instead. This has major consequences—as the landscape is moved within the `VirtualUniverse`, the texture coordinates of the vertices within the landscape are recomputed, for example, in the `TexCoordTest` example, by simply modifying the construction of the `TexCoordGeneration` object to be:

```
TexCoordGeneration texGen =
  new TexCoordGeneration( TexCoordGeneration.EYE_LINEAR,
                          TexCoordGeneration.TEXTURE_COORDINATE_2,
                          new Vector4f( 0,
                                        (float)
                                        (1.0/(2 * yMaxHeight)),
                                        0,
                                        0.5f ),
                          new Vector4f( 0,0,0,0 ),
                          new Vector4f( 0,0,0,0 ) );
```

We define a `VirtualUniverse` where the texture coordinate of the landscape is calculated from the *y* coordinate of the landscape in the `VirtualUniverse`'s coordinate system. In essence we have defined a band of texture coordinates (color) that ranges from –*y*MaxHeight to +*y*MaxHeight. When the landscape falls inside this range, it will have a texture coordinate applied to it.

In mathematical terms, this is equivalent to multiplying each vertex coordinate by the result of calling `Shape3D.getLocalToVworld` before computing the texture coordinate using:

s texture coordinate = (0.0 * vertex *x*) + (1.0/ 2 * *y*MaxHeight * vertex *y*) + (0.0 * vertex *z*) + 0.5;

Using the EYE_LINEAR mode allows you to define a field of texture coordinates that can produce dynamic contour lines on moving objects.

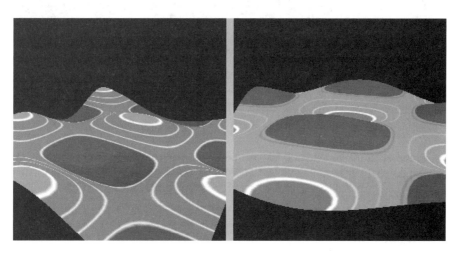

Figure 14.9   Using EYE_LINEAR texture coordinate generation. As the landscape is translated upward in the *y* axis, the texture coordinates change, resulting in a different frame. In the left-hand frame, only the peaks of the landscape are above the *y* = 0 plane; the rest of the landscape is either texture mapped with the water section of the texture image or does not have any texture applied since the calculated texture coordinate is less than 0.0. In the right-hand frame, most of the landscape is above the *y* = 0 plane, and only the deepest hollows in the landscape are textured using the water section of the texture image

SPHERE_MAP mode

The SPHERE_MAP mode is very different from the OBJECT_LINEAR or EYE_LINEAR modes in that it always generates 2D (*s*,*t*) texture coordinates irrespective of any mapping planes passed to the TexCoordGeneration constructor.

The SPHERE_MAP mode calculates texture coordinates based on the vector passing from the origin (in world coordinates) to a vertex. It creates a mapping that essentially paints an environment map onto the face of an object. Imagine that the object was a reflective sphere positioned in the center of a room. If the SPHERE_MAP texture coordinate generation mode was used, the sphere would appear to reflex the items within the room. By precomputing a spherical texture map using a ray-tracing program and using the SPHERE_MAP texture mode, a photorealistic reflective object can be created.

NOTE   Please refer to the OpenGL 1.1 Specification for the mathematical details of how the texture coordinates are calculated from the vector passing from the origin to each vertex.

Because the SPHERE_MAP mode always generates both *s* and *t* coordinates, we have to create a texture image to achieve the effect in figure 14.10. This texture image is shown in figure 14.11. However, because both the TexCoordTest example in EYE_LINEAR and OBJECT_LINEAR modes only use the *t* = 0 row of the image, their results are unchanged.

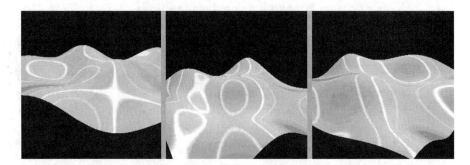

Figure 14.10 Using SPHERE_MAP **texture coordinate generation. Instead of the texture image being used to denote contour lines on the landscape, the landscape can now be considered to be a reflective surface within a spherical room that has the texture image applied as wallpaper to its inner walls**

Conclusions

Dynamic texture mapping is a very powerful mechanism for applications that can define a relatively simple mathematical relationship between vertex and texture coordinates. The SPHERE_MAP mode is useful for creating some special effects for the objects within your scene.

All three texture generation options can be confusing and are certainly more complex than simply using assigned texture coordinates. I suggest you experiment with the

Figure 14.11 Texture image used for SPHERE_MAP **texture coordinate generation**

TexCoordTest example, edit the texture images, and change the mapping planes until you are comfortable with the techniques and have an intuitive feel for the mathematics behind the texture coordinate generation options.

14.2 *3D TEXTURE COORDINATES*

The previous section included some hand waving on the subject of 3D texture coordinates. The 3D texture coordinates are fairly unusual and are at present supported by Java 3D only on the Solaris platform. Instead of a 2D texture image being *applied* to a surface, a 3D object can appear to have been carved from a 3D texture. Some textures are inherently 3D and are easiest to specify procedurally (such as the grain in wood). Using a 3D texture image defines a color (potentially with an alpha value) for each *x,y,z* location. Texels, instead of being 2D squares, are now 3D cubes within the three dimensions of the texture image (*s,t,r*).

For example, if a 2D wood grain texture were applied to the faces of a cube, the grain lines would not match up at the edges of the faces of the cube. By using a 3D texture image, the grain lines will appear to run *through* the cube in a realistic manner.

Similarly, in a 3D visualization application, such as MRI scanning, a 3D texture image might be used to represent the color of each voxel within a volume rendering. This might be used as a cheat to create a relatively coarse voxel resolution and apply a high-resolution 3D texture image to trade off accuracy against interactive performance.

14.3　TEXTURE AND MULTIPLE LEVELS OF DETAIL

```
java.lang.Object
  |
  +--javax.media.j3d.SceneGraphObject
       |
       +--javax.media.j3d.NodeComponent
            |
            +--javax.media.j3d.Texture
```

Capability Bits (OpenGL Reference: glTexImage2D, glTexParameter):

- BOUNDARY_COLOR
- ENABLE
- FILTER
- IMAGE
- MIPMAP_MODE

Texture is an abstract class and hence cannot be instantiated. The two derived classes Texture2D or Texture3D (used with 2D or 3D texture coordinates respectively) should be instantiated instead. Texture-derived objects are usually not created directly but are returned by the getTexture method of the TextureLoader utility class. See section 14.3.3 for more details.

14.3.1　Boundary color

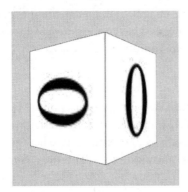

Figure 14.12
Boundary color set to black. The boundary was only visible when the boundary mode for _s_ and _t_ was set to CLAMP and the Min-Filter was set to NICEST

14.3.2　Boundary mode

Setting the boundary mode to Texture.WRAP allows texture coordinates greater than 1 to be used. The texture image will be repeated (tiled) along each axis (_s_, _t_, or _r_) that has the WRAP boundary mode. If CLAMP is used, texture coordinates outside the 0 to 1 range will be ignored. See figure 14.12 for an example of how CLAMP and MinFilter can be used.

Note that the texture image can be flipped in each axis by using the WRAP attribute and a texture coordinate of –1.

14.3.3 Setting the image

Setting the image within the `Texture` object is achieved using the `setImage` method. The `TextureLoader` utility class is usually used to create the `Texture` with an image applied:

From TextureTest.java

```
//Create TextureLoader and initialize it with an image file name
//and a mode
TextureLoader texLoader = new TextureLoader( texInfo.m_szImage,
 Texture.RGB, this );

//Extract a Texture object from the loader
Texture tex = texLoader.getTexture();

//Assign the Texture to the Appearance
Appearance app = new Appearance();
app.setTexture( tex );
```

The advantages of using the TextureLoader class are:

- Loading the image from disk (JPEG or GIF)
- Rescaling the image so that it is a power of 2, that is, width and height.
- Creating the appropriate `Texture` object, either `Texture2D` or `Texture3D`

If an `ImageComponent2D` or `ImageComponent3D` is passed to `Texture.setImage` directly and the `TextureLoader` class is not used, the application developer is responsible for ensuring that the images are a power of 2 (1, 2, 4, 8…) in both width and height. This is a requirement imposed by the underlying graphics API that is optimized to rescale images of this size.

14.3.4 MIPMAP mode, filter, and multiple texture images

One of the common problems of texture mapping is that the texture images become pixilated as resampling enlarges them. The quick fix to this is to ensure that all your texture images are large enough so that they can never become overly magnified.

Imagine a cube in your scene with a texture image applied to one face. If the cube's texture image is 64×64 pixels and the cube is very close to the viewer, it may end up taking up 300×300 pixels on the screen. A texture image that has been magnified by a factor of 5 is obviously not going to look very good—regardless of the sophistication of the sampling algorithm employed by the graphics hardware. A solution to this problem would be to assign a 256×256 pixel texture image to each face of the cube.

However, we are now using 16 times as much texture memory. To complicate matters, most of the time the cube is probably considerably further away from the viewer, and the graphics API will have to work hard to sample the 256×256 size image down to an appropriate size based on the cube's distance.

What we need, and what MIPMAPs provide, is the ability to specify *multiple* texture images. The graphics API will select the most appropriate one based on the size of the surface it is trying to render. We pay the penalty of storing multiple texture images— which is incidentally very small compared to storing the largest texture image.

For example,

$$64 \times 64 = 4096$$
$$32 \times 32 = 1024$$
$$16 \times 16 = 256$$
$$8 \times 8 = 64$$
$$4 \times 4 = 16$$
$$2 \times 2 = 4$$
$$1 \times 1 = 1$$

The cost of storing the 64 × 64 pixel image is proportional to 4096, while the cost of storing *all* the other images is proportional to 1365. So using MIPMAPs will improve performance for a very low memory penalty.

To use MIPMAPs you must specify *all* the texture images from your maximum size (which must be a power of 2, right down to the 1 × 1 image). So, if our largest texture image is 64 × 64 pixels, we require seven texture images. Usually, of course, the texture images will be increasingly low resolution images of the same feature. Texture images can be easily preprocessed using the resampling features of a bitmap editor such as PhotoShop (Adobe) or PaintShop Pro (JASC).

In figure 14.13, the `AppearanceTest` example uses texture images that are different so that the texture image that was chosen by the graphics API is apparent.

The individual texture images can be assigned to a `Texture` object as follows. Note that `Texture.MULTI_LEVEL_MIPMAP` was used to activate MIPMAP support.

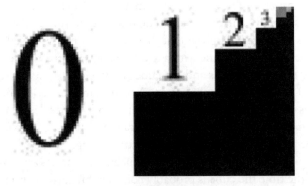

Figure 14.13   The seven texture images used in the `AppearanceTest` example to illustrate Java 3D MIPMAP support—64 x 64 pixels down to 1 x 1 pixels

```
//Create a texture loader and load the largest image (64x64-pixels)
TextureLoader texLoader =
  new TextureLoader( "texture00.jpg", m_Component );

//Retrieve the ImageComponent from the TextureLoader
ImageComponent2D image = texLoader.getImage();

//Create a MULTI_LEVEL_MIPMAP mode Texture2D object
//based on the size of the largest image
Texture2D tex2D =
  new Texture2D( Texture.MULTI_LEVEL_MIPMAP, Texture.RGBA,
  image.getWidth(), image.getHeight() );

//Now load each of the 7 images and assign to the Texture2D
for( int n = 0; n <= 6; n++ )
{
 texLoader = new TextureLoader(
  "texture0" + n + ".jpg", m_Component );
 tex2D.setImage( n, texLoader.getImage() );
}

//assign the Texture2D to the appearance
m_Appearance.setTexture( m_Texture );
```

Once the graphics API has multiple texture images to choose from, it needs some criteria to decide which texture image to display. The graphics API obviously uses the texture image that is easiest to resample to the desired size; however, some more advanced options are also available. These are controlled by the setMinFilter and setMagFilter methods (table 14.3).

Table 14.3 MinFilter and MagFilter

MinFilter Option	Effect
FASTEST	Equivalent to BASE_LEVEL_POINT
NICEST	Equivalent to MULTI_LEVEL_LINEAR
BASE_LEVEL_POINT	Finds nearest texel in the level 0 texture map
BASE_LEVEL_LINEAR	Performs bilinear interpolation on the four nearest texels in the level 0 texture map
MULTI_LEVEL_POINT	Selects the nearest texel in the nearest MIPMAP
MULTI_LEVEL_LINEAR	Performs trilinear interpolation of texels between four texels each from the two nearest MIPMAP levels
FASTEST	Equivalent to BASE_LEVEL_POINT
NICEST	Equivalent to BASE_LEVEL_LINEAR
BASE_LEVEL_POINT	Selects the nearest texel in the level 0 texture map
BASE_LEVEL_LINEAR	Performs a bilinear interpolation on the four nearest texels in the level 0 texture map

Figure 14.14 illustrates how complex blending of the MIPMAP texture images can be achieved. In frame 1 the left-hand face of the cube is dominated by the level 0 texture image, which progressively passes through the 1, 2, and 3 texture images as the size of the surface is reduced through rotation (frames 2 through 4). The blending of multiple texture images obviously requires more work on the part of the graphics API.

In contrast, when the MULTI_LEVEL_POINT mode is used, the texture images are not blended but rather different texture images are chosen for different pixels within the surface, based on the position of the pixel within the surface (figure 14.15). This is the fastest way for the graphics API to support multiple levels of detail texture images.

MIPMAPs are a relatively easy way to improve the appearance of the texture mapping in your application. Experiment with the AppearanceTest example application to strike a good balance between texture mapping appearance and performance. Most modern graphics hardware has built-in support for MIPMAPs, although the rendering quality varies greatly depending on hardware.

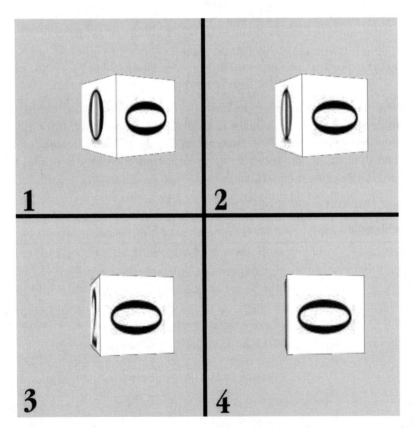

Figure 14.14 **Four frames from the AppearanceTest example illustrate how multiple texture images are blended when the MULTI_LEVEL_LINEAR MinFilter and BASE_LEVEL_LINEAR MagFilter are used**

CHAPTER 14 USING TEXTURE IMAGES

Figure 14.15
When the `MULTI_LEVEL_POINT` MinFilter mode is used, texture images are not blended, but rather separate images are used for different portions of the surface. The right-hand face of the cube uses the level 0 texture image at the front of the face and the level 1 texture image at the rear of the cube

14.4   *TEXTUREATTRIBUTES*

```
java.lang.Object
  |
  +--javax.media.j3d.SceneGraphObject
       |
       +--javax.media.j3d.NodeComponent
            |
            +--javax.media.j3d.TextureAttributes
```

Capability Bits (OpenGL Reference: glTexEnv):

- BLEND_COLOR
- MODE
- TRANSFORM

The `TextureAttributes` appearance component controls three parameters related to texture mapping: the color used for texture blending, how the texture image is combined with the material colors (`MODE`), and a geometric transform that is applied to the texture image during texture mapping.

14.4.1   Blend color

The blend color is *only* used when the `TextureAttributes.BLEND` mode is selected. Figures 14.16–14.18 are relatively self-explanatory and illustrate how the blend color affects the eventual applied texture.

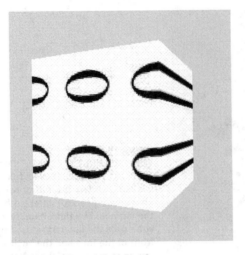

Figure 14.16 Texture image (subjected to texture coordinate generation, $s = 0,0,1,0$ and $t = 0,1,0,5$). No `TextureAttributes` assigned

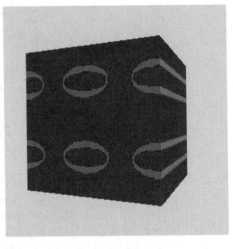

Figure 14.17 Applied texture image with TextureAttributes.BLEND and Blend color set to 100% blue

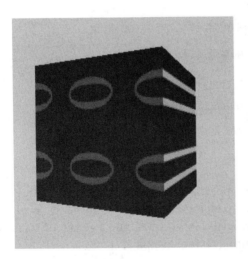

Figure 14.18 Applied texture image with Texture-Attributes.BLEND and Blend color set to 100% black, alpha 0.7

14.4.2 Mode

See figures 14.19–14.23 and table 14.4 for descriptions of the four modes in which a texture image can be applied to a surface:

Table 14.4   Texture modes

Mode	Effect
DECAL	Color value is the product of the surface color and 1 – alpha value for the surface plus texture color times texture alpha. The texture is applied to the surface in proportion to the alpha components of both the texture and the surface. The texture must either be in RGB or RGBA format.
MODULATE	Color value is the product of the color values of the texture and the surface color. If MODULATE is used with dark textures the surface may end up black.
BLEND	The color values on the surface are modulated by the color values of the texture and biased by the blend color.
REPLACE	Color value is simply the texture color.

Figure 14.19   Material colors set and no texture image applied

Figure 14.20   Material colors set as in figure 14.14 and texture image applied using DECAL mode

Figure 14.21 Material colors set as in figure 14.14 and texture image applied using MODULATE mode

Figure 14.22   Material colors set as in figure 14.14 and texture image applied using BLEND mode

Figure 14.23   Material colors set as in figure 14.14 and texture image applied using REPLACE mode

Refer to the Java 3D API Specification for more details on the texture mapping equations.

14.4.3   Transform

A rotational transformation can also be applied to the texture image prior to texture mapping. This is a fairly unusual operation but might prove useful for specialized operations or to implement special effects. The `TextureTransformTest` example creates a texture mapped `Box` and allows the user to interactively rotate the texture applied to the `Box` using the mouse (figure 14.24).

Note that only the rotational components of the `Transform3D` appear to be used.

From TextureTransformTest.java

```
//create a Box with an applied Texture image
//and a RotationInterpolator to rotate the box
protected BranchGroup createSceneBranchGroup()
{
 BranchGroup objRoot = super.createSceneBranchGroup();

 TransformGroup objTrans = new TransformGroup();
 objTrans.setCapability(TransformGroup.ALLOW_TRANSFORM_WRITE);
 objTrans.setCapability(TransformGroup.ALLOW_TRANSFORM_READ);

 Transform3D yAxis = new Transform3D();
 Alpha rotationAlpha = new Alpha(-1, Alpha.INCREASING_ENABLE,
  0, 0,
  4000, 0, 0,
  0, 0, 0);

 //create the rotation interpolator to rotate the scene
 RotationInterpolator rotator =
```

Figure 14.24   Applying a Transform to an applied texture image. TextureTransformTest allows a texture image to be interactively rotated using a MouseRotate behavior. The ColorCube at the lower left of the two frames shows the current rotation

```
  new RotationInterpolator(rotationAlpha,
    objTrans, yAxis, 0.0f, (float) Math.PI*2.0f);
rotator.setSchedulingBounds( createApplicationBounds() );
objTrans.addChild(rotator);

//create the box
final int nScale = 50;
Appearance app = new Appearance();
Box box = new Box( nScale, nScale, nScale,
                   Primitive.GENERATE_NORMALS |
                   Primitive.GENERATE_TEXTURE_COORDS, app );

//load the texture image
TextureLoader texLoader = new TextureLoader( "texture.gif", this );
app.setTexture( texLoader.getTexture() );

//set the texture attributes and ensure we can write
//to the Transform for the texture attributes
m_TextureAttributes = new TextureAttributes();
m_TextureAttributes.setCapability(
  TextureAttributes.ALLOW_TRANSFORM_WRITE );
app.setTextureAttributes( m_TextureAttributes );

//connect all the elements
objTrans.addChild( box );
objRoot.addChild( objTrans );
objRoot.addChild( createRotator() );

return objRoot;
}
```

```
//private TransformGroup createRotator()
{
 //create a ColorCube to illustrate the current rotation
 TransformGroup transTg = new TransformGroup();
 Transform3D t3d = new Transform3D();
 t3d.setTranslation( new Vector3d( -70, -70, 50 ) );
 transTg.setTransform( t3d );

 TransformGroup subTg = new TransformGroup();
 subTg.setCapability(TransformGroup.ALLOW_TRANSFORM_WRITE);

 subTg.addChild( new ColorCube(10.0) );

 //attach a MouseRotate behavior so we can rotate
 //the color cube with the left mouse button
 MouseRotate mouseRot = new MouseRotate( subTg );
 subTg.addChild( mouseRot );

//assign a transformChanged callback, because we want
//to be notified whenever the rotation of the ColorCube changed
//("this" implements MouseBehaviorCallback );

 mouseRot.setupCallback( this );
 mouseRot.setSchedulingBounds( getApplicationBounds() );

 transTg.addChild( subTg );

 return transTg;
}


//this is a callback method that the MouseRotate behavior calls
//when its Transform3D has been modified (by the user)
public void transformChanged(int type, Transform3D transform)
{
 //update the rotation of the TextureAttributes
 m_TextureAttributes.setTextureTransform( transform );
}
```

14.5 USING TRANSPARENT GEOMETRY WITH TRANSPARENT TEXTURE IMAGES

The Texture class allows texture images to have red, green, blue, and alpha (transparency) channels through the RGBA mode. Appearances (and hence geometry) can also have transparency information, either through per-vertex COLOR_4 colors, or through the TransparencyAtttributes NodeComponent. Figures 14.25–14.27 illustrate what happens when partially transparent images are applied to partially transparent Shape3Ds.

The easiest way to use transparent images is to use the GIF image format, which can include a transparent color. Most bitmap editors, such as JASC PaintShop Pro or Adobe Photoshop, can save GIF images with a transparent color.

Figures 14.25–14.27 were generated using the `AppearanceTest` example application. The `Box` had the appearance attributes shown on table 14.5.

Table 14.5 Box appearance attributes

Transparency: 0.5, NICEST

Material: Ambient = white, Diffuse = white, Emissive = blue, Specular = black, Shininess = 1

Texture: MagFilter = BASE_LEVEL_LINEAR, MinFilter = MULTI_LEVEL_LINEAR

MIPMAPs were enabled.

The front face (smaller) of the cube uses per-vertex colors with transparency and hence is unaffected by the overall TransparencyAttributes of the Box's Appearance.

Figure 14.25 is provided for contrast; it uses the opaque texture image (texture0n.jpg).

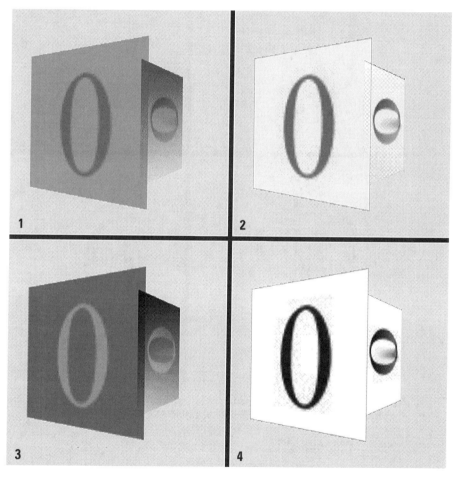

Figure 14.25 Shape3D with an opaque image applied (texture0n.jpg) from AppearanceTest. 1 = MODULATE, 2 = DECAL, 3 = BLEND, 4 = REPLACE

Figure 14.26 uses a transparent version (texture2n.gif) of the original texture image. The white background of the texture image has been marked as a transparent color in the GIF image.

Figure 14.27 uses the transparent texture image but also disables back-face removal using `PolygonAttributes.CULL_NONE`. Frame 2 (`DECAL`) suffered from continuous redraw because the back faces were redrawn over the front faces, and then the back faces were redrawn.

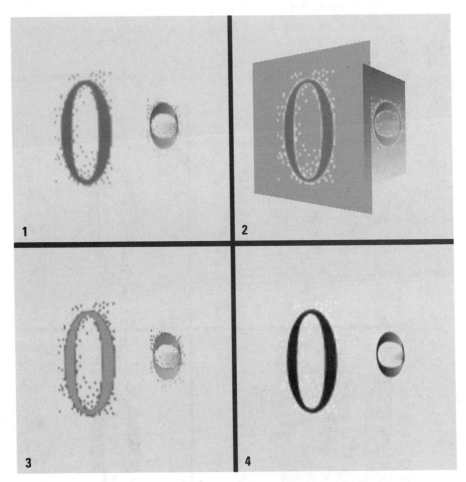

Figure 14.26   Shape3D with transparent image applied (texture2n.gif) from AppearanceTest. 1 = MODULATE, 2 = DECAL, 3 = BLEND, 4 = REPLACE

CHAPTER 14   USING TEXTURE IMAGES

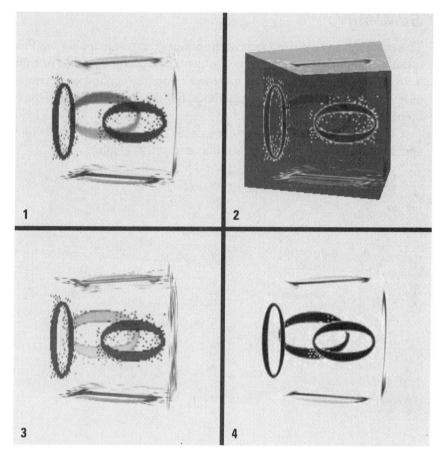

Figure 14.27   Transparency = 0.2, PolygonAttributes.CULL_NONE. Shape3D with transparent image applied (texture2n.gif) from AppearanceTest. 1 = MODULATE, 2 = DECAL, 3 = BLEND, 4 = REPLACE

14.6 *ANIMATED (VIDEO) TEXTURE MAPPING*

Many recent computer games use animated texture maps, for example, to map an MPEG video clip onto the face of a cube. 3D accelerator hardware is also starting to support video textures. Drawing animated textures is at present problematic in Java 3D because, although you can draw into an ImageComponent and use it as a texture image, the ImageComponent is *copied* into texture memory. Java 3D 1.2 should go some way to addressing this issue, but performance problems are likely to remain an issue for some time.

For very simple texture animations (a few frames), each frame of the animation can be pasted (either at runtime or as a preprocess) into a composite texture image. At run-time the texture coordinates of vertices can be modified to cycle through the various frames of the animation.

14.7 SUMMARY

This chapter has given you a taste of the power of texture mapping and the important role it plays in most 3D applications, be they educational, scientific, or entertainment. Texture mapping requires a little more work from the application developer, in terms of learning new terminology and methods, but the end results justify the extra development time.

Clever use of lighting and texture mapping sets the great, visually immersive 3D applications apart from flat, uninspiring "computer" graphics.

C H A P T E R   1 5

Geometry utility classes and object loaders

This chapter explains some of the utility classes that Java 3D supplies to help you import or generate geometry for your scenes.

15.1 INTRODUCTION

Java 3D comes with three utility classes that facilitate runtime geometry creation:

- `Triangulator` converts a list of points and connectivity information into a `GeometryArray` composed of triangles.

- `NormalGenerator` generates Normal vectors for a list of triangles.

- `Stripifier` redefines an existing triangle list such that the triangles are specified in longs strips, with adjacent triangles sharing as many vertices as possible. Triangle lists are stripified to speed rendering by graphics hardware and software underlying Java 3D.

The geometry compression classes allow Java 3D to create an internal compressed representation of geometry information. If the graphics hardware supports using compressed geometry, the result may be faster rendering time and lower memory usage. Geometry compression can also be useful for applications that need to send Java 3D geometry across network connections using serialization or Java RMI. Refer to the API documentation for further details.

The Java 3D object loaders define an architecture for writing files to import geometry data into Java 3D. Sun supplies two loaders as part of the Java 3D utilities package:

- Lightwave 3D
- Object file

In addition, the Java 3D/VRML working groups maintain a VRML loader to import VRML (WRL) files into Java 3D. The VRML loader must be downloaded separately (VRML97.JAR). The example `VrmlPickingTest` uses the VRML97 loader. The VRML97 loader is no longer being developed and is being replaced by the loaders being developed for the X3D standard, hosted at http://www.web3d.org.

15.2 TRIANGULATOR, NORMAL VECTOR GENERATOR, STRIPIFIER

Triangulation is a mechanism to convert arbitrary polygons to triangular surfaces for rendering. The `com.sun.j3d.utils.geometry.Triangulator` class can be used not only to convert an arbitrary *n*-sided polygon (which does not have to be planar) to triangular surfaces, but also to create holes in the generated composite surface. To use the `Triangulator`, put your vertex coordinates into a double or float array. This coordinate array should first define the outer boundary of the polygon, using counterclockwise winding.

Then define any polygons that are to be excluded from the generated composite triangular surface. This simple example in figure 15.1 defines two contours: the outer polygon and one hole. The `stripCountArray` is an array of integers that delineates one contour from the next. In figure 15.1, the `stripCountArray` would be

```
int[] stripCountArray = {4,3};
```

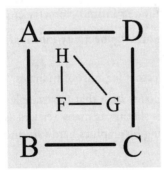

Figure 15.1   Counterclockwise winding for defining a polygon and a hole for Triangulation

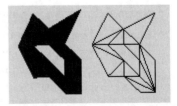

Figure 15.2   Output from TriangulatorTest: The surface generated rendered both as a solid (left) and as a wireframe (right)

The first contour (A,B,C,D) contains four vertices, and the hole (F,G,H) contains three vertices.

The `Triangulator` class is not very well documented, so the following example should illustrate the concepts of polygon triangulation using the `Triangulator` class. In particular, the `contourCountArray` element is misleadingly documented and should be set to the number of contours (1 + the number of holes). This is always the same as the length of the `stripCountArray`. Why the `contourCountArray` is necessary is not clear.

From TriangulatorTest.java

```
//Generate a surface from 10 vertices and
//create a hole in the surface by removing
//a hole defined using 5 vertices. Note that the hole
//must be entirely within the outer polygon.
private double[]m_VertexArray = {1,1,0, //0
        0,3,0, //1
        1,5,0, //2
        2,4,0, //3
        4,5,0, //4
        3,3,0, //5
        4,2,0, //6
        4,0,0, //7
        3,0,0, //8
        2,1,0, //9
//these are vertices for the hole
        1,3,0, //10
        2,3,0, //11
        3,2,0, //12
        3,1,0, //13
        2,2,0};//14
//triangulate the polygon
GeometryInfo gi = new GeometryInfo( GeometryInfo.POLYGON_ARRAY );

gi.setCoordinates( m_VertexArray );

//the first 10 points make up the outer edge of the polygon,
//the next five make up the hole
int[] stripCountArray = {10,5};
int[] countourCountArray = {stripCountArray.length};

gi.setContourCounts( countourCountArray );
gi.setStripCounts( stripCountArray );

Triangulator triangulator = new Triangulator();
triangulator.triangulate( gi );

//also generate normal vectors so that the surface can be light
NormalGenerator normalGenerator = new NormalGenerator();
normalGenerator.generateNormals( gi );

//create an appearance
Appearance ap = new Appearance();
```

```
//render as a wireframe
PolygonAttributes polyAttrbutes = new PolygonAttributes();
polyAttrbutes.setPolygonMode( PolygonAttributes.POLYGON_LINE );
polyAttrbutes.setCullFace( PolygonAttributes.CULL_NONE ) ;
ap.setPolygonAttributes( polyAttrbutes );

//add both a wireframe and a solid version
//of the triangulated surface
Shape3D shape1 = new Shape3D( gi.getGeometryArray(), ap );
Shape3D shape2 = new Shape3D( gi.getGeometryArray() );
```

■

After the geometry has been triangulated and normal vectors have been calculated, the geometry can be very easily stripified:

```
//invoke the Stripifier on the GeometryInfo
Stripifier st = new Stripifier()
st.stripify(gi);

//extract the stripified GeometryArray
Shape3D shape2 = new Shape3D( gi.getGeometryArray() );
```

15.3   OBJECT LOADERS

Sun has defined the com.sun.j3d.loaders.Loader interface that provides a standard set of methods for accessing the information read in from a 3D data file format. Because there is such a wide variety of 3D data file formats available, the Loader interface is fairly high level and does not return graphical information directly but encapsulates it in an object implementing the Scene interface.

15.3.1   LoaderBase

```
java.lang.Object
   |
   +--com.sun.j3d.loaders.LoaderBase
```

LoaderBase is a convenience class to manage the setting and retrieval of typical Loader information, such as base URL and load flags. Developers implementing their own Loader can populate, return, and interrogate a LoaderBase instance to provide a consistent API for end-user developers.

15.3.2   SceneBase interface

```
java.lang.Object
   |
   +--com.sun.j3d.loaders.SceneBase
```

SceneBase is a convenience class to manage the setting and retrieval of typical Scene information, such as:

- Background nodes
- Behavior nodes
- Description
- Fog nodes
- FOV parameters
- Lights
- Objects
- Sound nodes

Developers implementing their own `Loader` can populate, return, and interrogate a `SceneBase` instance to provide a consistent API for end-user developers.

15.3.3 Using the ObjectFile loader

The following example loads a simple Wavefront format .obj file (the hand1.obj file from the Sun Morphing demo). Note that it is also necessary to create lights for the scene and assign an `Appearance` and `Material` to the loaded Wavefront object. Figure 15.3 shows rendered output.

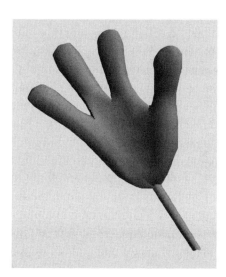

**Figure 15.3
A Wavefront OBJ file loaded using
the Sun ObjectFile loader**

From LoaderTest.java

```
protected BranchGroup createSceneBranchGroup()
{
 BranchGroup objRoot = super.createSceneBranchGroup();

 //create a TransformGroup to flip the hand onto its end
 //and enlarge it.
 TransformGroup objTrans1 = new TransformGroup();
```

```
Transform3D tr = new Transform3D();
objTrans1.getTransform( tr );
tr.rotX(90.0 * Math.PI / 180.0);
tr.setScale( 10.0 );
objTrans1.setTransform( tr );

//create a TransformGroup to rotate the hand
TransformGroup objTrans2 = new TransformGroup();
objTrans2.setCapability(TransformGroup.ALLOW_TRANSFORM_WRITE);
objTrans2.setCapability(TransformGroup.ALLOW_TRANSFORM_READ);

BoundingSphere bounds = new BoundingSphere(
                        new Point3d(0.0,0.0,0.0), 100.0);

//create a RotationInterpolator behavior to rotate the hand
Transform3D yAxis = new Transform3D();
Alpha rotationAlpha = new Alpha(-1, Alpha.INCREASING_ENABLE,
 0, 0,
 4000, 0, 0,
 0, 0, 0);
RotationInterpolator rotator = new RotationInterpolator(
 rotationAlpha, objTrans2, yAxis, 0.0f, (float) Math.PI*2.0f);
rotator.setSchedulingBounds(bounds); objTrans2.addChild(rotator);

//Set up the global lights
Color3f lColor1 = new Color3f(0.7f, 0.7f, 0.7f);
Vector3f lDir1  = new Vector3f(-1.0f, -1.0f, -1.0f);
Color3f alColor = new Color3f(0.2f, 0.2f, 0.2f);

AmbientLight aLgt = new AmbientLight(alColor);
aLgt.setInfluencingBounds(bounds);
DirectionalLight lgt1 = new DirectionalLight(lColor1, lDir1);
lgt1.setInfluencingBounds(bounds);

objRoot.addChild(aLgt);
objRoot.addChild(lgt1);

//load the object file
Scene scene = null;
Shape3D shape = null;

//read in the geometry information from the data file
ObjectFile objFileloader = new ObjectFile( ObjectFile.RESIZE );

try
{
 scene = objFileloader.load( "hand1.obj");
}
catch (Exception e)
{
 scene = null;
 System.err.println(e);
}

if( scene == null )
 System.exit(1);
```

```
//retrieve the Shape3D object from the scene
BranchGroup branchGroup = scene.getSceneGroup();
shape = (Shape3D) branchGroup.getChild(0);

//create an Appearance and Material
Appearance app = new Appearance();
Color3f objColor = new Color3f(1.0f, 0.7f, 0.8f);
Color3f black = new Color3f(0.0f, 0.0f, 0.0f);
app.setMaterial(new Material(objColor, black, objColor, black, 80.0f));

//assign the appearance to the Shape
shape.setAppearance( app );

//connect the scenegraph
objTrans2.addChild( scene.getSceneGroup() );
objTrans1.addChild( objTrans2 );
objRoot.addChild( objTrans1 );

return objRoot;
}
```

15.3.4   Third-party object loaders

There are a wide variety of object loaders available for use with Java 3D. The list of available loaders is maintained by Bill Day at http://www.j3d.org. Data file loaders available for most of the common 3D data file formats are listed in table 15.1.

Table 15.1   Data file loaders

Loader	Author	File Format(s)	Last Updated
Milkshape3D Loader	Gregory Pierce	Milkshape3D	30 Aug 2001
Milkshape3D Loader	Kevin Duling	Milkshape3D	28 Aug 2001
AC3D Loader	Ryan Wilhm/j3d.org	AC3D	28 Aug 2001
NCSA Portfolio	NCSA	3DS (3D-Studio) PDB (Protein Data Bank) DEM (Digital Elevation Map) IOB (Imagine) COB (Caligari trueSpace) OBJ (Wavefront) DXF (Drawing Interchange File) AutoCAD VRML 97 PLAY	15 Sept 2000
Xj3D Loader	Extensible 3D (X3D) Task Group (former VRML97-Java Working Group)	VRML97 X3D	15 Sept 2000

continued on next page

Table 15.1   Data file loaders (continued)

Loader	Author	File Format(s)	Last Updated
FullSail Open-FLT Loader	Shawn Kendall	OpenFLT	1 Aug 1999
Lw3dLoader	Sun	LWS (Lightwave Scene Format) uses LWO (Lightwave Object Format)	13 Jun 1998
ObjLoad	Sun	OBJ (Wavefront)	12 Jun 1998
NFF & OBJ Loader	Scott Metzger	NFF (WorldToolKit) OBJ (Wavefront)	15 Jun 1998
Loader3DS	Starfire Research	3DS(3D-Studio)	March 2001
Import3DS	Aaron Mulder	3DS (3D-Studio)	13 Jun 1998
Load3DS	Wesley Layne	3DS (3D-Studio)	25 Feb 2001
Load3DS	Rycharde Hawkes	3DS (3D-Studio)	16 Jun 1998
VTK Loader	Arish Ali	VTK (Visual Toolkit)	15 Sept 2000

Different loaders have different limitations and bugs. You should experiment with loaders and file formats until you find one that works for the files you need to display.

15.4   SUMMARY

Java 3D includes relatively basic support for processing geometry using the utility classes in the com.sun.j3d.utils.geometry package. The utilities are easy to use, and are useful for simple triangulation. For more powerful geometry manipulation operations (such as mesh generation or decimation you will have to convert one of the many utility libraries, usually written in C).

The interfaces and classes defined in the com.sun.j3d.loaders package however have proved to be very useful. They have defined a standard upon which many of the community Java 3D developers can build, and a large variety of loaders have been released—most are free.

C H A P T E R   1 6

Object interaction—picking and collision detection

Two example applications of Java 3D's support for picking are presented here. The first example, in section 16.7, loads a VRML scene and reports the name of the object from the VRML scene that was picked when a mouse click occurs. The second example uses Java 3D's Bounds-based picking to implement simple collision detection. The example creates four Sphere objects within a cube, which ricochet off each other and the walls of the cube.

16.1   INTRODUCTION TO PICKING

Picking is the act of identifying objects in the 3D scene, usually with a pointing device, such as the mouse. Java 3D's support for behaviors and picking can also be used to implement simple collision detection and response within a 3D scene. Picking is central to many of the *direct-manipulation* UI paradigms. Using direct manipulation, for example, you would translate an object by clicking it and moving the mouse, as opposed to typing the object ID and its new position into an edit field. For precision work, the edit field will work best; however, it abstracts the user from the 3D scene as compared to direct manipulation.

Java 3D 1.2 includes some new classes that make picking relatively easy. These classes are a big improvement over the 1.1 picking classes, which have been widely deprecated.

Before going into the details of the examples, I will describe the Java 3D 1.2 picking classes. The Java documentation for the picking classes is excellent, probably the best in Java 3D, so it is useful to familiarize yourself with it.

16.2 PICKSHAPES

```
java.lang.Object
  |
  +--javax.media.j3d.PickShape
```

PickShapes are used by the PickTool to provide information about the volume of space, segment, or infinite ray that the objects in the scene should be tested against. Java 3D supports the PickShapes listed in table 16.1:

Table 16.1   PickShapes supported by Java 3D

PickShapes	Description
PickBounds	PickBounds is a finite pick shape defined with a Bounds object.
PickConeRay	PickConeRay is an infinite cone ray pick shape.
PickConeSegment	PickConeSegment is a finite cone segment pick shape.
PickCylinderRay	PickCylinderRay is an infinite cylindrical ray pick shape.
PickCylinderSegment	PickCylinderSegment is a finite cylindrical segment pick shape.
PickPoint	PickPoint is a pick shape defined as a single point.
PickRay	PickRay is an infinite ray pick shape.
PickSegment	PickSegment is a line segment pick shape.

By using the appropriate PickShape you can find the objects in your scene that

- Fall within a given volume (PickBounds)
- Intersect with an infinite cone, such as a ray of light shining from a torch (PickConeRay)
- Intersect with a finite length cone, such as the objects within a torch ray, within a given distance (PickConeSegment)
- Intersect with a laser beam (PickCylinderRay)
- Intersect with a blind-man's stick (PickCylinderSegment)
- Intersect with a point (PickPoint)
- Intersect with a very narrow laser beam (PickRay)
- Intersect with a very narrow blind-man's stick (PickSegment)

16.3 PICKTOOL

```
java.lang.Object
  |
  +--com.sun.j3d.utils.picking.PickTool
```

`PickTool` is the base class for picking operations. The picking methods will return a `PickResult` object for each object picked, which can then be queried to obtain more detailed information about the specific objects that were picked. The pick mode specifies the detail level of picking before the `PickResult` is returned (see table 16.2).

Table 16.2 PickTools

PickTool Mode	Description
BOUNDS	Pick using the bounds of the pickable nodes. The PickResult returned will contain the SceneGraphPath to the picked Node.
GEOMETRY	Pick using the geometry of the pickable nodes. The PickResult returned will contain the SceneGraphPath to the picked Node. Geometry nodes in the scene must have the ALLOW_INTERSECT capability set for this mode.
GEOMETRY_INTERSECT_INFO	Same as GEOMETRY, but the PickResult will include information on each intersection of the pick shape with the geometry. The intersection information includes the subprimitive picked (i.e., the point, line, triangle, or quad), the closest vertex to the center of the pick shape, and the intersection's coordinate, normal, color, and texture coordinates. To allow this to be generated, Shape3D and Morph nodes must have the ALLOW_GEOMETRY_READ capability set, and GeometryArrays must have the ALLOW_FORMAT_READ, ALLOW_COUNT_READ, and ALLOW_COORDINATE_READ capabilities set, plus the ALLOW_COORDINATE_INDEX_READ capability for indexed geometry. To query the intersection color, normal, or texture coordinates, the corresponding READ capability bits must be set on the GeometryArray.

The utility method `PickTool.setCapabilities(Node, int)` can be used before the scenegraph is made live to set the capabilities of `Shape3D`, `Morph`, or `Geometry` nodes to allow picking.

A `PickResult` from a lower level of detail pick can be used to inquire about more detailed information if the capability bits are set. This can be used to filter the `Pick-Results` before the more computationally intensive intersection processing. For example, the application can do a BOUNDS pick and then selectively query intersections on some of the `PickResults`. This will save the effort of doing intersection computation on the other `PickResults`. However, querying the intersections from a GEOMETRY pick will make the intersection computation happen twice, so use `GEOMETRY_INTERSECT_INFO` if you want to inquire the intersection information on all the `PickResults`.

When using `pickAllSorted` or `pickClosest` methods, the picks will be sorted by the distance from the start point of the pick shape to the intersection point.

Morph nodes cannot be picked using the displayed geometry in GEOMETRY_INTER-SECT_INFO mode due to limitations in the current Java3D core API (the current geometry of the `Morph` cannot be queried). Instead, they are picked by using the geometry at index 0 in the `Morph`. This limitation may be eliminated in a future release of Java3D.

If the pick shape is a `PickBounds`, the pick result will contain only the scenegraph path, even if the mode is GEOMETRY_INTERSECT_INFO.

16.4   PICKCANVAS

```
java.lang.Object
   |
   +--com.sun.j3d.utils.picking.PickTool
        |
        +--com.sun.j3d.utils.picking.PickCanvas
```

`PickCanvas`, a subclass of `PickTool`, simplifies picking using mouse events from an AWT `Canvas`. This class allows picking using `Canvas` *x,y* locations by generating the appropriate pick shape.

The pick tolerance specifies the distance from the pick center to include in the pick shape. A tolerance of 0.0 may slightly speed up picking, but also makes it very difficult to pick points and lines. The pick canvas can be used to make a series of picks; for example, to initialize the pick canvas, do the following:

```
PickCanvas pickCanvas = new PickCanvas(canvas, scene);
pickCanvas.setMode(PickTool.GEOMETRY_INTERSECT_INFO);
pickCanvas.setTolerance(4.0f);
```

Then for each mouse event:

```
pickCanvas.setShapeLocation(mouseEvent);
PickResult[] results = pickCanvas.pickAll();
```

For the `pickAllSorted` or `pickClosest` methods, the picks will be sorted by the distance from the `ViewPlatform` to the intersection point.

16.5   PICKINTERSECTION

```
java.lang.Object
   |
   +--com.sun.j3d.utils.picking.PickIntersection
```

`PickIntersection` holds information about an intersection of a `PickShape` with a `Node` as part of a `PickResult`. Information about the intersected geometry, intersected primitive, intersection point, and closest vertex can be queried.

The intersected geometry is indicated by an index into the list of geometry arrays on the `PickResult`. It can also be queried from this object.

The intersected primitive indicates which primitive out of the GeometryArray was intersected (where the primitive is a point, line, triangle, or quad, not a com.sun.j3d.utils.geometry.Primitive). For example, the intersection would indicate which triangle out of a triangle strip was intersected. The methods which return primitive data will have one value if the primitive is a point, two values if the primitive is a line, three values if the primitive is a triangle, and four values if the primitive is quad.

The primitive's VWorld coordinates are saved when the intersection is calculated. The local coordinates, normal color, and texture coordinates for the primitive can also be queried if they are present and readable.

The intersection point is the location on the primitive which intersects the pick shape closest to the center of the pick shape. The intersection point's location in VWorld coordinates is saved when the intersection is calculated. The local coordinates, and the normal, color, and texture coordinates of the intersection can be interpolated if they are present and readable.

The closest vertex is the vertex of the primitive closest to the intersection point. The vertex index, VWorld coordinates, and local coordinates of the closest vertex can be queried. The normal, color, and texture coordinate of the closest vertex can be queried from the geometry array:

```
Vector3f getNormal(PickIntersection pi, int vertexIndex)
{
 int index;
 Vector3d normal = new Vector3f();
 GeometryArray ga = pickIntersection.getGeometryArray();
 if (pickIntersection.geometryIsIndexed())
 {
  index = ga.getNormalIndex(vertexIndex);
 }
 else
 {
  index = vertexIndex;
 }

 ga.getNormal(index, normal);
 return normal;
}
```

The color, normal, and texture coordinate information for the intersected primitive and the intersection point can be queried. The geometry includes them, and the corresponding READ capability bits are set. PickTool.setCapabilities(Node, int) can be used to set the capability bits to allow this data to be queried.

16.6 PICKRESULT

```
java.lang.Object
  |
  +--com.sun.j3d.utils.picking.PickResult
```

`PickResult` stores information about a pick hit. Detailed information about the pick and each intersection of the `PickShape` with the picked `Node` can be inquired. The `PickResult` is constructed with basic information, and more detailed information is generated as needed. The additional information is only available if capability bits on the scenegraph `Nodes` are set properly; `PickTool.setCapabilities(Node, int)` can be used to ensure correct capabilities are set. Inquiring data that is not available due to capabilities not being set will generate a `CapabilityNotSetException`.

A `PickResult` can be used to calculate intersections on `Node` which is not part of a live scenegraph using the constructor which takes a local to `VWorld` transformation for the `Node`.

Pick hits on `TriangleStrip` primitives will store the triangle points in the `PickIntersection` with the vertices in counterclockwise order. For triangles that start with an odd numbered vertex, this will be the opposite of the order of the points in the `TriangleStrip`. This way the triangle in the `PickIntersection` will be displayed the same way as the triangle in the strip.

If the `Shape3D` being picked has multiple geometry arrays, the arrays are stored in the `PickResult` and referred to by a geometry index. If the `Shape3D` refers to a `CompressedGeometry`, the geometry is decompressed into an array of `Shape3D` nodes that can be queried. The geometry `NodeComponents` for the `Shape3D` nodes are stored and used as if the `Shape3D` had multiple geometries. If there are multiple `CompressedGeometries` on the `Shape3D`, the decompressed `Shape3Ds` and `GeometryArrays` will be stored sequentially.

The intersection point for `Morph` nodes cannot be calculated using the displayed geometry due to limitations in the current Java3D core API (the current geometry of the `Morph` cannot be inquired). Instead, the geometry at index 0 in the `Morph` is used. This limitation may be eliminated in a future release of Java3D.

16.7 VRML PICKING EXAMPLE

The `VrmlPickingTest` example illustrates how the `PickCanvas` and `PickResult` classes can be used. The example loads a VRML format data file and allows the user to rotate, translate, and scale the loaded model. When the mouse is clicked, a list is generated of the intersections of the model with a `PickCylinderRay` that passes perpendicularly through the clicked screen location into the 3D scene. All the intersections with the model are reported, as well as the closest intersection.

When a mouse click occurs, `VrmlPickingTest` produces the following output (which corresponds to clicking the mouse in the position shown in figure 16.1. The output is a list of the `PickResult` objects (sorted from nearest to farthest):

`*** MouseClick ***`

First, the path through the scenegraph to the intersected node is displayed. In this case, the path is the `VirtualUniverse`'s `Locale`, a `BranchGroup`, the `Sphere` primitive (user data is "Sphere"), then finally a `Shape3D` containing a `TriangleStripArray`.

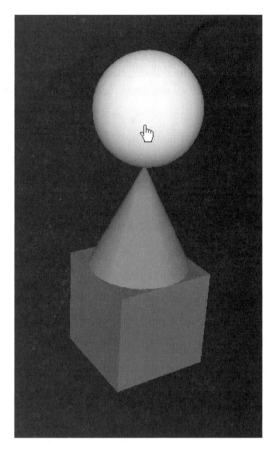

Figure 16.1
A VRML scene loaded into the
`VrmlPickingTest` **example. Note
the position of the cursor (the hand
icon), which corresponds to the scene
intersections in the code which follows**

```
Sorted PickResult 0: PickResult:
 sgp:javax.media.j3d.Locale@124fb8e :
 javax.media.j3d.BranchGroup :
 com.sun.j3d.utils.geometry.Sphere, Sphere :
 javax.media.j3d.Shape3D,
 Spherejavax.media.j3d.TriangleStripArray@12b486c
```

The transformation matrix required to convert the terminal node of the scenegraph
path (`Shape3D`) to Virtual World coordinates is displayed. This is the transformation
matrix that was in effect when the pick took place.

```
LocalToVworld Transform:
-0.5243562077058301, -0.8502316137753383, 0.04644104194946784,
0.35220520974733893
0.3928339572694004, -0.19315917400790997, 0.8990945531548112,
5.215472765774056
-0.7554680995624017, 0.4896894285499475, 0.4352840614012915,
0.5764203070064573
0.0, 0.0, 0.0, 1.0
```

Next, the intersection information for the ray is displayed. In this case, the ray intersected six Nodes in the model. For each intersection, the distance of the intersection from the ViewPlatform is calculated along with the point's coordinates in Virtual World coordinates. As you can see from the Z-coordinates and distances, five of the intersections were with Nodes at the front of the Sphere while one was with a node at the rear of the Sphere.

```
node:javax.media.j3d.Shape3D@12b485a
PickIntersection:  geomIndex = 0
 dist:13.190385327169809
 ptVW:(0.3082159939737674, 5.101595194311164, -0.40544525181089597)

PickIntersection:  geomIndex = 0
 dist:11.285273011880047
 ptVW:(0.2697997524391042, 4.782074528439611, 1.4723671948932975)

PickIntersection:  geomIndex = 0
 dist:11.28272787795884
 ptVW:(0.2766647006417829, 4.784127302928557, 1.4754390646997604)

PickIntersection:  geomIndex = 0
 dist:11.282690605316592
 ptVW:(0.26386760841671225, 4.797646503054273, 1.4773578620510737)

PickIntersection:  geomIndex = 0
 dist:11.279971427880689
 ptVW:(0.27735265885195876, 4.796380438058344, 1.4802262351804227)

PickIntersection:  geomIndex = 0
 dist:11.28272787795884
 ptVW:(0.2766647006417829, 4.784127302928557, 1.4754390646997604)


Sorted Object 0: Sphere

Closest Object: Sphere
```

The second illustrated pick intersection is more complex (figure 16.2). As you can see, the sphere is still the closest intersection; however, the pick ray passes through the entire model. In this example (output following), the VRML part intersections are (sorted from nearest to farthest):

1 Sphere: 2 intersections

2 Cone: 2 intersections

3 Cone: 2 intersections

4 Box: 2 intersections

5 Cone: 7 intersections

```
*** MouseClick ***
```

Sorted PickResult 0: PickResult:
```
sgp:javax.media.j3d.Locale@124fb8e :
javax.media.j3d.BranchGroup :
```

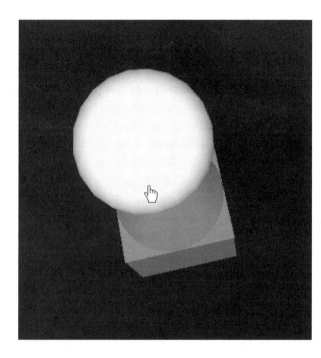

Figure 16.2
A VRML scene loaded into the `VrmlPickingTest` **example. Note the position of the cursor (the hand icon) which corresponds to the scene intersections in the code that follows**

```
com.sun.j3d.utils.geometry.Sphere, Sphere :
javax.media.j3d.Shape3D, Sphere
javax.media.j3d.TriangleStripArray@12b486c
LocalToVworld Transform:
0.974680683424301, -0.19810018807842686, -0.10370092016385302,
-0.5185046008192652
0.2217376557236817, 0.9160774460188752, 0.3341175316108114,
2.8105876580540574
0.028809328241108344, -0.34865230298798766, 0.9368092624581957,
3.084046312290978
0.0, 0.0, 0.0, 1.0

node:javax.media.j3d.Shape3D@12b485a
PickIntersection:  geomIndex = 0
 dist:10.31109258625374
 ptVW:(-0.503754844446497, 2.138046095717119, 2.3502490354035483)

PickIntersection:  geomIndex = 0
 dist:10.315735064224192
 ptVW:(-0.48806121433886257, 2.1446076441445165, 2.3442903032651294)

PickIntersection:  geomIndex = 0
 dist:10.311507103034156
 ptVW:(-0.46680214250863505, 2.1403178766932185, 2.3478813387527073)

PickIntersection:  geomIndex = 0
 dist:8.737141773923474
 ptVW:(-0.41919205110931124, 2.265854783380931, 3.916754614302066)

PickIntersection:  geomIndex = 0
```

```
 dist:8.771580342395431
 ptVW:(-0.41919205110931124, 2.265854783380931, 3.916754614302066)

PickIntersection:  geomIndex = 0
 dist:8.732273133281984
 ptVW:(-0.41290180559136586, 2.275910225691348, 3.9205080490411017)

PickIntersection:  geomIndex = 0
 dist:8.73669779993455
 ptVW:(-0.4106277895151771, 2.2691852339960756, 3.916514821486335)
```

Sorted Object 0: Sphere

Sorted PickResult 1: PickResult:
```
sgp:javax.media.j3d.Locale@124fb8e :
javax.media.j3d.BranchGroup :
javax.media.j3d.Shape3D, Cone
javax.media.j3d.TriangleFanArray@1262519
LocalToVworld Transform:
0.974680683424301, -0.19810018807842686, -0.10370092016385302,
-0.3111027604915591
0.2217376557236817, 0.9160774460188752, 0.3341175316108114,
2.1423525948324347
0.028809328241108344, -0.34865230298798766, 0.9368092624581957,
1.2104277873745866
0.0, 0.0, 0.0, 1.0

node:javax.media.j3d.Shape3D@1261cac
PickIntersection:  geomIndex = 0
 dist:10.943688351941072
 ptVW:(-0.510896717862459, 2.1149716954978928, 1.7318035261186269)

PickIntersection:  geomIndex = 0
 dist:10.92767850911496
 ptVW:(-0.5066210416916537, 2.112735307161519, 1.7330744444918968)
```

Sorted Object 1: Cone

Sorted PickResult 2: PickResult:
```
sgp:javax.media.j3d.Locale@124fb8e :
javax.media.j3d.BranchGroup :
javax.media.j3d.Shape3D, Cone
javax.media.j3d.TriangleFanArray@1262519
LocalToVworld Transform:
0.974680683424301, -0.19810018807842686, -0.10370092016385302,
-0.3111027604915591
0.2217376557236817, 0.9160774460188752, 0.3341175316108114,
2.1423525948324347
0.028809328241108344, -0.34865230298798766, 0.9368092624581957,
1.2104277873745866
0.0, 0.0, 0.0, 1.0

node:javax.media.j3d.Shape3D@1261cac
PickIntersection:  geomIndex = 0
```

```
dist:10.943688351941072
ptVW:(-0.510896717862459, 2.1149716954978928, 1.7318035261186269)

PickIntersection:  geomIndex = 0
 dist:10.92767850911496
 ptVW:(-0.5066210416916537, 2.112735307161519, 1.7330744444918968)
```

Sorted Object 2: Cone

Sorted PickResult 3: PickResult:
```
sgp:javax.media.j3d.Locale@124fb8e :
javax.media.j3d.BranchGroup :
javax.media.j3d.Shape3D, Box
javax.media.j3d.QuadArray@1264877
LocalToVworld Transform:
0.974680683424301, -0.10370092016385303, 0.19810018807842686,
-0.10370092016385303
0.2217376557236817, 0.3341175316108115, -0.9160774460188752,
1.4741175316108115
0.028809328241108344, 0.9368092624581957, 0.3486523029879877,
-0.6631907375418048
0.0, 0.0, 0.0, 1.0

node:javax.media.j3d.Shape3D@1264cfe
PickIntersection:  geomIndex = 0
 dist:12.494425040536017
 ptVW:(-0.5914732681836042, 1.9639480320061125, 0.17556762285086336)

PickIntersection:  geomIndex = 0
 dist:14.587993543333791
 ptVW:(-0.6908450104199546, 1.7903467955691152, -1.9084230065569017)
```

Sorted Object 3: Box

Sorted PickResult 4: PickResult:
```
sgp:javax.media.j3d.Locale@124fb8e :
javax.media.j3d.BranchGroup :
javax.media.j3d.Shape3D, Cone
javax.media.j3d.TriangleFanArray@124fa1a
LocalToVworld Transform:
0.974680683424301, -0.19810018807842686, -0.10370092016385302,
-0.2074018403277061
0.2217376557236817, 0.9160774460188752, 0.3341175316108114,
1.8082350632216233
0.028809328241108344, -0.34865230298798766, 0.9368092624581957,
0.2736185249163908
0.0, 0.0, 0.0, 1.0

node:javax.media.j3d.Shape3D@124fa08
PickIntersection:  geomIndex = 0
 dist:12.494425040536019
 ptVW:(-0.5914732681836044, 1.9639480320061125, 0.17556762285086158)

PickIntersection:  geomIndex = 0
```

```
dist:12.500884811804253
ptVW:(-0.5720301373107639, 1.9989535603646984, 0.16523500707364264)
```

Sorted Object 4: Cone

Closest PickResult: PickResult:
```
sgp:javax.media.j3d.Locale@124fb8e :
javax.media.j3d.BranchGroup :
com.sun.j3d.utils.geometry.Sphere, Sphere :
javax.media.j3d.Shape3D, Sphere
javax.media.j3d.TriangleStripArray@12b486c
```

```
LocalToVworld Transform:
0.974680683424301, -0.19810018807842686, -0.10370092016385302,
-0.5185046008192652
0.2217376557236817, 0.9160774460188752, 0.3341175316108114,
2.8105876580540574
0.028809328241108344, -0.34865230298798766, 0.9368092624581957,
3.084046312290978
0.0, 0.0, 0.0, 1.0
```

```
node:javax.media.j3d.Shape3D@12b485a
PickIntersection:  geomIndex = 0
 dist:10.31109258625374
 ptVW:(-0.503754844446497, 2.138046095717119, 2.3502490354035483)

PickIntersection:  geomIndex = 0
 dist:10.315735064224192
 ptVW:(-0.48806121433886257, 2.1446076441445165, 2.3442903032651294)

PickIntersection:  geomIndex = 0
 dist:10.311507103034156
 ptVW:(-0.46680214250863505, 2.1403178766932185, 2.3478813387527073)

PickIntersection:  geomIndex = 0
 dist:8.737141773923474
 ptVW:(-0.41919205110931124, 2.265854783380931, 3.916754614302066)

PickIntersection:  geomIndex = 0
 dist:8.771580342395431
 ptVW:(-0.41919205110931124, 2.265854783380931, 3.916754614302066)

PickIntersection:  geomIndex = 0
 dist:8.732273133281984
 ptVW:(-0.41290180559136586, 2.275910225691348, 3.9205080490411017)

PickIntersection:  geomIndex = 0
 dist:8.73669779993455
 ptVW:(-0.4106277895151771, 2.2691852339960756, 3.916514821486335)
```

Closest Object: Sphere

Note that multiple intersections can be reported because the pick ray used for inter-section testing actually has a width (tolerance). The tolerance makes it easier for users to pick small objects or lines at the expense of absolute accuracy. You should also note that generating all the picking information in the preceding code is computationally quite expensive, so you should use simple BOUNDS picking whenever possible, unless you need to know the exact location within a shape that was picked.

A method to generate the picking output is shown in the following example:

From VrmlPickingTest.java

```
//This example loads a VRML file, automatically computes
//the view point to view the objects in the file,
//and then mouse picks. For each pick, all the selected components
//of the scene are reported (by their VRML name).
//The VRML scene can be rotated, scaled, and
//translated using the mouse.
public class VrmlPickingTest extends Java3dApplet implements
  MouseListener
{
 PickCanvas        pickCanvas = null;

 public VrmlPickingTest()
 {
 }

 public VrmlPickingTest( String[] args )
 {
  saveCommandLineArguments( args );
  initJava3d();
 }

 protected void addCanvas3D( Canvas3D c3d )
 {
  setLayout( new BorderLayout() );
  add( "Center", c3d );
  doLayout();

  if ( m_SceneBranchGroup != null )
  {
   c3d.addMouseListener( this );

   pickCanvas = new PickCanvas( c3d, m_SceneBranchGroup );
   pickCanvas.setMode( PickTool.GEOMETRY_INTERSECT_INFO );
   pickCanvas.setTolerance( 4.0f );
  }

  c3d.setCursor( new Cursor( Cursor.HAND_CURSOR ) );
 }

 public TransformGroup[] getViewTransformGroupArray()
 {
  TransformGroup[] tgArray = new TransformGroup[1];
  tgArray[0] = new TransformGroup();

  Transform3D viewTrans = new Transform3D();
  Transform3D eyeTrans = new Transform3D();

  BoundingSphere sceneBounds = (BoundingSphere)
```

```
   m_SceneBranchGroup.getBounds();

   //point the view at the center of the object
   Point3d center = new Point3d();
   sceneBounds.getCenter( center );
   double radius = sceneBounds.getRadius();
   Vector3d temp = new Vector3d( center );
   viewTrans.set( temp );

   //pull the eye back far enough to see the whole object
   double eyeDist = 1.4 * radius /
    Math.tan( Math.toRadians( 40 ) / 2.0);
   temp.x = 0.0;
   temp.y = 0.0;
   temp.z = eyeDist;
   eyeTrans.set( temp );
   viewTrans.mul( eyeTrans );

   //set the view transform
   tgArray[0].setTransform( viewTrans );

   return tgArray;
 }

protected BranchGroup createSceneBranchGroup()
{
 BranchGroup objRoot = super.createSceneBranchGroup();

 Bounds lightBounds = getApplicationBounds();

 AmbientLight ambLight =
  new AmbientLight( true, new Color3f( 1.0f, 1.0f, 1.0f) );
 ambLight.setInfluencingBounds( lightBounds );
 objRoot.addChild( ambLight );

 DirectionalLight headLight = new DirectionalLight();
 headLight.setInfluencingBounds( lightBounds );
 objRoot.addChild( headLight );

 TransformGroup mouseGroup = createMouseBehaviorsGroup();

 String vrmlFile = null;

 try
 {
  URL codebase = getWorkingDirectory();
  vrmlFile = codebase.toExternalForm() + "/VRML/BoxConeSphere.wrl";
 }
 catch( MalformedURLException mue )
 {
 }

 if ( m_szCommandLineArray != null )
 {
  switch ( m_szCommandLineArray.length )
  {
   case 0:
```

```
    break;

    case 1:
     vrmlFile = m_szCommandLineArray[0];
    break;

    default:
     System.err.println("Usage: VrmlPickingTest [pathname|URL]");
     System.exit( -1 );
  }
 }

 BranchGroup sceneRoot = loadVrmlFile( vrmlFile );

 if ( sceneRoot != null )
  mouseGroup.addChild( sceneRoot );

 objRoot.addChild( mouseGroup );

 return objRoot;
}

private TransformGroup createMouseBehaviorsGroup()
{
 TransformGroup examineGroup = new TransformGroup();
 examineGroup.setCapability(TransformGroup.ALLOW_TRANSFORM_READ);
 examineGroup.setCapability(TransformGroup.ALLOW_TRANSFORM_WRITE);

 Bounds behaviorBounds = getApplicationBounds();

 MouseRotate mr = new MouseRotate( examineGroup );
 mr.setSchedulingBounds( behaviorBounds );
 examineGroup.addChild( mr );

 MouseTranslate mt = new MouseTranslate( examineGroup );
 mt.setSchedulingBounds( behaviorBounds );
 examineGroup.addChild( mt );

 MouseZoom mz = new MouseZoom( examineGroup );
 mz.setSchedulingBounds( behaviorBounds );
 examineGroup.addChild( mz );

 return examineGroup;
}


private BranchGroup loadVrmlFile( String location )
{
 BranchGroup sceneGroup = null;
 Scene scene = null;

 VrmlLoader loader = new VrmlLoader();

 try
 {
  URL loadUrl = new URL(location);
  try
  {
   //load the scene
```

```
   scene = loader.load(new URL(location));
  }
  catch (Exception e)
  {
   System.out.println("Exception loading URL:" + e);
  }
 }
 catch (MalformedURLException badUrl)
 {
  //location may be a path name
  try
  {
   //load the scene
   scene = loader.load(location);
  }
  catch (Exception e)
  {
   System.out.println("Exception loading file from path:" + e);
  }
 }

 if (scene != null)
 {
  //get the scene group
  sceneGroup = scene.getSceneGroup();

  sceneGroup.setCapability( BranchGroup.ALLOW_BOUNDS_READ );
  sceneGroup.setCapability( BranchGroup.ALLOW_CHILDREN_READ );

  Hashtable namedObjects = scene.getNamedObjects();
  System.out.println("*** Named Objects in VRML file:
     \n" + namedObjects);

  //recursively set the user data here so we can find our objects
  //when they are picked
  java.util.Enumeration enumValues = namedObjects.elements();
  java.util.Enumeration enumKeys = namedObjects.keys();

  if( enumValues != null )
  {
   while( enumValues.hasMoreElements() != false )
   {
    Object value = enumValues.nextElement();
    Object key = enumKeys.nextElement();

    recursiveSetUserData( value, key );
   }
  }
 }

 return sceneGroup;
}
//Method to recursively set the user data for objects
//in the scenegraph tree we also set the capabilities
```

```
//on Shape3D and Morph objects required by the PickTool
void recursiveSetUserData( Object value, Object key )
{
 if( value instanceof SceneGraphObject != false )
 {
  //set the user data for the item
  SceneGraphObject sg = (SceneGraphObject) value;
  sg.setUserData( key );

  //recursively process group
  if( sg instanceof Group )
  {
   Group g = (Group) sg;

   //recurse on child nodes
   java.util.Enumeration enumKids = g.getAllChildren();

   while( enumKids.hasMoreElements() != false )
    recursiveSetUserData( enumKids.nextElement(), key );
  }
  else if ( sg instanceof Shape3D || sg instanceof Morph )
  {
   PickTool.setCapabilities( (Node) sg, PickTool.INTERSECT_FULL );
  }
 }
}

public void mouseClicked(MouseEvent e)
{
 System.out.println("*** MouseClick ***");

 pickCanvas.setShapeLocation( e );
 PickResult[] results = pickCanvas.pickAllSorted();

 if( results != null )
 {
  for (int n = 0; n < results.length; n++ )
  {
   PickResult pickResult = results[n];

   System.out.println(
     "Sorted PickResult " + n + ": " + pickResult );

   Node actualNode = pickResult.getObject();

   if( actualNode.getUserData() != null )
   {
    System.out.println(
      "Sorted Object " + n + ": " + actualNode.getUserData() );
   }
  }
 }

 PickResult pickResult = pickCanvas.pickClosest();

 if( pickResult != null )
```

```
  {
    System.out.println( "Closest PickResult: " + pickResult );

    Node actualNode = pickResult.getObject();

    if( actualNode.getUserData() != null )
    {
      System.out.println(
        "Closest Object: " + actualNode.getUserData() );
    }
  }

}

public void mouseEntered(MouseEvent e) {}

public void mouseExited(MouseEvent e) {}

public void mousePressed(MouseEvent e) {}

public void mouseReleased(MouseEvent e) {}

public static void main( String[] args )
{
  VrmlPickingTest pickingTest = new VrmlPickingTest( args );

  new MainFrame( pickingTest, 400, 400 );
}
}
```

The `VrmlPickingTest` example sets up a simple AWT application or applet, loads a VRML file into it and when an AWT `MouseEvent` is generated calculates `Pick-Results` for each intersection between the ray perpendicular to the Canvas and the loaded VRML model.

The `initJava3D` method initializes Java 3D—it creates a `VirtualUniverse` from scratch, and does not use the `SimpleUniverse` utility class. By overriding `Java3dApplet` methods, users of the class can customize the functionality and configuration of the `VirtualUniverse` created by the base class. In this example, the `addCanvas3D` method is overridden to assign a `Canvas3D` to a AWT `Container`, the `getViewTransformGroupArray` method creates an array of `TransformGroups` to be used on the view side of the scenegraph, while the `createSceneBranchGroup` method returns a `BranchGroup` containing all the scenegraph elements for the scene side of the scenegraph. The remaining methods are utility methods defined by the `VrmlPickingTest` class to implement the example functionality.

The `addCanvas3D` method sets up the AWT UI elements; specifically it assigns a `BorderLayout` algorithm and adds a `Canvas3D` to the center area of the AWT `Component`. Additionally the `addCanvas3D` method adds a `MouseListener` instance of this to the `Canvas3D` so that the `VrmlPickingTest` class will receive a callback from AWT when mouse events occur. A `PickCanvas` is created for the

Canvas3D using the PickTool.GEOMETRY_INTERSECT_INFO intersection mode to calculate PickResults. The tolerance for picking is set to 4.0. Finally, the cursor for the Canvas3D is set to the standard AWT hand-cursor icon.

The createSceneBranchGroup method loads the VRML file using the VRML 97 VrmlLoader class. After having been loaded from a URL or File, the named objects in the VRML file are iterated and the User Data field is set to the VRML name of the object. Assigning the VRML name to the User Data will make it easy to identify which object in the scene has been picked with the mouse—we can just grab the picked Node and examine its user data field.

The PickResult calculation is performed within the AWT mouse callback method mouseClicked. When a mouse click occurs AWT will invoke the method passing in a MouseEvent object that describes the position of the mouse and button states when the click took place. We merely have to call pickCanvas.setShape-Location to assign the MouseEvent to the PickCanvas and then call pick-Canvas.pickAllSorted for the PickCanvas to return an array of PickResults with all the intersections sorted from furthest to nearest.

16.8   USING PICKING FOR COLLISION DETECTION

The Java 3D 1.2 picking utilities can also be used to implement simple collision detection with a scene. The basic idea is to create a custom behavior that checks for picking intersections at runtime. By triggering the behavior in every frame, it is possible to detect collisions between objects and add application logic to respond to them. Unfortunately this is not a 100 percent robust mechanism for detecting collisions—it is possible for an object to be moving so fast that in the time between frames it passes right *through* an object in the scene. By the time the behavior is invoked again, the object is no longer in collision, and the intersection will have been missed. One possible application-specific workaround is to do a single frame look ahead (or look behind) to check whether an intersection was missed. A commercial collision detection engine (such as VCollide) provides much more scaleable collision detection and can handle cases such as that just described. If your application relies heavily on collision detection (and there are no cheats that you can use), you should probably investigate a commercial library. Defining a scene with thousands of objects, which could all potentially collide with one another, requires specialized collision detection algorithms that fall outside of Java 3D.

The remainder of this chapter will discuss an example that uses picking to implement simple collision detection. There are a limited number of collidable objects in the scene (10), and the speed of the moving objects has been defined such that it is not possible for the objects to pass through one another between frames (figure 16.3).

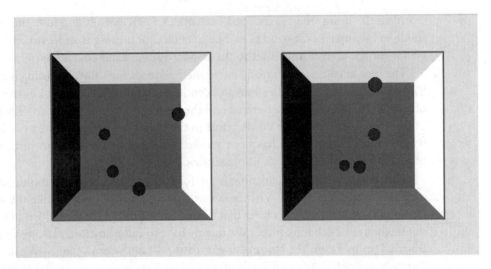

Figure 16.3 Two frames from the `PickCollisionTest`. The spheres bounce around within a large box, each side of which is defined by a scaled and translated `ColorCube` object. The spheres can bounce off one another as well as the sides of the box

From PickCollisionTest.java

```
/*
 * This example creates a large hollow box (out of ColorCubes,
 * one for each side of the box). Within the box, four Spheres are
 * created. Each Sphere has a behavior attached that detects
 * collisions with the sides of the box, and the other Spheres.
 * When a collision is detected, the trajectory of the Sphere is
 * reversed and the color of the Sphere changed. When a collision
 * is not detected, the Sphere is advanced along its
 * current trajectory.
 */
class PickCollisionTest extends Java3dApplet
  implements ActionListener
{
 private static int     m_kWidth = 400;
 private static int     m_kHeight = 400;

 private static final int  boxSize = 10;

 public PickCollisionTest()
 {
  initJava3d();
 }

 public void actionPerformed( ActionEvent event )
 {
 }

 protected void addCanvas3D( Canvas3D c3d )
 {
  add( c3d );
```

```
  doLayout();
 }

 protected double getScale()
 {
  return 0.5;
 }


 //recursively set the user data for objects in the scenegraph tree
 void recursiveSetUserData( SceneGraphObject root, Object value )
 {
  root.setUserData( value );

  //recursively process group
  if( root instanceof Group )
  {
   Group g = (Group) root;

   //recurse on child nodes
   java.util.Enumeration enumKids = g.getAllChildren();

   while( enumKids.hasMoreElements() != false )
    recursiveSetUserData( (SceneGraphObject)
      enumKids.nextElement(), value );
  }
 }

 protected void addCube( BranchGroup bg, double x, double y,
                         double z, double sx, double sy,
                         double sz, String name,
                         boolean wireframe )
 {
  //create four ColorCube objects
  TransformGroup cubeTg = new TransformGroup();
  Transform3D t3d = new Transform3D();
  t3d.setTranslation( new Vector3d( x, y, z ) );
  t3d.setScale( new Vector3d( sx, sy, sz ) );
  cubeTg.setTransform( t3d );
  ColorCube cube = new ColorCube( 1.0 );

  //we have to make the front face wireframe
  //we can't see inside the box!
  if ( wireframe )
  {
   Appearance app = new Appearance();
   app.setPolygonAttributes(
     new PolygonAttributes( PolygonAttributes.POLYGON_LINE,
                            PolygonAttributes.CULL_NONE, 0 ) );
   cube.setAppearance( app );
  }

  cubeTg.addChild( cube );
  recursiveSetUserData( cubeTg, name );

  bg.addChild( cubeTg );
 }
```

```
protected void addSphere( BranchGroup bg, double x,
                          double y, double z,
                          Vector3d incVector, String name )
{
 Appearance app = new Appearance();

 TransformGroup sphereTg = new TransformGroup();
 Transform3D t3d = new Transform3D();
 t3d.setTranslation( new Vector3d( x, y, z ) );
 sphereTg.setTransform( t3d );

 sphereTg.setCapability(TransformGroup.ALLOW_TRANSFORM_WRITE);
 sphereTg.setCapability(TransformGroup.ALLOW_TRANSFORM_READ);

 sphereTg.addChild( new Sphere( 1, app ) );
 bg.addChild( sphereTg );
 recursiveSetUserData( sphereTg, name );

 //create the collision behavior
 CollisionBehavior collisionBehavior =
  new CollisionBehavior( bg, sphereTg, app,
   new Vector3d( x,y,z ), incVector );
 collisionBehavior.setSchedulingBounds( getApplicationBounds() );
 bg.addChild( collisionBehavior );
}

protected BranchGroup createSceneBranchGroup()
{
 BranchGroup objRoot = super.createSceneBranchGroup();

 Bounds lightBounds = getApplicationBounds();

 AmbientLight ambLight =
   new AmbientLight( true, new Color3f(1.0f, 1.0f, 1.0f) );
 ambLight.setInfluencingBounds( lightBounds );
 objRoot.addChild( ambLight );

 DirectionalLight headLight = new DirectionalLight();
 headLight.setInfluencingBounds( lightBounds );
 objRoot.addChild( headLight );

 //create ColorCube objects, one for each side of a cube
 addCube( objRoot, 0,boxSize,0, boxSize,0.1,boxSize,
          "Top", false );
 addCube( objRoot, 0,-boxSize,0, boxSize,0.1,boxSize,
          "Bottom", false );
 addCube( objRoot, boxSize,0,0, 0.1,boxSize,boxSize,
          "Right", false );
 addCube( objRoot, -boxSize,0,0, 0.1,boxSize,boxSize,
          "Left", false );
 addCube( objRoot, 0,0,-boxSize, boxSize,boxSize,0.1,
          "Back", false );
 addCube( objRoot, 0,0,boxSize, boxSize,boxSize,0.1,
          "Front", true );
```

```java
    //create the spheres
    addSphere( objRoot, 0,3,4, new Vector3d( 0.1,0.3,0.1),
            "Sphere 1" );
    addSphere( objRoot, 3,0,-2, new Vector3d( 0.4,0.1,0.2),
            "Sphere 2" );
    addSphere( objRoot, 0,-3,0, new Vector3d( 0.2,0.2,0.6),
            "Sphere 3" );
    addSphere( objRoot, -3,0,-4, new Vector3d( 0.1,0.6,0.3),
            "Sphere 4" );

    return objRoot;
    }


  public static void main(String[] args)
  {
   PickCollisionTest pickCollisionTest = new PickCollisionTest();
   pickCollisionTest.saveCommandLineArguments( args );

   new MainFrame( pickCollisionTest, m_kWidth, m_kHeight );
  }
}


/*
 * This behavior detects collisions between the branch of a scene,
 * and a collision object. The Java 3D 1.2 picking utilities are used
 * to implement collision detection. The objects in the scene
 * that are collidable should have their user data set. The collision
 * object's user data is used to ignore collisions between the object
 * and itself.
 *
 * When a collision is detected the trajectory of the collision object
 * is reversed (plus a small random factor) and an Appearance object
 * is modified.
 *
 * When a collision is not detected the collision object is moved
 * along its current trajectory and the Appearance color is reset.
 *
 * Collision checking is run after every frame.
 */
class CollisionBehavior extends Behavior
{
 //the wake up condition for the behavior
 protected WakeupCondition m_WakeupCondition = null;

 //how often we check for a collision
 private static final int ELAPSED_FRAME_COUNT = 1;

 //the branch that we check for collisions
 private BranchGroup pickRoot = null;

 //the collision object that we are controlling
 private TransformGroup collisionObject = null;

 //the appearance object that we are controlling
```

```java
private Appearance objectAppearance = null;

//cached PickBounds object used for collision detection
private PickBounds pickBounds = null;

//cached Material objects that define the collided and
//missed colors
private Material collideMaterial = null;
private Material missMaterial = null;

//the current trajectory of the object
private Vector3d incrementVector = null;

//the current position of the object
private Vector3d positionVector = null;

public CollisionBehavior( BranchGroup pickRoot,
                          TransformGroup collisionObject,
                          Appearance app,
                          Vector3d posVector,
                          Vector3d incVector )
{
 //save references to the objects
 this.pickRoot = pickRoot;
 this.collisionObject = collisionObject;
 this.objectAppearance = app;

 incrementVector = incVector;
 positionVector = posVector;

 //create the WakeupCriterion for the behavior
 WakeupCriterion criterionArray[] = new WakeupCriterion[1];
 criterionArray[0] =
  new WakeupOnElapsedFrames( ELAPSED_FRAME_COUNT );

 objectAppearance.setCapability( Appearance.ALLOW_MATERIAL_WRITE );

 collisionObject.setCapability(
   TransformGroup.ALLOW_TRANSFORM_WRITE );
 collisionObject.setCapability( Node.ALLOW_BOUNDS_READ );

 //save the WakeupCriterion for the behavior
 m_WakeupCondition = new WakeupOr( criterionArray );
}

public void initialize()
{
 //apply the initial WakeupCriterion
 wakeupOn( m_WakeupCondition );

 Color3f objColor = new Color3f(1.0f, 0.1f, 0.2f);
 Color3f black = new Color3f(0.0f, 0.0f, 0.0f);
 collideMaterial  = new Material(objColor, black, objColor,
                                  black, 80.0f);

 objColor = new Color3f(0.0f, 0.1f, 0.8f);
 missMaterial  = new Material(objColor, black, objColor,
                                black, 80.0f);
```

```java
    objectAppearance.setMaterial( missMaterial );
  }

  protected void onCollide()
  {
    objectAppearance.setMaterial( collideMaterial );

    incrementVector.negate();

    //add a little randomness
    incrementVector.x += (Math.random() - 0.5) / 20.0;
    incrementVector.y += (Math.random() - 0.5) / 20.0;
    incrementVector.z += (Math.random() - 0.5) / 20.0;
  }
  protected void onMiss()
  {
    objectAppearance.setMaterial( missMaterial );
  }

  protected void moveCollisionObject()
  {
    Transform3D t3d = new Transform3D();

    positionVector.add (incrementVector );
    t3d.setTranslation( positionVector );

    collisionObject.setTransform( t3d );
  }

  public boolean isCollision( PickResult[] resultArray )
  {
    if( resultArray == null || resultArray.length == 0 )
      return false;
/*
 * We use the user data on the nodes to ignore the case
 * of the collisionObject having collided with itself!
 * The user data also gives us a good mechanism for reporting
 * the collisions.
 */
    for( int n = 0; n < resultArray.length; n++ )
    {
      Object userData = resultArray[n].getObject().getUserData();

      if ( userData != null && userData instanceof String )
      {
        //check that we are not colliding with ourselves...
        if ( ((String) userData).equals( (String)
          collisionObject.getUserData() ) == false )
        {
          System.out.println( "Collision between: " +
            collisionObject.getUserData() + " and: " + userData );
          return true;
        }
      }
    }
```

```
    return false;
}

public void processStimulus( java.util.Enumeration criteria )
{
 while( criteria.hasMoreElements() )
 {
  WakeupCriterion wakeUp = (WakeupCriterion)
    criteria.nextElement();

  //every N frames, check for a collision
  if( wakeUp instanceof WakeupOnElapsedFrames )
  {
   //create a PickBounds
   PickTool pickTool = new PickTool( pickRoot );
   pickTool.setMode( PickTool.BOUNDS );

   BoundingSphere bounds = (BoundingSphere)
     collisionObject.getBounds();
   pickBounds = new PickBounds(
    new BoundingSphere( new Point3d( positionVector.x,
                                     positionVector.y,
                                     positionVector.z ),
   bounds.getRadius() ) );
   pickTool.setShape( pickBounds, new Point3d( 0,0,0 ) );
   PickResult[] resultArray = pickTool.pickAll();

   if ( isCollision( resultArray ) )
    onCollide();
   else
    onMiss();

   moveCollisionObject();
  }
 }

 //assign the next WakeUpCondition, so we are notified again
  wakeupOn( m_WakeupCondition );
}
```

16.9 CONCLUSIONS

Java 3D includes fairly good high-level support for user interaction through the extensive picking API. For fairly simple applications, the picking API also provides a basis for simple collision detection. For more complex applications, or applications that require the simulation-level accuracy, a dedicated collision detection library should be investigated. There are a number of commercial collision detection libraries that have been used with Java 3D. Please refer to the Java 3D interest email list for the latest references.

C H A P T E R   1 7

Java 3D, Swing, and applets

We have reached the point where we can build a complete Java 3D application that integrates Swing for the 2D interface components and Java 3D for a 3D rendering window.

In addition, we will attempt to deploy the application as an applet using the Java 2 SDK plug-in. This is an ambitious and challenging deployment environment, but improvements in the runtime installation of Java 2 and the Java 2 plug-in are making this an increasingly viable possibility. Java WebStart represents an exciting development in this area, which may make one-click distribution, installation, and launch of Java 2-based applications a reality. A high level overview of the SwingTest example is presented along with extensive source code annotations. Please refer to http://java.sun.com/products/javawebstart/ for Java WebStart documentation.

17.1 BUILDING THE JAVA 3D SWING APPLICATION

Rather than embarking on a theoretical HelloUniverse-type example using Swing, we will dive straight in and start building a much more realistic Java 3D application. The application (SwingTest) has the following features:

- It uses Swing components, including a JmenuBar-based menu system, for the UI.
- The Java 3D scene is modified at runtime through the UI.

- The Java 3D scenegraph, used for rendering, is built from scratch rather than using the `SimpleUniverse` utility class.
- It uses Java 3D 1.2 off-screen rendering support to render frames into an image.
- It saves the captured images to disk in JPEG format.
- It supports running as an applet.

The Java 3D demo applications from Sun used the `SimpleUniverse` utility class to build the scenegraph for the applications. `SwingTest` will build the whole scenegraph from scratch, so you can relate the various classes to each other and how they are combined to produce screen output (figure 17.1). The `SimpleUniverse` class is useful for quick Java 3D prototypes; however, it hides many of the interesting and powerful features of Java 3D's view model.

The code in this example is all in one class, `SwingTest`, which is actually a Swing `JPanel`. This is the approach that has been taken for much of the example code, but you should not emulate it for your applications. You should aim to break your application's functionality into far more discrete pieces, pushing the functionality down the class hierarchy as much as possible. Other examples use utility classes defined in the `org.selman.java3d.book` package, which you should be able to reuse in building your applications. This example does not rely on any external library code, so you can see the entire application and how all the pieces relate to one another.

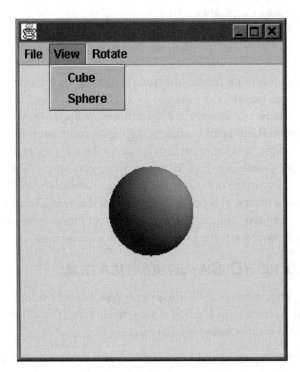

Figure 17.1
The `SwingTest` example running as an application. Combines Swing, Java 3D, dynamic scenegraph modifications, and off-screen rendering

```
//These are the fairly standard imports that we will be using
//for many of the examples in the book. The "core" Java 3D code
//resides in the javax.media.j3d package.
import java.applet.Applet;
import java.awt.*;
import java.awt.event.*;
import java.awt.image.*;
import java.io.*;

import javax.media.j3d.*;
import javax.vecmath.*;
import javax.swing.*;

import com.sun.image.codec.jpeg.*;

/*
 * The SwingTest class extends the Swing JPanel and
 * can therefore be added to a Swing JFrame or JPanel as a component
 * of the user interface. The SwingTest class contains the 3D display,
 * and responds to Swing user interface events by implementing
 * the ActionListener interface. The main entry point for the
 * application creates the JFrame that will house the SwingTest JPanel
 * as well as the JmenuBar, which will generate the User Interface
 * events.
 */
public class SwingTest extends JPanel implements ActionListener
{
 /*
  * Java 3D applications describe a 3D scene to the rendering system
  * that produces the rendered frames. The 3D scene description
  * is added to a tree (directed-acyclic-graph) data structure
  * called a scenegraph. The scenegraph tree has two major branches:
  * the scene branch describes the objects and lights in the scene
  * as well as any behaviors that act upon the scene. The view branch
  * of the scenegraph describes the viewer of the scene, including
  * their position, screen device, and viewing parameters.
  *
  * SwingTest needs to modify the objects on the scene side
  * of the scenegraph at runtime, so we keep a reference to it in the
  * sceneBranchGroup member variable below.
  */
 private BranchGroup    sceneBranchGroup = null;

 /*
  * SwingTest rotates the objects in the scene using a
  * RotationInterpolator behavior that will automatically modify
  * the rotation components of a 4 × 4 transformation matrix.
  * Objects that are attached to the transformation matrix object
  * (TransformGroup) will therefore be automatically rotated.
  */
 private RotationInterpolator  rotator = null;
```

```
/* Java 3D will render the scene into a Canvas3D component.
 * To perform frame captures and save the frames to disk, we keep
 * a reference to an offscreen (nonvisible) Canvas3D component that
 * can be explicitly called to render individual frames.
 */
private Canvas3D      offScreenCanvas3D = null;

/*
 * The image that is attached to the off-screen Canvas3D and
 * contains the results of screen captures
 */
private ImageComponent2D   imageComponent = null;

//The width of the offscreen Canvas3D
private static final int  offScreenWidth = 400;

//The height of the offscreen Canvas3D
private static final int  offScreenHeight = 400;

//Constructor.
//Set the layout algorithm for the panel and initialize Java 3D
//and the scene.
public SwingTest()
{
 setLayout( new BorderLayout() );
 init();
}

//The init method does all of the work of setting up and
//populating the scenegraph.
protected void init()
{
 /*
  * Every Java 3D application has an instance of a class derived from
  * VirtualUniverse. The VirtualUniverse class contains a number of
  * Locales objects, each of which describes a discrete region
  * within the scene, and has its own coordinate system. By deriving
  * your own class from VirtualUniverse you can define utility methods
  * or additional datastructures for your application.
  */
 VirtualUniverse universe = createVirtualUniverse();

/*
 * A Locale object allows a coordinate system to be specified
 * for a region within the scene. By having multiple Locales
 * in your scene you can have multiple levels of detail without
 * losing coordinate precision due to rounding errors.
 */
 Locale locale = createLocale( universe );

/*
 * A BranchGroup is a branch of the scenegraph tree. A BranchGroup
 * has a single parent Node and can have multiple child Nodes. The
 * sceneBranchGroup created below contains the graphical objects,
 * lights, and behaviors that will compose the rendered scene.
```

```
      */
      BranchGroup sceneBranchGroup = createSceneBranchGroup();

      /*
       * A Background Node allows you to specify a colored background,
       * background image, or background geometry for your application.
       * In this example we simply create a light-gray background color and
       * add it to the scene side of the scenegraph. Java 3D will
       * automatically detect that it is a Background Node and
       * paint the background color into the Canvas3D prior to rendering
       * the scene geometry.
       */
      Background background = createBackground();

      if( background != null )
       sceneBranchGroup.addChild( background );

      /*
       * We must now define the view side of the scenegraph. First
       * we create a ViewPlatform. The ViewPlatform defines a location
       * in the scene from which the scene can be viewed. The scene
       * can contain multiple ViewPlatforms, and View objects can be moved
       * between them at runtime.
       */
      ViewPlatform vp = createViewPlatform();

      /*
       * To contain the ViewPlatform we create a scenegraph branch.
       * We create a BranchGroup that is the top of the view branch.
       * Underneath it we create a series of TransformGroup, and then
       * finally we attach the ViewPlatform to the lowest TransformGroup.
       * The TransformGroups (which contain a 4 × 4 transformation matrix)
       * allow the ViewPlatform to be rotate, scaled, and translated within
       * the scene.
       */
      BranchGroup viewBranchGroup =
       createViewBranchGroup( getViewTransformGroupArray(), vp );

      //We then have to add the scene branch to the Locale
      //we added previously to the VirtualUniverse.
      locale.addBranchGraph( sceneBranchGroup );

      //Add the view branch to the Locale
      addViewBranchGroup( locale, viewBranchGroup );

      /*
       * Finally, create the View object and attach it to
       * the ViewPlatform. The View object has an associated
       * PhysicalEnvironment and PhysicalBody that defines the
       * characteristics of the viewer and their display hardware.
       * A Canvas3D rendering component is attached to the View which
       * is used to display the frames rendered.
       */
      createView( vp );
   }
```

```
/*
 * Callback to allow the Canvas3D to be added to a Panel. This method
 * is called by createView and allows the Canvas3D to be added to its
 * parent GUI components, in this can as SwingTest is extends JPanel we
 * can just add it directly to SwingTest.
 */
protected void addCanvas3D( Canvas3D c3d )
{
 add( "Center", c3d );
}

 //Helper method to create a Java 3D View and
 //attach it to a ViewPlatform .
protected View createView( ViewPlatform vp )
{
 View view = new View();

 //We create a default PhysicalBody and PhysicalEnvironment and
 //associate them with the View.
 PhysicalBody pb = createPhysicalBody();
 PhysicalEnvironment pe = createPhysicalEnvironment();

 view.setPhysicalEnvironment( pe );
 view.setPhysicalBody( pb );

 //Add the View to the ViewPlatform
 if( vp != null )
  view.attachViewPlatform( vp );

 /*
  * Set the locations of the clipping planes for the View.
  * Java 3D uses a finite number of bits (in a depth-buffer) to
  * track the relative distances of objects from the viewer.
  * These depth-buffer bits are used to track objects between
  * the front clipping plane and the rear clipping plane. Only objects
  * that fall between the two clipping planes will be rendered. As the
  * depth-buffer bits have a finite length (usually 16 or 24 bits)
  * the ratio between the front clipping plane and the rear clipping
  * plane should be less than about 1000, or the depth-buffer will be
  * very coarsely quantized and accuracy will be lost. In this example
  * we use 1.0 for the front clipping plane and 100.0 for the rear
  * clipping plane.
  */
 view.setBackClipDistance( getBackClipDistance() );
 view.setFrontClipDistance( getFrontClipDistance() );

 //Create the Canvas3D used to display the rendered scene
 Canvas3D c3d = createCanvas3D( false );

 //Add the Canvas3D to the View so that the View has a component
 //to render into.
 view.addCanvas3D( c3d );

 //Here we create and add on the offscreen Canvas3D instance
 //that we use for screen captures.
```

```
view.addCanvas3D( createOffscreenCanvas3D() );

//Finally, invoke the addCanvas3D callback method that will add
//the visible Canvas3D to a GUI component (JPanel)
addCanvas3D( c3d );

return view;
}

/Simple utility method to create a solid colored background for
//the Canvas3D.
protected Background createBackground()
{
 //We create a color by specifying the Red, Green, and Blue
 //components, in this case a light gray.
 Background back = new Background(
  new Color3f( 0.9f, 0.9f, 0.9f ) );

 //We need to set the volume within the scene within which the
 //Background is active
 back.setApplicationBounds( createApplicationBounds() );
 return back;
}

/*
 * Simple utility method that returns a bounding volume
 * for the application. In this case we create a spherical volume,
 * centered at 0,0,0 and with a radius of 100.
 */
protected Bounds createApplicationBounds()
{
 return new BoundingSphere(new Point3d(0.0,0.0,0.0), 100.0);
}

//Utility method to create a Canvas3D GUI component. The Canvas3D
//is used by Java 3D to output rendered frames.
protected Canvas3D createCanvas3D( boolean offscreen )
{
 /*
  * First we query Java 3D for the available device information.
  * We set up a GraphicsConfigTemplate3D and specify that we would
  * prefer a device configuration that supports antialiased output.
  */
 GraphicsConfigTemplate3D gc3D = new GraphicsConfigTemplate3D();
 gc3D.setSceneAntialiasing( GraphicsConfigTemplate.PREFERRED );

 //We then get a list of all the screen devices for the
 //local graphics environment
 GraphicsDevice gd[] = GraphicsEnvironment.
                       getLocalGraphicsEnvironment().
                        getScreenDevices();

 //We select the best configuration supported by the first screen
 //device, and specify whether we are creating an onscreen or
 //an offscreen Canvas3D.
```

```
Canvas3D c3d = new Canvas3D( gd[0].getBestConfiguration(
  gc3D ), offscreen );

/*
 * Here we have hard-coded the initial size of the Canvas3D.
 * However, because we have used a BorderLayout layout algorithm,
 * this will be automatically resized to fit—as the parent JFrame
 * is resized.
 */
c3d.setSize( 500, 500 );

return c3d;
}

//Callback to get the scale factor for the View side of the
//scenegraph
protected double getScale()
{
 return 3;
}

/*
 * Get a TransformGroup array for the View side of the scenegraph.
 * We create a single TransformGroup (which wraps a 4 × 4 transformation
 * matrix) and modify the transformation matrix to apply a scale to
 * the view of the scene, as well as move the ViewPlatform back
 * by 20 meters so that we can see the origin (0,0,0). The objects
 * that we create in the scene will be centered at the origin, so if
 * we are going to be able to see them, we need to move the
 * ViewPlatform backward.
 */
public TransformGroup[] getViewTransformGroupArray()
{
 TransformGroup[] tgArray = new TransformGroup[1];
 tgArray[0] = new TransformGroup();

/*
 * Here we move the camera BACK a little so that we can see
 * the origin (0,0,0). Note that we have to invert the matrix as
 * we are moving the viewer not the scene.
 */
 Transform3D t3d = new Transform3D();
 t3d.setScale( getScale() );
 t3d.setTranslation( new Vector3d( 0.0, 0.0, -20.0 ) );
 t3d.invert();
 tgArray[0].setTransform( t3d );

 return tgArray;
}

//Simple utility method that adds the View side of the scenegraph
//to the Locale
protected void addViewBranchGroup( Locale locale, BranchGroup bg )
{
 locale.addBranchGraph( bg );
```

```java
}

//Simple utility method that creates a Locale for the
//VirtualUniverse
protected Locale createLocale( VirtualUniverse u )
{
 return new Locale( u );
}

//Create the PhysicalBody for the View. We just use a default
//PhysicalBody.
protected PhysicalBody createPhysicalBody()
{
 return new PhysicalBody();
}

//Create the PhysicalEnvironment for the View. We just use a
//default PhysicalEnvironment.
protected PhysicalEnvironment createPhysicalEnvironment()
{
 return new PhysicalEnvironment();
}

//Return the View Platform Activation Radius.
protected float getViewPlatformActivationRadius()
{
 return 100;
}

//Create the View Platform for the View.
protected ViewPlatform createViewPlatform()
{
 ViewPlatform vp = new ViewPlatform();
 vp.setViewAttachPolicy( View.RELATIVE_TO_FIELD_OF_VIEW );
 vp.setActivationRadius( getViewPlatformActivationRadius() );

 return vp;
}

//Return the distance to the rear clipping plane.
protected double getBackClipDistance()
{
 return 100.0;
}

//Return the distance to the near clipping plane.
protected double getFrontClipDistance()
{
 return 1.0;
}

//Create the View side BranchGroup. The ViewPlatform is wired in
//beneath the TransformGroups.
protected BranchGroup createViewBranchGroup(
 TransformGroup[] tgArray, ViewPlatform vp )
```

```
{
 BranchGroup vpBranchGroup = new BranchGroup();

 if( tgArray != null && tgArray.length > 0 )
 {
  Group parentGroup = vpBranchGroup;
  TransformGroup curTg = null;

  for( int n = 0; n < tgArray.length; n++ )
  {
   curTg = tgArray[n];
   parentGroup.addChild( curTg );
   parentGroup = curTg;
  }

  tgArray[tgArray.length-1].addChild( vp );
 }
 else
  vpBranchGroup.addChild( vp );

 return vpBranchGroup;
}

//Create the VirtualUniverse for the application.
protected VirtualUniverse createVirtualUniverse()
{
 return new VirtualUniverse();
}

//Utility method that performs some additional initialization
//for an offscreen Canvas3D.
protected Canvas3D createOffscreenCanvas3D()
{
 //First we create a Canvas3D and specify that it is to be used
 //for offscreen rendering.
 offScreenCanvas3D = createCanvas3D( true );

 //We then need to explicitly set the size of the off screen
 //Canvas3D.
 offScreenCanvas3D.getScreen3D().setSize( offScreenWidth,
                                          offScreenHeight );

 //This calculation returns the physical size of the screen and
 //is based on 90 display pixels per inch
 offScreenCanvas3D.getScreen3D().
  setPhysicalScreenHeight( 0.0254/90 * offScreenHeight );
 offScreenCanvas3D.getScreen3D().
  setPhysicalScreenWidth( 0.0254/90 * offScreenWidth );

 //We then create an AWT RenderedImage that the Canvas3D will
 //render into. We create a simple 3 Byte RGB format image.
 RenderedImage renderedImage =
  new BufferedImage( offScreenWidth, offScreenHeight,
                     BufferedImage.TYPE_3BYTE_BGR );

 //The AWT RenderedImage needs to be wrapped in a Java 3D
```

```
//ImageComponent2D before it can be assigned to the
//Canvas3D for rendering
imageComponent =
 new ImageComponent2D( ImageComponent.FORMAT_RGB8,
                         renderedImage );

//This call notifies Java 3D that we require read-access to the
//ImageComponent2D. We will be reading the pixels in the image
//when we output it to disk.
imageComponent.setCapability( ImageComponent2D.ALLOW_IMAGE_READ );

//Finally, we assign the ImageComponent2D to the offscreen
//Canvas3D for rendering
offScreenCanvas3D.setOffScreenBuffer( imageComponent );

return offScreenCanvas3D;
}

//Create the scene side of the scenegraph. This method does
//all the work of creating the scene branch—containing graphical
//objects, lights, and rotation behaviors to rotate the objects.
protected BranchGroup createSceneBranchGroup()
{
 //First we create the root of the scene side scenegraph. We will
 //add other Nodes as children of this root BranchGroup.
 BranchGroup objRoot = new BranchGroup();

/*
 * Create a TransformGroup to rotate the objects in the scene
 * and set the capability bits on the TransformGroup so that
 * it can be modified at runtime by the rotation behavior.
 */
TransformGroup objTrans = new TransformGroup();
objTrans.setCapability(TransformGroup.ALLOW_TRANSFORM_WRITE);
objTrans.setCapability(TransformGroup.ALLOW_TRANSFORM_READ);

//Create a spherical bounding volume that will define the volume
//within which the rotation behavior is active.
BoundingSphere bounds = new BoundingSphere(
                          new Point3d(0.0,0.0,0.0), 100.0);

//Create a 4 × 4 transformation matrix
Transform3D yAxis = new Transform3D();

/*
 * Create an Alpha interpolator to automatically generate
 * modifications to the rotation component of the transformation
 * matrix. This Alpha loops indefinitely and generates numbers
 * from 0 to 1 every 4000 milliseconds.
 */
Alpha rotationAlpha = new Alpha(-1, Alpha.INCREASING_ENABLE,
 0, 0,
 4000, 0, 0,
 0, 0, 0);

/*
```

```
 * Create a RotationInterpolator behavior to effect the
 * TransformGroup. Here we will rotate from 0 to 2π degrees about
 * the Y-axis based on the output of rotationAlpha.
 */
rotator = new RotationInterpolator( rotationAlpha,
                                    objTrans, yAxis, 0.0f,
                                    (float) Math.PI*2.0f );

//Set the scheduling bounds on the behavior. This defines the
//volume within which this behavior will be active.
rotator.setSchedulingBounds( bounds );

//Add the behavior to the scenegraph so that Java 3D
//can schedule it for activation.
objTrans.addChild(rotator);

/*
 * Create the BranchGroup which contains the objects we add/remove
 * to and from the scenegraph. We store a reference to this subbranch
 * of the scene side of the scenegraph in a member variable
 * as we need to modify the contents of the branch at runtime.
 */
sceneBranchGroup = new BranchGroup();

//Allow the BranchGroup to have children added and removed
//at runtime
sceneBranchGroup.setCapability( Group.ALLOW_CHILDREN_EXTEND );
sceneBranchGroup.setCapability( Group.ALLOW_CHILDREN_READ );
sceneBranchGroup.setCapability( Group.ALLOW_CHILDREN_WRITE );

//Add the subbranches for both the cube and the sphere to
//the BranchGroup
sceneBranchGroup.addChild( createCube() );
sceneBranchGroup.addChild( createSphere() );

//Create the colors for the lights
Color3f lColor1 = new Color3f( 0.7f,0.7f,0.7f );
Vector3f lDir1  = new Vector3f( -1.0f,-1.0f,-1.0f );
Color3f alColor = new Color3f( 0.2f,0.2f,0.2f );

//Create an ambient light
AmbientLight aLgt = new AmbientLight( alColor );
aLgt.setInfluencingBounds( bounds );

//Create a directional light
DirectionalLight lgt1 = new DirectionalLight( lColor1, lDir1 );
lgt1.setInfluencingBounds( bounds );

//Add the lights to the scenegraph
objRoot.addChild(aLgt);
objRoot.addChild(lgt1);

/*
 * Wire the scenegraph together. It is useful to do this
 * in the reverse order that the branches were created—
 * rather like closing parentheses, that way you will not forget
```

```
 * to add a child branch to its parent. If you forget to add a branch
 * that you have created and populated then it will just not
 * show up in the scene!
 */
objTrans.addChild( sceneBranchGroup );
objRoot.addChild( objTrans );

//Return the root of the scene side of the scenegraph
return objRoot;
}

/*
 * Create a BranchGroup that contains a Cube. The User Data
 * for the BranchGroup is set so the BranchGroup can be
 * identified later. User Data is a field that you can set
 * on all Nodes in the scenegraph to allow you to associate
 * your own data with particular scenegraph elements. The Cube
 * must wrapped in a BranchGroup as only BranchGroups can be
 * added and removed from the scenegraph at runtime—
 * not Shape3Ds themselves which describe the geometry.
 */
protected BranchGroup createCube()
{
//Create a parent BranchGroup for the Cube
BranchGroup bg = new BranchGroup();

//Tell Java 3D that we need the ability to detach this BranchGroup
//from its parent Node.
bg.setCapability( BranchGroup.ALLOW_DETACH );

//Add a Shape3D (geometry) Node to the BranchGroup
bg.addChild( new com.sun.j3d.utils.geometry.ColorCube() );

//Set the User Data on the BranchGroup so that we can easily
//identify this BranchGroup later, when we need to remove it.
bg.setUserData( "Cube" );
return bg;
}

//Create a BranchGroup that contains a Sphere. The user data for
//the BranchGroup is set so the BranchGroup can be identified.
protected BranchGroup createSphere()
{
BranchGroup bg = new BranchGroup();

//Tell Java 3D that we need the ability to detach this BranchGroup
//from its parent Node.
bg.setCapability( BranchGroup.ALLOW_DETACH );

//So that the Sphere is nicely shaded and responds to the lights
//in the scene, we create an Appearance with a Material
//for the Sphere.
Appearance app = new Appearance();
Color3f objColor = new Color3f(1.0f, 0.7f, 0.8f);
Color3f black = new Color3f(0.0f, 0.0f, 0.0f);
```

```java
app.setMaterial(new Material(objColor, black, objColor, black, 80.0f));

//Create the Sphere and assign the Appearance.
bg.addChild( new com.sun.j3d.utils.geometry.Sphere( 1, app ) );

//Set the User Data on the BranchGroup so that we can easily
//identify this BranchGroup later, when we need to remove it.
bg.setUserData( "Sphere" );
return bg;
}

//Remove a BranchGroup from the scene based on the User Data.
//This allows us to dynamically remove the "Cube" or "Sphere"
//BranchGroups at runtime.
protected void removeShape( String name )
{
 try
 {
  //First we get all the child Nodes from the parent of the Cube
  //and/or Sphere BranchGroups
  java.util.Enumeration enum = sceneBranchGroup.getAllChildren();
  int index = 0;

  //We then need to iterate through the Nodes to find the one with
  //the User Data that we would like to remove
  while ( enum.hasMoreElements() != false )
  {
   SceneGraphObject sgObject = (SceneGraphObject)
    enum.nextElement();

   //Get the User Data for the ScenegraphObject
   Object userData = sgObject.getUserData();

   //Compare the current ScenegraphObject's User Data with
   //what we are looking for, if they match then we can remove
   //the BranchGroup.
   if ( userData instanceof String &&
    ((String) userData).compareTo( name ) == 0 )
   {
    System.out.println( "Removing: " + sgObject.getUserData() );
    sceneBranchGroup.removeChild( index );
   }

   index++;
  }
 }
 catch( Exception e )
 {
  /*
   * The scenegraph may not have yet been synchronized. It is possible
   * for an exception to be thrown here as the removing a BranchGroup
   * is not instantaneous.
   */
 }
}
```

```
//Called to render the scene into the offscreen Canvas3D and
//save the image (as a JPEG) to disk.
protected void onSaveImage()
{
 offScreenCanvas3D.renderOffScreenBuffer();
 offScreenCanvas3D.waitForOffScreenRendering();
 System.out.println( "Rendered to offscreen" );

 try
 {
  FileOutputStream fileOut = new FileOutputStream( "image.jpg" );

  JPEGImageEncoder encoder =
   JPEGCodec.createJPEGEncoder( fileOut );
  encoder.encode( imageComponent.getImage() );

  fileOut.flush();
  fileOut.close();
 }
 catch( Exception e )
 {
  System.err.println( "Failed to save image: " + e );
 }

 System.out.println( "Saved image." );
}

/*
 * AWT callback to indicate that an items has been selected
 * from a menu. This is not the way to implement menu handling
 * for a large application (!) but it serves for our simple example.
 */
public void actionPerformed( ActionEvent ae )
{
 System.out.
  println( "Action Performed: " + ae.getActionCommand() );

 java.util.StringTokenizer toker =
  new java.util.StringTokenizer( ae.getActionCommand(), "|" );

 String menu = toker.nextToken();
 String command = toker.nextToken();

 if ( menu.equals( "File" ) )
 {
  if ( command.equals( "Exit" ) )
  {
   System.exit( 0 );
  }
  else if ( command.equals( "Save Image" )  )
  {
   onSaveImage();
  }
 }
```

```java
else if ( menu.equals( "View" ) )
{
 if ( command.equals( "Cube" ) )
 {
  removeShape( "Sphere" );
  sceneBranchGroup.addChild( createCube() );
 }
 else if ( command.equals( "Sphere" ) )
 {
  removeShape( "Cube" );
  sceneBranchGroup.addChild( createSphere() );
 }
}
else if ( menu.equals( "Rotate" ) )
{
 if ( command.equals( "On" ) )
 {
  rotator.setEnable( true );
 }
 else if ( command.equals( "Off" ) )
 {
  rotator.setEnable( false );
 }
}
}

//Helper method to creates a Swing JmenuItem and set the action
//command to something we can distinguish while handling menu events.
private JMenuItem createMenuItem( String menuText,
                                  String buttonText,
                                  ActionListener listener )
{
 JMenuItem menuItem = new JMenuItem( buttonText );
 menuItem.addActionListener( listener );
 menuItem.setActionCommand( menuText + "|" + buttonText );
 return menuItem;
}

/*
 * Registers a window listener to handle ALT+F4 window closing.
 * Otherwise the Swing application will just be made invisible when
 * the parent frame is closed.
 */
static protected void registerWindowListener( JFrame frame )
{
 //Disable automatic close support for Swing frame.
 frame.
  setDefaultCloseOperation( WindowConstants.DO_NOTHING_ON_CLOSE );

 //Add the window listener
 frame.addWindowListener(
  new WindowAdapter()
  {
```

```java
    //Handles the system exit window message
    public void windowClosing( WindowEvent e )
    {
     System.exit( 1 );
    }
   }
  );
}

/*
 * Main entry point for the application. Creates the parent JFrame,
 * the JMenuBar and creates the JPanel which is the application
 * itself.
 */
public static void main( String[] args )
{
 /*
  * Tell Swing that we need Popup Menus to be heavyweight. The Java 3D
  * window is a heavyweight window - that is, the window is a native
  * window, and therefore any windows that must overlap it must also be
  * native. Our menu items will be dropped down in front of the
  * Java 3D Canvas3D so they must be created as heavyweight windows.
  */
JPopupMenu.setDefaultLightWeightPopupEnabled( false );

  /*
   * Similarly we can declare that ToolTip windows are created
   * as heavyweight. Our application does not use tooltips. However,
   * if a toolbar was added the tooltips would overlap the Canvas3D
   * and would also need to be heavyweight windows.
   */
ToolTipManager ttm = ToolTipManager.sharedInstance();
ttm.setLightWeightPopupEnabled( false );

//Create the outermost frame for the application
JFrame frame = new JFrame();
//Create the application JPanel, which contains the Canvas3D
//with the 3D view.
SwingTest swingTest = new SwingTest();

/*
 * Create a JMenuBar that will generate the events for the
 * application. We register the swingTest instance as a listener
 * for the action events generated by the menu items.
 */
JMenuBar menuBar = new JMenuBar();
JMenu menu = null;

//Create some menu items and add them to the JMenuBar
menu = new JMenu( "File" );
menu.add(
 swingTest.createMenuItem( "File", "Save Image", swingTest ) );
menu.add(
 swingTest.createMenuItem( "File", "Exit", swingTest ) );
```

```
        menuBar.add( menu );

        menu = new JMenu( "View" );
        menu.add(
         swingTest.createMenuItem( "View", "Cube", swingTest ) );
        menu.add(
         swingTest.createMenuItem( "View", "Sphere", swingTest ) );
        menuBar.add( menu );

        menu = new JMenu( "Rotate" );
        menu.add(
         swingTest.createMenuItem( "Rotate", "On", swingTest ) );
        menu.add(
         swingTest.createMenuItem( "Rotate", "Off", swingTest ) );
        menuBar.add( menu );

        //Assign the JMenuBar to the parent frame.
        frame.setJMenuBar( menuBar );

        //Add the SwingTest JPanel to the parent frame.
        frame.getContentPane().add( swingTest );

        //Set the initial size of the parent frame
        frame.setSize( 550, 550 );

        //Register a window listener to intercept the closing
        //of the parent frame.
        registerWindowListener( frame );

        //Finally, make the parent frame visible!
        frame.setVisible( true );
    }
}
```

17.2   ADDING SUPPORT FOR RUNNING AS AN APPLET

If you are running a flavor of Windows and you navigate to a web page that contains a Java applet (e.g., figure 17.2), the Java applet will be launched using the web browser's JVM. On a Windows machine, this will be the Microsoft VM, which does not implement the Java 2 (SDK 1.2) release of the J2SE platform. Your applets based on Java 2 will therefore not be started by the Microsoft VM.

As the relationship between Sun and Microsoft has been a little frosty of late, it is unlikely that Sun can negotiate with Microsoft to get its JVM shipped with new installations of Windows. This has forced Sun to develop the Java plug-in product. The Java plug-in is a web-browser plug-in that installs on a Windows machine and can download the Java 2 JRE and launch a Java 2 JVM capable of running Java 2 applications.

Because web-browser plug-ins can be installed with little user intervention by the web browser, the idea is that the installation and launch of the plug-in should be made as simple as possible.

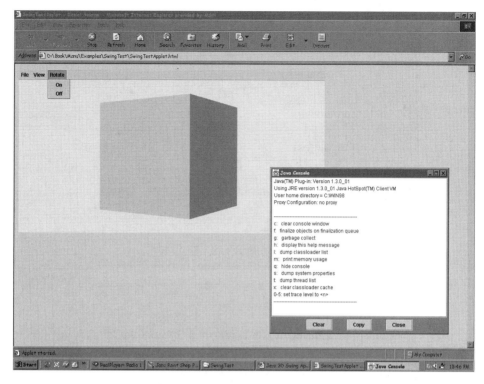

Figure 17.2 The `SwingTest` example running as an applet inside Internet Explorer.
Note Java 2 plug-in Swing console and the Duke icon in the system tray

17.2.1 Original HTML applet code

For example, when you are developing your applet you might have an HTML page
like that shown in figure 17.3 to launch it. This HTML page would work fine with
Sun's Java 2 applet viewer utility.

```html
<html>
  <head>
      <title>SwingTestApplet - Daniel Selman</title>
  </head>
  <body>

<APPLET  CODE = SwingTestApplet WIDTH = 760 HEIGHT = 390 >
<PARAM NAME = ARCHIVE VALUE  = SwingTest.jar>

<!--"UNUSED PARAMETERS..."-->
<PARAM NAME = "IMAGE_WIDTH" VALUE  = "256">
<PARAM NAME = "IMAGE_HEIGHT" VALUE  = "256">

</APPLET>

</body>
</html>
```

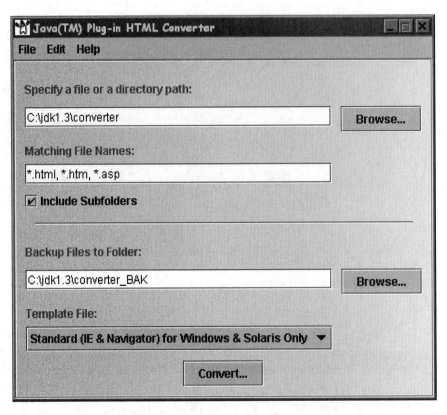

Figure 17.3 Running the `HTMLConverter`. Note the template file option allows you to tailor your converted files to particular operating systems or browsers

17.2.2   Using the Java 2 plug-in HTMLConverter

To get the same applet to run with Internet Explorer or Netscape, your HTML page must first be converted to use the Java 2 plug-in. The HTML conversion process will take your original `<APPLET>` tags and wrap them in a web-browser plug-in `<OBJECT>` tag. The original `<APPLET>` parameters will be passed to the plug-in instead of invoked directly on the applet.

At the time of writing the latest version of the plug-in is: Java 2 SDK, Standard Edition (J2SE), Version 1.3.0_01 which also supports Netscape 6.0.

The limitations of the plug-in tend to change quite quickly, here are some references:

- http://java.sun.com/products/plugin/
- http://java.sun.com/products/plugin/1.3/docs/tags.html
- http://java.sun.com/products/plugin/1.3/converter.html

After you have installed the plug-in, you can invoke the HTML converter application and supply your original HTML file.

The output from the conversion process will produce a file similar to the following:

```html
<html>
  <head>
     <title>SwingTestApplet - Daniel Selman</title>
  </head>
  <body>

<!--"CONVERTED_APPLET"-->
<!-- HTML CONVERTER -->
<OBJECT classid="clsid:E19F9330-3110-11d4-991C-005004D3B3DB"
WIDTH = 760 HEIGHT = 390  codebase="http://java.sun.com/products/plugin/
1.3.0_
 01/jinstall-130_01-win32.cab#Version=1,3,0,1">
<PARAM NAME = CODE VALUE = SwingTestApplet >

<PARAM NAME="type"
 VALUE="application/x-java-applet;jpi-version=1.3.0_01">
<PARAM NAME="scriptable" VALUE="false">
<PARAM NAME = ARCHIVE VALUE   = SwingTest.jar>
<PARAM NAME = "IMAGE_WIDTH" VALUE   = "256">
<PARAM NAME = "IMAGE_HEIGHT" VALUE   = "256">
<COMMENT>
<EMBED type="application/x-java-applet;jpi-version=1.3.0_01"  CODE = Swing-
TestApplet WIDTH = 760 HEIGHT = 390 ARCHIVE =  SwingTest.jar IMAGE_WIDTH =
"256" IMAGE_HEIGHT =  "256"  scriptable=false pluginspage="http://
java.sun.com/products/plugin/1.3.0_01/plugin-install.html"><NOEMBED>
<!--"UNUSED PARAMETERS..."-->
</NOEMBED>
</EMBED>
</COMMENT>
</OBJECT>

<!--
<APPLET CODE = SwingTestApplet WIDTH = 760 HEIGHT = 390>
<PARAM NAME = ARCHIVE VALUE   = SwingTest.jar>
<PARAM NAME = "IMAGE_WIDTH" VALUE   = "256">
<PARAM NAME = "IMAGE_HEIGHT" VALUE   = "256">
<!--"UNUSED PARAMETERS..."-->
</APPLET>
-->

<!--"END_CONVERTED_APPLET"-->

</body>
</html>
```

17.2.3 The end-user experience

When a user with a virgin machine hits your web page, the following sequence of steps will occur:

1 User prompted to install the correct version of the Java plug-in (figure 17.4).

2 User accepts and the plug-in installation process begins (figure 17.5).

3 Plug-in is installed and can be configured through the Windows Control Panel (figure 17.6).

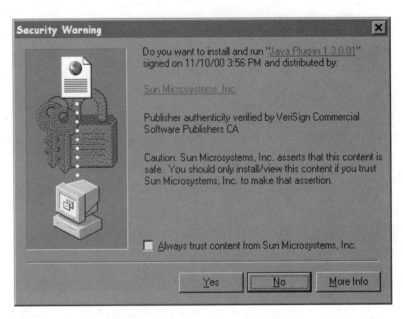

Figure 17.4 If the end user requires a newer JRE the Java plug-in installation will be activated

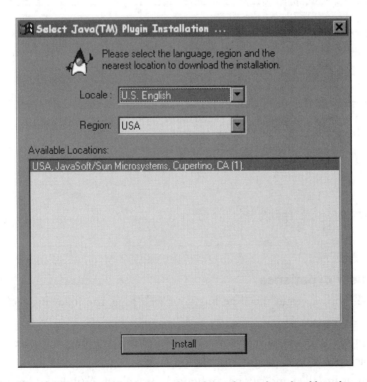

Figure 17.5 The end user is prompted to select a download location and begin the download and installation process

CHAPTER 17   JAVA 3D, SWING, AND APPLETS

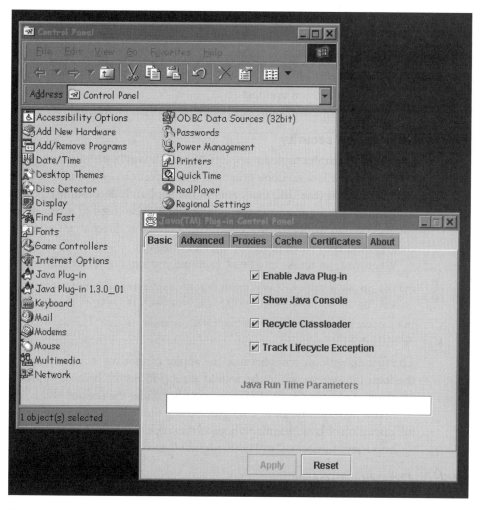

Figure 17.6   After installation the Java 2 plug-in icon will be available in the Windows Control Panel

17.2.4   Automatic Java 3D installation

At the time of this writing it was not possible to confirm that Java 3D could be automatically installed by the Java 2 plug-in. Sun claims that this will work, but I experienced a number of problems running on Windows 98, which prevented me from verifying this.

It *should* be possible to create a Java 3D applet that would install the Java 2 SDK, then install Java 3D and the Java 3D applet or application into the Java 2 extension directory and finally run the applet.

There are a number of useful articles on Sun's web sites covering the Java 2 extension mechanism:

- Tutorial on the Java 2 extensions mechanism:
  http://java.sun.com/docs/books/tutorial/ext/index.html
- Java 2 SDK extensions documentation:
  http://java.sun.com/products/jdk/1.2/docs/guide/extensions/
- JAR file extension options:
  http://java.sun.com/docs/books/tutorial/jar/index.html

17.2.5 Applets and security

Security is a complex topic for applets. When `SwingTest` is running as an applet, it is subject to the Java sandbox principle. The applet can only read and write files from its own codebase (the URL that contains the applet). Indeed, some care must be taken while programming to ensure that applet-safe APIs are used to access files. In general, you will need to work exclusively with URL objects, as direct access using files does not always work, even when using the applet's codebase.

When you run the `SwingTest` example you will notice the following exceptions:

```
Failed to save image: java.security.AccessControlException:
 access denied (java.io.FilePermission image.jpg write)

java.security.AccessControlException: access denied (java.lang.RuntimePer-
mission exitVM)
```

The first exception occurs because the applet cannot write the captured image onto the local file system, while the second exception occurs because applets cannot call `System.exit` to exit the JVM, but are rather under the control of the Java 2 plug-in.

Access permissions can be configured using the Java 2 security policy descriptors. A full discussion of Java 2 security is beyond the scope of this book. For more details refer to
http://java.sun.com/j2se/1.3/docs/guide/security/

17.3 CONCLUSIONS

Installation of Java 2 client-side applications, particularly those requiring other extensions (such as Java 3D applications) is still undergoing changes and improvements. This is a bit of a mixed blessing since some of this work has been going on for about two years. However, the Java WebStart initiative demonstrates that Sun is taking the installation issue seriously.

Java 3D system architecture

By now I hope you are curious to know *how* Java 3D achieves what it does. In this chapter we gallop through some of the implementation details behind the Java 3D API gaining insight into getting the most from Java 3D and maximizing the performance of your applications. This chapter gives you some clues for implementing your own 3D graphics API in Java.

Sun's Java 3D internal implementation details are all subject to change at any time. The version described here is Java 3D 1.2 running on the Win32 platform.

18.1   INTRODUCTION

The implementation of the Java 3D API has undergone considerable revision between the 1.1 and 1.2 versions of the API. About 70 percent of the Java code was rewritten between these two versions! The Java 3D 1.1 architecture was fairly simplistic and could be considered a proof-of-concept implementation of the API.

Version 1.2 moved to a message-based architecture and took tighter control of the various worker threads created by the API implementation. The collision detection thread was removed in 1.2, and collision detection is carried out by the new `TimerThread` functionality. By explicitly activating the threads in the system, the 1.2 API has removed the free-running threads (behaviors and collision detection) that caused 100 percent CPU utilization in Java 3D 1.1.

18.2 *THREADS RUNNING A JAVA 3D APPLICATION*

As you can see from tables 18.1 through 18.3, a typical Java 3D application contains many threads, some concerned with system behavior, some running the GUI event processing, and some (13) controlling the Java 3D runtime environment. The two `ThreadGroups`, "main" and "Java 3D," are subgroups of the top-level "system" `ThreadGroup`.

The Java 3D threads have the default thread priority of 5, although this can be controlled using the `VirtualUniverse.setJ3DThreadPriority` method. The priority must fall between `Thread.MAX_PRIORITY` and `Thread.MIN_PRIORITY`. The default is `Thread.NORM_PRIORITY`. The priority of the parent `ThreadGroup` (Java 3D) cannot be exceeded. Note that unlike nondaemon threads, daemon threads do not have to exit their `Runnable`'s run method for the JVM to exit.

Table 18.1 Thread Group: System

Name	Priority	Daemon
Reference Handler	10	Yes
Finalizer	8	Yes
Signal Dispatcher	10	Yes

Table 18.2 Thread Group: Main

Name	Priority	Daemon
Main	5	No
AWT-EventQueue-0	6	No
SunToolkit.PostEventQueue-0	5	No
AWT-Windows	5	No
Image Fetcher 1	8	No
Image Fetcher 0	8	No

Table 18.3 Thread Group: Java3D

Name	Priority	Daemon
J3D-MasterControl	5	No
J3D-RenderingAttributesStructureUpdateThread	5	No
J3D-TimerThread	5	No
J3D-BehaviorStructureUpdateThread-1	5	No
J3D-GeometryStructureUpdateThread-1	5	No
J3D-SoundStructureUpdateThread-1	5	No

continued on next page

CHAPTER 18 JAVA 3D SYSTEM ARCHITECTURE

Table 18.3   Thread Group: Java3D (continued)

Name	Priority	Daemon
J3D-RenderingEnvironmentStructureUpdateThread-1	5	No
J3D-TransformStructureUpdateThread-1	5	No
J3D-BehaviorScheduler-1	5	No
J3D-RenderStructureUpdateThread-1	5	No
J3D-SoundSchedulerUpdateThread-1	5	No
J3D-InputDeviceScheduler-1	5	No
J3D-Renderer-1	5	No

The Java 3D implementation is heavily multithreaded. Typically each thread controls access to a particular data structure. The threads use the MasterControl thread to periodically synchronize and exchange notifications and messages across threads. Each thread maintains a subclass of the J3dStructure member, which contains the messages to be processed by the thread. The J3dStructure.processMessages abstract method is implemented by each subclass to examine the message queue and process messages as appropriate.

Once a message is posted to a thread by the MasterControl thread, the receiving thread is marked as having work to do and scheduled for activation. See the discussion of the MasterControl class for details of the message dispatch and processing mechanism.

Most threads are associated with an instance of a VirtualUniverse (threads with the -1 suffix), while the MasterControl, RenderingAttributesStructure-UpdateThread, and TimerThread are systemwide and maintain data structures that apply across all VirtualUniverse instances.

The multithreaded nature of Java 3D allows it to leverage multiple CPUs if available; however, it does make synchronizing certain operations difficult or impossible.

18.2.1   Native Windows threads running a Java 3D application

As illustrated in figure 18.1 a Windows Java 3D application creates five threads above normal priority and three Time Critical threads. This will cause other applications running simultaneously to experience a dramatic slowdown when the Java 3D application is in the foreground.

18.3   MASTERCONTROL

The MasterControl class is Java 3D's central message dispatch and thread scheduling mechanism. The MasterControl object is a static member of the Virtual-Universe class, and is initialized by a static initializer on the VirtualUniverse class. All instances of the VirtualUniverse class therefore share the same Master-Control instance.

The first time a message is posted to the MasterControl class, it creates the MasterControlThread. The MasterControlThread runs the main message-processing loop for the MasterControl class.

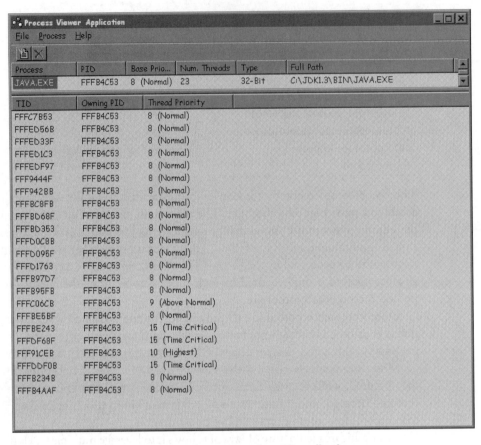

Figure 18.1 Native (Windows) threads running a Java 3D application

```
class MasterControlThread extends Thread
{

    MasterControlThread(ThreadGroup threadgroup)
    {
        super(threadgroup, "J3D-MasterControl");
        VirtualUniverse.mc.createMCThreads();
        start();
    }

    public void run()
    {
        do
            while(VirtualUniverse.mc.running)
            {
                VirtualUniverse.mc.doWork();
```

```
                Thread.yield();
        }

    while(!VirtualUniverse.mc.mcThreadDone());
    }
}
```

■

The constructor for the MasterControl class loads the J3D.DLL native DLL and reads the Java 3D system properties (see table 18.4).

Message processing and threading architecture

The MasterControl class is a message exchange mechanism between the various subsystems that compose the Java 3D runtime. The MasterControl thread maintains five UnorderList members, each containing Java 3D worker threads.

- stateWorkThreads:

    RenderingAttributesStructure calls updateMirrorObject on the NodeComponentRetained passed with the message.

    GeometryStructure maintains a binary hash tree of GeometryAtom objects and Groups. Maintains the wakeupOnCollisionEntry, Exit, and Movement lists.

    BehaviorStructure maintains a list of behaviors and marks them for activation.

    RenderingEnvironmentStructure maintains a list of the lights, fog, alternate appearances, clipping regions, and backgrounds to be used for each RenderAtom.

    SoundStructure maintains a list of sounds and soundscapes and schedules them for activation with the View's SoundScheduler.

    BehaviorScheduler, for all VirtualUniverse instances, maintains a list of BillBoard behaviors and behaviors in the system and calls the processStimulus method on each if marked for activation.

    Inputdevicescheduler maintains lists of nonblocking and blocking input devices and calls the pollAndProcessInput method on the non-blocking devices. A new thread is created to handle the input from each blocking InputDevice.

    RenderBin, for each View, maintains lists of RenderAtoms that describe rendering operations to be performed. The RenderBin implements methods such as renderOpaque, renderBackground, renderOrdered, and renderTransparent, which are called by the Render class.

SoundScheduler, for each View, maintains a list of SoundScheduler-Atoms and marks each for activation. The render method iterates the scheduled SoundSchedulerAtoms and calls the start method on each.

- renderWorkThreads:

  Renderer for each Canvas3D's Screen3D. The Render class runs the main Java 3D rendering loop by calling methods on the Canvas3D class and processing the RenderBin for the Canvas3D's View.

- requestRenderWorkThreads:

  Renderer for each Screen3D in the device render map.

- renderThreadData:

  Renderer for each Screen3D for each View, including offscreen Renderers.

- inputDeviceThreads:

  A single Inputdevicescheduler.

Each UnorderList member contains an array of J3dThreadData objects, containing a J3dThread member and additional scheduling information.

The MasterControl.doWork method (invoked by the MasterControl-Thread.run method) runs in two phases. The first phase checks for any pending messages to be executed and returns if there is nothing to execute. The second phase runs the threads under the control of the MasterControl class.

```
void doWork()
{
    runMonitor( CHECK_FOR_WORK, null, null, null, null);

    if(pendingRequest)
        handlePendingRequest();

    if(!running)
        return;

    if(threadListsChanged)
        updateWorkThreads();

    updateTimeValues();

    View aview[] = (View[])views.toArray(false);
    for(int i = views.size() - 1; i >= 0; i--)
        if(aview[i].active)
            aview[i].updateViewCache();

    runMonitor( RUN_THREADS, stateWorkThreads,
renderWorkThreads, requestRenderWorkThreads, null);
    if(renderOnceList.size() > 0)
        clearRenderOnceList();
}
```

The actual `runMonitor` method is fairly complex, and it seems to perform the four functions shown in table 18.4, depending on the value of the first argument.

Table 18.4   runMonitor

Identifier	Index	Purpose
CHECK_FOR_WORK	0	Evaluates each thread and set the MasterControlThread to wait if none of the threads needs to be processed.
SET_WORK	1	Calls notify() on the MasterControlThread
RUN_THREADS	2	Iterates through all the J3dThreadData under the control of the MasterControl. The notify() method is called on each thread associated with each J3dThreadData object.
SET_WORK_FOR_REQUEST_RENDERER	5	Sets the requestRenderWorkToDo member to true and calls notify on the MasterControl thread.

The other arguments are (in order): the array of State Work Threads, the array of Render Work Threads, and the array of Request Render Work Threads. As you can see in the following pseudocode, Java 3D has the ability to call the `doWork` method on each worker thread directly. This enables Java 3D to perform the work of multiple threads within a single thread.

```
For all Render Work Threads
   If the Thread needs to be run (J3dThreadData member),
   Check whether the View should be rendered based on its Minimum Frame
   Cycle Time
   Update the OrientatedShape3Ds in each View
   If specified lock the geometry from updates,
   If the CPU limit is 1, call the doWork method of the J3dThreadData's
   J3dThread directly
   Otherwise call the runMonitor method (NOTIFY) to notify the thread
   If specified release the lock on the geometry,
   If specified, grab the current time and put it into the View's RenderBin
Next Rendering Thread
If specified, wait for all Rendering threads to complete

For all State Work Threads
 If the CPU limit is 1, call the doWork method of the J3dThreadData's
 J3dThread directly
 Otherwise call the runMonitor method (NOTIFY) to notify the thread
Next State Thread
If specified, wait for all State threads to complete

For all Request Render Work Threads
 If the CPU limit is 1, call the doWork method of the J3dThreadData's
 J3dThread directly
 Otherwise call the runMonitor method (NOTIFY) to notify the thread
Next State Thread
If specified, wait for all State threads to complete
```

```
Update the View Frame Timing Values
Update all the Mirror Objects registered with the MasterControl

Wait for Request Rendering to complete
Update the frame timestamps for each rendered View
```

J3dMessage

Java 3D communicates between its various worker threads using a message dispatch mechanism. Messages are instances of the J3dMessage class. Each message contains an identifier and a target VirtualUniverse as well as up to five parameters for the message (generic Objects). Certainly not the most OO of designs—in fact it reminds me of the WPARAM and LPARAM attributes on the MESSAGE structure used to propagate messages under Windows.

The message identifiers are defined in table 18.5.

Table 18.5 Message identifiers

Message	Identifier
INSERT_NODES	0
REMOVE_NODES	1
RUN	2
TRANSFORM_CHANGED	3
UPDATE_VIEW	4
STOP_THREAD	5
COLORINGATTRIBUTES_CHANGED	6
LINEATTRIBUTES_CHANGED	7
POINTATTRIBUTES_CHANGED	8
POLYGONATTRIBUTES_CHANGED	9
RENDERINGATTRIBUTES_CHANGED	10
TEXTUREATTRIBUTES_CHANGED	11
TRANSPARENCYATTRIBUTES_CHANGED	12
MATERIAL_CHANGED	13
TEXCOORDGENERATION_CHANGED	14
TEXTURE_CHANGED	15
MORPH_CHANGED	16
GEOMETRY_CHANGED	17
APPEARANCE_CHANGED	18
LIGHT_CHANGED	19
BACKGROUND_CHANGED	20
CLIP_CHANGED	21

continued on next page

Table 18.5   Message identifiers *(continued)*

Message	Identifier
FOG_CHANGED	22
BOUNDINGLEAF_CHANGED	23
SHAPE3D_CHANGED	24
TEXT3D_TRANSFORM_CHANGED	25
TEXT3D_DATA_CHANGED	26
SWITCH_CHANGED	27
COND_MET	28
BEHAVIOR_ENABLE	29
BEHAVIOR_DISABLE	30
INSERT_RENDERATOMS	31
ORDERED_GROUP_INSERTED	32
ORDERED_GROUP_REMOVED	33
COLLISION_BOUND_CHANGED	34
REGION_BOUND_CHANGED	35
MODELCLIP_CHANGED	36
BOUNDS_AUTO_COMPUTE_CHANGED	37
SOUND_ATTRIB_CHANGED	38
AURALATTRIBUTES_CHANGED	39
SOUNDSCAPE_CHANGED	40
ALTERNATEAPPEARANCE_CHANGED	41
RENDER_OFFSCREEN	42
RENDER_RETAINED	43
RENDER_IMMEDIATE	44
SOUND_STATE_CHANGED	45
ORIENTEDSHAPE3D_CHANGED	46
TEXTURE_UNIT_STATE_CHANGED	47
UPDATE_VIEWPLATFORM	48
BEHAVIOR_ACTIVATE	49

The type member refers to one of the predefined message types from the table.

Each `J3dMessage` maintains a reference count so that it can clear the references to its arguments when its reference count reaches zero. Messages with a reference count of zero are placed back into a list of free messages, for subsequent reuse. This message instance cache minimizes the number of message objects created by the Java 3D at run-time in an attempt to prevent excessive garbage collection. Interestingly this type of Object pooling is no longer favored as Sun's HotSpot compiler performs object pooling and reuse automatically.

The `MasterControl` method `getMessage` will either return a message from the free list if one is available or allocate a new `J3dMessage` instance, which will get added to the free list once its reference count reaches zero. The `J3dMessage` also maintains a reference to a `View` object and contains a thread identifier (bit-field) that identifies the threads that should receive the message, as shown in table 18.6.

Table 18.6   Java 3D Threads

Identifier	Java 3D Thread	Java 3D Thread Name
0x1	BEHAVIOR_SCHEDULER	J3D-BehaviorScheduler-INSTANCE#
0x2	SOUND_SCHEDULER	J3D-SoundSchedulerUpdateThread-INSTANCE#
0x4	INPUT_DEVICE_SCHEDULER	J3D-InputDeviceScheduler-INSTANCE#
0x10	RENDER_THREAD	J3D-Renderer-INSTANCE#
0x40	UPDATE_GEOMETRY	J3D-GeometryStructureUpdateThread-INSTANCE#
0x80	UPDATE_RENDER	J3D-RenderStructureUpdateThread-INSTANCE#
0x100	UPDATE_BEHAVIOR	J3D-BehaviorStructureUpdateThread-INSTANCE#
0x200	UPDATE_SOUND	J3D-SoundStructureUpdateThread-INSTANCE#
0x400	UPDATE_RENDERING_ATTRIBUTES	J3D-RenderingAttributesStructureUpdate-Thread
0x1000	UPDATE_RENDERING_ENVIRONMENT	J3D-RenderingEnvironmentStructure-UpdateThread-INSTANCE#
0x2000	UPDATE_TRANSFORM	J3D-TransformStructureUpdateThread-INSTANCE#

The `sendMessage` method updates appropriate message queue data structures based on the value of the thread identifier (table 18.7).

Table 18.7   Target thread identifiers for messages

Thread Identifier	Effect
UPDATE_RENDERING_ATTRIBUTES	Appends the message to the global (across Virtual-Universes) RenderingAttributesStructure.
UPDATE_GEOMETRY	Appends the message to the VirtualUniverses' GeometryStructure
UPDATE_TRANSFORM	Appends the message to the VirtualUniverses' TransformStructure
UPDATE_BEHAVIOR	Appends the message to the VirtualUniverses' BehaviorStructure
UPDATE_SOUND	Appends the message to the VirtualUniverses' SoundStructure

continued on next page

Table 18.7 Target thread identifiers for messages *(continued)*

Thread Identifier	Effect
UPDATE_RENDERING_ENVIRONMENT	Appends the message to the VirtualUniverses' RenderingEnvironmentStructure
SOUND_SCHEDULER	Appends the message to the View's SoundScheduler (if a View is not specified, the message is added to the SoundScheduler for all registered Views)
UPDATE_RENDER	Appends the message to the View's RenderBin (if a View is not specified, the message is added to the RenderBin for all registered Views that are attached to the specified VirtualUniverse)

18.3.1   System properties read by Java 3D

Java 3D reads a number of system properties, some documented and some internal. A list of these properties is also maintained on the J3D.ORG site at http://www.j3d.org/implementation/properties.html.

Table 18.8 lists the system properties that are referenced in the Java code of the Java 3D distribution. Many more system properties are available which are specific to the OpenGL or DirectX versions of Java 3D. Please refer to the J3D.ORG website for the latest information on these properties.

Table 18.8 Java 3D System Properties

Name	Default	Purpose
java.version	None	Check to see whether Java 3D is running under SDK 1.3
j3d.sharedctx	False	Use shared display contexts when rendering
j3d.renderLock	True	Disable the render lock
j3d.g2ddrawpixel	True	
j3d.threadLimit	Processors + 1	Number of concurrent threads that Java 3D can use.
j3d.deviceSampleTime	0	Input device sampling time.
j3d.debug	False	Switch on Java 3D debug output. Currently only used by the MasterController.
Javax.media.j3d.compileStats	None	Output scenegraph compilation statistics
Javax.media.j3d.compileVerbose	None	Output verbose message when compiling scenegraph

18.4   *BEHAVIORSCHEDULER*

The BehaviorScheduler is responsible for activating all the Behaviors registered with a VirtualUniverse. For active and activated Behaviors, the process-Stimulus method is called on the Behavior.

The `BehaviorScheduler` integrates tightly with the `BehaviorStructure` class, which maintains lists of all the `Behaviors` that have been created for a `Virtual-Universe` instance. The `BehaviorStructure` also contains much of the logic to determine when a `Behavior` has been activated, whether due to an AWT event, `Behavior ID` being posted, `Bounds` intersection, `Sensor` condition, or a `Transform3D` change.

18.5 *INPUTDEVICESCHEDULER*

The `InputDeviceScheduler` maintains lists of nonblocking and blocking Java 3D `InputDevices`. It calls `pollAndProcessInput` on each nonblocking `InputDevice`.

18.6 *RENDERER*

Name: `J3D-Renderer-INSTANCE#`

A `Renderer` instance is created for each screen device that is to be rendered into. The `Renderer` instances are kept in a static `Hashtable` in the `Screen3D` class. The `Renderer` calls into the `Canvas3D` instances (second `JThreadData` argument) that are available for rendering. If a device supports swapping, there may be multiple `Canvas3Ds` in the second argument.

`Renderer` uses the first argument, which is one of the `GraphicsContext3D` rendering commands (see table 18.9). The `Renderer` extracts the messages from the `RendererStructure` and calls methods on the `GraphicsContext3D` as appropriate.

The complex `Renderer doWork` method implements the main Java 3D rendering loop. It sets up the projection matrices, handles stereoscopic rendering, and performs the main rendering loop; specifically, it:

1 Clears the background using the background fill color

2 Calls `preRender` on the `Canvas3D`

3 Renders the background geometry

4 Sets the frustrum planes for rendering

5 Renders the opaque geometry

6 Renders the ordered geometry

7 Calls `renderField` on the `Canvas3D`

8 Renders the semitransparent geometry

9 Calls `postRender` on the `Canvas3D`

10 Performs offscreen rendering

18.6.1 GraphicsContext3D commands

Table 18.9 lists the rendering commands that are used along with a `Renderer-Structure` instance to determine which methods on the `GraphicsContext3D` need to be invoked to execute a given command.

Table 18.9 GraphicsContext3D commands

Command	Index
CLEAR	0
DRAW	1
SWAP	2
READ_RASTER	3
SET_APPEARANCE	4
SET_BACKGROUND	5
SET_FOG	6
SET_LIGHT	7
INSERT_LIGHT	8
REMOVE_LIGHT	9
ADD_LIGHT	10
SET_HI_RES	11
SET_MODEL_TRANSFORM	12
MULTIPLY_MODEL_TRANSFORM	13
SET_SOUND	14
INSERT_SOUND	15
REMOVE_SOUND	16
ADD_SOUND	17
SET_AURAL_ATTRIBUTES	18
SET_BUFFER_OVERRIDE	19
SET_FRONT_BUFFER_RENDERING	20
SET_STEREO_MODE	21
FLUSH	22
FLUSH2D	23
SET_MODELCLIP	24

18.6.2 RenderAtoms and RenderMolecule

`RenderAtoms` are self-contained rendering units that can be passed to the underlying rendering engine. The `RenderAtom` contains lights, fog, model clipping information, an `Appearance`, and a model transformation matrix. `RenderAtoms` can be linked using double linked-list `RenderAtom` members within the `RenderAtom` class.

Higher level rendering operations are described using the RenderMolecule class. In addition to maintaining a list of RenderAtoms, RenderMolecules are able to remove redundant changes in Appearance between consecutive RenderAtoms. In this way, the number of Appearance state changes (Appearance, Material, Transparency, etc.) performed by the underlying rendering engine is minimized.

18.7 STRUCTUREUPDATETHREAD

The StructureUpdateThread is a J3dThread that can be attached to a J3dStructure object to perform message processing. The StructureUpdate-Thread instances are:

- J3D-GeometryStructureUpdateThread
- J3D-RenderStructureUpdateThread
- J3D-BehaviorStructureUpdateThread
- J3D-SoundStructureUpdateThread
- J3D-RenderingAttributesStructureUpdateThread
- J3D-RenderingEnvironmentStructureUpdateThread
- J3D-TransformStructureUpdateThread
- J3D-SoundSchedulerUpdateThread

The StructureUpdateThread is attached to an instance of a J3dStructure object, and its doWork method calls the processMessages method on the J3dStructure. The various classes derived from J3dStructure (such as SoundStructure) implement structure specific message execution.

18.8 TIMERTHREAD

The J3D-TimerThread manages:

- Any number of WakeupOnElapsedTime objects, stored in a WakeupOn-ElaspedTimeHeap (sorted, resizable array)
- 1 InputDeviceScheduler (sampling time loaded from System property)
- 1 SoundScheduler (WakeupOnElapsedTime every 2 minutes, by default)

The TimerThread will call the setTriggered method on each WakeupOn-ElapsedTime as appropriate.

18.9 SCENEGRAPHOBJECT

SceneGraphObject is the base class for all the objects that can be added to a Java 3D scenegraph. It includes a number of interesting capabilities and defines some general architectural principals for Java 3D (such as capability bits and the *retained* delegate class pattern). The attributes of the SceneGraphObject class are described in more detail next.

BitSet capabilities

A `BitSet` is an object that contains the capability bits that have been set on the `SceneGraphObject`.

SceneGraphObjectRetained retained

The retained field holds the private Java 3D implementation object for this `SceneGraphObject`. The `SceneGraphObjectRetained` maintains a reference to its source object and implements several `setLive` methods that can be overridden to respond in a `Node` specific manner. By having an internal delegate class separate from the public implementation class defined by the specification Sun has more leeway in modifying the implementation without breaking the API or exposing protected or package level access to methods or fields.

private boolean compiled

This field is `true` if this node has been compiled.

private boolean live

This field is `true` if this node has been attached to a live scenegraph.

private boolean liveOrCompiled

This field is `true` if this node has been attached to a live scenegraph or has been compiled.

private Object userData

This field holds a reference to the User Data object for this scenegraph node.

Hashtable nodeHashtable

Some `ScenegraphObjects` have a `Hashtable` of `NodeComponents` associated with them.

18.10 NODE TYPES

Table 18.10 contains a list of `Node` types and their identifiers.

Table 18.10 Node types

Name	Identifier	Name	Identifier
BACKGROUND	1	LINK	9
CLIP ·	2	MORPH	10
LINEARFOG	3	SHAPE	11
EXPONENTIALFOG	4	BACKGROUNDSOUND	12

continued on next page

Table 18.10   Node types *(continued)*

Name	Identifier	Name	Identifier
AMBIENTLIGHT	5	POINTSOUND	13
DIRECTIONALLIGHT	6	CONESOUND	14
POINTLIGHT	7	SOUNDSCAPE	15
SPOTLIGHT	8	VIEWPLATFORM	16
BEHAVIOR	17	GROUP	23
SWITCH	18	TRANSFORMGROUP	24
BRANCHGROUP	19	BOUNDINGLEAF	25
ORDEREDGROUP	20	MODELCLIP	26
DECALGROUP	21	ALTERNATEAPPEARANCE	27
SHAREDGROUP	22	ORIENTEDSHAPE3D	28

18.11 EXCEPTION STRINGS

Read from ExceptionStrings.properties (inside J3DCORE.JAR).

```
Appearance0=Appearance: no capability to set material
Appearance1=Appearance: no capability to get material
Appearance2=Appearance: no capability to set texture
Appearance3=Appearance: no capability to get texture
Appearance4=Appearance: no capability to set textureAttributes
Appearance5=Appearance: no capability to get textureAttributes
```

And so forth...

18.12 J3D DLL

The native methods within the Java 3D implementation are packaged within J3D.DLL (for Windows) and called using JNI from the Java code. The native code implements a procedural API for both OpenGL and DirectX rendering.

There are many programming tools that can list the signatures of the methods exported from a Windows DLL. The native method listings which follow are useful in that they not only expose where Java 3D calls down into native code but they also provide a blueprint for how an ambitious programmer might patch or hook a native DLL to implement an alternative rendering scheme or produce debugging output.

18.12.1 Exported methods

The following lists are sorted by ordinal (the numeric index of an exported method within a DLL) and arranged by Java 3D class. Prepend `java_javax_media_j3d` to the names in the following lists. For example J3D.DLL exports a method called `java_javax_media_j3d_Canvas3D_callDisplayList` which implements the method `callDisplayList` which was declared as native within the `Canvad3D` class.

Canvas3D

_Canvas3D_accum@16
_Canvas3D_accumReturn@12
_Canvas3D_callDisplayList@20
_Canvas3D_clear@28
_Canvas3D_clearAccum@28
_Canvas3D_composite@40
_Canvas3D_createContext@28
_Canvas3D_createOffScreenBuffer@28
_Canvas3D_createQueryContext@24
_Canvas3D_ctxUpdateEyeLightingEnable@16
_Canvas3D_decal1stChildSetup@12
_Canvas3D_decalNthChildSetup@12
_Canvas3D_decalReset@16
_Canvas3D_destroyContext@20
_Canvas3D_destroyOffScreenBuffer@20
_Canvas3D_disableFog@12
_Canvas3D_disableModelClip@12
_Canvas3D_endDisplayList@12
_Canvas3D_freeDisplayList@16
_Canvas3D_freeTexture@16
_Canvas3D_getNumCtxLights@12
_Canvas3D_getTextureColorTableSize@12
_Canvas3D_getTextureUnitCount@12
_Canvas3D_newDisplayList@16
_Canvas3D_readOffScreenBuffer@24
_Canvas3D_resetColoringAttributes@32
_Canvas3D_resetLineAttributes@12
_Canvas3D_resetPointAttributes@12
_Canvas3D_resetPolygonAttributes@12
_Canvas3D_resetRenderingAttributes@20
_Canvas3D_resetTexCoordGeneration@12
_Canvas3D_resetTextureAttributes@12
_Canvas3D_resetTextureNative@16
_Canvas3D_resetTransparency@24
_Canvas3D_setBlendFunc@20
_Canvas3D_setDepthBufferWriteEnable@16
_Canvas3D_setDepthFunc@16
_Canvas3D_setFogEnableFlag@16
_Canvas3D_setLightEnables@24
_Canvas3D_setLightingEnable@16
_Canvas3D_setModelViewMatrix@20
_Canvas3D_setProjectionMatrix@16
_Canvas3D_setRenderMode@20
_Canvas3D_setSceneAmbient@24
_Canvas3D_setViewport@28
_Canvas3D_swapBuffers@20
_Canvas3D_syncRender@16
_Canvas3D_texturemapping@48
_Canvas3D_updateMaterial@28
_Canvas3D_useCtx@20
_Canvas3D_useSharedCtx@8

ColoringAttributesRetained

```
_ColoringAttributesRetained_updateNative@48
```

CompressedGeometryRetained

```
_CompressedGeometryRetained_decompressByRef@12
_CompressedGeometryRetained_decompressHW@20
_CompressedGeometryRetained_execute@40
```

DirectionalLightRetained

```
_DirectionalLightRetained_updateLight@40
```

ExponentialFogRetained

```
_ExponentialFogRetained_update@28
```

GeometryArrayRetained

```
_GeometryArrayRetained_buildGA@64
_GeometryArrayRetained_defineByteColorPointer@44
_GeometryArrayRetained_defineDoubleVertexPointer@20
_GeometryArrayRetained_defineFloatColorPointer@44
_GeometryArrayRetained_defineFloatVertexPointer@20
_GeometryArrayRetained_defineNormalPointer@20
_GeometryArrayRetained_defineTexCoordPointer@28
_GeometryArrayRetained_disableGlobalAlpha@24
_GeometryArrayRetained_execute@76
_GeometryArrayRetained_executeInterLeaved@72
_GeometryArrayRetained_executeVA@32
_GeometryArrayRetained_globalAlphaSUN@8
_GeometryArrayRetained_setVertexFormat@20
```

GraphicsContext3D

```
_GraphicsContext3D_readRasterNative@48
```

LineAttributesRetained

```
_LineAttributesRetained_updateNative@32
```

LinearFogRetained

```
_LinearFogRetained_update@40
```

MasterControl

```
_MasterControl_getMaximumLights@8
_MasterControl_getNumberOfProcessor@8
_MasterControl_getThreadConcurrency@8
_MasterControl_initializeJ3D@8
_MasterControl_setThreadConcurrency@12
```

MaterialRetained

_MaterialRetained_updateNative@84

ModelClipRetained

_ModelClipRetained_update@52

NativeConfigTemplate3D

_NativeConfigTemplate3D_choosePixelFormat@16
_NativeConfigTemplate3D_isDoubleBufferAvailable@24
_NativeConfigTemplate3D_isSceneAntialiasingAvailable@24
_NativeConfigTemplate3D_isStereoAvailable@24

NativeWSInfo

_NativeWSInfo_subclass@12

PointAttributesRetained

_PointAttributesRetained_updateNative@20

PointLightRetained

_PointLightRetained_updateLight@52

PolygonAttributesRetained

_PolygonAttributesRetained_updateNative@32

RasterRetained

_RasterRetained_execute@56

Renderer

_Renderer_freeContext@16

RenderingAttributesRetained

_RenderingAttributesRetained_updateNative@48

Screen3D

_Screen3D_getDisplayParameters@24

SpotLightRetained

_SpotLightRetained_updateLight@72

TexCoordGenerationRetained

_TexCoordGenerationRetained_updateNative@76

Texture3DRetained

```
_Texture3DRetained_bindTexture@20
_Texture3DRetained_updateTextureFields@52
_Texture3DRetained_updateTextureImage@44
```

TextureAttributesRetained

```
_TextureAttributesRetained_updateNative@44
_TextureAttributesRetained_updateTextureColorTableNative@
```

TextureRetained

```
_TextureRetained_bindTexture@20
_TextureRetained_updateTextureFields@48
_TextureRetained_updateTextureImage@40
_TextureRetained_updateTextureSubImage@44
```

TextureUnitStateRetained

```
_TextureUnitStateRetained_updateTextureUnitState@20
```

Texture

```
_Texture_freeTexture@16
```

TransparencyAttributesRetained

```
_TransparencyAttributesRetained_updateNative@40
```

18.12.2   Imported methods

The J3D.DLL Windows library of course also imports methods from other Windows libraries. The list that follows describes the methods that the J3D.DLL library relies upon from other Windows libraries. This information is not particularly relevant except for the imports from OPENGL32.DLL (which is the standard OpenGL library on Windows). By looking at these imports you can see exactly which OpenGL functions the Sun Java 3D requires and uses.

KERNEL32.dll

```
GetLastError
GetSystemInfo
LCMapStringW
RtlUnwind
LCMapStringA
CloseHandle
SetFilePointer
SetStdHandle
LoadLibraryA
SetEnvironmentVariableA
GetACP
CompareStringW
```

```
GetOEMCP
GetCPInfo
CompareStringA
GetStringTypeA
MultiByteToWideChar
GetStringTypeW
InterlockedIncrement
InterlockedDecrement
FlushFileBuffers
GetEnvironmentStringsW
GetEnvironmentStrings
WriteFile
FreeEnvironmentStringsA
GetModuleFileNameA
FreeEnvironmentStringsW
GetModuleHandleA
GetProcAddress
WideCharToMultiByte
TlsGetValue
SetLastError
TlsAlloc
TlsSetValue
TlsFree
HeapReAlloc
GetCurrentThreadId
VirtualFree
HeapCreate
VirtualAlloc
HeapAlloc
GetStartupInfoA
HeapDestroy
GetStdHandle
SetHandleCount
GetFileType
DeleteCriticalSection
InitializeCriticalSection
GetCommandLineA
HeapFree
GetVersion
EnterCriticalSection
GetCurrentProcess
LeaveCriticalSection
TerminateProces
FormatMessageA
ExitProcess
```

USER32.dll

```
GetSystemMetrics
CallWindowProcA
SetWindowLongA
```

GDI32.dll

```
ChoosePixelFormat
SwapBuffers
CreateDCA
DeleteObject
DescribePixelFormat
CreateCompatibleDC
SetPixelFormat
CreateDIBSection
SelectObject
DeleteDC
```

OPENGL32.dll

```
glLogicOp
glAlphaFunc
glPolygonMode
glLightModelfv
glPolygonOffset
glViewport
glLineWidth
glMultMatrixd
glPointSize
glTexGenfv
glTexGeni
glHint
glCullFace
glFogfv
glPopAttrib
glLoadIdentity
glPushAttrib
glMaterialfv
glPolygonStipple
glShadeModel
glTexParameterfv
glTexSubImage2D
glStencilOp
glStencilFunc
glClearStencil
glDepthFunc
glLightf
glLightfv
glClipPlane
glFogi
GlColor4fv
glFogf
glNormal3fv
glTexCoord3fv
glColor3fv
glTexCoord2fv
glNormalPointer
```

```
glVertex3fv
glInterleavedArrays
glEnableClientState
glColorPointer
glVertexPointer
glDrawArrays
glTexCoordPointer
glDisableClientState
glDeleteTextures
glReadPixels
wglGetProcAddress
glEndList
glDeleteLists
glCallList
GlFlush
glNewList
glFinish
glDrawBuffer
glAccum
glClearAccum
glBindTexture
glClearColor
glPixelStorei
GlOrtho
glTexParameterf
glTexEnvf
glTexCoord2f
glTexImage2D
glBegin
glGetBooleanv
glVertex2f
glEnd
glBlendFunc
glIsEnabled
glDisable
glRasterPos3f
glMatrixMode
glLoadMatrixd
glDepthMask
glPixelZoom
glDrawPixels
wglShareLists
glClear
glGetIntegerv
glReadBuffer
glEnable
glColorMaterial
wglMakeCurrent
wglDeleteContext
wglCreateContext
glTexEnvi
glGetString
```

```
glTexEnvfv
glLightModeli
glLineStipple
```

18.13 SUMMARY

I hope this quick summary of Sun's Java 3D implementation has given you an appreciation for how it works and has piqued your interest. Poking around, using fairly simple tools and a little guesswork you can learn a lot–either purely for education or to help performance tune or debug your Java 3D applications.

One of the criticisms of Java 3D has been the lack of information on the implementation of the API. Parts of the Java 3D Specification are vague and the semantics of how changes to the scenegraph are propagated across the runtime, synchronized, and rendered are largely undocumented. I hope this chapter will spur on others at Sun, or elsewhere, to further document some of these more advanced aspects of the implementation.

Since this is the last chapter, I say well done! I'm sure it's been a hard slog, especially if you are new to Java 3D, but I hope it has been worth it. Don't hesitate to contact me through the Manning Authors Online forum, or we may run into each other on Sun's Java 3D email list. May all your capability bits be set correctly!

A P P E N D I X   A

Example code

A.1 LIST OF EXAMPLES

Table A.1 lists the example code that appears throughout this book. The code itself may be downloaded from http://www.manning.com/selman.

Table A.1

Title	Description	Chapter
AlphaTest	Plots an interactive graph of the parameterized Java 3D Alpha function.	12
AppearanceTest	Allows the elements of the Appearance attribute to be interatively modified.	14, 11, 9
AvatarTest	Creates a simple virtual world that implements simple collision detection and includes sound. Demonstrates Java 3D platform geometry support using the SimpleUniverse class.	11, 6
BehaviorTest	Defines six custom behaviors: rotation interpolator, stretch (springs and masses geometry modification), size reporting, exploding geometry, frames-per-second display, bounds display.	13
BillboardTest	Displays geometry and attaches a simple billboard behavior.	11, 8
BoundsTest	Creates a variety of geometry and displays the Java 3D bounds information.	5

continued on next page

Table A.1 *(continued)*

Title	Description	Chapter
common	A shared package of reusable code for Java 3D.	
CompileTest	Creates a simple scene and compiles the scene.	
CuboidTest	Demonstrates the geometry differences between the Box and Cuboid objects.	A3
CustomAlphaTest	Plots an interactive graph of a custom alpha function that loads its values from an external text file.	12
HiResCoordTest	Creates a scene using the Java 3D Locale to define different coordinates within the virtual world.	6
ImmediateTest	Performs Immediate Mode rendering using Java 3D.	4
InterpolatorTest	Uses a SwitchInterpolator to switch between a range of Java 3D interpolators.	12, 5
JavaMet	Sample Swing based Java 3D application (applet). Run run.bat to start the applet. Configuration parameters are read from JavaMet_App.properties.	7
KeyNavigateTest	A DOOM style immersive 3D world that demonstrates simple collision detection and an external map file.	11
LightTest	An interactive preview application that allows you to edit all the light parameters.	10
LoaderTest	Demonstrates using the Java 3D Object (obj) file loader.	15
MixedTest	Uses Java 3D mixed mode: rendering in immediate and retained mode.	4
MouseNavigateTest	Demonstrates direct object manipulation using the mouse.	11
MultiView	Creates multiple `Canvas3D` based views into the same 3D world.	
MyJava3D	Implements simple wire frame 3D rendering using a homegrown graphics API.	2
NodesTest	Creates a scene that illustrates using many of the Java 3D Nodes.	5
PickCollisionTest	Creates a 3D box with spheres bouncing around within it. Uses picking-based collision detection to respond to sphere-sphere and sphere-box collisions.	16
PlatformTest	Uses multiple views and platform geometry support (on SimpleUniverse). Each viewer can interact with the scene and see the other.	6
PointTest	Demonstrates rendering points in many styles.	9
RasterTest	Draws an image into the 3D scene as a Raster and reads the depth components of the 3D scene into a Raster.	8
ScenegraphTest	Builds a simple hierarchical model of the upper torso and uses RotationInterpolators to crudely animate the model.	4

continued on next page

Table A.1 *(continued)*

Title	Description	Chapter
SimpleTest	Builds a simple scene using the SimpleUniverse class and demonstrates lighting, textures, and background geometry.	3
SplineInterpolatorTest	Creates a 3D flyover of the city of Boston rendered from satellite images. Uses 3D spatial sound to associate sounds with helicopters in the scene.	12, 11
SwingTest	Displays a Swing- and Java 3D-based application that illustrates using JMenus with Java 3D. Allows you to capture screen shots and saves them as JPEG files.	5, 17
SwitchTest	Illustrates using the Switch node to interactively select geometry for display.	5
TexCoordTest	Demonstrates Java 3D texture mapping, including OBJECT_LINEAR, EYE_LINEAR and SPHERE_MAP modes	14
Text2DTest	Uses Text2D nodes to render labels into the 3D scene.	
Text3DTest	Uses Text3D nodes to render 3D labels into the 3D scene.	8
TextureTest	Reads texture coordinates and a texture image from disc and generates texture mapped geometry for rendering.	14
TextureTransformTest	Uses texture transformation to interactively rotate a texture around a Box using the mouse.	14
TriangulatorTest	Uses the Java 3D triangulation and normal generation utilities to triangulate geometry (including a hole).	15
VrmlPickingTest	Loads a VRML file using the VRML loader and illustrates using the Java 3D picking utilities to identify components of the model that are clicked with the mouse.	15, 16

A.2   INSTALLATION NOTES

Before running any of the included examples, please complete the general Java 3D installation instructions described in chapter 3. Verify that Sun's Java 3D demo applications run from the command line. For example:

```
C:\jdk1.3\demo\java3d\HelloUniverse>java HelloUniverse
```

should pop up a window with a rotating cube.

Next, download and unzip the examples for the book to a suitable directory. Copy the utility JAR files:

- j3dtree.jar (open-source Java 3D scenegraph viewer, written by the author)
- vrml97.jar (Java 3D VRML loader)

to the JDK extensions directory. For example, copy them to

C:\JDK1.3\JRE\LIB\EXT

This will make the classes within the JAR files available to Java applications without referencing them in the CLASSPATH, making it easier to run the examples.

A.3   INSTRUCTIONS FOR RUNNING THE EXAMPLES

Set the SELMAN_CLASSPATH environment variable to the installation location:

   set SELMAN_CLASSPATH="C:\dselman\classes"

Set the location of your JDK installation:

   set JAVA_HOME=c:\jdk1.3

Running the examples should now be as easy as switching to the relevant directory and typing run.bat.

Most of the examples have been formatted to run comfortably on fairly modest hardware without hardware acceleration. If you have a fast machine and hardware acceleration, you should be able to increase the size of the rendering window by simply resizing it.

In addition to the rendering window, many of the examples use J3dTree to pop up a scenegraph introspection window that will show you the structure of the Java 3D scenegraph being rendered.

A.3.1   Running applet examples

Some of the examples are available as both an application and an applet. Applets use the JDK 1.2 plug-in and include an HTML file in their example directory. If you have followed the installation instructions in chapter 2, the examples should run by just double-clicking the HTML file to open it in your Netscape or Internet Explorer web browser.

Note that the dselman.jar file containing all the class files for the book should be copied into the JRE\LIB\EXT directory.

The following examples are available in applet and application form:

- AlphaTest: Simple 2D display using Java 3D Alpha class.
- CustomAlphaTest: 2D display of a custom Alpha class with a popup Java 3D rendering Canvas.
- JavaMet: Large 2D/3D Swing application.
- VrmlPickingTest: Loads a VRML file into the browser and activates picking (mouse selection). Use the mouse buttons to rotate, translate, and scale the VRML model.

A P P E N D I X   B

Programming and graphics resources online

This appendix contains a list of resources and sources for Java 3D programming and graphics information.

Java 3D home page
> http://java.sun.com/products/java-media/3D/index.html

Java 3D API Specification
> http://java.sun.com/products/java-media/3D/forDevelopers/j3dguide/
> j3dTOC.doc.html

Java WebStart documentation
> http://java.sun.com/products/javawebstart/

Java 2 extensions mechanism tutorial
> http://java.sun.com/docs/books/tutorial/ext/index.html

Java 2 SDK extensions documentation
> http://java.sun.com/products/jdk/1.2/docs/guide/extensions/

JAR file extension options
> http://java.sun.com/docs/books/tutorial/jar/index.html

JDK 1.3.1
> http://www.javasoft.com/j2se/1.3/

Java 3D Forum

http://forum.java.sun.com/list/discuss.sun.java.3d

Matrix and Quaternion FAQ

http://www.cs.ualberta.ca/~andreas/math/matrfaq_latest.html

Web3D Consortium

http://www.web3d.org/

Core Web3D

http://www.coreweb3d.com/

Bill Day's articles on Java 3D

http://www.javaworld.com/javaworld/jw-12-1998/jw-12-media.html

http://www.javaworld.com/javaworld/jw-01-1999/jw-01-media.html

http://www.javaworld.com/javaworld/jw-05-1999/jw-05-media.html

J3D.ORG

http://www.j3d.org/

3D graphics glossaries

http://www.mondomed.com/mlabs/glossary.html (Mondo Media)

http://www.3dgaming.com/fps/techshop/glossary/ (3Dgaming.com)

http://oss.medialab.chalmers.se/dictionary/ (Chalmers MediaLab)

3D graphics engines list

http://cg.cs.tu-berlin.de/~ki/engines.html

3D file formats

http://www.cica.indiana.edu/graphics/3D.objects.html

VRML links and models

http://hiwaay.net/~crispen/vrml/worlds.html

Java development portal

http://www.governmentit.com/development/java.htm

GL4Java

http://www.jausoft.com/gl4java/

3D Ark

www.3dark.com/resources/faqs.html.

OpenGL FAQ and troubleshooting guide

www.frii.com/~martz/oglfaq/depthbuffer.htm

OpenGL "Red Book"

> http://ask.ii.uib.no/ebt-bin/nph-dweb/dynaweb/SGI_Developer/
> OpenGL_PG/

Visible Human Project

> http://www.nlm.nih.gov/research/visible/visible_human.html

Cosm

> http://www.cosm-game.com

Virtual Terrain site

> http://www.vterrain.org

Edinburgh Virtual Environment Centre

> http://www.edvec.ed.ac.uk

Volume Graphics Research Group, Department of Computer and Information Science, Ohio State University

> http://www.cis.ohio-state.edu/volviz

Visualization Laboratory, Department of Computer Science, State University of New York at Stony Brook

> http://www.cs.sunysb.edu/~vislab/

Amapi 3D (http://www.eovia.com)

Adaptive meshes and the ROAM Algorithm

> "ROAMing Terrain: Real-time Optimally Adapting Meshes"
> http://www.llnl.gov/graphics/ROAM

BSP applet

> http://symbolcraft.com/pjl/graphics/bsp/

BSP FAQ

> ftp://ftp.sgi.com/other/bspfaq/faq/bspfaq.html

Online courses

> University Course, Stefan Rufer
> Computer Science Department, Biel School of Engineering and Architecture (Berne)
>
> > http://www.hta-bi.bfh.ch/~rfs/pwf/java3/home.html

Introduction to Computer Graphics

> Department of Computer Sciences, University of North Carolina at Chapel Hill
> www.cs.unc.edu/~davemc/Class/136/

Reading resources

Illustrated Java 3D bibliography in French
http://www-iiuf.unifr.ch/~schweizp/infogra/BiblioJava3D.htm

Java books reviewed
http://www.javacoffeebreak.com/books/

List of Java books
http://www.non.com/books/Java_cc.html

Book reviews by Brian Hook
http://www.wksoftware.com/publications/3dbooks.html

Sébastien Loisel's *Zed3D, A compact reference for 3d computer graphics programming*
www.math.mcgill.ca/~loisel/

Matrix and quaternion FAQ, Department of Computing Science, University of Alberta
http://www.cs.ualberta.ca/~andreas/math/matrfaq_latest.html

Software and software companies

Allaire (Kawa)
http://www.allaire.com/

Borland (Jbuilder)
http://www.inprise.com/jbuilder/

Eclipse (Open Source, IBM)
http://www.eclipse.org/

GNU (Emacs)
http://www.gnu.org/software/emacs/

IntelliJ IDEA
http://www.intellij.com/

JAD (decompiler)
http://www.geocities.com/SiliconValley/Bridge/8617/jad.html.

NetBeans
http://www.netbeans.org

Sitraka (Jprobe)
http://www.sitraka.com/software/jprobe/

Visual Café, WebGain
http://www.webgain.com/Products/VisualCafe_Overview.html

VMGEAR (OptimizeIt)
http://www.vmgear.com/

APPENDIX C

Primitives, the geometry cache, and GeomBuffer

C.1   BOX OBJECTS AND GEOMBUFFER

Arguably there is a bug in the Box class because the faces of the cube are defined using two triangles. TriangleArrays are quicker to render than QuadArrays, but when the Box is rendered as a wireframe (i.e., only the edges of the Box are drawn), an extra diagonal line is drawn that separates the two triangles that define a face. This bug was not present in Java 3D 1.1 and was introduced in Java 3D 1.1.1. With luck, the bug will be rectified in subsequent releases.

If you require that your Box objects be rendered as wireframes, the following class can be used instead of Box to ensure the faces are rendered correctly. The Box class must be simply modified to create an OldGeomBuffer object instead of a GeomBuffer.

From CuboidTest\Cuboid.java

```
/*
 * Based on Sun's Box.java 1.13 98/11/23 10:23:02
 * Work around for the Box bug when rendered in Wireframe mode.
 * override this method
 */
public Cuboid( float xdim, float ydim, float zdim,
               int primflags, Appearance ap)
```

```
{
    int i;
    double sign;

    xDim = xdim;
    yDim = ydim;
    zDim = zdim;
    flags = primflags;

    //Depends on whether normal inward bit is set.
    if ((flags & GENERATE_NORMALS_INWARD) != 0)
      sign = -1.0;
    else
      sign = 1.0;

    TransformGroup objTrans = new TransformGroup();
    objTrans.setCapability(ALLOW_CHILDREN_READ);
    this.addChild(objTrans);

    Shape3D shape[] = new Shape3D[6];

    for (i = FRONT; i <= BOTTOM; i++)
    {
      OldGeomBuffer gbuf = new OldGeomBuffer(4);
      gbuf.begin(OldGeomBuffer.QUAD_STRIP);

      for (int j = 0; j < 2; j++)
      {
       gbuf.normal3d( (double) normals[i].x*sign,
          (double) normals[i].y*sign,
          (double) normals[i].z*sign);

       gbuf.texCoord2d(tcoords[i*8 + j*2], tcoords[i*8 + j*2 + 1]);
       gbuf.vertex3d( (double) verts[i*12 + j*3]*xdim,
          (double) verts[i*12+ j*3 + 1]*ydim,
          (double) verts[i*12+ j*3 + 2]*zdim );
      }

      for (int j = 3; j > 1; j--)
      {
       gbuf.normal3d( (double) normals[i].x*sign,
          (double) normals[i].y*sign,
          (double) normals[i].z*sign);
       gbuf.texCoord2d(tcoords[i*8 + j*2], tcoords[i*8 + j*2 + 1]);
       gbuf.vertex3d( (double) verts[i*12 + j*3]*xdim,
          (double) verts[i*12+ j*3 + 1]*ydim,
          (double) verts[i*12+ j*3 + 2]*zdim );
      }

      gbuf.end();
      shape[i] = new Shape3D(gbuf.getGeom(flags));
      numVerts = gbuf.getNumVerts();
      numTris = gbuf.getNumTris();

      if ((flags & ENABLE_APPEARANCE_MODIFY) != 0)
      {
       (shape[i]).setCapability(Shape3D.ALLOW_APPEARANCE_READ);
```

```
      (shape[i]).setCapability(Shape3D.ALLOW_APPEARANCE_WRITE);
    }
    objTrans.addChild(shape[i]);
  }
  if (ap == null)
  {
   setAppearance();
  }
  else
   setAppearance(ap);
}
```

GeometryBuffer must also be simply modified (in fact, the original 1.1 version can be used), to create a QuadArray inside processQuadStrips—newer versions create a TriangleStripArray. Copy the GeomBuffer file (defined in the com.sun.j3d.utils.geometry package, for which there is source code). Save the file as OldGeomBuffer and replace the processQuadStrips method from GeomBuffer with the method which follows.

From CuboidTest\OldGeomBuffer.java

```
/*
 * OldGeometryBuffer.java - based on Sun's GeomBuffer.java.
 * Work around for the Box bug when rendered in Wireframe mode.
 * This version actually returns Quadstrips for a Quadstrip array,
 * unlike the newer version that returns TriangleStrips....
 * override this method
 */
private GeometryArray processQuadStrips()
  {
    GeometryArray obj = null;
    int i;
    int totalVerts = 0;

    for (i = 0; i < currPrimCnt; i++)
    {
      int numQuadStripVerts;

      numQuadStripVerts = currPrimEndVertex[i] - currPrimStartVertex[i];
      totalVerts += (numQuadStripVerts/2 - 1) * 4;
    }
    if (debug >= 1) System.out.println("totalVerts " + totalVerts);

    if (((flags & GENERATE_NORMALS) != 0) &&
      ((flags & GENERATE_TEXTURE_COORDS) != 0))
    {
     obj = new QuadArray(totalVerts,
     QuadArray.COORDINATES |
     QuadArray.NORMALS |
     QuadArray.TEXTURE_COORDINATE_2);
    }
```

```
else if (((flags & GENERATE_NORMALS) == 0) &&
  ((flags & GENERATE_TEXTURE_COORDS) != 0))
{
 obj = new QuadArray(totalVerts,
   QuadArray.COORDINATES |
   QuadArray.TEXTURE_COORDINATE_2);
}
else if (((flags & GENERATE_NORMALS) != 0) &&
  ((flags & GENERATE_TEXTURE_COORDS) == 0))
{
 obj = new QuadArray(totalVerts,
   QuadArray.COORDINATES |
   QuadArray.NORMALS);
}
else
{
 obj = new QuadArray(totalVerts,
    QuadArray.COORDINATES);
}

Point3f[] newpts = new Point3f[totalVerts];
Vector3f[] newnormals = new Vector3f[totalVerts];
Point2f[] newtcoords = new Point2f[totalVerts];
int currVert = 0;

for (i = 0; i < currPrimCnt; i++)
{
  for (int j = currPrimStartVertex[i] + 2;
      j < currPrimEndVertex[i];j+=2)
 {
  outVertex(newpts, newnormals, newtcoords, currVert++,
   pts, normals, tcoords, j - 2);
  outVertex(newpts, newnormals, newtcoords, currVert++,
   pts, normals, tcoords, j - 1);
  outVertex(newpts, newnormals, newtcoords, currVert++,
   pts, normals, tcoords, j + 1);
  outVertex(newpts, newnormals, newtcoords, currVert++,
   pts, normals, tcoords, j);
  numTris += 2;
 }
}
numVerts = currVert;

obj.setCoordinates(0, newpts);
if ((flags & GENERATE_NORMALS) != 0)
  obj.setNormals(0, newnormals);
if ((flags & GENERATE_TEXTURE_COORDS) != 0)
  obj.setTextureCoordinates(0, newtcoords);

geometry = obj;
return obj;
}
```

C.2 PRIMITIVES AND THE GEOMETRY CACHE

A feature of the `Primitive`-derived classes is that they support the geometry cache (or some of them do). The geometry cache is intended to save CPU time when building `Primitive`-derived objects by caching `GeomBuffer` objects and returning them as appropriate. For example, if your application requires 100 `Spheres` with radius 50, the geometry cache will create the geometry for the first sphere and return this geometry for the remaining 99. Mysteriously, only the `Cone`, `Cylinder`, and `Sphere` `Primitives` use the geometry cache.

The source code to implement the geometry cache is useful because it presents an object lesson in how *not* to design such a facility. The geometry cache is implemented using a static hashtable of `String` keys that are used to retrieve an `Object` instance (in this case, `GeomBuffer`). The `Strings` that are used as keys are built from four `int` and three `float` parameters. Problems with this crude, inefficient, and simplistic design are:

- The design is not extensible. Three `ints` and three `floats` were arbitrarily chosen to uniquely designate a geometric `Primitive`. If a `Primitive`-derived object cannot be uniquely described using these parameters, the architecture will fail. A better architecture would have been to store each `Primitive` type in its own Hashtable and use the relevant object's `hashCode` function to generate an `int` key to reference the geometry. In this way, responsibility for generating hash codes is delegated to the derived class (as is customary in Java), and there can be no interaction between derived classes since they are stored in separate Hashtables.

- Using `Strings` to look up the objects in the geometry cache wastes memory as well as CPU time. `String` manipulations are relatively costly and are wholly unnecessary in this context.

- The geometry cache can help with saving only a few CPU cycles involved with *creating* the geometry—it does not save any runtime memory or help consolidate objects.

- Since the static Hashtable is never emptied, memory consumption is increased because cached `Geometry` objects are never dereferenced and garbage collected.

From Primitive.java

```
//The data structure used to cache GeomBuffer objects
static Hashtable geomCache = new Hashtable();

String strfloat(float x)
{
 return (new Float(x)).toString();
}

// Add a GeomBuffer to the cache
protected void cacheGeometry( int kind, float a, float b, float c,
```

```
                                  int d, int e, int flags,
                                  GeomBuffer geo)
{
 String key = new String(kind+strfloat(a)+strfloat(b)+
   strfloat(c)+d+e+flags);

geomCache.put(key, geo);
}

// Retrieve a GeomBuffer object
protected GeomBuffer getCachedGeometry( int kind, float a, float b,
                                        float c, int d, int e,
                                        int flags)
{
 String key = new String(kind+strfloat(a)+strfloat(b)+ strfloat(c)
   +d+e+flags);
 Object cache = geomCache.get(key);

 return((GeomBuffer) cache);
}
```

From Cylinder.java

```
//The Geometry Cache in use
GeomBuffer cache =
 getCachedGeometry( Primitive.CYLINDER, radius, radius height,
                    xdivision, ydivision, primflags);

if (cache != null)
{
 shape[BODY] = new Shape3D(cache.getComputedGeometry());
 numVerts += cache.getNumVerts();
 numTris += cache.getNumTris();
}
```

C.3   GEOMBUFFER

Java 3D programmers coming from an OpenGL background will recognize much of the code used to define the vertices and normal vectors of the Box primitive, defined in com.sun.j3d.utils.geometry.Box.

```
GeomBuffer gbuf = new GeomBuffer(4);

//extract of code to generate the geometry of a Box
gbuf.begin(GeomBuffer.QUAD_STRIP);
gbuf.normal3d( (double) normals[i].x*sign, (double)
 normals[i].y*sign, (double) normals[i].z*sign);
gbuf.texCoord2d(tcoords[i*8 + j*2], tcoords[i*8 + j*2 + 1]);
gbuf.vertex3d(  (double) verts[i*12 + j*3]*xdim, (double)
verts[i*12+ j*3 + 1]*ydim,
  (double) verts[i*12+ j*3 + 2]*zdim );
gbuf.end();
```

```
//create a Shape3D object to wrap the GeomBuffer
Shape3D shape =
 new Shape3D( gbuf.getGeom( GeomBuffer.GENERATE_NORMALS ) );
```

The GeomBuffer class has been designed to allow OpenGL programmers to quickly and easily generate Java 3D geometry in a manner similar to defining an OpenGL display list (for example). In the preceding example a GeomBuffer is created to hold four vertices defined as a *quad strip* which draws a connected group of quadrilaterals. One quadrilateral is defined for each pair of vertices presented after the first pair. Vertices $2n - 1$, $2n$, $2n + 2$, and $2n + 1$ define quadrilateral n, and n quadrilaterals are drawn.

The GeomBuffer class is used in many of the classes derived from Primitive since, I suspect, this code has been ported from an OpenGL-based implementation and the GeomBuffer was created to simplify porting.

```
int QUAD_STRIP = 0x01;
int TRIANGLES = 0x02;
int QUADS = 0x04;
```

At present, an instance of a GeomBuffer can contain only a single primitive type; that is, one cannot mix quad strips and Triangles (for example) in a single GeomBuffer.

Except for a bug that causes the GeomBuffer to generate a TriangleStrip-Array for a QUAD_STRIP instead of a QuadStripArray, the class is easy to use and allows OpenGL code to be quickly inserted into a Java 3D application.

bibliography

Angell, Ian. *High Resolution Computer Graphics Using C.* Halstead Press, 1990.

Arvo, James (ed.). *Graphics Gems II.* Academic Press, 1991.

Barrilleaux, Jon. *3D User Interfaces with Java 3D.* Manning Publications, 2000.

DeLoura, Mark, ed. *Game Programming Gems,* Charles River Media, 2000.

DeLoura, Mark, ed. *Game Programming Gems 2,* Charles River Media, 2001.

Eberly, David H. *3D Game Engine Design : A Practical Approach to Real-Time Computer Graphics,* Morgan-Kaufmann, 2000.

Ebert, David, et al. *Texturing and Modeling: A Procedural Approach.* Academic Press, 1994.

Foley, J.D., et al. *Computer Graphics: Principles and Practice, 2nd ed.* Addison-Wesley, 1990.

Foley, J.D., et al. *Introduction to Computer Graphics,* Addison-Wesley, 1993.

Glaeser, Georg. *Fast Algorithms for 3D Graphics.* Springer-Verlag, 1994.

Glassner, Andrew (ed.). *Graphics Gems.* Academic Press, 1990.

Glassner, Andrew, *Principles of Digital Image Synthesis, Vols. 1 and 2.* Morgan-Kaufman, 1995.

Gonzalez, Rafael and Richard Woods. *Digital Image Processing.* Addison-Wesley, 1992.

Harrington, Steve. *Computer Graphics: A Programming Approach, 2nd ed.* McGraw-Hill, 1987.

Heckbert, Paul. *Graphics Gems IV.* Academic Press, 1994.

Hoffman, Christoph. *Geometric and Solid Modeling: An Introduction.* Morgan-Kaufman, 1989.

Kirk, David (ed.). *Graphics Gems III.* Academic Press, 1992.

Laszlo, Michael J. *Computational Geometry and Computer Graphics in C++.* Prentice Hall, 1996.

Magnenat-Thalmann, Nadia and Daniel Thalmann. *Image Synthesis: Theory and Practice.* Springer-Verlag, 1987.

Moller, Tomas. *Real-Time Rendering,* A. K. Peters Ltd, 1999.

Mortenson, Michael. *Computer Graphics: An Introduction to the Mathematics and Geometry.* Industrial Press, 1989.

Neider, Jackie, et al. *OpenGL Programming Guide.* Addison-Wesley, 1994.

OpenGL ARB *OpenGL Reference Manual.* Addison-Wesley, 1994.

O'Rourke, Joseph. *Computational Geometry in C.* Cambridge University Press, 1994.

Robinson, Mathew et al. *Swing,* Manning Publications, 1999.

Rogers, David F. and J. Alan Adams. *Mathematical Elements for Computer Graphics, 2nd Ed.* McGraw-Hill, 1990.

Rogers, David and Rae Earnshaw (ed.). *State of the Art in Computer Graphics: Visualization and Modeling.* Springer-Verlag, 1991.

Sowizral, Henry, et al. *The Java 3D API Specification.* Addison-Wesley, 2000.

Vince, John. *3D Computer Animation.* Addison-Wesley, 1992.

Watt, Alan. *3D Computer Graphics,* 2nd ed. Addison-Wesley, 1993.

Watt, Alan, et al. *3D Games, Volume 1: Real-time Rendering and Software Technology.* Addison-Wesley, 2000.

Watt, Alan et al. *Advanced Animation and Rendering Techniques.* Addison-Wesley, 1993.

Wolberg, George. *Digital Image Warping,* IEEE Computer Science Press, 1990 .

Woo, Mason, et al. *OpenGL Programming Guide, 3rd Ed.,* Addison-Wesley, 1999.

Wright, Richard S. Jr., et al. *OpenGL Super Bible, 2nd Ed.,* Waite Group, 1999.

index